Human Behavioral Ecology and Coastal Environments

Society and Ecology in Island and Coastal Archaeology

UNIVERSITY PRESS OF FLORIDA

Florida A&M University, Tallahassee
Florida Atlantic University, Boca Raton
Florida Gulf Coast University, Ft. Myers
Florida International University, Miami
Florida State University, Tallahassee
New College of Florida, Sarasota
University of Central Florida, Orlando
University of Florida, Gainesville
University of North Florida, Jacksonville
University of South Florida, Tampa
University of West Florida, Pensacola

HUMAN BEHAVIORAL ECOLOGY AND COASTAL ENVIRONMENTS

Edited by Heather B. Thakar and Carola Flores Fernandez

Foreword by Victor D. Thompson and Scott M. Fitzpatrick

UNIVERSITY PRESS OF FLORIDA

Gainesville / Tallahassee / Tampa / Boca Raton

Pensacola / Orlando / Miami / Jacksonville / Ft. Myers / Sarasota

28 27 26 25 24 23   6 5 4 3 2 1

Library of Congress Cataloging-in-Publication Data
Names: Thompson, Victor D., author of foreword. | Fitzpatrick, Scott M., author of foreword. |
   Thakar, Heather B., editor. | Flores Fernandez, Carola, editor.
Title: Human behavioral ecology and coastal environments / edited by Heather B. Thakar and
   Carola Flores Fernandez ; foreword by Victor D. Thompson and Scott M. Fitzpatrick.
Description: Gainesville : University Press of Florida, [2022] | Series: Society and ecology in island
   and coastal archaeology | Includes bibliographical references and index.
Identifiers: LCCN 2022026787 (print) | LCCN 2022026788 (ebook) | ISBN 9780813069586
   (hardback) | ISBN 9780813070322 (pdf)
Subjects: LCSH: Coastal settlements. | Coastal archaeology. | Human ecology—History. | Human
   behavior—History. | Coastal ecology—History. | Environmental management. | BISAC: SOCIAL
   SCIENCE / Archaeology | SOCIAL SCIENCE / Anthropology / Cultural & Social
Classification: LCC GN784 .H85 2022 (print) | LCC GN784 (ebook) | DDC 304.2—dc23/
   eng/20220715
LC record available at https://lccn.loc.gov/2022026787
LC ebook record available at https://lccn.loc.gov/2022026788

The University Press of Florida is the scholarly publishing agency for the State University System
of Florida, comprising Florida A&M University, Florida Atlantic University, Florida Gulf Coast
University, Florida International University, Florida State University, New College of Florida,
University of Central Florida, University of Florida, University of North Florida, University
of South Florida, and University of West Florida.

University Press of Florida
2046 NE Waldo Road
Suite 2100
Gainesville, FL 32609
http://upress.ufl.edu

Contents

Figures

Tables

Foreword

For most archaeologists, the phrase "human behavioral ecology" conjures up images of societies in places such as the Great Basin of the United States or Australian deserts or its early application in explaining foraging strategies and, later, agricultural development. In fact, as a whole, most archaeologists who employ human behavioral ecology in their research work in decidedly terrestrial environments. And indeed, many of the concepts and models related to this theoretical perspective have implicit terrestrial underpinnings, given their history of use and development. However, models and concepts such as patch choice, prey encounter rates, and optimal foraging, of course, are not limited to use in one type of environment. In fact, that is the strength of these concepts—that they are portable to a number of different situations, environments, economies, and political organizations.

As the editors point out in their introduction, archaeologists have greatly expanded the use of human behavioral ecology to a broad swath of cases, moving beyond the traditional settings of terrestrial hunter-gatherers. As this book demonstrates, coastal and island societies represent one of the forefronts where these ideas produce key insights into human adaptation in such regions. As the scholars in this volume discuss, through various lenses, human settlement and use of particular marine environments are as much about the transitions and movement through them as they are about the unique resources they hold. One of the most important points relating to the former is that movement within and around these landscapes is defined by water. And while groups that are situated along rivers use canoes, rafts, and other vessels, the coast and open sea present another degree of complexity that, as many authors in this volume note, both challenges and facilitates the search, collection, harvest, and capture of food in these environments.

The myriad species found in these landscapes also present unique circumstances for foraging groups and other economies. It is critical to understand how people acquire such resources. This is true for some of the most widely harvested species such as shellfish, which often necessitates knowledge of bed location and tidal cycles, but whose collection can be done with both limited technology and by group members not often considered in foraging models (e.g., children, the elderly). Conversely, there are species that require sophisticated knowledge and technology (e.g., hook and line, harpooning) and are often difficult and sometimes dangerous to procure (e.g., large sharks, swordfish, pinnipeds, whales). Such species fit well within concepts of costly signaling and the like. The primary question the authors ask in this volume is this: how can we most productively apply a diversity of concepts and models from human behavioral ecology to coastal landscapes? As readers will note as they peruse these case studies, each chapter highlights differing nuanced points about how people have lived in and adapted to these ever-changing places.

Perhaps one of the most important aspects of this book is that the editors have assembled an impressive mix of both junior and senior scholars who examine distinct cases from around the globe, all of which demonstrate the utility of applying human behavior ecology to island and coastal settings. Together, these chapters encompass a host of differentially organized groups that include issues related to resource acquisition within open-ocean and tropical estuarine coastlines from the Arctic to the Mediterranean, the Australian coast, Europe, Chile, the Pacific, and beyond.

There are three key points that emerge from this volume that demonstrate why we should be thinking about human behavioral ecology in the context of coastal and island settings. The first is that people adapted very early to coastal environments and such situations are thought to be key in behavioral modernity among humans. Second, many of the largest and most politically complex groups of hunter-gatherers emerged in these types of environs. And third, the settlement of remote areas around the world was facilitated by—and required—adaptation to coastal environments; it is from these settlements that large complex societies emerged. As a result, understanding human decision-making and cultural behaviors among these groups is critical to exploring how humans lived in and adapted to these environments through time and across space.

The chapters presented here aptly demonstrate the antiquity and diversity of the human condition as it relates to exploration and survival in the aquatic realm. While archaeologists are continually pushing back the time at which hominins first engaged with, roamed adjacent to, and exploited marine environments, they are also refining the ways in which these data can be collected methodologically and interpreted theoretically. As is continually becoming apparent, human behavioral ecology represents one of the most useful ways in which the behavior of our ancient ancestors can be examined, the tenets of which are becoming firmly embedded within the fabric of the subfield we know as island and coastal archaeology.

This volume represents a significant step forward both for applications of human behavioral ecology and for our understanding of island and coastal archaeology. In these pages, readers will find both case studies and a synthesis regarding the state of knowledge and research that is on the horizon in these areas. Not only do the volume's authors make a substantial contribution regarding the nature of island and coastal societies—explicitly rooted in their articulation with these unique environments—but they also pave a way for future generations to build on and explore.

Where would we be without the sea? As readers will acknowledge in the pages that follow, human behavioral ecology is well suited for examining Earth's islands and coasts and provide us with much greater insight into what it means to live along dynamic coastal interfaces, which were pivotal to our evolutionary past and continue to influence human societies today. We hope you enjoy the chapters within this volume and find their content both interesting and informative. This is a book that will help move this theoretical perspective forward in a positive direction and provide a robust interpretive foundation for years to come.

Victor D. Thompson
Scott M. Fitzpatrick
Series Editors

Preface

The volume before you provides an unparalleled framework for exploring the evolutionary history of coastal and maritime societies worldwide. Case studies demonstrate how human behavioral ecology (HBE) can be used to frame research questions in different political, social, economic, and environmental settings and how its expanding toolkit (assumptions and models) can be deployed to reconstruct past human behavior in maritime settings and beyond. HBE starts with the assumption that the last 7 million years of human evolution has resulted in a tendency for rational decision-making, optimization, and the ability to assess risk. Humans are imperfect decision makers and navigating changing political, social, and environmental situations is complex. HBE provides a starting point for exploring this complexity, and it is often the observations that are not explained by modeled predictions that are the most interesting. In my opinion, HBE provides one of the best paths forward for productive archaeological science.

For more than 45 years, HBE has proven to be a productive conceptual framework for analyzing hunter-gatherer subsistence behavior in living and past societies. In fact, one of the earliest archaeological applications of optimal foraging theory and the prey choice model was for understanding past taxonomic changes in shellfish assemblages from coastal California middens through time (Beaton 1973). Since that time, the use of HBE models in coastal and island settings has become more sophisticated and now includes subsistence choice optimization, central place foraging, discounting, risk minimization, and costly signaling to study the complexity of subsistence-oriented decision-making. Ethnoarchaeological work in contemporary coastal societies provides an increasingly clearer picture of the material manifestations of human behavior. The repertoire of models has also expanded to address questions regarding colonization, settlement and land tenure, the adoption of domesticates and agriculture by coastal populations, the emergence of hereditary inequality, and even the development of state-level societies in rich coastal environments. HBE's appeal is its flexibility of application and its attention to model building to generate predictions to be tested with archaeological data.

Although HBE has been used in coastal contexts for many years, this volume is the first to consistently apply the framework to questions of maritime adaptations globally. The chapter authors share a range of case studies exploring the opportunities and constraints on past societies living in close proximity to nearshore or coastal environments. Many of the authors start with more traditional HBE issues of subsistence behavior but quickly expand to broader and more complex questions of social and political complexity. I found it personally fulfilling to see the expanded use of our early attempts to apply the ideal free distribution model to issues of colonization, settlement, and sociopolitical organization in multiple regions. The innovative integration of HBE and traditional ecological knowledge is visionary, as is the first attempt to explore the aggregate effects of optimal foraging logic within coastal environments using agent-based modeling. The volume has something for everyone, and it is an extraordinary contribution to archaeological science.

Reference Cited

Beaton, J. 1973. The Nature of Aboriginal Exploitation of Mollusc Populations in Southern California. Master's thesis, Department of Anthropology, University of California, Los Angeles.

Douglas J. Kennett

Acknowledgments

Three years ago we embarked upon this project, beginning with the success of a symposium titled "Human Behavioral Ecology at the Coastal Margins: Global Perspectives on Coastal and Maritime Adaptations." We acknowledge all of the original contributors, including chapter authors who have been with us throughout this journey (Catherine West, Ben Fitzhugh, Shannon Tushingham, Colin Wren, Curtis Marean, Jimmy Daniels, and Hector Neff), as well as the presenters whose contributions are not in this final manuscript (Jessi Halligan, Javier Fernandez Lopez de Pablo, Genevieve Dewar, Brian Steward, Hiroto Takamiya, John Crock, César Méndez, Paulo DeBlasis, Manuel San Roman). Our collective discussion alongside the apt commentary of Daniel Sandweiss helped us to synthesize our goals, guiding questions, and approach to this final manuscript.

Our passion for coastal archaeology was (and continues to be) nurtured by our mentors Michael Glassow, Barbara Voorhies, and Michael Jochim. These three remarkable scholars influenced our career paths and the development of this manuscript in multitudinous ways. Michael Glassow also read and commented on early drafts of various chapters. His insights significantly improved this work. Other colleagues, including three reviewers, deserve a very special thanks for their constructive feedback. In particular, we are indebted to Chris Jazwa, who went above and beyond his duties as a reviewer, offering discussion and reference materials that greatly improved the final manuscript. Flores Fernandez also recognizes Diego Salazar and the whole research team of Fondecyt 1151203 for sharing the mysteries of the Taltal desert coast.

Institutional support from the Department of Anthropology and the Melbern G. Glasscock Center for Humanities Research at Texas A&M University (Thakar), The National Fund for Scientific and Technological Development, FONDECYT 11200953, and ANID–Millennium Science Initiative Program UPWELL–NCN19_153 (Flores Fernandez) facilitated our collaborative efforts by supporting everything from travel for in-person writing and editing to research space and subvention funds.

Introduction

Behavioral Ecology at the Coastal Margins

HEATHER B. THAKAR, CAROLA FLORES FERNANDEZ,
AND SHANNON TUSHINGHAM

Human Behavioral Ecology and Coastal Environments uses the concepts and models of behavioral ecology to understand the adaptations of diverse coastal and maritime societies that live at the margins of the terrestrial landscape and rely on aquatic resources. Human behavioral ecology is not a new approach for anthropologists and archaeologists; scholars in these disciplines have been applying concepts from human behavioral ecology to research on human societies for more than four decades. Behavioral ecology models also have been used to address human ecological and economic behavior in nearshore and marine ecosystems, such as shellfish collecting (Beitl 2015; Bird and Bliege Bird 2000; de Boer et al. 2000; Thomas 2007a, 2007b), shrimp and lobster harvesting (Béné and Tewfik 2001; Chimello de Oliveira and Begossi 2011; McCay 1981), nearshore fishing (Aswani 1998; Begossi 1992, 1995; Beckerman 1991; de Boer et al. 2001; McCay 1981; Smith 1991), pelagic fishing (Gillis et al. 1995; Sosis 2000, 2001, 2002), turtle hunting (Bird et al. 2001; Smith and Bliege Bird 2000), and whale hunting (Alvard and Nolin 2002; Nolin 2010; Smith 1991). While humans adapt and interact with coasts and oceans in different ways than they do with the terrestrial environment, they form an integral component of the interlocking ecosystems in both environments. Thus, the application of primarily terrestrial-based models varies with respect to the unique conditions, constraints, and context of coastlines. We briefly review these models alongside supporting examples from behavioral ecology to think generally about coastal adaptations. The chapters in this volume expand on these efforts by applying the theory of human behavioral ecology in the context of regional syntheses and case studies from nine sites around the globe.

Volume Overview

Human behavioral ecology has provided a general conceptual framework for analyzing and interpreting hunter-gatherer subsistence behavior in living and prehistoric societies. In anthropology, this research tradition originated as foraging theory focused on the study of more mobile terrestrial hunter-gatherer populations (Winterhalder and Smith 1981), but the focus has expanded to include evaluations of societies engaged in other modes of production. Anthropological research in this tradition also now includes resource storage and distribution, group size and structure, specialized gender roles, and life history evolution. We believe that the basic concepts of behavioral ecology theoretical models have much to offer those who study coastal adaptations of the past. This is not to say that there is not significant room for growth. As detailed below, our position is that there are important critiques of human behavioral ecology that can help refine models.

This book includes perspectives from North and South America, Europe, Africa, Polynesia, and Australia. Topics include the unique challenges coastal societies face, including ecological risks and the variability of coastal environments (e.g., extreme seasonality and natural hazards); balancing coastal and terrestrial resource needs; aquatic technological innovation; and multiscale environmental change. The authors use a variety of analytical approaches, including resource and patch-choice optimization, central place foraging, ideal free distribution, costly signaling theory, and niche construction. They present regional overviews and case studies that address past coastal adaptations from a conceptual framework informed by neo-Darwinian theory, which allows us to interrogate both past developments and future directions in coastal archaeology.

This introductory chapter provides a brief review of the behavioral ecology framework and the particular value of this approach in coastal contexts. The rest of the volume is presented first as three regional overviews:

Arctic and Subarctic (West, Gjesfjeld, Anderson, and Fitzhugh)
Pacific Northwest (Tushingham)
Mediterranean (Plekhov, Levine, and Leppard)

These are followed by a series of six case studies:

Pacific southern Mexico (Daniels, Thakar, and Neff)
Atacama Desert of Chile (Flores Fernandez and Olguín)
Southwestern France (Gauthier-Bérubé and Thakar)
South Africa (Wren, Janssen, Hill, and Marean)

Northern Australia (Wright, Faulkner, and Westaway)
Pacific Islands of American Sāmoa (Morrison, DiNapoli, Allen,
Rieth)

These chapters explicitly acknowledge regional research legacies that influence the application of broad conceptual models, including which models are commonly used, which variables are emphasized, and which modifications are considered most critical.

The concluding chapter by Thakar and Flores Fernandez integrates insights from the volume and offers an updated appraisal of the theoretical contributions of behavioral ecology to reconstructions of past coastal societies. In keeping with the exploratory nature of the volume, this final chapter is part essay and part commentary; we seek to identify conceptual gaps in the application of theoretical models and highlight useful modifications from regional approaches.

Significance of the Coast

The significance of the coast as both a natural and an anthropogenic landscape cannot be overstated. This complex and ever-changing boundary between the land and sea, where life and diversity abound, is critical in supporting (and shaping) human societies. Recent research suggests that the beginning of coastal adaptations marked a transformative point in the evolution of our species (Marean 2014) and in our demographic and geographic expansion out of Africa and across the globe (Erlandson 2001). Aquatic resources supported some of the largest and most complex sedentary hunter-gatherer groups on Earth (Arnold and Walsh 2010); intensive fisheries fueled early agricultural civilizations (Leppard 2014; Kennett and Kennett 2006); and maritime exploration, trade, and conquest drove historic empires (Killingray et al. 2004). Even today, it is estimated that almost a quarter of the world's population lives within 100 km of a coast and up to half the world's population depends directly or indirectly on coastal resources (Berkes 2015).

People rely on coasts for subsistence and economic resources. From the northern latitudes of the Arctic Circle to the southern latitudes of Tierra del Fuego, high primary productivity means that a wide variety of aquatic resources (seaweed, littoral plants, shellfish, fish) is concentrated along coastlines. These resources draw sea mammals and migratory birds to these rich ecological zones seasonally (Berkes 2015). Distinct coastal features and ecosystems such as rocky coasts, beaches, barriers and sand dunes, estuaries and lagoons, deltas, river mouths, wetlands, and coral reefs punctuate coastlines, blurring the boundaries of the land and sea. These diverse coastal environments offer high-resource biomass, large resource diversity, and ecological stability. Coastal habitats also vary greatly, resulting in uneven spatial and temporal distribution of resources (Blanchette et al. 2008). Rocky intertidal zones and estuaries can be up to ten times more productive than other coastal habitats. Coastal upwelling of nutrient-rich water results in highly localized marine productivity, and submarine canyons can funnel nutrient-rich water to productive patches along the coast (Chavez and Messié 2009). Dwelling by the shore offers a measure of security from seasonal famine that is rarely found inland (Wickham-Jones 2014).

Interlocking marine and terrestrial ecosystems juxtapose a variety of environments and habitats that provide shelter, water, and fuel for humans. Rocky outcrops, caves, and rock shelters offer natural shelter from the wind and elements, as do high dunes next to sandy bays and natural depressions formed by abandoned lagoons and riverbeds (Wickham-Jones 2014). Freshwater seeps, streams, and rivers tend to be a reliable resource. Undeveloped coastlines contain an abundant supply of driftwood drawn from near and far, supplies of seaweed, and timber from coastal scrub and woodlands (Wickham-Jones 2014). The availability and proximity of these critical resources and the diversity, productivity, and seasonal availability of terrestrial foods draw humans to coasts (Perlman 1980). For example, the Atacama Desert of South America's Pacific coast is a hyperarid environment that is bordered by an exceptionally rich marine environment (Thiel et al. 2007). In such cases, coasts offer refuge for populations confronted by much harsher environments inland. Along the coast, people are sheltered by more moderate temperature regimes, increased levels of moisture produced by coastal fogs, and freshwater seeps that emerge along bedrock beyond the high-tide level (see Borrero and Barberena 2006).

People rely on coasts and their associated waterways for transportation and exchange. Boats, canoes, and even rafts made of materials that are often available in the coastal environment provide some of the most efficient means of transport available to people (Ames 2001). The unique geomorphology of coastlines, which are convoluted in ways that create large bays and sheltered harbors or that open up and expose the shore to the heavy surf and gusty wind, both facilitates and constrains travel (Ames 2001). Interconnected lagoons, estuaries, rivers, and lakes at the boundary between the land and sea provide protected routeways along the coast and entry well into the hinterland. Prominent topographic features facilitate the cultural development of mental maps of the coast and its waterways (Anderson 2004; Wickham-Jones 2014). People with the knowledge and skill to navigate the coastline used the sea as a highway in order to maintain social and economic connection between populations (Anderson 2004; Moss 2004). However, strong currents, adverse weather conditions, and tidal range also constrain access to the sea and its exchange routes and may even imperil life (Rainbird 1999).

Peoples' adaptation to the coast and their reliance on its resources carry the potential of both risk and reward. The ethnographic and archaeological records demonstrate the dramatic impact of coastal adaptations on human diet, technology, mobility, and social behavior (Marean 2014). Comparative ethnographic analyses demonstrate that coastal hunter-gatherers tend to have larger, denser populations that reside in more sedentary communities. These populations have more elaborate forms of social differentiation that is supported by greater craft specialization and more extensive trade networks than do terrestrial hunter-gatherers (Binford 1980, 1990; Keeley 1988; Kelly 2013; Kroeber 1939). Coastal hunter-gatherers also experience relatively high levels of conflict (Lambert 1997; Moss and Erlandson 1992), more costly investments in complex technology (Ames 1994, 2001; Arnold 1996; Arnold and Walsh 2010), and a greater need to defend food storage that results in increased territoriality (Kennett and Clifford 2004; Tushingham and Bettinger 2019). These unique trajectories, which are conditioned by local environments and regional cultural histories, hold vital clues to our understanding of the full spectrum of human adaptive capacities.

Definitions

Coastlines and coastal resources vary significantly through space and time, defying general or simplistic categorization. Instead of trying to determine lines between aquatic and terrestrial, we accept the premise that coastal people made use of all resources they found in this dynamic environmental zone. Beginning with the most basic geographic definitions, we use "littoral" to refer to the shoreline, "coastal" to encompass the zone where sea and land processes intermix, and "maritime" to reference the open waters of the oceans and seas. Authors in this volume examine the full expression of human lifeways in relationship to these geographic contexts. In each chapter, authors describe how people who lived along the coast transformed subsistence practices, settlement and mobility patterns, use of technology, exploitation of lithic raw material, social relationships, and mechanisms of exchange. These human societies can only be understood in terms of how they relate to the coast. Maritime adaptation includes all of these issues and includes lifeways that center on fishing, hunting, and voyaging in the open ocean. Those lifeways require sophisticated watercraft and specialized technologies that are not required for exploitation of the littoral and coastal zones.

Critically, focus on these zones does not preclude the use of inland resources. To varying degrees, littoral, coastal, and maritime adaptations around the world incorporate wild, cultivated, and domesticated terrestrial plants and animals. Even societies that practice the most intensive forms of maritime adaptations may access raw materials such as lithics or timber found in terrestrial habitats far from the coast. Dried fish, fish oil, and other marine products could also be produced as commodities for trade and exchange by coastal-dwelling communities with interior groups, particularly in fat-poor northern climes (e.g., Ames 1998; Kuhnlein et al. 1982; Tushingham et al. 2021). Indeed, maritime adaptations often hinged on access to well-developed woodlands and forests that people accessed directly or through a network of social interactions and material exchange (Wickham-Jones 2014). In some case studies presented in this volume, the authors had to explore social, economic, and ecological processes at a broader spatial scale than the coastal margins alone. However, in each example, coastal resources are "so important that the mobility system is designed to intercept the coast as a planned part of the annual mobility strategy, sometimes moving between the interior and the coast, or even staying there all year" (Marean 2014). Scheduling around coastal rhythms is a fine balancing act that requires deep understanding, planning, and foresight. It is this knowledge that underpins our definition of coastal adaptations.

In the broader archaeological literature, littoral, coastal, and maritime adaptations are often lumped together as "aquatic adaptations" or "coastal adaptations." For the sake of brevity, we also use these phrases as shorthand for the complex set of behaviors associated with human societies whose lifeways revolve around the coast and its resources. Coastal peoples with such aquatic adaptations are often interchangeably referred to as "hunter-gather-fishers," "aquatic hunter-gatherers," "aquatic foragers," "coastal foragers," "coastal collectors," "seafarers," "voyagers, "mariners," and much more. You will see such terms in these chapters as we integrate our case studies with past research. Regardless of the particular phraseology used to describe them, all of the human societies presented in this work demonstrate a clear and transformative reliance on the coast and its resources.

Human Behavioral Ecology Research in Coastal Adaptations

Binford's (1990:134) earlier evaluation of coastal adaptations considered the "correlated shift to the increasing use of aquatic resources to be one of the major problems archaeologists have yet to address realistically in terms of the issues of complexity and human evolution. Importantly, this shift would be *favored in simple energetic terms* and would not necessarily be a response to density-dependent 'frustration' of mobility—the fundamental hunter-gatherer positioning strategy for gaining a living" (emphasis added). Since then, human behavioral ecology, which commonly considers energetic costs and returns, as well as other currencies, has been widely used as a theoretical framework. This neo-Darwinian approach is grounded in natural selection theory. It focuses on the evolution and adaptive design of human behavior in specific ecological contexts (Krebs and Davies 2009; Winterhalder and Smith 1992, 2000). Human behavioral ecology is rooted in the microeconomic logic of foraging theory, although it has expanded to encompass analyses of societies engaged in other modes of production and a diversity of economic, social, reproductive, and life history topics (Winterhalder and Kennett 2006). The theory now offers an expanding suite of models based on ethnographic research and evolutionary theory for exploring complex ecological interactions in changing social and natural environments and for constructing hypotheses that can be tested with archaeological data (Bettinger and Richerson 1996; Winterhalder and Smith 2000).

While anthropologists have used human behavioral ecology to interpret and predict human behavior in a variety of terrestrial contexts (e.g., Hawkes et al. 1982, 1991; Kaplan and Hill 1992; Simms 1987; Winterhalder 1981, 1986), their use of the theory in the context of coastal adaptation has developed more slowly, possibly due to the complexities associated with the spatial distribution of coastal resources and the difficulties involved with prey detection and mobility in diverse coastal habitats (Aswani 1998). Similarly, storage logistics can be complicated to model for less mobile aquatic foragers living at mid-latitudes and require reevaluation of simple central place frameworks. Nonetheless, researchers have used human behavioral ecology to analyze coastal adaptations and economies with favorable results. This work is ethnographic (e.g., Aswani 1998; Bird and Bliege Bird 1997; Thomas 2007a, 2007b), ethnoarchaeological (e.g., Bird 1997; Thomas 2002), and archaeological (e.g., Kennett 2005). Here, we review the general assumptions, fundamental concepts, models, and predictions of the theory and the insights gleaned from behavioral ecology studies of coastal adaptations and economies.

This review is not comprehensive. Rather, we outline the broad parameters of each model in order to establish the basic framework that each chapter author builds upon. We do not claim that the human behavioral ecology research tradition is a complete replacement for other approaches. Rather, we seek to explore its role as a complementary explanation that has much to offer archaeologists interested in exploring changes in human coastal adaptations. Individual chapters explore application of well-established traditional foraging models (diet breadth, patch choice, patch residence, central place, ideal free distribution, and costly signaling) and emergent perspectives derived from niche construction, traditional ecological knowledge, and nutritional and reproductive ecology focused on dynamic processes, alternative currencies, and gender-based strategies. These topics reflect current trends in behavioral ecology.

Traditional Foraging Models

Optimal foraging theory and the models derived from it rely on the concepts of optimization, marginal value, opportunity costs, discounting, and risk sensitivity. The optimization assumption posits that human behavior will tend toward (but may not always achieve) optimization and efficiency, particularly as the value of a behavior changes in relationship to its duration (if it is an activity) or quantity (if it is a resource; Winterhalder and Kennett 2006). Diminishing value is expected to prompt changes in behavior, especially if the cost of not pursuing an alternative behavior is greater than the valuation of the current behavior. Discounting future rewards diminishes the value of behaviors with up-front costs and delayed returns. Similarly, risk sensitivity results in a lower perceived value of behaviors with unpredictable returns. When these two concepts have been integrated, they have proved useful for studying adaptive decision-making (Winterhalder and Kennett 2006).

Based on these concepts, optimal foraging theory assumes that humans tend to make economically rational decisions that optimize returns while minimizing investment costs and risk (Stephens and Krebs 1986). Each optimal foraging theory model defines 1) a range of possible behavioral actions, 2) the internal and external constraints, 3) a specific measure of currency humans use to assess costs and benefits, and 4) an overarching goal, such as maximizing energy capture or enhancing reproductive success (Winterhalder and Kennett 2006). Contingency models based on these four features purposefully reduce decision-making to the most basic variables. Environmental, technological, and social constraints are treated as givens. Even though this simplification has been criticized, it forces researchers to evaluate the assumptions and underlying logic of each model. Mismatches between theoretical predictions and the observed or reconstructed behavior offer insights about other variables that may influence decision-making. Thus, optimal foraging theory can be used productively to explore questions about long-term change in the proposed constraints and the broader historical contingencies involved in the changing processes of a culture (Kaplan and Hill 1992).

Using energy (kcals) as the primary measurement of optimization, anthropologists use optimal foraging theory models to formulate testable predictions that can account for the decisions people make about the array of resources they use (diet breadth and costly signaling), the resource areas they use (patch choice), the amount of time they spend in a resource area (patch residence), and the places they choose to live in relationship to resources (central place) and to other people (the ideal free distribution). In this volume, we acknowledge that energy is not always the most appropriate currency when applying foraging models to coastal contexts and resources. Significant advances in the application of human behavioral ecology involve the use of other currencies such as nutrient content or social prestige (Flores Fernandez and Olguín, this volume). Yet the focus on the costs and benefits associated with individual-level decisions in localized ecological settings provides a robust framework for understanding coastal adaptations (Wren et al., this volume). Each model has the potential to be adapted to particular circumstances and to the parameters between humans, the resources they exploit, and the environments they occupy. This perspective stresses the dynamic management of trade-offs that occur in temporal and spatial relationship to the abundance, distribution, accessibility, and predictability of resources and to broader environmental, technological, and social constraints. These basic concepts may be regarded as fundamental to the analysis of any economy, ranging from coastal foragers to industrial shipbuilders (Plekhov et al. and Gauthier-Bérubé and Thakar, this volume).

Coastal Diet Choice (Resource Selection)

The diet breadth model focuses on people's decision to pursue or harvest a resource they encounter or to pass it over in favor of a more profitable one (Emlen 1966; MacArthur and Pianka 1966). In this model, humans rank alternative sets of potential resources within a homogenous environment based on their potential profitability or net benefit. Whether or not a group will include a resource type depends on the abundance and distribution of resources in the environment, the frequency of encounters with high-ranked resources, the technology used, and human populations dynamics. Assuming that people know, on the basis of past experience, the mean encounter rate, average energy returns, and handling costs associated with different resource types, the variety of resource types they exploit should be more restricted or specialized when high-ranked resources are more abundant, encounter rates are high, and search time is low. Inversely, the variety of resource types exploited should become broader or more diversified when high-ranked resources are less abundant, encounter rates are low, and search time is high. For example, in the artisanal fishery of Inhaca Island, Mozambique, fishermen added a greater quantity of small fish to the daily catch as the catch rate for favored piscivorous fish declined alongside an overall decrease in general catch rates (de Boer et al. 2001). Critically, the diet breadth model assumes that in both productive and nonproductive environments, whether or not a group includes a resource in the diet depends only on the availability of higher-ranked resources and not on the availability of that particular resource. An assumption of this model is that people will ignore resources that fall outside the optimal resource set regardless of how abundant those resources are and how frequently the group encounters them (MacArthur and Pianka 1966).

The misconception that bigger is better, or that larger animals offer greater returns, contributed to the development of resource rankings that relegated many smaller coastal resources to the position of "starvation foods" that were consumed in the absence of all other alternatives (Erlandson 2001). However, many types of small coastal resources are found in highly productive and predictable aggregations that require minimal search time, risk, or technological investment to capture or process (Bird and Bliege Bird 1997, 2000). Indeed, modern foragers are known to exploit a wide range of coastal resources, including shellfish, fish, sea mammals, seabirds, amphibians, turtles, and waterfowl (Bliege Bird et al. 2001; de Boer et al. 2000). Mass harvesting of small-bodied forage fish (e.g., herring, smelt) for storage seems to have been intensified for storage prior to or in tandem with harvests of larger-bodied fishes. Fine-grained sieving and flotation analyses are demonstrating their ubiquity at sites throughout the Pacific Northwest Coast (McKechnie and Moss 2016; Tushingham and Christiansen 2016). Foraging decisions in coastal habitats depend on the character and availability of the resources in both aquatic and terrestrial environments and the costs of procuring them given the available technology. Despite this divergence, the diet breadth model offers a robust set of conceptual tools for exploring both what coastal resources people exploit and how and why they chose to exploit particular types of resources in coastal habitats.

For example, the fact that intertidal mollusks (bivalves and gastropods) are predictably available and sessile enhances the profitability of exploiting them given that dense aggregations are available throughout much of the year (Wright et al., this volume). Bird's (1996) study among the Meriam of Torres Strait demonstrated that shellfish-gathering activities can be explained in terms of the variable costs and benefits foragers face while collecting prey (see de Boer et al. 2000 and Thomas 2002 for similar conclusions). All members of a group, including both men and women and children and the elderly, can participate in procuring this resource with minimal risk and little technology. People who practice optimal foraging (that is, passing over lower-ranked shellfish) may achieve net return rates comparable to those associated with medium-sized or small game and plants (Bird and Bliege Bird 2000). Thomas (2007a) demonstrated that several atoll communities in Kiribati, Micronesia, increased the rate of shellfish gathering relative to other subsistence activities during periods of daytime low tides at new or full moons (spring tides), when encounter rates were highest. During intertidal foraging bouts, they consistently focused on collecting the high-ranked taxa that were always taken when they were encountered. Although technological constraints (e.g., not having a knife or crowbar) and unfavorable tidal conditions limited efficient harvest, shellfish gatherers consistently foraged in a way that matched the predictions of the diet breadth model (Thomas 2007a). Diverse studies that range from the coastal ethnography of marine mammal hunting among the Inujjuamiut (Smith 1991) to artisanal fisheries of Inhaca Island, Mozambique (de Boer et al. 2001), and modern commercial fisheries in New Jersey (McCay 1981) demonstrate both the flexibility and utility of the diet breadth model as a good predictor of which coastal resources a group will select in specific resource patches.

Coastal Patch Choice and Patch Residence Time

The patch choice model focuses on whether a group will decide to exploit a resource patch once it is encountered or pass it over for a more profitable one in a heterogenous environment (MacArthur and Pianka 1966). In this model, a patch is an isolated area of resource opportunities, or a resource clump. An individual can encounter several discontinuous resource patches in their daily foraging range and will rank them according to their net profitability. Thus, as with the predictions of the diet breadth model regarding resource use, the patch choice model indicates that people will exploit the highest-ranking and most profitable resource patches. This prediction is critical for understanding mass harvest strategies in aquatic environments that target resources that are linked through local food webs and are likely to include both high- and low-ranked taxa (Monks 1987). Whether or not people include alternative patches in the foraging range depends on the availability and productivity of higher-ranked patches. Thomas (2007b) found that Kiribati shellfish gatherers might ignore or drop a patch containing high-ranked resources in favor of another patch with dense concentrations of low-ranked resources. Bird (1996) documented that the foraging decisions of mollusk gatherers on Mer Island in the Torres Strait were conditioned by predictable variability in returns among resource patches. In each scenario, the ranking of the coastal resource patch as a whole is more predictive of foraging decisions than the ranking of individual resources.

However, unlike individual resources, which have a fixed value, resource patches have a marginal value. As resources are harvested or as prey become increasingly evasive, encounter rates decrease and the overall value of a resource patch is diminished. The marginal value theorem predicts that the value of a patch decreases in inverse proportion to the time a person spends harvesting a patch (Charnov 1976). Therefore, given the interdependence of the patch choice model and the marginal value theorem, use of one requires assumptions about the other (Stephens and Krebs 1986).

The patch choice model predicts where a person will forage, and the patch residence model complements it by predicting how much time a person will spend harvesting resources in a patch (Charnov 1976). In this model, the net profitability of patch residence times relates to the marginal value of the current patch, the average return rate of all patches in the foraging area, and the unfavorable opportunity costs of not moving on. The patch residence model anticipates that people will leave a patch when its marginal value drops below the average foraging rate. Staying longer would incur unfavorable opportunity costs because higher returns are available elsewhere. Similarly, staying for a shorter time is also suboptimal because average rates of return are higher than the costs of moving to another resource patch (Winterhalder and Kennett 2006).

Many coastal resources can be very productive and predictable, but they are also scattered across the landscape and are found in many habitat types. Similarly, the superiority of coastal habitats is not a given; in some contexts, terrestrial environments are extremely productive relative to adjacent marine ecozones. Such patchiness is characteristic of highly heterogeneous edge environments. In this context, the patch choice model and the patch residence model provide a robust set of tools for analyzing the dynamic movement of resource users across a heterogenous environment. For example, Smith's (1991) behavioral ecology study of Inujjuamiut fishing strategies documented that as overall productivity in the environment increased, short travel times (and reduced costs) were associated with short patch residence, during which people took the highest return opportunities and moved on quickly. Conversely, as overall productivity decreased within the environment, long travel times (and higher costs) were associated with longer residence times, during which people harvested a wider array of resources that included lower-return opportunities before they moved on. This study indicates that the optimal set of patches and patch residence times was achieved by adding patches of decreasing quality until foraging time (between and within patches) per unit harvested was minimized. Ultimately, both strategies produced the same results: 1) the marginal value of harvested patches was the same, approximating the average foraging rate of the area, when they were abandoned; and 2) patches with marginal values that were less than the average foraging rate were ignored (sensu Aswani 1998). Sosis (2002) similarly argues that Ifaluk fishers switch to alternative fishing grounds when catch rates drop below the per capita mean of the average catch rate for all patches.

Prey mobility in aquatic environments presents a challenge in terms of considering marine habitats as patches. For example, Aswani (1998) analyzes the daily and seasonal movement of Solomon Islanders in Roviana Lagoon in New Georgia. A mosaic of local microenvironments in the lagoon create bounded resource patches that may become depleted from sustained predation on sedentary species, such as mollusks, coral reef fish, and certain crustaceans. Although prey mobility in the aquatic lagoon environment challenges people's ability to assess changes in the productivity of a patch, the patch choice and patch resource models predict that people will select fishing areas (or patches) and spend time in them according to the average return rates they expect. Fishermen spend less time in high-quality patches when the cost of travel between patches is low, and they spend more time fishing in patches with declining yields when travel costs are too high (Aswani 1998).

The patch choice and patch resource models have proven to be robust in predicting spatial behavior and time allocation in a diversity of littoral, coastal, and marine environments. Lopes and colleagues' (2011) behavioral ecology study of riverine and coastal fishers of the Brazilian Amazon found that the patch choice and patch resource models best predicted fishing behavior in habitats with well-defined boundaries such as lakes and backwaters. In these well-defined patches, people who traveled farther to reach a fishing area tended to stay longer and return with more fish. Similarly, Begossi (1992), Chimello de Oliveira and Begossi (2011), and Lopes and colleagues (2011) found that small-scale shrimp fishers in Brazil moved on to different fishing grounds when the return rate of the previous trip dropped below average. Cockle collectors in coastal Ecuador also move to new fishing grounds when catch rates fall below the average (Beitl 2015) and mollusk gatherers in western Kiribati, Micronesia, switch patches when faced with diminishing returns (Thomas 2007b). In this particular context, prey mobility is not a critical factor in patch depletion; it is tidal movements that depress local resources.

Coastal Residence Location (Central Place Foraging)

The central place foraging model focuses on people's decisions about where to establish and how to provision a residential home base in relation to the distribution of resources across a heterogenous landscape (Orians and Pearson 1979; Stephens and Krebs 1996). People tend to forage in a pattern that radiates from a central location they return to each day, bringing foodstuffs and other resources to share (Kelly 2013:65). In this model, the net profitability of alternative residential locations is estimated as people calculate the energy gains from a foraging trip minus the energy costs of round-trip travel to procurement sites and the costs of collecting, processing, and transporting a resource. Central place foraging theory predicts that people will locate their residential base to increase the efficiency of foraging for local and distant resources, including the costs required to deliver resources back to the residential base (Zeanah 2000). Variables that change the distribution, accessibility, or productivity of key resources include changing seasons and ocean currents (environmental) or technological investment and niche construction (anthropogenic). These may influence the delivery rate to the central place and prompt people to relocate their residential base.

The central place foraging model predicts that people will tend to optimize their delivery rate by maximizing transportation efficiency, which operates independently of resource encounter or procurement rates (Bettinger et al. 1997). Therefore, the farther people must travel, the more selective they should become about the resources they transport back to the central place. Nonetheless, factors such as the technology available for handling resources in the field or the nonfood value of some resources may contribute to some variability in the array of resources people deliver to the residential base (Bird and Bliege Bird 1997).

People can choose to increase the value of a load they must transport by processing resources near the procurement site. Removing low-value parts (e.g., mollusk shells) prior to transport maximizes delivery of high-quality material to the central base. However, time spent in field processing incurs potential opportunity costs by forgoing additional foraging time. Alternatively, time in field processing could also be spent in transport (Metcalfe and Barlow 1992). The field-processing variant of the central place foraging model predicts that people will process resources in the field when the associated costs are low enough and the resulting increase in load value is high enough to increase the net value of resources delivered to the central place. In all scenarios, foraging distance is the most critical factor. Travel and transport costs are relatively lower over shorter distances. Therefore, people may prefer to make multiple trips, transporting many lower-value loads of unprocessed resources. However, over long distances, people may prefer to make fewer trips, transporting fewer higher-value loads of processed resources. The central place foraging model predicts that this relationship between processing and foraging distance is proportional. Importantly, central place foraging assumes pedestrian transport by individuals, yet transport costs may have been significantly offset (and load sizes increased) when other forms of transport were available (e.g., boats; Ames 2002; Fulkerson and Tushingham 2021).

In general, the farther people must travel to acquire a specific set of resources, the higher the costs of processing in the field they should accept (Metcalfe and Barlow 1992). Bird and Bliege Bird's (1997) study of Meriam shell fishers in the Torres Strait Islands evaluated the travel distance at which field processing increased the rate of delivery of edible meat to a central place. Analysis of foraging bouts in two distinct resource patches demonstrated that Meriam Islanders need to travel only 70–120 m beyond the central place before field processing would increase the rate of delivery. Bird and Bliege Bird found that people consistently process key high-ranked taxa with low processing costs at the procurement site. Even though this behavior conformed with the predictions of the central place foraging model, Bird and Bliege Bird cautioned that people may deviate from the expectations of the central place foraging model. For example, they may transport unprocessed shells over great distances to keep the meat fresh for later consumption, trade, or other uses.

Studies of small-scale fishers that return to a central place (their residences or their landing points) with their catch also demonstrate the utility of central place foraging as a good predictor of delivery rate maximization (Alvard 1993; Aswani 1998; Begossi 1992, 1995; Begossi and Richerson 1992; Begossi et al. 2005; Seixas and Begossi 2000). In a study of four small fishing communities that exploit a variety of coastal habitats (marine, estuarine, and riverine) in Brazil, Begossi and colleagues (2009) indicated a significant correlation in round-trip travel time and catch size. In this study, delivery rate is proportional to the quantity of resources returned to the central place because the fishers' catch does not exceed their load capacity. In contrast,

Gillis and colleagues (1995) indicated that deep-water trawl fishermen who use nets to catch fish en masse face significant constraints on load capacity. In this context, fishermen choose to increase the value of a transported load by sorting and discarding fish of lower value to make more room for more valuable fish. In the context of open-ocean fishing, the option of making multiple trips is removed from the equation, and transport efficiency is determined by the value of a single load. On-ship processing (sorting and discard) of each haul maximizes the total value of the landed catch at the end of each trip.

In archaeological contexts, field processing of fish and marine mammals also took place through butchery, drying, and similar weight-reducing strategies that significantly increased load utility prior to transport. Whether processing occurred at field camps or at home bases, the risk of spoilage was also an important consideration. Storage timing is often glossed over in most central place foraging models, although it was a critical decision-making element in the intensification of aquatic resources. For instance, as clarified in the front-back-loaded model (Bettinger 2009), fish, marine mammals, and shellfish were "front-loaded" resources, insofar as they required up-front labor costs and rapid and expert processing so the harvest did not go rancid prior to storage. More mobile communities may have avoided investing in front-loaded storage practices, particularly when such stores would have been vulnerable to seizure by others (Tushingham and Bettinger 2019). Although overall costs could be higher, back-loaded resources such as nuts and seeds could provide less risky alternatives because harvesters could delay processing costs before storage. This seems to have been the case in much of California, where intense harvesting of acorns seems to have preceded intense harvesting of salmon and pine nuts (Tushingham and Bettinger 2013). Women's strategic decision-making was also likely influenced by the opportunity costs of childcare, which could be decreased by selecting more back-loaded foods and strategies for storage (Fulkerson and Tushingham 2021; Whelan et al. 2013).

Coastal Habitat Settlement (The Ideal Free Distribution Model)

The ideal free distribution model focuses on the decisions people make about whether to establish a settlement in a habitat or migrate to a new habitat (Fretwell and Lucas 1970). When people encounter alternative habitats, they can rank them based on suitability, which generally includes the abundance of resources, the density of the population that inhabits and uses them, and other local factors. Recent application incorporates explicit consideration of natural (e.g., availability of fresh water, volcanism) and anthropogenic (e.g., investments in niche construction) variables that enhance the utility of this model for understanding behavioral responses to changing social and environmental conditions. In a recent *Environmental Archaeology* special issue on ideal free distribution, Weitzel and Codding (2020) stated that "there seem to be no geographic or temporal bounds to the utility of IDMs, and we look forward to the application of these models in ever more diverse settings." Among these more diverse settings, recent coastal research emphasizes that the suitability of habitats may be connected to the water rather than the land (e.g., Giovas and Fitzpatrick 2014; Hanna and Giovas 2019; Jazwa et al. 2013; Winterhalder et al. 2010). Thus, assessments of settlement locations may have been linked to how currents take boats in and offshore, the size and structure of nearshore marine habitats, or how deep or shallow the continental shelf is near the wharf. For example, the latter will define how far away from the shore larger fish prey might be encountered. In maritime societies, places with good landing conditions and wind protection were highly ranked habitats. Not surprisingly big shell midden sites and port cities are located near closed bays and geographic features protected from wind.

Similar to patch choice model predictions, the ideal free distribution model assumes that initial settlers or colonizers (assuming they are able to move freely) will choose to reside first in the highest-ranking and most suitable habitat. However, habitat value is dependent on density, and the model treats the presence of other people as part of what makes a habitat desirable or undesirable. At low population density, the Allee effect predicts a positive density effect in which further immigration or in situ population growth may increase habitat value (Sutherland 1996). Yet at high population density, further immigration or in situ growth can prompt a negative density effect that diminishes habitat value. As more people move into a habitat, crowding increases both direct and indirect competition for resources (Sutherland 1996). The resultant resource depletion drives down the marginal value of the highest-ranked habitat until it approximates the value of a second-ranked habitat that has not been settled yet (Winterhalder and Kennett 2006). At this point, when the marginal values of the first- and second-ranked habitats are equalized, people should migrate to the second-ranked habitat (Tremayne and Winterhalder 2017). Staying longer in the higher-ranked habitat would incur unfavorable opportunity costs because higher returns are available elsewhere. Lower-ranked habitats will continue to be settled in their rank order until there is no advantage to further spread.

This model predicts that the relative number of residents present in a habitat will match the relative abundance of resources available in the habitat (Pulliam and Caraco 1984; Tregenza 1994). This process is both dynamic and cumulative. Changes in population density will lead to changes in habitat value and vice versa. Assuming that the costs associated with relocation are negligible in comparison to the opportunity costs of not moving, migration enables people to continuously readjust settlement distribution toward the ideal distribution. People are not expected to abandon high-ranking habitats as lower-ranking ones are occupied (although cf. Winterhalder et al. 2010). In the optimal solution, whether settlements are distributed over one or more habitats, the marginal value of all occupied habitats is comparable and all residents experience equal gains.

Recent application of the ideal free distribution model has significantly advanced stagnant debate regarding the timing and nature (i.e., gradual vs. punctuated change) of increasing complexity throughout the Santa Barbara Channel region. According to this model, explanation is derived from understanding the general ecological processes that shape relationships between internal and external factors. This effort initially examined the colonization and subsequent resettlement dynamics but has since expanded to include the origins of social hierarchy, inequality, and territoriality (Jazwa et al. 2013, 2019; Jazwa, Duffy, et al. 2016; Jazwa, Kennett, et al. 2016; Kennett et al. 2009, 2013; Winterhalder et al. 2010). The ideal free distribution model integrates internal and external dynamics and offers a more sophisticated understanding of how slow and continuous change in environmental or demographic variables causes abrupt and discontinuous change in population-level responses (Winterhalder et al. 2010:485). Proponents of this approach argue that long-term increases in island population density led to infilling, environmental saturation, and declines in suitability of high-ranked habitats settled during the middle Holocene. Abrupt relocation of significant portions of the population occurred as individuals perceived the opportunity to do better by moving into less suitable but also less densely occupied habitats. Island residents expanded into secondary and tertiary habitats during the late Holocene as settlement opportunities became increasingly rare and relatively poor in their prospects (Winterhalder et al. 2010).

Winterhalder and colleagues (2010) showed that human settlement of the Northern Channel Islands of California conformed to an ideal free distribution using watershed attributes such as drainage size and beach length as suitability proxies. Detailed quantitative application of this model provides three critical insights: 1) emergence of sociopolitical complexity on the Northern Channel Islands likely occurred prior to 650 cal BP, 2) marginal change in one variable (i.e. demography or environment) may produce discontinuous change in related variables (i.e. settlement or foraging decisions), and 3) concepts of gradual or punctuated change better describe specific variables rather than whole systems (Winterhalder et al. 2010:485). Extending this approach to include concepts drawn from the despotic variant of ideal free distribution, Kennett and colleagues (2009:309; 2013:129) argue that cascading impacts on human health and increasing violence reflect heightened social and environmental circumscription exacerbated by climatic instability of the late Holocene—conditions primed for corporate group formation, asymmetrical access to resources, and institutionalized inequality between 1350 and 650 cal BP. Thus, ideal free distribution dynamics gave way to despotism as increased population packing and subsistence intensification led to unequal access to resources. Individuals resisted settling in the most marginal habitats in favor of subordinating themselves to despotic control in higher-suitability locations.

Coastal Costly Signaling

Costly signaling theory focuses on people's decision to pursue a resource even at a cost to the potential overall efficiency of foraging (Grafen 1990; Zahavi 1975, 1977). In this approach, the neo-Darwinian goal of reproductive fitness may be enhanced by foraging decisions that promote social opportunities for mating and partnerships. Thus, even a seemingly suboptimal foraging effort can increase fitness by contributing to a group's ability to acquire mates or allies. This logically shifts resource value away from energy derived from food. Resource value is instead predicated on social prestige (Winterhalder and Kennett 2006). Costly signaling theory assumes that not all calories are equal; some forms of energy are more prestigious than others (Bliege Bird and Smith 2005). Thus, the value of resources and how those resources are acquired or distributed will sometimes be predicated on the prestige associated with their use or the reliable information their capture signals about the underlying abilities of an individual (Smith and Bliege Bird 2000). Shifting the currency of the foraging models to social value shifts the modeling effort of human behavioral ecology from the narrow question of resource selection to broader anthropological issues such as the roles of gender, prestige, and power in structuring economic activity (Hawkes and Bliege Bird 2002).

Costly signaling theory predicts that individuals who engage in signaling behavior should target prestigious, hard-to-acquire resources that are large enough to be widely distributed within the community (Smith 2010). Such individuals benefit from enhanced desirability as a mate or an ally and the audience that receives the resources benefits from useful information about the quality of potential competitors, mates, and allies (Hawkes and Bliege Bird 2002). For example, Bliege Bird and colleagues (2001) documented how Meriam turtle hunters in the Torres Strait of Australia signal their abilities as marine hunters, risk takers, and leaders by giving away turtle meat at public events without any expectation of reciprocity. As turtle hunting involves a competitive and costly activity without an immediate benefit, the explanations for the provisioning of this collective good was the efficiency of sending a reliable signal about the quality of hunters as mates, allies, or competitors (Smith and Bliege Bird 2005; Smith et al. 2003). On the Ifaluk atoll of Micronesia, Sosis (2002) examined the seemingly poor foraging choice of torch fishing for dog-toothed tuna. Sosis concluded that torch fishing was a costly display that enhanced the status of the fishers in which the social benefit (mating gain) was not for the fishers themselves but for their younger matrilineal kin. Similarly, Alvard and Gillespie (2004) found that male whale hunters in Lamalera, Indonesia, had a selective advantage regarding marrying and reproducing earlier in their lives and thus having significantly more offspring.

Coastal Niche Construction

Niche construction theory emphasizes the reciprocal causality of changes in an ecosystem in which ecological and evolutionary processes shape human behavior and human behavior shapes the environment (Laland et al. 2015). The theory encompasses the niche-altering activities of all organisms but characterizes humans as "the ultimate niche constructors" (Zeder 2017:3). While niche construction theory recognizes that not all modifications humans make constitute niche construction and that niche construction can occur without influencing evolution (Bliege Bird and Codding 2015; Mohlenhoff and Codding 2017), it provides a testable framework for assessing the coevolution of ecosystems and human societies.

In human societies, the evolutionary consequences of niche-constructing behaviors may significantly alter the net benefits of different subsistence practices over the long term (Odling-Smee and Laland 2011). Accordingly, feedback between optimal behavior in the present, the structure of an ecosystem, and optimal behavior in the future creates interdependencies between human behavior and the coastal ecosystems in which people operate. One example is the habitat expansion that was the result of the construction of "clam gardens" along the Northwest Coast of North America. These were intertidal rack-walled terraces that increased prey abundance and improved harvest efforts through landscape modification (Groesbeck et al. 2014; Lepofsky et al. 2021). Another example is human foragers' use of fire to increase short-term gains by lowering search costs and increasing foraging efficiency, particularly for small game that favor disturbance habitats (Bird et al. 2005; Bliege Bird et al. 2008). Shifts from lightning to anthropogenic fire regimes have been linked to both positive effects (greater biodiversity, increased nutrient availability, and enhanced productivity of herbaceous plants; Bliege Bird et al. 2008) and negative effects (population extinctions, declines in mammal populations, and trophic cascades). Both the positive and negative impacts of niche construction contribute to ecological inheritances that act as directional forces for human adaptation (Odling-Smee et al. 2013).

Kluiving (2015) argued that transitional landscapes (i.e., coastlines, lakeshores, and rivers) where land meets water, saltwater mixes with freshwater, and mountains grade to river valleys were both attractive to early settlers and susceptible to the unintended impacts of subsistence pursuits (Daniels et al., this volume). Efforts to enhance relative abundance, buffer variation, or reduce scheduling conflicts of key resources generate changes to the ecosystem structure and alter the selection pressures future generations inherit. However, it is not possible to predict whether the effects of niche construction will be systematic or orderly (Constant et al. 2018). Unique local environmental, adaptive, and historical contexts shape these dynamic processes.

Emerging Directions

These foraging models are supported by a growing list of ethnographic and ethnoarchaeological studies of coastal societies that provide critical insights into the application of these concepts to the coast and its resources. However, it is important to acknowledge and perhaps lean into several important critiques. Human behavioral ecology is often perceived as an androcentric Western approach that is overly engaged with economic returns, does not regularly engage with Indigenous peoples, and overlooks or glosses over colonial forces that continue to impact these communities. We see these important critiques as foreshadowing emerging directions both in the field of human behavioral ecology and our own discipline of archaeology. Chapter authors throughout this book highlight opportunities for future growth that may help address these critiques.

A primary opportunity for human behavioral ecology is increased engagement with Indigenous communities and the incorporation of traditional ecological knowledge frameworks and collaborative research methodologies. Such work can provide valuable insights into sustainable practices, resource management, and humans' construction of niche coastal resources and habitats. Traditional ecological knowledge consists of continually updated cognitive maps of resource distributions, information about the life cycles of economically important resources, the seasons when resources are available, and how environments or biotic communities can be manipulated to enhance the supply and predictability of target resources. This knowledge is conveyed in stories, myths, ritual performance, and the lessons elders pass on to younger members of social groups. Traditional ecological knowledge provides a coherent framework for how the world works and the place of humans within it. Including these cultural behaviors among the variables that shape evolutionary trajectories, then, provides fresh insight into how the generation and transmission of traditional ecological knowledge plays a catalytic role in human adaptations (Zeder 2017). This is exemplified in recent studies that address anthropogenic "built landscapes" and practices that enhance resource productivity. Prey mobility in open waters can provide a conceptual challenge for prey choice models where well-defined boundaries are absent. In reality, the application of "built patches" or landscapes could be created through technology (e.g., weirs, traps, dams) to enhance capture rates or to signal or define ownership of resource patches; through resource management; or through niche construction (e.g., clam gardens, kelp gardens) that modify local ecologies and enhance sustainable resource production (Brown and Brown 2009; Groesbeck et al. 2014; Moss and Wellman 2017). While human behavioral ecology is often set in opposition to traditional ecological knowledge approaches, this does not need to be the case. For example, Fitzhugh and colleagues (2019:1079) propose a "human ecodynamics" approach that marries human behavioral ecology, traditional ecological knowledge, and other complementary frameworks.

Indigenous people and local experts can provide great insight into human behavioral ecology models because they often have firsthand knowledge of procurement, processing, and storage activities. Research collaborations and coauthorship with such individuals are opportunities to establish more realistic models, for instance by improving cost-benefit data, testing models through collaborative field research and experimental archaeology, and discussing how to establish the most appropriate currencies and values. Community-based archaeology often provides important insights about decision-making based on social interaction with landscapes that goes beyond economic productivity. For instance, in a study of limpet (*opihi*) foraging at sites on Moloka'i Island, Hawaii, Rodgers and Weisler (2021) found that optimal foraging theory models could not explain archaeological patterns. Low-ranked *Cellana sandwicensis* was the most common species. Working with modern Indigenous shellfish gatherers with extensive knowledge of *opihi* gathering and local ecologies led the authors to conclude that ancient shell-fishing practices followed social and cultural preferences over basic caloric returns. For instance, the community prioritized *C. sandwicensis*, which they ranked as having superior taste and texture. Another possible motivation was that the species was considered to be one of the most challenging of the *opihi* to procure (the community referred to it as the "fish of death"). So, as is the case today, its procurement may have been associated with costly signaling of "risk-taking behavior among men, as a social indicator of prowess" (Rodgers and Weisler 2021).

On the scale of the landscape, ideal free distribution models that recognize the role of humans in transforming ecological niches can help us better understand settlement in places that might not appear optimal at first glance. For instance, social and culturally specific variables and concepts of Indigenous relationality can be incorporated in frameworks that explain why people persist in inhabiting certain locales over long time scales—not because they offer better returns but because they are tied to ancestral landscapes (e.g., Helmer and Brown 2021).

In addition to building more realistic models, collaborative historical archaeology practices can help archaeologists develop research questions that interest local communities and have real-world consequences (Tushingham et al. 2019). For instance, many North American tribal and First Nations communities are actively engaged with the management (or comanagement) of ancestral fisheries and coastal resources and locations. While formal economic models are common in modern fisheries and coastal wildlife management, human behavioral ecology would seem to be a fruitful area of potential interdisciplinary collaboration, particularly in terms of conservation efforts (Low and Heinen 1993). Yet the deep-time archaeological data and human behavioral ecology insights can inform modern management, sustainable use practices of coastal environments, and similar topics that are often overlooked or are not presented adequately to land managers and Indigenous communities. This can be a missed opportunity for interdisciplinary collaboration that can maintain the relevancy of archaeological work that has real-world impacts.

Human behavioral ecology models can be a powerful way to understand the division of labor and decision-making by varied age and gender groups. Costly signaling and evolutionary leadership models tend to emphasize the decision-making of men and the social dynamics and formation of higher-level political structures, often at the expense of understanding women's contributions in these arenas. For example, women's roles in coastal adaptations are often glossed over or poorly explored. Women are often assumed to be primarily shell fishers whose participation in fishing was low. But this can be a stereotype, since women were clearly engaged with a variety of tasks and responsibilities (Kleiber et al. 2015; Moss 1993). Women played a major role in decisions about procuring, processing, and storing resources and about settlement patterns. Human behavioral ecology frameworks about risk-averse strategies are poised to help us understand such dynamics. For example, childcare opportunity costs—which are rarely explicitly considered in central place model applications—were likely critical to women's decisions about diet choice and food storage (e.g., see Fulkerson and Tushingham 2021; Hawkes et al. 1997; Hurtado et al. 1985, 1992; Whelan et al. 2013:665–666). Finally, while intensification scenarios often portray women as "drudges" who must endure more costly processing, evolutionary theory, particularly when informed by feminist thought, can help us understand some of the benefits and motivations behind women's decisions. The benefits of plant intensification and front-loaded storage strategies include greater reliability and thus enhanced provisioning for dependent offspring. Yet in addition to avoidance of potential food shortfalls and provisioning, it is likely that decisions were influenced by advantages related to power and status (Ackerman 2003; Frink 2007) and to an overall desire for household and personal autonomy relating to reproduction, social status, and subsistence (see also Tushingham, this volume).

Conclusions

Critical research traditions in coastal archaeology (reviewed in detail in Erlandson 2001, Erlandson and Fitzpatrick 2006, and Fitzpatrick et al. 2015) focus on 1) the environment and ecology of coastal communities, which are often at the frontlines of environmental change; 2) patterns of colonization, dispersal, and migration; 3) innovations made to specialized maritime technology; 4) patterns of settlement and resource use; and 5) the development of social and political complexity, including increased conflict and territoriality. In recent decades, increasing recognition of the unique and diverse evolutionary trajectories of coastal societies and their role in social transformation has moved coastal archaeology from the margins of anthropological debate to the center of methodological and theoretical advancements (Erlandson and Fitzpatrick 2006). The authors in this volume make substantive contributions to these research traditions, highlighting the many ways that human behavioral ecology contributes to theoretical interpretation and to our understanding of past coastal societies.

Volume Editors' Note

Carola Flores Fernandez

This book is dedicated to Domingo and Bernardo Broitman for their company and support in every single new path I take, and also to Barbara Voorhies and Michael Glassow for their guidance through my graduate training and beyond.

Heather B. Thakar

This book is dedicated to Michael Glassow and Barbara Voorhies for their generous mentorship and unwavering friendship.

References Cited

Ackerman, Lillian Alice. 2003. *A Necessary Balance: Gender and Power among Indians of the Columbia Plateau*. University of Oklahoma Press, Norman.

Alvard, Michael S. 1993. Testing the "Ecologically Noble Savage" Hypothesis: Interspecific Prey Choice by Piro Hunters of Amazonian Peru. *Human Ecology* 21(4):355–387.

Alvard, Michael S., and Allen Gillespie. 2004. Good Lamalera Whale Hunters Accrue Reproductive Benefits. *Research in Economic Anthropology* 23:225–247.

Alvard, Michael S., and David A. Nolin. 2002. Rousseau's Whale Hunt? Coordination among Big-Game Hunters. *Current Anthropology* 43(4):533–559.

Ames, Kenneth M. 1994. The Northwest Coast: Complex Hunter-Gatherers, Ecology, and Social Evolution. *Annual Review of Anthropology* 23(1):209–229.

———. 1998. Economic Prehistory of the Northern British Columbia Coast. *Arctic Anthropology* 35(1):68–87.

———. 2001. Slaves, Chiefs and Labour on the Northern Northwest Coast. *World Archaeology* 33(1):1–17.

———. 2002. Going by Boat: The Forager-Collector Continuum at Sea. In *Beyond Foraging and Collecting: Evolutionary Change in Hunter Gatherer Settlement Systems*, edited by Ben Fitzhugh and Junko Habu, pp. 19–52. Kluwer Academic/Plenum, New York.

Anderson, David G. 2004. Archaic Mounds and the Archaeology of Southeastern Tribal Societies. In *Signs of Power: The Rise of Cultural Complexity in the Southeast*, edited by Kenneth E. Sassaman, Michael J. Heckenberger, Jon L. Gibson, and Philip J. Carr, pp. 270–299. University of Alabama Press, Tuscaloosa.

Arnold, Jeanne E. 1996. The Archaeology of Complex Hunter-Gatherers. *Journal of Archaeological Method and Theory* 3(1):77–126.

Arnold, Jeanne E., and M. R. Walsh. 2010. *California's Ancient Past: From the Pacific to the Range of Light*. SAA Press, Washington, DC.

Aswani, Shankar. 1998. Patterns of Marine Harvest Effort in Southwestern New Georgia, Solomon Islands: Resource Management or Optimal Foraging? *Ocean & Coastal Management* 40(2–3):207–235.

Beckerman, Stephen. 1991. Barí Spear Fishing: Advantages to Group Formation? *Human Ecology* 19(4):529–554.

Begossi, Alpina. 1992. The Use of Optimal Foraging Theory in the Understanding of Fishing Strategies: A Case from Sepetiba Bay (Rio de Janeiro State, Brazil). *Human Ecology* 20(4):463–475.

———. 1995. Fishing Spots and Sea Tenure: Incipient Forms of Local Management in Atlantic Forest Coastal Communities. *Human Ecology* 23(3):387–406.

Begossi, Alpina, Mariana Clauzet, Natalia Hanazaki, P. Lopes, Milena Ramires, and Renato A. M. Silvano. 2009. Fishers' Decision Making, Optimal Foraging and Management. *III Seminário de Gestão Socioambiental Para o Desenvolvimento Sustentável da Aqüicultura e da Pesca no Brasil* 3:1–5.

Begossi, Alpina, and Peter J. Richerson. 1992. The Animal Diet of Families from Búzios Island (Brazil): An Optimal Foraging Approach. *Journal of Human Ecology* 3(2):433–458.

Begossi, A., R. A. M. Silvano, and R. M. Ramos. 2005. Foraging Behavior among Fishermen from the Negro and Piracicaba Rivers, Brazil: Implications for Management. *WIT Transactions on Ecology and the Environment* 83:503–513.

Beitl, Christine M. 2015. Mobility in the Mangroves: Catch Rates, Daily Decisions, and Dynamics of Artisanal Fishing in a Coastal Commons. *Applied Geography* 59:98–106.

Béné, Christophe, and Alexander Tewfik. 2001. Fishing Effort Allocation and Fishermen's Decision-Making Process in a Multi-Species Small-Scale Fishery: Analysis of the Conch and Lobster Fishery in Turks and Caicos Islands. *Human Ecology* 29(2):157–186.

Berkes, Fikret. 2015. *Coasts for People: Interdisciplinary Approaches to Coastal and Marine Resource Management*. Routledge, New York.

Bettinger, Robert L. 2009. *Hunter-Gatherer Foraging: Five Simple Models*. Eliot Werner, Clinton Corners, New York.

Bettinger, Robert L., Ripan Malhi, and Helen McCarthy. 1997. Central Place Models of Acorn and Mussel Processing. *Journal of Archaeological Science* 24(10):887–899.

Bettinger, R. L., and P. J. Richerson. 1996. The State of Evolutionary Archaeology. In *Darwinian Archaeologies*, edited by Herbert D. G. Machner, pp. 221–231. Plenum, New York.

Binford, Lewis R. 1980. Willow Smoke and Dogs' Tails: Hunter-Gatherer Settlement Systems and Archaeological Site Formation. *American Antiquity* 45(1):4–20.

———. 1990. Mobility, Housing, and Environment: A Comparative Study. *Journal of Anthropological Research* 46(2):119–152.

Bird, Douglas W. 1996. Intertidal Foraging Strategies among the Meriam of the Torres Strait Islands, Australia: An Evolutionary Ecological Approach to the Ethnoarchaeology of Tropical Marine Subsistence. PhD dissertation, University of California, Davis.

———. 1997. Behavioral Ecology and the Archaeological Consequences of Central Place Foraging among the Meriam. *Archeological Papers of the American Anthropological Association* 7(1):291–306.

Bird, Douglas W., and Rebecca Bliege Bird. 2000. The Ethnoarchaeology of Juvenile Foragers: Shellfishing Strategies among Meriam Children. *Journal of Anthropological Archaeology* 19(4):461–476.

Bliege Bird, Rebecca L., and Douglas W. Bird. 1997. Delayed Reciprocity and Tolerated Theft: The Behavioral Ecology of Food-Sharing Strategies. *Current Anthropology* 38(1):49–78.

Bliege Bird, Rebecca, Douglas W. Bird, Jane Balme, Nurit Bird-David, Benjamin Campbell, Kristin Hawkes, and Ian Keen. 2008. Why Women Hunt: Risk and Contemporary Foraging in a Western Desert Aboriginal Community. *Current Anthropology* 49(4):655–693.

Bliege Bird, Rebecca L., and Brian F. Codding. 2015. The Sexual Division of Labor. In *Emerging Trends in The Social and Behavioral Sciences*, edited by Robert Scott and Stephan Kosslyn, pp. 1–16. John Wiley & Sons, New York.

Bliege Bird, Rebecca L., Eric Smith, and Douglas W. Bird. 2001. The Hunting Handicap: Costly Signaling in Human Foraging Strategies. *Behavioral Ecology and Sociobiology* 50(1):9–19.

Bliege Bird, Rebecca L., and Eric Alden Smith. 2005. Signaling Theory, Strategic Interaction, and Symbolic Capital. *Current Anthropology* 46:221–248.

Borrero, Luis A., and Ramiro Barberena. 2006. Hunter-Gatherer Home Ranges and Marine Resources: An Archaeological Case from Southern Patagonia. *Current Anthropology* 47(5):855–867.

Brown, F., and Y. K. Brown. 2009. *Staying the Course, Staying Alive—Coastal First Nations Fundamental Truths: Biodiversity, Stewardship and Sustainability*. Biodiversity BC, Victoria, British Columbia.

Charnov, Eric L. 1976. Optimal Foraging: The Marginal Value Theorem. *Theoretical Population Biology* 9(2):129–136.

Chavez, Francisco P., and Monique Messié. 2009. A Comparison of Eastern Boundary Upwelling Ecosystems. *Progress in Oceanography* 83(1–4):80–96.

Chimello de Oliveira, Luiz Eduardo, and Alpina Begossi. 2011. Last Trip Return Rate Influence Patch Choice Decisions of Small-Scale Shrimp Trawlers: Optimal Foraging in São Francisco, Coastal Brazil. *Human Ecology* 39(3):323–332.

Codding, Brian F., and Douglas W. Bird. 2015. Behavioral Ecology and the Future of Archaeological Science. *Journal of Archaeological Science* 56:9–20.

Constant, Axel, Maxwell J. D. Ramstead, Samuel P. L. Veissière, John O. Campbell, and Karl J. Friston. 2018. A Variational Approach to Niche Construction. *Journal of the Royal Society Interface* 15(141):20170685.

de Boer, Willem F., Tania Pereira, and Almeida Guissamulo. 2000. Comparing Recent and Abandoned Shell Middens to Detect the Impact of Human Exploitation on the Intertidal Ecosystem. *Aquatic Ecology* 34(3):287–297.

de Boer, Willem F., Annemieke M. P. van Schie, Domingos F. Jocene, Alzira B. P. Mabote, and Almeida Guissamulo. 2001. The Impact of Artisanal Fishery on a Tropical Intertidal Benthic Fish Community. *Environmental Biology of Fishes* 61(2):213–229.

Ellis, Erle C. 2015. Ecology in an Anthropogenic Biosphere. *Ecological Monographs* 85(3):287–331.

Emlen, J. Merritt. 1966. The Role of Time and Energy in Food Preference. *American Naturalist* 100(916):611–617.

Erlandson, Jon M. 2001. The Archaeology of Aquatic Adaptations: Paradigms for a New Millennium. *Journal of Archaeological Research* 9(4):287–350.

Erlandson, J. M., and S. M. Fitzpatrick. 2006. Oceans, Islands, and Coasts: Current Perspectives on the Role of the Sea in Human Prehistory. *Journal of Island & Coastal Archaeology* 1(1):5–32.

Fitzhugh, Ben, Virginia L. Butler, Kristine M. Bovy, and Michael A. Etnier. 2019. Human Ecodynamics: A Perspective for the Study of Long-Term Change in Socioecological Systems. *Journal of Archaeological Science: Reports* 23:1077–1094.

Fitzpatrick, Scott M., Torben C. Rick, and Jon M. Erlandson. 2015. Recent Progress, Trends, and Developments in Island and Coastal Archaeology. *Journal of Island and Coastal Archaeology* 10(1):3–27.

Fretwell, S. D., and H. L. Lucas Jr. 1970. On Territorial Behavior and Other Factors Influencing Habitat Distribution in Birds. I. Theoretical Development. *Acta Biotheoretica* 19:16–36.

Frink, Lisa. 2007. Storage and Status in Precolonial and Colonial Coastal Western Alaska. *Current Anthropology* 48(3):349–374.

Fulkerson, Tiffany J., and Shannon Tushingham. 2021. Geophyte Field Processing, Storage, and Women's Decision-Making in Hunter-Gatherer Societies: An Archaeological Case Study from Western North America. *Journal of Anthropological Archaeology* (62):101299.

Gillis, Darren M., Ellen K. Pikitch, and Randall M. Peterman. 1995. Dynamic Discarding Decisions: Foraging Theory for High-Grading in a Trawl Fishery. *Behavioral Ecology* 6(2):146–154.

Giovas, Christina M., and Scott M. Fitzpatrick. 2014. Prehistoric Migration in the Caribbean: Past Perspectives, New Models and the Ideal Free Distribution of West Indian Colonization. *World Archaeology* 46(4):569–589.

Grafen, A. 1990. Biological Signals as Handicaps. *Journal of Theoretical Biology* 144:517–546.

Groesbeck, Amy S., Kirsten Rowell, Dana Lepofsky, and Anne K. Salomon. 2014. Ancient Clam Gardens Increased Shellfish Production: Adaptive Strategies from the Past Can Inform Food Security Today. *PLOS ONE* 9(3):91235.

Hanna, Jonathan A., and Christina M. Giovas. 2019. An Islandscape IFD: Using the Ideal Free Distribution to Predict Pre-Columbian Settlements from Grenada to St. Vincent Eastern Caribbean. *Environmental Archaeology* 27(4):402–419.

Hawkes, Kristen, and Rebecca Bliege Bird. 2002. Showing Off, Handicap Signaling, and the Evolution of Men's Work. *Evolutionary Anthropology: Issues, News, and Reviews* 11(2):58–67.

Hawkes, Kristen, Kim Hill, and James F. O'Connell. 1982. Why Hunters Gather: Optimal Foraging and the Ache of Eastern Paraguay. *American Ethnologist* 9(2):379–398.

Hawkes, Kristen, James F. O'Connell, and N. G. Jones. 1997. Hadza Women's Time Allocation, Offspring Provisioning, and the Evolution of Long Postmenopausal Life Spans. *Current Anthropology* 38(4):551–577.

———. 1991. Hunting Income Patterns among the Hadza: Big Game, Common Goods, Foraging Goals and the Evolution of the Human Diet. *Philosophical Transactions of the Royal Society of London Series B: Biological Sciences* 334(1270):243–250.

Helmer, E. and J. W. Brown. 2021. Site Suitability Modeling with Culturally-Specific Variables: A Southern Northwest Coast Case Study. *Journal of Archaeological Science: Reports* 36(1270):243–251.

Hurtado, A. Magdalena, Kristen Hawkes, Kim Hill, and Hillard Kaplan. 1985. Female Subsistence Strategies among Ache Hunter-Gatherers of Eastern Paraguay. *Human Ecology* (13):1–28.

Hurtado, A. Magdalena, Kim Hill, Ines Hurtado, and Hillard Kaplan. 1992. Trade-Offs between Female Food Acquisition and Child Care among Hiwi and Ache Foragers. *Human Nature* 3(3):185–216.

Jazwa, Christopher S., Christopher J. Duffy, Lorne Leonard, and Douglas J. Kennett. 2016. Hydrological Modeling and Prehistoric Settlement on Santa Rosa Island, California, USA. *Geoarchaeology: An International Journal* 31:101–120.

Jazwa, Christopher S., Douglas J. Kennett, and Bruce Winterhalder. 2013. The Ideal Free Distribution and Settlement History at Old Ranch Canyon, Santa Rosa Island. In *California's Channel Islands: The Archaeology of Human-Environment Interactions*, edited by C. S. Jazwa and J. E. Perry, pp. 75–96. University of Utah Press, Salt Lake City.

———. 2016. A Test of Ideal Free Distribution Predictions Using Targeted Survey and Excavation on California's Northern Channel Islands. *Journal of Archaeological Method and Theory* (23):1242–1284.

Jazwa, Christopher S., Douglas J. Kennett, Bruce Winterhalder, and Terry L. Joslin. 2019. Territoriality and the Rise of Despotic Social Organization on Western Santa Rosa Island, California. *Quaternary International* (518):41–56.

Kaplan, Hillard, and Kim Hill. 1992. The Evolutionary Ecology of Food Acquisition. In *Evolutionary Ecology and Human Behaviour*, edited by E. A. Smith and B. Winterhalder, pp. 167–201. Routledge, New York.

Keeley, Lawrence H. 1988. Hunter-Gatherer Economic Complexity and "Population Pressure": A Cross-Cultural Analysis. *Journal of Anthropological Archaeology* 7(4):373–411.

Kelly, Robert L. 2013. *The Lifeways of Hunter-Gatherers: The Foraging Spectrum*. Cambridge University Press, Cambridge.

Kennett, Douglas J. 2005. *The Island Chumash: Behavioral Ecology of a Maritime Society*. University of California Press, Los Angeles.

Kennett, Douglas J., and Robert A. Clifford. 2004. Flexible Strategies for Resource Defense on the Northern Channel Islands of California: An Agent-Based Model. In *Voyages of Discovery: The Archaeology of Islands*, edited by Scott Fitzpatrick, pp. 21–50. Greenwood, Westport, Connecticut.

Kennett, Douglas J., and James P. Kennett. 2006. Early State Formation in Southern Mesopotamia: Sea Levels, Shorelines, and Climate Change. *Journal of Island & Coastal Archaeology* 1(1):67–99.

Killingray, David, Margarette Lincoln, and Nigel Rigby (editors). 2004. *Maritime Empires: British Imperial Maritime Trade in the Nineteenth Century*. Boydell, Rochester, New York.

Kleiber, Danika, Leila M. Harris, and Amanda C. J. Vincent. 2015. Gender and Small-Scale Fisheries: A Case for Counting Women and Beyond. *Fish and Fisheries* 16(4):547–562.

Krebs, John R., and Nicholas B. Davies (editors). 2009. *Behavioural Ecology: An Evolutionary Approach*. John Wiley & Sons, New York.

Kroeber, Alfred Louis. 1939. *Cultural and Cultural Areas of Native North America*. University of California Press, Berkeley.

Kuhnlein, Harriet V., Alvin C. Chan, J. Neville Thompson, and Shuryo Nakai. 1982. Ooligan Grease: A Nutritious Fat Used by Native People of Coastal British Columbia. *Journal of Ethnobiology* 2(2):154–161.

Laland, Kevin N., Tobias Uller, Marcus W. Feldman, Kim Sterelny, Gerd B. Müller, Armin

Moczek, Eva Jablonka, and John Odling-Smee. 2015. The Extended Evolutionary Synthesis: Its Structure, Assumptions and Predictions. *Proceedings of the Royal Society B: Biological Sciences* 282(1813):20151019.

Lambert, Patricia M. 1997. Patterns of Violence in Prehistoric Hunter-Gatherer Societies of Coastal Southern California. In *Troubled Times: Violence and Warfare in The Past,* edited by David Frayer and Debra L. Martin, pp. 77–109. Routledge, New York.

Lepofsky, Dana, Ginevra Toniello, Jacob Earnshaw, Christine Roberts, Louis Wilson, Kirsten Rowell, and Keith Holmes. 2021. Ancient Anthropogenic Clam Gardens of the Northwest Coast Expand Clam Habitat. *Ecosystems* 24:248–260.

Leppard, Thomas P. 2014. Modeling the Impacts of Mediterranean Island Colonization by Archaic Hominins: The Likelihood of an Insular Lower Palaeolithic. *Journal of Mediterranean Archaeology* 27:231–254.

Lopes, Priscila F. M., Renato A. M. Silvano, and Alpina Begossi. 2011. Extractive and Sustainable Development Reserves in Brazil: Resilient Alternatives to Fisheries? *Journal of Environmental Planning and Management* 54(4):421–443.

Low, Bobbi S., and Joel T. Heinen. 1993. Population, Resources, and Environment: Implications of Human Behavioral Ecology for Conservation. *Population and Environment* 15(1):7–41.

Macarthur, Robert H., and Eric R. Pianka. 1966. On Optimal Use of a Patchy Environment. *American Naturalist* 100(916):603–609.

Marean, Curtis W. 2014. The Origins and Significance of Coastal Resource Use in Africa and Western Eurasia. *Journal of Human Evolution* 77(1):17–40.

McCay, Bonnie J. 1981. Optimal Foragers or Political Actors? Ecological Analyses of a Jersey Fishery. *American Ethnologist* 8(2):356–382.

McKechnie, Iain, and Madonna L. Moss. 2016. Meta-analysis in Zooarchaeology Expands Perspectives on Indigenous Fisheries of the Northwest Coast of North America. *Journal of Archaeological Science: Reports* 8:470–485.

Metcalfe, Duncan, and K. Renee Barlow. 1992. A Model for Exploring the Optimal Trade-Off between Field Processing and Transport. *American Anthropologist* 94(2):340–356.

Mohlenhoff, Kathryn A., and Brian F. Codding. 2017. When Does It Pay to Invest in a Patch? The Evolution of Intentional Niche Construction. *Evolutionary Anthropology: Issues, News, and Reviews* 26(5):218–227.

Monks, Gregory G. P. 1987. Prey as Bait: The Deep Bay Example. *Canadian Journal of Archaeology/Journal Canadien d'Archéologie* 11:119–142.

Moss, Madonna L. 1993. Shellfish, Gender, and Status on the Northwest Coast: Reconciling Archeological, Ethnographic, And Ethnohistorical Records of the Tlingit. *American Anthropologist* 95(3):631–652.

———. 2004. Island Societies Are Not Always Insular: Tlingit Territories in the Alexander Archipelago and the Adjacent Alaska Mainland. In *Voyages of Discovery: The Archaeology of Islands,* edited by Scott Fitzpatrick, pp. 165–183. Greenwood, Westport, Connecticut.

Moss, Madonna L., and Jon M. Erlandson. 1992. Forts, Refuge Rocks, and Defensive Sites: The Antiquity of Warfare along the North Pacific Coast of North America. *Arctic Anthropology* 29(2):73–90.

Moss, Madonna L., and Hannah P. Wellman. 2017. The Magoun Clam Garden near Sitka,

Alaska: Niche Construction Theory Meets Traditional Ecological Knowledge, but What about the Risks of Shellfish Toxicity? *Alaska Journal of Anthropology* 15(1–2):7–24.

Nolin, David A. 2010. Food-Sharing Networks in Lamalera, Indonesia. *Human Nature* 21(3):243–268.

Odling-Smee, J., D. H. Erwin, E. P. Palkovacs, M. W. Feldman, and K. N. Laland. 2013. Niche Construction Theory: A Practical Guide for Ecologists. *Quarterly Review of Biology* 88(1):3–28.

Odling-Smee, John, and Kevin N. Laland. 2011. Ecological Inheritance and Cultural Inheritance: What Are They and How Do They Differ? *Biological Theory* 6(3):220–230.

Orians, Gordon H., and Nolan E. Pearson. 1979. On the Theory of Central Place Foraging. In *Analysis of Ecological Systems*, edited by D. J. Horn and R. D. Mitchell, pp. 155–177. Ohio State University Press, Columbus.

Perlman, Stephen M. 1980. An Optimum Diet Model, Coastal Variability, and Hunter-Gatherer Behavior. *Advances in Archaeological Method and Theory* 3:257–310.

Pulliam, H. R., and T. Caraco. 1984. Living in Groups: Is There an Optimal Group Size? In *Behavioural Ecology: An Evolutionary Approach*, edited by J. R. Krebs and N. B. Davies, pp. 122–47. Blackwell Scientific, Oxford.

Rainbird, Paul. 1999. Islands Out of Time: Towards a Critique of Island Archaeology. *Journal of Mediterranean Archaeology* 12(2):216–234.

Rindos, D. 1984. *The Origins of Agriculture: An Evolutionary Perspective.* Academic Press, New York.

Rogers, Ashleigh J. and Marshall I. Weisler. 2021. *He iʻa make ka ʻopihi:* Optimal Foraging Theory, Food Choice, and the Fish of Death. *Journal of Archaeological Method and Theory* 28:1314–1347.

Seixas, Cristiana S., and A. Begossi. 2000. Central Place Optimal Foraging Theory: Population and Individual Analyses of Fishing Strategies at Aventureiro (Ilha Grande, Brazil). *Ciência e Cultura* 52(2):85–92.

Simms, Steven R. 1987. *Behavioral Ecology and Hunter-Gatherer Foraging: An Example from the Great Basin.* British Archaeological Reports International Series 381. British Archaeological Reports, Oxford.

Small, Christopher, and Robert J. Nicholls. 2003. A Global Analysis of Human Settlement in Coastal Zones. *Journal of Coastal Research* 19(3):584–599.

Smith, Eric Alden. 1991. *Inujjiamiut Foraging Strategies: Evolutionary Ecology of an Arctic Hunting Economy.* Aldine de Gruyter, New York.

———. 2010. Communication and Collective Action: Language and the Evolution of Human Cooperation. *Evolution and Human Behavior* 31(4):231–245.

Smith, Eric Alden, and Rebecca L. Bliege Bird. 2000. Turtle Hunting and Tombstone Opening: Public Generosity as Costly Signaling. *Evolution and Human Behavior* 21(4):245–261.

———. 2005. Costly Signaling and Cooperative Behavior. In *Moral Sentiments and Material Interests: The Foundations of Cooperation in Economic Life*, edited by Herbert Gintis, Samuel Bowles, Robert T. Boyd, and Ernst Fehr, pp. 115–132. MIT Press, Cambridge, Massachusetts.

Smith, Eric Alden, Rebecca Bliege Bird, and Douglas W. Bird. 2003. The Benefits of Costly Signaling: Meriam Turtle Hunters. *Behavioral Ecology* 14(1):116–126.

Sosis, Richard. 2000. Costly Signaling and Torch Fishing on Ifaluk Atoll. *Evolution and Human Behavior* 21(4):223–244.

———. 2001. Sharing, Consumption, and Patch Choice on Ifaluk Atoll. *Human Nature* 12(3):221–245.

———. 2002. Patch Choice Decisions among Ifaluk Fishers. *American Anthropologist* 104(2):583–598.

Stephens, David W., and John R. Krebs. 1986. *Foraging Theory*. Vol. 1. Princeton University Press, Princeton, New Jersey.

Sutherland, William J. 1996. Predicting the Consequences of Habitat Loss for Migratory Populations. *Proceedings of the Royal Society of London: Series B: Biological Sciences* 263(1375):1325–1327.

Thiel, M., E. C. Macaya, E. Acuña, W. Arntz, H. Bastias, K. Brokordt, P. Camus, J. C. Castilla, L. Castro, M. Cortés, C. Dumont, R. Escribano, M. Fernandez, J. Gajardo, C. Gaymer, I. Gómez, A. González, H. Gonzalez, P. Haye, J. E. Illanes, J. L. Iriarte, D. Lancellotti, G. Luna-Jorquera, C. Luxoro, P. Manriquez, V. Marín, P. Muñoz, S. A. Navarrete, E. Perez, E. Poulin, J. Sellanes, H. Sepúlveda, W. Stotz, F. Tala, A. Thomas, C. Vargas, J. Vásquez, and A. Vega. 2007. The Humboldt Current System of Northern and Central Chile, Oceanographic Processes, Ecological Interactions and Socioeconomic Feedback. *Oceanographic Marine Biology* 45:195–344.

Thomas, Frank R. 2002. An Evaluation of Central-Place Foraging among Mollusk Gatherers in Western Kiribati, Micronesia: Linking Behavioral Ecology with Ethnoarchaeology. *World Archaeology* 34(1):182–208.

———. 2007a. The Behavioral Ecology of Shellfish Gathering in Western Kiribati, Micronesia, 1: Prey Choice. *Human Ecology* 35:179–194.

———. 2007b. The Behavioral Ecology of Shellfish Gathering in Western Kiribati, Micronesia, 2: Patch Choice, Patch Sampling, and Risk. *Human Ecology* 35:515–526.

Tregenza, Tom. 1994. Common Misconceptions in Applying the Ideal Free Distribution. *Animal Behaviour* 47(2):485–487.

Tremayne, Andrew H., and Bruce Winterhalder. 2017. Large Mammal Biomass Predicts the Changing Distribution of Hunter-Gatherer Settlements in Mid-Late Holocene Alaska. *Journal of Anthropological Archaeology* 45:81–97.

Tushingham, Shannon. 2020. The Ordered Anarchy Frontier: Storage, Sedentism, and the Evolution of Plank House Villages on the Southern Pacific Northwest Coast. In *Cowboy Ecologist: Papers in Honor of Robert L. Bettinger*, edited by Michael G. Delacorte, Terry L. Jones, and Roshanne S. Bakhtiary, 49–69. Center for Archaeological Research, University of California at Davis.

Tushingham, Shannon, Loukas Barton, and R. L. Bettinger. 2021. How Ancestral Subsistence Strategies Solve Salmon Starvation and the "Protein Problem" of Pacific Rim Resources. *American Journal of Physical Anthropology* 175(4):741–761.

Tushingham, Shannon, and Robert L. Bettinger. 2013. Why Foragers Choose Acorns before Salmon: Storage, Mobility, and Risk in Aboriginal California. *Journal of Anthropological Archaeology* 32(4):527–537.

———. 2019. Storage Defense: Expansive and Intensive Territorialism in Hunter-Gatherer Delayed Return Economies. *Quaternary International* 518:21–30.

Tushingham, Shannon, and Colin Christiansen. 2015. Native American Fisheries of the

Northwestern California and Southwestern Oregon Coast: A Synthesis of Fish-Bone Data and Implications for Late Holocene Storage and Socio-Economic Organization. *Journal of California and Great Basin Anthropology* 35(2):189–215.

Tushingham, Shannon, Justin Hopt, Colin Christiansen, Me'lash-ne Loren Bommelyn, John Green, Michael Peterson, Suntayea Steinruck, Crista Stewart. 2020. In the Footsteps of Amelia Brown: Collaborative Historical Ecology at Shin-yvslh-sri~, a Tolowa Village on the North Coast of California. *Journal of Island and Coastal Archaeology* 15(1):3–27.

Weitzel, Elic M., and Brian F. Codding. 2020. The Ideal Distribution Model and Archaeological Settlement Patterning. *Environmental Archaeology* 27(4):349–356. https://doi.org/10.1080/14614103.2020.1803015.

Whelan, Carly S., Adrian R. Whitaker, Jeffrey S. Rosenthal, and Eric Wohlgemuth. 2013. Hunter-Gatherer Storage, Settlement, and the Opportunity Costs of Women's Foraging. *American Antiquity* 78(4):662.

Wickham-Jones, Caroline. 2014. Coastal Adaptations. In *The Oxford Handbook of the Archaeology and Anthropology of Hunter-Gatherers*, vol. 1, edited by Vicki Cummings, Peter Jordan, and Marek Zvelebil. Oxford University Press, Oxford.

Winterhalder, Bruce. 1981. Foraging Strategies in the Boreal Environment: An Analysis of Cree Hunting and Gathering. In *Hunter-Gatherer Foraging Strategies: Ethnographic and Archeological Analyses*, edited by B. Winterhalder and E. A. Smith, pp. 66–98. University of Chicago Press, Chicago.

———. 1986. Diet Choice, Risk, and Food Sharing in a Stochastic Environment. *Journal of Anthropological Archaeology* 5(4):369–392.

Winterhalder, Bruce, and Douglas J. Kennett. 2006. Behavioral Ecology and the Transition from Hunting and Gathering to Agriculture. In *Behavioral Ecology and the Transition to Agriculture*, edited by Douglas J. Kennett and Bruce Winterhalder, pp. 1–21. University of California Press, Los Angeles.

Winterhalder, Bruce, Douglas J. Kennett, Mark N. Grote, and Jacob Bartruff. 2010. Ideal Free Settlement of California's Northern Channel Islands. *Journal of Anthropological Archaeology* 29(4):469–490.

Winterhalder, Bruce, and Eric Alden Smith. 1981. *Hunter-Gatherer Foraging Strategies: Ethnographic and Archeological Analyses.* University of Chicago Press, Chicago.

———. 1992. Evolutionary Ecology and The Social Sciences. In *Evolutionary Ecology and Human Behavior*, edited by Eric Alden Smith and Bruce Winterhalder, pp. 3–24. Routledge, New York.

———. 2000. Analyzing Adaptive Strategies: Human Behavioral Ecology at Twenty-Five. *Evolutionary Anthropology: Issues, News, and Reviews* 9(2):51–72.

Zahavi, Amotz. 1975. Mate Selection—A Selection for a Handicap. *Journal of Theoretical Biology* 53(1):205–214.

———. 1977. The Cost of Honesty: Further Remarks on The Handicap Principle. *Journal of Theoretical Biology* 67(3):603–605.

Zeanah, David W. 2000. Transport Costs, Central Place Foraging, and Hunter-Gatherer Alpine Land Use Strategies. *Intermountain Archaeology* 122:1–14.

Zeanah, David W., Brian F. Codding, Douglas W. Bird, Rebecca Bliege Bird, and Peter M. Veth. 2015. Diesel and Damper: Changes in Seed Use and Mobility Patterns Following

Contact amongst the Martu of Western Australia. *Journal of Anthropological Archaeology* 39:51–62.

Zeder, Melinda A. 2017. Domestication as a Model System for the Extended Evolutionary Synthesis. *Interface Focus* 7:20160133.

I

Regional Overviews

1

Human Behavioral Ecology and the Complexities of Arctic Environments

CATHERINE F. WEST, ERIK GJESFJELD, SHELBY
ANDERSON, AND BEN FITZHUGH

Human populations are well adapted to coastal environments across the Arctic and Subarctic (Figure 1.1). However, they frequently face difficult and unpredictable conditions that place a premium on the strategies people choose for subsistence, reproduction, and settlement. For example, extreme seasonality dramatically changes the Arctic landscape as sea ice freezes and thaws, and seasonal storminess in the Subarctic significantly restricts human movement and resource availability. Human behavioral ecology has been used to understand human-environmental dynamics across these environments in a variety of ways.

In this chapter, we focus principally on the region between the ice-free North Pacific Ocean and the ice-dominated Arctic Ocean. We use the term "Beringian Corridor" to refer to this ecologically complex region (Figure 1.2). The Beringian Corridor is a transect that captures much of the environmental and seasonal variability around the circumpolar Arctic and the Subarctic. It also captures diverse hunter-gatherer lifeways and resource availability. We review three key contributions of human behavioral ecology models to our understanding of past hunter-gatherer behavior in these places, including applications of the optimal foraging prey choice model to zooarchaeological datasets; paleodemographic approaches to reconstructing and interpreting fluctuations in the size and density of human populations; and use of the ideal free distribution model to help us understand shifting settlement patterns in northern Alaska. While these approaches have expanded our understanding of lifeways in the North, we believe that human behavioral ecology models that consider extreme seasonality, the resulting need to store and share food, and the degree to which climate

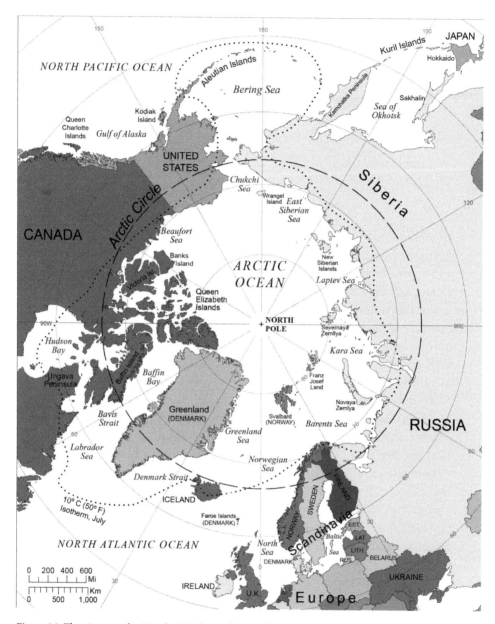

Figure 1.1. The circumpolar North. Map by Kathryn Killackey.

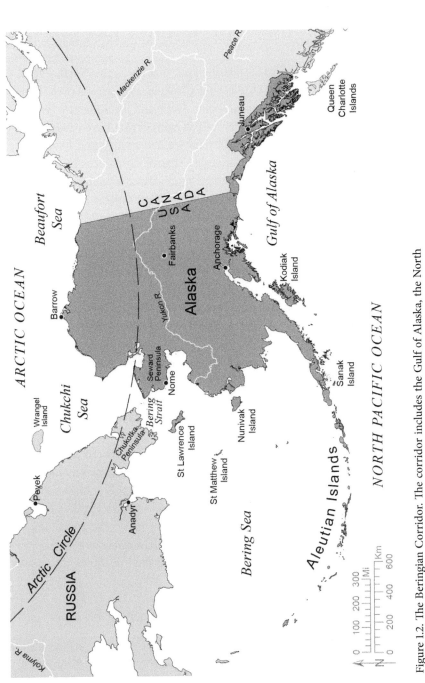

Figure 1.2. The Beringian Corridor. The corridor includes the Gulf of Alaska, the North Pacific Ocean, the Sea of Okhotsk, and the Bering, Chukchi, and Beaufort Seas. Map by Kathryn Killackey.

change has influenced both population dynamics and settlement patterns are necessary to move this research forward.

The Beringian Corridor

We define the Beringian Corridor as the Gulf of Alaska, the North Pacific Ocean, the Sea of Okhotsk, and the Bering, Chukchi, and Beaufort Seas (Figure 1.2). This corridor, like the circumpolar Arctic and the Subarctic (Figure 1.1), includes highly variable geographies and habitats that have conditioned the different adaptive strategies used by the human groups that have lived in this region for millennia. This variability shaped differences in technology, human population density, residential aggregation, foraging group size, storage practices, and, ultimately, social and political aspects of territoriality and competitiveness (e.g., Anderson et al. 2011; Davis and Knecht 2010; Fitzhugh 2003; Mason 1998). For example, modes of travel, patchiness, and the timing of available resources differ throughout the Beringian Corridor on a seasonal basis. In the past, travel costs were determined in part by the presence or absence of sea ice on the landscape. In the south, open water conditions meant that coastal waters were available mostly year-round, while in the north, travel costs demanded seasonal adaptations to both open water and sea ice. The seasonally abundant and patchy geographic distribution of many key subsistence species—such as migratory caribou, salmon, and marine species—contributed to diverse hunter-gatherer subsistence adaptations across the region. Northern peoples developed innovative mass capture and food storage technologies (e.g., drying, smoking, oil rendering) and complex social systems of exchange, sharing, and seasonal movement that can ameliorate the cycles of abundance and scarcity of critical northern subsistence resources. In the Beringian Corridor, Alaska Native communities include the Alutiiq/Sugpiaq, Unanga (Aleuts), southern Yupik, northern Alaska Yupik and Iñupiaq, and, on the Asian side, the Chukchi, Siberian Yupik, Koryak, and Kuril Ainu (Fitzhugh and Crowell 1988; Takase 2018). The archaeological record of maritime lifeways across this region demonstrates a long-term intimate relationship between people and coastal environments that goes back thousands of years (Fitzhugh 2016).

Human Behavioral Ecology in the Circumpolar North

Human behavioral ecology applies the principles of evolutionary ecology to studies of human behavior as it relates to ecological context (Smith and Winterhalder 1992). Kelly (2013:31) summarizes the approach: "Human behavioral ecology is . . . concerned with understanding how different human behaviors are adaptive in a particular environmental or social context." Applications of human behavioral ecology assume that the capacity to change behavior, with its expensive cognitive demands, arose in hominin development as a consequence of evolution by natural selection in environments where flexibility would have conferred evolutionary advantages (e.g., in highly varying and unpredictable settings). For such behavioral plasticity to have evolved and stabilized in a population or species, it would also have had to have been paired with a biologically anchored inclination to seek adaptive over maladaptive solutions to environmental challenges. Human behavioral ecologists predict that human behavior will change in pursuit of optimal outcomes, or the best net benefit to cost. In the past 45 years, human behavioral ecology has been constructively applied to questions of human foraging, mobility and sedentism, intensification and origins of agriculture, group size, emergent inequalities, and prestige (see the summary in Codding and Bird 2015).

However, human behavioral ecology is widely criticized for its biological reductionism, ecological materialism, and neglect of the culture concept (e.g., Smith 2006). While these criticisms are understandable, they often fail to recognize that human behavioral ecology is most often used heuristically to differentiate between activities that can be explained with biological and economic principles and those that cannot. While we cannot speak for others who have used human behavioral ecology models in their work, we readily acknowledge that human behavior is embedded in and rationalized according to cultural meanings and social logics that cannot be fully reduced to evolutionary or economic principles. Nevertheless, we believe that human behavioral ecology models are useful starting points, especially for studying aggregate patterns of human behaviors through time archaeologically and in relation to environmental dynamics.

Among those who study high-latitude environments, there is a strong emphasis on using human behavioral ecology models to reconstruct three long-term processes: 1) changes in diet and resource use; 2) fluctuations in the size and density of human populations; and 3) shifting settlement patterns. This emphasis is partly a product of the assumption that changes in the environment strongly influenced how communities lived in Arctic and Subarctic regions. Here, we present these processes as examples of how the archaeological evidence of these regions can be interpreted through human behavioral ecology models to examine the fundamental question of how ecological forces influence long-term changes in diet, population, and settlement. However, these examples also highlight the opportunity to expand human behavioral ecology models to incorporate the impact of seasonal variability in resources across the landscape more fully. Seasonality is discussed most often in terms of foraging decisions, but in northern latitudes it is valuable to consider how seasonal changes in resources may also influence social networks, territoriality, and even social inequality.

Subsistence: Resource Use and Diet Breadth

Optimal foraging theory is a subfield of behavioral ecology that seeks to predict how people (and nonhuman animals) make optimal choices while foraging. These choices include which prey to pursue upon encounter, whether or not to transport all or parts of a carcass back to camp, when to stay in a patch and continue diminishing the available resources or move to another patch, and what resources to pursue from central campsites. Diet breadth models have served as the workhorse for human behavioral ecology zooarchaeological analyses around the world, including the Beringian Corridor (e.g., Betts and Friesen 2006; Darwent 2002). In general, the diet breadth model of optimal foraging theory predicts that as encounters with high-ranked resources decrease, people will incorporate lower-ranked resources into their diet, increasing the diet breadth (Kaplan and Hill 1992; Kelly 2013). The model anticipates that changes in encounter rates correlate with changes in the relative abundance of identified taxa in the archaeological record. Along the Beringian Corridor, these models have been applied most widely in the Gulf of Alaska, where they have been used to predict how increasing social complexity, harvest pressure, and late Holocene climate change should have influenced human foraging strategies (Betts et al. 2008, 2011; Kopperl 2003; Shaw 2012; West 2009).

Drawing on optimal foraging theory models, Fitzhugh (2003) argued that increasing social complexity among hunter-gatherers in the Gulf of Alaska could be explained—in part—as a consequence of resource intensification. He predicted that as hunter-gatherer populations in the Kodiak archipelago grew and became more densely packed over time, resource intensification should have led to a decrease in the number of high-ranked and slow-reproducing marine mammals. Those pressures should then have triggered technological intensification that made it more efficient to harvest lower-ranked resources and shuffled the optimal diet rankings. In an effort to evaluate this model, Kopperl (2003) tested for resource intensification in the zooarchaeological record of the Kodiak archipelago. He found that decreases in marine mammal abundance did precede increases in marine fish abundance at the Rice Ridge site 6,000–4,000 years ago. However, he was not able to say whether the relative decrease in marine mammal use and increase in marine fish was attributable to the overhunting of highly ranked marine mammals (as he had predicted) or to a shift in available taxa due to the influence of climate change on local habitats.

Building on this work, diet breadth models have been used in the Gulf of Alaska to tease apart the effects of climate change, resource availability, and human harvest pressure on human subsistence strategies. West (2009) used a diet breadth model to predict how changes in climate and the availability of Pacific salmon (*Oncorhynchus* spp.) should have influenced fishing strategies on the Karluk River in the Kodiak archipelago over the last 2,000 years. Drawing on local climate records (West 2009; West et al. 2011) and the independent paleolimnological record of salmon abundance that Finney and colleagues (2002) produced, West found that observed decreases in salmon productivity did not consistently correspond with increases in diet breadth over this period. Similar studies from the Sanak Biocomplexity Project used diet breadth models to predict how highly ranked Otariidae (the northern fur seal and the Steller sea lion) and Pacific cod (*Gadus macrocephalus*) should have been influenced by both climate change and human harvesting on Sanak Island over the last 4,500 years (Betts et al. 2008, 2011). Changes in otariid use relative to smaller-bodied marine mammals varied over time: there was an increase in the relative frequency of otariids in the archaeological record from 4,500 to 3,500 years ago, followed by a decline at 1,000 years ago and a slight increase at 500 years ago. Based on the expectations of diet breadth models, Betts and colleagues (2008) argued that after the initial colonization of Sanak Island before 4,500 years ago, otariids showed the effects of human harvesting. They argued that after this interval of harvest pressure, however, changes in otariid abundance reflected broader fluctuations in the regional climate and human and otariid populations reached a "natural predator/prey equilibrium" (Betts et al. 2008:106). They also concluded that cod abundance relative to smaller-bodied fish seemed to reflect changes in the climate of the Gulf of Alaska over time rather than the effects of human overexploitation (Betts et al. 2011).

While the data are limited, the research summarized here suggests a lack of clear regional trends in resource exploitation across the Gulf of Alaska. As in other regions, hunter-gatherers may have been faced with a number of forces that influenced their subsistence strategies, including social and political demands, population increase, climate change and seasonal variability, behavioral changes of prey, and local resource depression. This work raises a number of unanswered questions: beyond caloric value, what social and economic demands informed people's food choices? How did people throughout the Beringian Corridor use their foraging decisions to mitigate risk in this variable environment and to adapt to extreme seasonality?

To answer these questions, archaeologists must move beyond simple diet breadth models to examine resource selection in a way that considers the extreme seasonal variability throughout the Beringian Corridor. Human behavioral ecology provides models for assessing how families prepare for lean seasons by properly processing and storing resources, maintaining social networks, and, in some cases, investing in defensive or competitive social interactions. For example, Fitzhugh (2001) used optimality models of risk and opportunity cost to propose that technological adaptations for mass harvesting and food storage on Kodiak Island facilitated population growth and changes in social complexity. Such adaptations reorganized subsistence priorities and settlement patterns. They enabled people to settle in more permanent locations, control resources, and support larger populations over more seasons. To understand how food choices were influenced by extreme seasonality, researchers could apply future discounting/delay models (e.g., Kennett and Winterhalder 2006), lazy-L models (Stephens and Krebs 1986), or front-back-loaded models (Tushingham and Bettinger 2013) in this region to assess how foragers built up or stored enough energy to survive periods when foraging was not possible. Such work would rely on a combination of archaeological, ethnohistoric, ethnographic, and paleoenvironmental data plus traditional ecological knowledge to test for successful planning and storage for lean seasons.

In addition to food storage, food sharing plays an important role in contemporary Arctic and Subarctic communities as a way of avoiding energy shortfalls (e.g., Winterhalder 1986). For example, in his ethnographic study in east Hudson Bay, Smith (1991) found that like other hunter-gatherer groups, the Inujjuamiut mitigated risk by sharing food and foraging cooperatively. However, he argued that maintaining these activities went beyond optimizing foraging decisions and relied on complex social and political mechanisms that must be viewed from a political economic perspective (Smith 1991:303–305). To test this idea, Ready and Power (2018) used social network analysis to demonstrate that food sharing among contemporary Inuit people is not just an economic interaction but also a complex social interaction based on hierarchies and political influence. This practice has deep roots in the Arctic, as Waguespack (2002) illustrated. Using the zooarchaeological record and human behavioral ecology models of food sharing, she argued that caribou sharing in northern Alaska likely occurred both as a way of mitigating risk in a variable environment and as a consequence of "tolerated theft," or the passive sharing of a resource that can be defended only at an unreasonable cost.

One common critique of optimal foraging models is that food choices are not driven by calories alone (e.g., Lupo 2007). Instead, food can be viewed as material culture that is closely tied to identity and social dynamics (e.g., Twiss 2007). One way that human behavioral ecology models address social dynamics is by drawing on gendered foraging models to test the strategies men, women, and children use. These three groups may tolerate different levels of risk, may have different fitness goals, and likely make different contributions to the diet (e.g., Bird 1999; Codding et al. 2011; Zeanah 2004). In the Arctic and Subarctic, gender-based models could be used to understand the archaeological signatures of foraging strategies that depend on and inform social structures. As Frink (2009) notes, gender-based production is well documented in northern communities. Frink (2009:22) writes that among the Yup'ik people of Alaska, "[a person's] sense of self was and continues to be intimately associated with gender- and age-based production." Men's and women's contributions overlap significantly, though some tasks tend to fall to women and men separately across the North American Arctic (Frink 2009; Stopp 2002). The resources that women collect and process—plants, individually collected fish, and shellfish—tend to be ignored by current dietary analyses in northern contexts, which generally continue to correlate body size with prey rank (but see Fitzhugh 2003 and West 2009). Taking a gendered perspective of Arctic and Subarctic foraging could elevate previously low-ranked foods and reconsider their contributions to the overall diet. Tests of this hypothesis could challenge traditional measures of foraging efficiency and abundance indices based on body size prey ranks (e.g., Codding et al. 2011; Zeanah 2004).

Paleodemography

Human behavioral ecologists have long argued that ecological circumstances should have a strong influence on residential group sizes, foraging group sizes, and population densities and that population densities impose unique adaptive challenges on human communities (see Kelly 2013 for an extended discussion). Human behavioral ecology research also has expanded to focus on ecological factors that influence human demography and reproduction in populations of varying size and density (Nettle et al. 2013; Winterhalder and Smith 2000). Archaeologists have adopted human behavioral ecology principles to examine longer-term changes in demographic processes, in an approach sometimes referred to as evolutionary demography (Shennan 2009).

An evolutionary demography approach builds from the assumption that reproductive decisions, like foraging decisions, are based on the logic of trade-offs. For example, researchers assume that parents (or potential parents) consider the trade-offs of the benefit of multiple children with the economic and energy costs associated with raising more children successfully. They predict that a population will grow when food supplies are unlimited. Accordingly, increase, decrease, or stability in regional populations can be interpreted as a consequence of the relative availability of food resources in the local ecological setting, although mortality and in-migration and out-migration must also be considered.

In a recent study, Briere and Gajewski (2020) addressed the correlation between human population dynamics and climate variability across the entirety of the North American Arctic and Subarctic. Using the frequency of radiocarbon dates as a proxy for population size, the authors examined the relationship among population size, temperature, and sea-ice conditions across multiple regions and subregions. Their results suggest that population size was generally larger during warm periods and smaller during colder periods, but the overall population of the region increased over the Holocene at an accelerated rate. This apparent growth in population occurred despite a long-term cooling of the region during the late Holocene. The authors highlighted the widespread decline in population size across the Arctic and Subarctic that began in the late Holocene (3,900 years ago), a period marked by a major transition in the global climate and increased cooling throughout northern latitudes. This cooling period and Arctic-wide population decline generally corresponds with the population declines in western Alaska (Tremayne and Brown 2017) and northern Alaska (Anderson et al. 2019). Furthermore, Anderson and colleagues argued that demographic shifts may have been a driver for the development of marine adaptations and late Holocene marine intensification in northern Alaska.

In similar studies farther south, Fitzhugh and colleagues (2016) and Gjesfjeld and colleagues (2019) examined the population dynamics of the Kuril Islands in combination with detailed paleoenvironmental evidence. Using more than 350 radiocarbon dates obtained by the Kuril Biocomplexity Project and the International Kuril Islands Project, Fitzhugh and colleagues (2016) identified major trends in the population history of the archipelago. The most prominent of these trends are two periods of population increase followed by two periods of decline associated with the Epi-Jomon (2400–1300 cal BP) and Okhotsk cultural periods (1300–700 cal BP). This includes a dramatic population decline between 1000 and 700 cal BP that ultimately left the Kuril archipelago more or less abandoned (Figure 1.3). Despite the trends identified in the radiocarbon database, clear correlation with climate changes was not demonstrated. Fitzhugh and colleagues (2016:186–187) suggest that "it is tempting to see a relationship between late Holocene climate

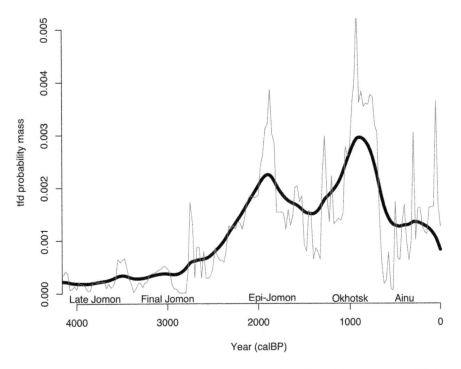

Figure 1.3. Summed probability distribution (gray line) and kernel density estimate (black line) for the Kuril archipelago based on 364 radiocarbon dates provided in Fitzhugh and colleagues (2016). The broadly accepted cultural periods for the region are also provided for reference. ("Tfd" in the *y*-axis label means total frequency distribution.) Figure by Ben Fitzhugh.

and population trends in the Kurils. While the remote islands were significantly occupied after the end of the Holocene Climatic Optimum, possibly hinting at poor conditions associated with extreme warming, human populations appear to have achieved peak sizes during the moderately cool periods that characterized the late Holocene's neoglacial period, and may have declined or completely abandoned the remote islands in the coldest periods." Fitzhugh and colleagues (2020) compared this Kuril proxy model with paleodemographic models for the Kodiak archipelago, Sanak Island, and the Aleutian Islands, identifying patterns that they argue could reflect more specific basin-scale, east-west oscillations in marine productivity and food security.

The paleodemographic approach hints at the long-term impact of environmental changes on the size and density of coastal hunter-gatherer populations, particularly those living in marginal, circumpolar environments.

While the studies described here draw on human behavioral ecology theory to interpret the results of these population studies, human behavioral ecology models have not been explicitly developed or tested in the cases presented. For example, Anderson and colleagues (2019) emphasized that "complexity" or marine intensification may explain the relationship between population growth and settlement or mobility, while Tremayne and Brown (2017) looked to the relationship among technology, culture change, and population dynamics to explain intensification. Despite the focus on the relationships among demographic, subsistence, social, and technological variables, the underlying evolutionary and adaptive logics are grounded in human behavioral ecology principles and more explicit modeling might be instructive.

Shennan and Sear (2021) suggest that the field of archaeological demography has made relatively little use of developments in ecological evolutionary demography and, more specifically, life history theory. For example, life history theory may provide a valuable source of expectations to help explain the boom-and-bust cycles of population, such as those seen in the Kuril Islands. Broadly speaking, humans demonstrate "slow" life histories, which are defined as strategies that prioritize investing in the quality of offspring through parenting effort as opposed to the quantity of offspring through mating effort. From a life history perspective, the presence of boom-and-bust cycles should be fairly unusual for species with slow life histories, yet they seem to appear often in studies of archaeological demography. One hypothesis is that slow life histories may be favored in environments that are highly variable and where some periods of population decline are inevitable (Jones 2011). The combination of changing environmental conditions and a slow life history strategy would favor the emergence of density-dependent mechanisms in which population size would track environmental carrying capacity (Shennan and Sear 2021). In this theory, it is perhaps unreasonable to expect human population growth to be stable, and perhaps paleodemographic models, especially in northern latitudes, need to be sensitive to population fluctuations and changing environmental conditions.

Paleodemographic approaches offer a largely untapped potential to test human behavioral ecology expectations about population growth, decline, and stability in relation to climatic changes and other variables. Radiocarbon-based paleodemographic results provide only one source of evidence, and explanations for cultural change based on population dynamics will require greater attention to expectations from life history theory and engagement with other archaeological and paleoenvironmental data.

Settlement Patterns

Human behavioral ecology models have also helped inform interpretations of the spatial distribution of Arctic settlements. Archaeologists have applied ideal free distribution, ideal despotic distribution, and patch choice models to the Arctic and Subarctic in order to understand how and why people chose to settle in coastal or inland environments, when they chose to develop more permanent settlements, and the role of seasonality in settlement patterns (Fitzhugh 2003; Tremayne and Winterhalder 2017). The ideal free distribution model adds social competition to optimal foraging theory, patch choice, and central place foraging models to predict where individuals should choose to live depending on the productivity of available habitats and the number of individuals occupying them (Boone 1992; Codding and Bird 2015; Fretwell and Lucas 1969). This model predicts that the most productive habitats will be occupied first and will tend to have the highest population density (Codding and Bird 2015:15). The ideal despotic distribution model theorizes that as decreasing productive habitats continue to fill up across the landscape, increased competition and the effects of crowding may lead to restrictions on people's ability to move and settle freely across the landscape.

These concepts have been used to argue that the spread of Arctic maritime traditions was the result of a shift to previously untapped maritime resources and that this shift supported population growth and denser settlements in resource-rich coastal environments (Gerlach and Mason 1992; Mason 1998; Mason and Barber 2003; Mason and Gerlach 1995a, 1995b). As these coastal populations grew and competed for resources, people would have been faced with the decision to move to less desirable but also less populated tundra and boreal habitats in the interior (Anderson et al. 2019). Tremayne and co-authors (Tremayne and Brown 2017; Tremayne and Winterhalder 2017) use a paleodemographic approach to explore the trade-off between inhabiting coastal and interior settlements during the mid- to late Holocene in western Alaska. In a pioneering study, Tremayne and Winterhalder (2017) used 775 archaeological radiocarbon dates from 6000 to 1000 cal BP to construct a proxy record for changes in metapopulation sizes in Alaska over time. Using the ideal free distribution model, they ranked Alaskan ecozones according to the highest to lowest productivity and argued that the immigration of Arctic Small Tool tradition populations stressed the capacities of the top-ranked forest interior zone, driving surplus population to the coasts. As the technologies needed to harvest marine resources developed, this excess population found that they could settle the coast of Arctic Alaska, opening up the Arctic maritime ecological niche and expanding human populations.

In a follow-up study, Tremayne and Brown (2017) expanded the sample to 1,180 radiocarbon dates from more than 350 archaeological sites. Based on these data, they suggested that population declines beginning around 3600 cal BP were more pronounced in interior settings than in coastal landscapes. Broadly speaking, coastal settings appear to demonstrate less demographic volatility over time: population sizes in interior regions of Alaska completely collapsed from 3600 to 2700 cal BP, while population size in coastal locations first increased but then only gradually declined during this same period (Tremayne and Brown 2017). This suggests that populations took refuge in coastal habitats, likely because coastal environments offered a more stable resource base than interior locations.

The logic of the ideal free distribution model suggests that once people settled the coastal regions and had the capacity to extract energy from the marine system, the communities with the most stable and productive resources had the most secure lives and may have even developed some level of patronage with less secure families from the region. The ideal despotic distribution model predicts that such a system would develop as some individuals or families gained greater access to stable resources.

Fitzhugh (2002, 2003) used human behavioral ecology models in the Subarctic to predict how hunter-gatherers in the Kodiak archipelago developed from mobile, small-scale foraging groups of the Ocean Bay period more than 7,000 years ago to sedentary and politically differentiated "complex hunter-gatherers" by the eighteenth century. Drawing on Boone's synthesis of optimal group size models, ideal free distribution and ideal despotic distribution models, and asymmetrical bias theory (Vehrencamp 1983), he proposed that social inequality, territorial defense, warfare, and captive slavery emerged after unprecedented population growth and crowding. Fitzhugh (2002) argued that before mass harvesting, processing, and storage of fish began approximately 4500 BP (at the start of the Early Kachemak phase), Ocean Bay communities would have lived in small and relatively mobile groups in the winter, aggregating and spending longer intervals at productive resource hotspots in the summer. This pattern is the reverse of those of the late prehistoric to the historic era, when people congregated in winter villages and were more mobile in the summer. Fitzhugh predicted that in the absence of stored food for the lean winter season, communities would have depended on the more evenly distributed and more easily depressed overwintering resources that were available close to shore (e.g., nearshore fish, gulls, shellfish). In the summer, in contrast, the Kodiak environment would have transformed into a landscape with more productive but patchily distributed harvesting locations that increased the marginal utility of resource patches. Accordingly, people would have been less mobile in the summer than they were in the winter. This prediction arguably helps explain the persistence of portable tents and equipment through the Ocean Bay phase and the rapid shift to sedentary winter villages soon after the invention of the delayed-return fishing economy after 4500 BP.

These applications of optimal foraging models—ideal free distribution, ideal despotic distribution, and patch choice—are productive in that we can combine resource distribution and group dynamics with environmental information to predict why and under what conditions settlement practices may change. These models provide insights into the strategies Arctic and Subarctic communities may have used in the past, but, like many behavioral ecology models, the ideal free distribution and ideal despotic distribution models are only the first steps toward a more thorough accounting of factors that influenced the settlement patterns in and long-term habitation of Arctic and Subarctic regions. Several questions arise from this research. How can models derived from human behavioral ecology be used to sharpen research into the pace of adaptation to new landscapes? Could these models be used to better understand how settlement patterns responded to the needs for social networking in remote or high-risk landscapes or under competitive circumstances?

To answer these questions, human behavioral ecology models could incorporate GIS, zooarchaeological records, technological data, and oral histories to illuminate the choices that people made about where to settle. For example, Monteleone (2016) used GIS and statistical analyses in the context of human behavioral ecology models to examine the consistency of site locations on Prince of Wales Island in southeast Alaska. She argued that site location reflects how people chose to settle the island when they were constrained by both ecological and social dynamics. Her results show that people chose to live in the same locations consistently for 5,000 years. This study used measurable parameters to explain decision-making: people chose where to situate their villages or camps depending on the location of freshwater sources, the type of shoreline or beach nearby, and proximity to individual resources (clam beds, salmon runs, etc.). Oral histories confirm some of these decisions. Additional diversity could be examined by expanding these parameters (Monteleone 2016). Such studies could be expanded across the Subarctic and Arctic to understand in greater detail the choices people made about where to settle.

Similar methodological approaches combined with human behavioral ecology models could be used more widely to predict how the North American Arctic was settled. Archaeologists have long sought to understand the two waves of migration into and across the North American and Greenlandic Arctic (~4500 cal BP and ~800 BP, respectively). However, little explicit theoretical attention has been given to predicting or interpreting the ways Paleo-Inuit and Neo-Inuit moved through the Arctic, how boat- and sled-based mobility conditioned colonization, the degree to which mobility strategies were terrestrial or maritime, where people settled, and how settlement patterns evolved in relation to environmental and social changes. While the broad patterns of these histories are known, human behavioral ecology models could be used to predict the locations of early settlements in combination with paleoecological mapping of high-productivity locations. This could be especially useful for locating sites on now-submerged (or emerged) coastlines and interior riverine areas that are only minimally surveyed. The broader contribution of ideal free distribution and ideal despotic distribution models in this context is that they can test whether early Paleo-Inuit and early Neo-Inuit settlement patterns deviate from our expectation of optimal habitat choice.

Conclusions and Future Directions of Human Behavioral Ecology in Arctic Archaeology

Our goal in this chapter was to illustrate the utility of human behavioral ecology models in Arctic and Subarctic archaeological research concerning questions about the ecological forces that drive long-term changes in diet, population, and settlement patterns. The rich zooarchaeological record of this region reveals that different hunter-gatherer groups adapted to localized climate change in different ways, but regional studies are rare and human behavioral ecology models could help clarify the relationships among climate, extreme seasonality, animal availability, risk aversion, and northern peoples' complex foodways on a broader scale. Paleodemography and settlement studies suggest that the marine environment played an important role in the growth and mobility of human populations across the Arctic and Subarctic, but the relationship between environmental changes and demographic changes remains elusive and human behavioral ecology models could be used more widely to understand how population dynamics, resource use, and technological change could improve our understanding of cultural change.

It would serve interested practitioners to consider how high seasonality modulates the costs and benefits of food harvesting, food storage, travel, and social interactions and aggregations. From a specifically archaeological perspective, these questions should consider how changes in climate and polar landscapes have rearranged the payoffs for alternative strategies for hunting and gathering people. Future research might give more explicit attention to how seasonal sea ice changes the costs and benefits of foraging, mobility, storage, and competition on an annual basis and how human behavioral ecology models might guide additional research to understand human-ecological dynamics in seasonally frozen environments or places that exist at the ice edge between frozen and temperate environments. We propose that standard optimal foraging models might not address some of the key variables that drove the dynamics of Arctic and Subarctic lifeways under extreme weather conditions and seasonality, the demands of food storage for lean seasons, and the preservation of social networks in this context. A human behavioral ecology perspective offers a number of ways to address these dynamics in northern environments, including modeling future discounting, intragroup relationships, sharing, life history theory, and methodological advances. We suggest that application of these tools may further illuminate how people selected resources and adapted to seasonal extremes across these regions.

Finally, Arctic people have a rich oral history and deep knowledge of local ecology. In addition, they are often very engaged in archaeology. There is strong potential for working together in a way that combines human behavioral ecology modeling and Indigenous knowledge frameworks in a complementary fashion. This would result in archaeology that meets community priorities, needs, and interests and communicates this work in a way that appeals to Indigenous partners while at the same time advancing and refining our understanding of the applicability of human behavioral ecology models in these contexts. Local knowledge and the consideration of extreme seasonal variability could help us go beyond idiosyncratic applications and further develop and evaluate human behavioral ecology models that are applicable to coastal high-latitude contexts.

Acknowledgments

We thank the editors of this volume, Heather Thakar and Carola Flores Fernandez, for organizing this volume, for their generosity, and for their excellent contributions to this chapter.

References Cited

Anderson, Shelby L., Matthew T. Boulanger, and Michael D. Glascock. 2011. A New Perspective on Late Holocene Social Interaction in Northwest Alaska: Results of a Preliminary Ceramic Sourcing Study. *Journal of Archaeological Science* 38(5): 943–955.

Anderson, Shelby L., Thomas Brown, Justin Junge, and Jonathan Duelks. 2019. Demographic Fluctuations and the Emergence of Arctic Maritime Adaptations. *Journal of Anthropological Archaeology* 56:101100.

Betts, Matthew W., and T. Max Friesen. 2006. Declining Foraging Returns from an Inexhaustible Resource? Abundance Indices and Beluga Whaling in the Western Canadian Arctic. *Journal of Anthropological Archaeology* 25(1):59–81.

Betts, Matthew W., Herbert D. G. Maschner, and Donald S. Clark. 2011. Zooarchaeology of the "Fish That Stops": Using Archaeofaunas to Construct Long-Term Time Series of Atlantic and Pacific Cod Populations. In *The Archaeology of North Pacific Fisheries*, edited by Madonna L. Moss and Aubrey Cannon, pp. 171–194. University of Alaska Press, Fairbanks.

Betts, Matthew W., Herbert D. G. Maschner, and Veronica Lech. 2008. A 4500-Year Time Series of Otariid Abundance on Sanak Islands, Western Gulf of Alaska. In *Human Impacts on Seals, Sea Lions, and Sea Otters: Integrating Archaeology and Ecology in the Northeast Pacific*, edited by Todd J. Braje and Torben C. Rick, pp. 93–110. University of California Press, Berkeley.

Bird, Rebecca. 1999. Cooperation and Conflict: The Behavioral Ecology of the Sexual Division of Labor. *Evolutionary Anthropology: Issues, News, and Reviews* 8(2):65–75.

Boone, James L. 1992. Competition, Conflict, and the Development of Social Hierarchies. In *Evolutionary Ecology and Human Behavior*, edited by Eric A. Smith and B. Winterhalder, pp. 301–337. Aldine Transactions, Brunswick, New Jersey.

Briere, Michelle D., and Konrad Gajewski. 2020. Human Population Dynamics in Relation to Holocene Climate Variability in the North American Arctic and Subarctic. *Quaternary Science Reviews* 240:106370.

Codding, Brian F., and Douglas W. Bird. 2015. Behavioral Ecology and the Future of Archaeological Science. *Journal of Archaeological Science* 56:9–20.

Codding, Brian F., Rebecca Bliege Bird, and Douglas W. Bird. 2011. Provisioning Offspring and Others: Risk-Energy Trade-Offs and Gender Differences in Hunter-Gatherer Foraging Strategies. *Proceedings of the Royal Society B: Biological Sciences* 278(1717):2502–2509.

Darwent, Christyann M. 2002. High Arctic Paleoeskimo Fauna: Temporal Changes and Regional Differences (Canada, Greenland). PhD dissertation, University of Missouri.

Davis, Richard S., and Richard A. Knecht. 2010. Continuity and Change in the Eastern Aleutian Archaeological Sequence. *Human Biology* 82(5/6):507–524.

Finney, Bruce P., Irene Gregory-Eaves, Marianne S. V. Douglas, and John P. Smol. 2002. Fisheries Productivity in the Northeastern Pacific Ocean over the Past 2,200 Years. *Nature* 416(6882):729–733.

Fitzhugh, Ben. 2001. Risk and Invention in Human Technological Evolution. *Journal of Anthropological Archaeology* 20(2):125–167.

———. 2002. Residential and Logistical Strategies in the Evolution of Complex Hunter-Gatherers on the Kodiak Archipelago. In *Beyond Foraging and Collecting*, edited by Ben Fitzhugh and Junko Habu, pp. 257–304. Springer US, Boston.

———. 2003. *The Evolution of Complex Hunter-Gatherers: Archaeological Evidence from the North Pacific*. Kluwer Academic/Plenum, New York.

———. 2016. The Origins and Development of Arctic Maritime Adaptations in the Subarctic and Arctic Pacific. In *The Oxford Handbook of Maritime Art*, edited by Max Friesen and Owen Mason, pp. 253–278. Oxford University Press, Oxford.

Fitzhugh, Ben, William A. Brown, and Nicole Misarti. 2020. Archaeological Paleodemography: Resilience, Robustness and Population Crashes around the North Pacific Rim. In *Arctic Crashes: People and Animals in the Changing North*, edited by Igor Krupnik and Aron Crowell, pp. 43–60. Smithsonian Scholarly Press, Washington, DC.

Fitzhugh, Ben, Erik W. Gjesfjeld, William A. Brown, Mark J. Hudson, and Jennie D. Shaw. 2016. Resilience and the Population History of the Kuril Islands, Northwest Pacific: A Study in Complex Human Ecodynamics. *Quaternary International* 419:165–193.

Fitzhugh, William W., and Aron Crowell. 1988. *Crossroads of Continents: Cultures of Siberia and Alaska*. Smithsonian Institution Press, Washington, DC.

Fretwell, Stephen Dewitt, and Henry L. Lucas. 1969. On Territorial Behavior and Other Factors Influencing Habitat Distribution in Birds. *Acta Biotheoretica* 19(1):16–36.

Frink, Lisa. 2009. The Identity Division of Labor in Native Alaska. *American Anthropologist* 111(1):21–29.

Gerlach, Craig, and Owen K. Mason. 1992. Calibrated Radiocarbon Dates and Cultural Interaction in the Western Arctic. *Arctic Anthropology* 29(1):54–81.

Gjesfjeld, Erik, Michael A. Etnier, Katsunori Takase, William A. Brown, and Ben Fitzhugh. 2019. Biogeography and Adaptation in the Kuril Islands, Northeast Asia. *World Archaeology* 51:429–453.

Jones, James Holland. 2011. Primates and the Evolution of Long, Slow Life Histories. *Current Biology* 21(18):R708–R717.

Kaplan, Hillard, and Kim Hill. 1992. The Evolutionary Ecology of Food Acquisition. In *Evolutionary Ecology and Human Behavior*, edited by Eric A. Smith and Bruce Winterhalder, pp. 167–202. Aldine de Gruyter, Brunswick, New Jersey.

Kelly, Robert. 2013. *The Lifeways of Hunter-Gatherers: The Foraging Spectrum*. Cambridge University Press, Cambridge.

Kennett, Douglas J., and Bruce Winterhalder (editors). 2006. *Behavioral Ecology and the Transition to Agriculture*. University of California Press, Berkeley.

Kopperl, Robert E. 2003. Cultural Complexity and Resource Intensification on Kodiak Island, Alaska. PhD dissertation, University of Washington.

Lupo, Karen D. 2007. Evolutionary Foraging Models in Zooarchaeological Analysis: Recent Applications and Future Challenges. *Journal of Archaeological Research* 15(2):143–189.

Mason, Owen K. 1998. The Contest between the Ipiutak, Old Bering Sea, and Birnirk Polities and the Origin of Whaling during the First Millennium A.D. along Bering Strait. *Journal of Anthropological Archaeology* 17(3):240–325.

Mason, Owen K., and Valerie Barber. 2003. A Paleo-Geographic Preface to the Origins of Whaling: Cold Is Better. In *Indigenous Ways to the Present: Native Whaling in the Western Arctic*, edited by Allen P. McCartney, pp. 69–108. University of Utah Press, Salt Lake City.

Mason, Owen K., and S. Craig Gerlach. 1995a. The Archaeological Imagination, Zooarchaeological Data, the Origins of Whaling in the Western Arctic, and "Old Whaling" and Choris Cultures. In *Hunting the Largest Animals: Native Whaling in the Western Arctic and Subarctic*, edited by Allen P. McCartney, pp. 1–31. Studies in Whaling 3. Canadian Circumpolar Institute, Alberta.

———. 1995b. Chukchi Hot Spots, Paleo-Polynyas, and Caribou Crashes: Climatic and Ecological Dimensions of North Alaska Prehistory. *Arctic Anthropology* 32(1):101–130.

Monteleone, Kelly. 2016. Exploring the Consistency of Archaeological Site Locations in the Prince of Wales Area in Southeast Alaska over the Last 5000 Years. *Alaska Journal of Anthropology* 14(1–2):1–15.

Nettle, Daniel, Mhairi A. Gibson, David W. Lawson, and Rebecca Sear. 2013. Human Behavioral Ecology: Current Research and Future Prospects. *Behavioral Ecology* 24(5):1031–1040.

Ready, Elspeth, and Eleanor A. Power. 2018. Why Wage Earners Hunt: Food Sharing, Social Structure, and Influence in an Arctic Mixed Economy. *Current Anthropology* 59(1):74–97.

Shaw, Jennie. 2012. Economies of Driftwood: Fuel Harvesting Strategies in the Kodiak Archipelago. *Études/Inuit/Studies* 36(1):63–88.

Shennan, Stephen. 2009. Evolutionary Demography and the Population History of the European Early Neolithic. *Human Biology* 81(3):339–355.

Shennan, Stephen, and Rebecca Sear. 2021. Archaeology, Demography and Life History Theory Together Can Help Us Explain Past and Present Population Patterns. *Philosophical Transactions of the Royal Society B* 376(1816):20190711.

Smith, Bruce D. 2006. Human Behavioral Ecology and the Transition to Food Production. In *Behavioral Ecology and the Transition to Agriculture*, edited by Douglas J. Kennett and Bruce Winterhalder, pp. 289–303. University of California Press, Berkeley.

Smith, Eric A. 1991. *Inujjuamiut Foraging Strategies: Evolutionary Ecology of an Arctic Hunting Economy.* A. de Gruyter, New York.

Smith, Eric A., and Bruce Winterhalder (editors). 1992. *Evolutionary Ecology and Human Behavior.* Routledge, New York.

Stephens, David W., and John R. Krebs. 1986. *Foraging Theory.* Princeton University Press, Princeton, New Jersey.

Stopp, Marianne P. 2002. Ethnohistoric Analogues for Storage as an Adaptive Strategy in Northeastern Subarctic Prehistory. *Journal of Anthropological Archaeology* 21(3):301–328.

Takase, Katsunori. 2018. Pit Dwellings of the Nalychevo Culture in Southern Kamchatka and the Northern Kuril Islands. *Journal of the Graduate School of Letters* 13:11–33.

Tremayne, Andrew H., and William A. Brown. 2017. Mid to Late Holocene Population Trends, Culture Change and Marine Resource Intensification in Western Alaska. *Arctic* 70(4):365–380.

Tremayne, Andrew H., and Bruce Winterhalder. 2017. Large Mammal Biomass Predicts the Changing Distribution of Hunter-Gatherer Settlements in Mid-Late Holocene Alaska. *Journal of Anthropological Archaeology* 45:81–97.

Tushingham, Shannon, and Robert L. Bettinger. 2013. Why Foragers Choose Acorns before Salmon: Storage, Mobility, and Risk in Aboriginal California. *Journal of Anthropological Archaeology* 32(4):527–537.

Twiss, Katheryn C. (editor). 2007. *The Archaeology of Food and Identity.* Center for Archaeological Investigations, Southern Illinois University, Carbondale.

Vehrencamp, Sandra L. 1983. A Model for the Evolution of Despotic versus Egalitarian Societies. *Animal Behaviour* 31(3):667–682.

Waguespack, Nicole M. 2002. Caribou Sharing and Storage: Refitting the Palangana Site. *Journal of Anthropological Archaeology* 21(3):396–417.

West, Catherine F. 2009. Kodiak Island's Prehistoric Fisheries: Human Dietary Response to Climate Change and Resource Availability. *Journal of Island and Coastal Archaeology* 4(2):223–239.

West, Catherine F., Stephen Wischniowski, and Christopher Johnson. 2011. Little Ice Age Climate: Gadus Macrocephalus Otoliths as a Measure of Local Variability. In *The Archaeology of North Pacific Fisheries*, edited by Madonna L. Moss and Aubrey Cannon, pp. 31–44. University of Alaska Press, Fairbanks.

Winterhalder, Bruce. 1986. Diet Choice, Risk, and Food Sharing in a Stochastic Environment. *Journal of Anthropological Archaeology* 5(4):369–392.

Winterhalder, Bruce, and Eric A. Smith. 2000. Analyzing Adaptive Strategies: Human Behavioral Ecology at Twenty-Five. *Evolutionary Anthropology: Issues, News, and Reviews* 9(2):51–72.

Zeanah, D. W. 2004. Sexual Division of Labor and Central Place Foraging: A Model for the Carson Desert of Western Nevada. *Journal of Anthropological Archaeology* 23(1):1–32.

2

Aquatic Hunter-Gatherer-Fishers

Evolutionary Frameworks in Northeast Pacific Rim Archaeology

SHANNON TUSHINGHAM

The northeast Pacific Rim coast, which extends from far northern Alaska to northwestern California, is a vast and diverse area, both culturally and ecologically. At the time of Euro-American contact, the region was inhabited by Indigenous hunting, gathering, and fishing communities associated with three culture areas (e.g., as defined by Kroeber 1939): 1) the western coast of the Arctic, 2) the western coast of the Subarctic, and 3) the Pacific Northwest Coast. These groups are aquatic hunter-gatherers, or communities whose primary mode of subsistence centered on the hunting, gathering, and fishing of aquatic resources (sensu Ames 2002).

The development of the rich and varied cultures of the northeast Pacific Rim has long fascinated archaeologists. Work in the region has had an enormous impact on how we think about how human foragers who lived at middle to high latitudes interacted with their environments. Prominent models from the region center on variation in environmental circumstances and how this might have influenced various aspects of human subsistence, organization, mobility, and what are often seen as developments unique to or characteristic of hunter-gatherer-fishers of the region, in particular sedentism, storage, and the development of complex sociopolitical structures (e.g., Binford 1980, 1990; Schalk 1977, 1981; Suttles 1968). At contact, groups throughout the region practiced collector-type logistical strategies (sensu Binford 1980), which are postulated to be associated with "the aquatic resource revolution" (Binford 1990:138) and the emergence of boat technology (Binford 1990; Ames 2002).

Human behavioral ecology frameworks and models have the potential to elucidate many of these important processes that led to the intensification of aquatic resources, particularly given Binford's suggestion that the shift to aquatic resource dependency can be understood in "simple energetic terms" (Binford 1990:134) as opposed to in terms of population pressure. Yet human behavioral ecology modeling of aquatic foraging dynamics is not without challenges and in many critical areas of research has not gained as much traction among archaeologists working in the northeast Pacific Rim. Several recent regional reviews note that the place and legitimacy of human behavioral ecology frameworks has come under substantial scrutiny (e.g., Campbell and Butler 2010a; Fitzhugh et al. 2019; Grier et al. 2017; Moss 2011).

This chapter addresses the current status and potential of human behavioral ecology frameworks for the northeast Pacific Rim. The guiding questions of the chapter are How useful are human behavioral ecology approaches and models for research on aquatic hunter-gatherers? and What are some of the challenges and opportunities for understanding the evolution of northeast Pacific Rim societies? To shed light on these questions, I review human behavioral ecology research from the region, both current and potential. I have organized the review into four general areas: 1) studies that draw from the ideal free distribution model and address basic questions about mobility, where people situate themselves on the landscape, and the logic behind colonization decision-making; 2) studies that draw upon resource intensification or depression schema and technological investment and niche construction models and discuss aquatic diet choice or elucidate how foragers make decisions about what resources to pursue; 3) studies that use the front-back-loading model, field-processing models, and storage defense models that investigate central place storage and organization of logistics in aquatic contexts; and (4) studies that use the costly signaling model and highlight the gender division of labor and differing foraging goals. I then discuss storage models that elucidate women's decision-making and childcare opportunity costs and why understanding such dynamics are critical to understanding mid- to late Holocene developments in much of western North America. This chapter is regional in scope but emphasizes the Pacific Northwest Coast and northern California.

Aquatic Foragers and Collectors: Early Models and Concepts

The forager-collector model (Binford 1980), easily one of the most influential models of hunter-gatherer mobility (and in Americanist archaeology in general) was initially formulated in the northeast Pacific Rim by influential archaeologist Lewis R. Binford. The model equates environmental productivity—measured by effective temperature—with certain settlement and subsistence strategies of hunter-gatherers. A key insight is that hunter-gatherers who live in more seasonal middle- to high-latitude environments (e.g., the northeast Pacific Rim) tend to follow collector-type strategies. The model was always conceived as a spectrum of hunter-gatherer adaptations among collectors who engaged in the logistics of resource procurement and food storage and foragers who tended to live in less seasonal environments, were generally more mobile, lived in smaller groups, had more expedient or more portable tools, and moved from place to place or mapped on to seasonal resources as they became available.

Later, Binford (1990) expanded on the forager-collector model, theorizing that groups that lived at higher latitudes (i.e., in areas with lower effective temperature values) in temporally and spatially patchy environments would be more dependent on aquatic resources. Binford (1990:132) argued that logistical collector-type strategies reduced mobility and subsistence variability to a "habitat trade-off (between aquatic and terrestrial resources) . . . particularly among people living in the higher latitudes." Embedded in Binford's original forager-collector model are assumptions about how people make decisions about settlement location, mobility, subsistence, and storage, based on the perspective that the environment is a major force in driving the adaptive strategies of hunter-gatherers (Bettinger et al. 2015:81–86). Major explanatory limitations and difficulties in applying this model to the archaeological record have led Binford and others to make numerous important revisions and critiques of this middle-range (bridging) theory. For the northeast Pacific Rim, key schema include the terrestrial versus aquatic forager dichotomy (Binford 1990) and frameworks that explore the social aspects of storage in immediate- versus delayed-return economies (Woodburn 1980) or storing versus nonstoring economies (Testart 1982).

The publication of *Beyond Foraging and Collecting: Evolutionary Change in Hunter-Gatherer Settlement Systems* (Fitzhugh and Habu 2002) was a watershed moment in the development of evolutionary theory in northeast Pacific Rim archaeology. This important collection of papers—including many on aquatic foragers in the eastern and western Pacific Rim—addresses ways that evolutionary frameworks can improve on Binford's schema. For example, Ames (2002) made the important observation that boats revolutionized transport and completely changed human settlement and mobility dynamics. Other contributions based on evolutionary theory and human behavioral ecology frameworks have been used in regional archaeological studies.

Mobility, Colonization, and Transport: Settlement Choice and the Ideal Free Distribution Model

Contingency models that address where people situate themselves on the landscape and the logic behind colonization decision-making draw primarily from the ideal free distribution model. This model provides a framework that predicts how organisms make decisions about where to live or settle (Fretwell and Lucas 1970). The basic premise is that organisms will distribute themselves in places that are ideal or most suitable to a point where all individuals are situated in equally ideal places. The model posits that since population increases (packing) can lead to declines in habitat suitability (more organisms, fewer resources to go around), individuals will move to new places.

An increasing number of archaeologists are using the ideal free distribution model (e.g., Bettinger et al. 2015:122–123; Codding and Jones 2013; Kennett et al. 2006; Winterhalder et al. 2010), but archaeologists of the northeast Pacific Rim have used it only rarely. A notable exception is Tremayne and Winterhalder's (2017) elegant study that involved an analysis of site distribution in habitats that were ranked based on densities of mammal populations. They concluded that, as the ideal free distribution model predicts, early settlements were primarily associated with areas with higher densities of mammal populations (higher-ranked locations) and that these densities influenced Arctic and Subarctic settlement decisions, the distribution of Arctic Small Tool tradition sites, and the origin of the Arctic maritime tradition.

The logic of the ideal free distribution model can be expanded in research that investigates initial late Pleistocene colonization of the Americas. Some of the strongest arguments along these lines have emerged, for instance, with the kelp highway hypothesis, or the idea that early migrants mapped on to highly productive aquatic environments as they entered the Americas during the late Pleistocene (Erlandson 2001). A great deal of recent work is occurring in the northeast Pacific Rim, the initial frontier for migrations to the New World via Beringia. This includes studies backed by the Hakai Institute. These researchers have made several high-profile discoveries along the coast of British Columbia that provide data to support early (>14,000 years ago) habitation sequences along the Pacific coastal corridor (e.g., McLaren et al. 2018). Great strides are also being made as regional archaeologists integrate discoveries from coastal and inland locations in large high-resolution datasets. Potter and colleagues (2018) mapped sites in Alaska and western Canada that date to more than 10,000 years ago and tracked their presence in relation to the location of the proposed ice-free corridor and North Pacific Coast. They concluded that migrations via coastal and inland routes are possible (similar dates, multiple sites along both corridors) and showed that continued application of ideal free distribution models provide a framework for understanding why both terrestrial and coastal routes provided suitable habitats or solutions.

Subsistence, Prey Choice, Patch Theory, and Technological Investment

The most common group of human behavioral ecology models used in studies of the northeast Pacific Rim are optimal foraging models that address how foragers make decisions about prey and resource patches and provide criteria for evaluating resource intensification or depression, technological investment, and niche construction. In northeast Pacific Rim archaeology, straightforward applications of prey choice contingency models often involve evaluations of zooarchaeological data in relation to energetic returns and time investment based on ethnohistoric, ethnoarchaeological, and experimental data (Butler 2000; Butler and Campbell 2004; Etnier 2007; Lyman 2003). These and other studies illustrate how reductive models can force researchers to evaluate assumptions, leading to surprising and powerful results.

Such studies also highlight the basic challenges of working with diet breadth models in this region. Studies of anadromous fish, including several species of Pacific salmon (*Oncorhynchus* spp.), offer a good example of how basic optimal foraging theory models overlook important variables and circumstances that influenced foraging decisions in this region. These cultural keystone species were once widely viewed as prime movers in Pacific Northwest societies; that is, they were a low-cost, high-ranking resource. Researchers theorized that salmon storage developed in tandem with the emergence of sociopolitical complexity and sedentary village life. However, archaeologists now have a more realistic understanding of the many organizational, labor, and technological costs associated with efficient mass harvest and storage that significantly impact actual return rates and likely delay intensification of the resource (see the recent review in Tushingham et al. 2021).

In more northern latitudes and interior zones, abundant salmon can be encountered seasonally in many streams, but they are less predictable and are available for short periods. Thus, exploitation requires mobilization and coordination of a significant labor force (Schalk 1977; Suttles 1968).

Compared to other types of fishing (e.g., a single person capturing salmon with spears and harpoons), successful mass harvest of periodic salmon abundance also involves considerable technological investment (e.g., costs related to constructing and maintaining weirs, nets, and basketry traps). Additional processing and storage costs, including the coordination, labor, and expertise required to rapidly butcher, dry, and pack fish for transport and storage (e.g., Hewes 1947; Kroeber and Barrett 1960), which was typically the realm of women among Pacific Rim ethnohistoric groups, have been historically overlooked but must be considered as a critical component of decision-making. Moreover, once fish was processed, the potential for loss of labor and capital (e.g., the fish or expensive technology) would have been high without well-built, costly-to-make storage facilities to ensure that stores were kept safe from pests and freeloaders and to prevent human and animal predation (Tushingham and Bettinger 2019).

In many circumstances, maximizing (or minimizing) certain nutrients might have been as important for guiding diet decisions as meeting basic energy needs. Hunter-gatherers around the world consistently avoid diets with greater than 35% of energy from protein (Speth 2010). This seems to reflect a physiological threshold that limits intake of any lean meat. In places where protein is a major component of the diet, people must obtain complementary caloric energy through fat- and/or carbohydrate-rich resources to avoid protein toxicity, an acute situation that can lead to illness and even death (Cordain et al. 2000; Speth 1989, 2010; Speth and Spielmann 1983). While salmon dried for storage is a significant resource, preparing it involves removal of most fat to prevent it from going rancid. Thus, groups in areas where fish is a major part of the overwintering diet had to circumvent the dietary protein ceiling by accessing foods rich in carbohydrates and/or fat. Where plant biomass was high (e.g., in more southerly latitudes), consumption of nuts, seeds, berries, and root foods was critical. In more northern areas, fat-heavy foods were critical, in particular forage fish (e.g., eulachon), marine mammals, and even bears. In the far north interior, where salmon runs can reach thousands of miles inland, people circumvented "salmon starvation" (protein toxicity due to overconsumption of salmon and other lean meat) by trading for oil with coastal peoples or by obtaining fat by processing bone marrow. Without such solutions, increased mortality and reproductive rates would have meant that relying on salmon was unsustainable (Tushingham et al. 2021; Figure 2.1). More complex models (e.g., linear programming) are a potential avenue for future work as they can incorporate multiple variables and maximum and minimum limits.

SALMON INTENSIFICATION

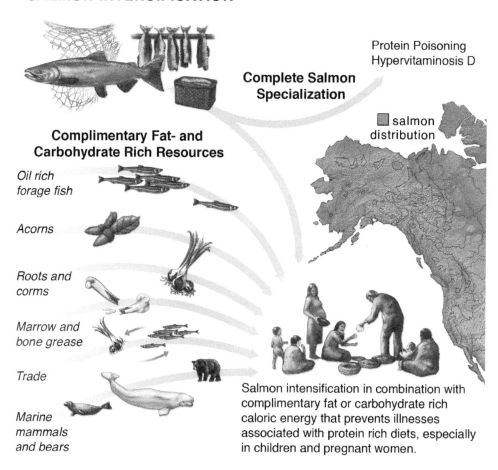

Protein Poisoning
Hypervitaminosis D

**Complete Salmon
Specialization**

salmon
distribution

**Complimentary Fat- and
Carbohydrate Rich Resources**

Oil rich
forage fish

Acorns

Roots and
corms

Marrow and
bone grease

Trade

Marine
mammals
and bears

Salmon intensification in combination with
complimentary fat or carbohydrate rich
caloric energy that prevents illnesses
associated with protein rich diets, especially
in children and pregnant women.

Figure 2.1. As Tushingham and colleagues (2021) have shown, many Pacific Rim Indigenous communities relied on stored salmon for overwintering, but they avoided protein toxicity through subsistence strategizing informed by ancestral nutrition knowledge. Such factors were critical to group survival, and the authors argue that salmon intensification was contingent on the simultaneous intensification of secondary carbohydrate-rich or fat-rich resources, not as backup resources but as major dietary components. Image by Kathryn Killackey.

Although size of prey body is typically taken as a proxy for ranking in diet choice models, several complications are particularly relevant to using foraging models in the northeast Pacific Rim. Even when only a single taxon is targeted, using size of prey body as a proxy for ranking is complicated when prey is sexually dimorphic in size and/or behavior. For instance, Lyman (2003:378–379) presents the complications of prey choice ranking of several Pacific pinniped species whose adult males can have an average live weight that is twice the size of females and differ markedly from females in terms of territorialism and seasonal availability. Further, prey choice model ordering that does not take into account between- and within-species variation in escape behaviors might erroneously assume it was "no more difficult or dangerous for a predator to pursue a 900 kg male Steller sea lion than it is to pursue a 65 kg female northern fur seal," as Lyman (2003:378) points out. Marine mammal hunters of the past were undoubtedly well aware of such fundamental differences in behaviors and body size, so realistic human behavioral ecology models must also take these factors into account.

Small-bodied species can also complicate matters. For example, despite their small individual body size (which simple diet breadth models would rank as low), herring and smelt were major staples in the northeast Pacific Rim from very early in the archaeological record (e.g., McKechnie et al. 2014; Thornton et al. 2010; Tushingham et al. 2013). Such resources can have enormous return rates when they are taken in large numbers (Ugan 2005). Macronutrient considerations might have also made such forage fish more attractive. For example, eulachon and other fat-rich forage fish were highly prized by groups that relied heavily on salmon and other protein-rich stored foods for the reasons discussed above (Kuhnlein et al. 1982; Tushingham et al. 2021).

Prey choice models assume that prey are distributed homogenously and that foragers had an unweighted or equal chance of encountering of any prey type. Of course, it is very typical for resources to be clumped in certain ecological niches or patches, and humans take advantage of such distributions. Aquatic foragers often invested in mass harvest strategies that might have involved "prey as bait" strategies, might have involved targeting resources that are linked through local food webs, and might have included both high- and low-ranked taxa (Monks 1987). In such cases, patch choice scenarios might be most appropriate. These are developed around the idea that as foragers encounter multiple patches, they likely make decisions about patches of resources (which the group ranks based on foraging efficiency, distance from home bases, etc.) rather than prey rank (Bird and O'Connell 2006; Charnov 1976).

Technological Investment and Niche Construction

Across the northeast Pacific Rim, aquatic hunter-gatherers engaged with a wide array of often highly complex technologies such as nets, traps, and harpoons to improve the return rates of mass harvests. Significant investment in technology can increase the return rates of highly clumped resources, but producing and maintaining such items can be quite costly. When technological costs offset overall post-encounter return rates, then seemingly high-ranked prey might not be worth pursuing. Fish nets, for instance, improve mass harvest return rates and might be used many times, but production and repair costs might offset the overall cost and thus make investment in netting technology unworthy of pursuit (Ugan et al. 2003).

Technological investment is also related to perception of environmental risk. In an exploration of technological change in the Kodiak archipelago, Fitzhugh (2001) suggested that risk taking in technological innovation might be favored during times of increased stress (e.g., during environmental calamity or resource collapse). Fitzhugh (2001:157) theorizes that technological solutions and variations proliferate rapidly in response to perceived urgency, in contrast to the limited technological change that is associated with perceived security.

One of the more interesting avenues of research in the northeast Pacific Rim explores when it pays for a group to invest in a patch. For instance, there are many examples of built landscapes, anthropogenic constructions, and practices that enhance production, such as clam gardens to increase shellfish production (Groesbeck et al. 2014; Moss and Wellman 2017). Niche construction models can provide useful frameworks for understanding when it would make sense to engage in such practices (Mohlenhoff and Codding 2017; Smith 2011). However, Grier (2014:233) has argued that that niche construction theory doesn't permit analysis of the "critical social dimensions" of constructed cultural landscapes.

Resource Depression, Resource Management, and Traditional Ecological Knowledge

Traditional optimal foraging theory predicts that high-ranked prey will always be taken on encounter and are thus susceptible to resource depression. Studies that have investigated resource depletion scenarios in the Pacific Northwest Coast include zooarchaeological investigations of pinniped reductions due to a hypothesized tragedy of the commons (Hildebrandt and Jones 2002; Hildebrandt and Jones 1992; Jones et al. 2002). Also, the combination of declines in the number of high-ranked fish and marine mammals and the expansion of lower-ranked prey in sites on the lower Columbia (Butler 2000) offer evidence of resource depletion in the northwest Pacific Rim. However, other studies suggest that pinniped populations were not overhunted (Lyman 2003). Etnier (2007) documents 500 years of sustainable pinniped harvest at Ozette, and a synthesis of fish bone data from 63 sites in the Columbia River drainage suggests long-term stability despite population increases and technological innovations (Butler and Campbell 2004). Such data suggest that precontact salmon fisheries seem to have been sustainably harvested for thousands of years (Campbell and Butler 2010a).

Resource management or stewardship practices, use rights, and ownership of resource patches might have been factors that buffered the depletion of coveted resources (e.g., Butler and Campbell 2004; Campbell and Butler 2010a, 2010b). Management might have included prescribed anthropogenic burning and sustainable harvesting practices that promoted the long-term growth and stability of particular resources (e.g., Hoffmann et al. 2016; Rosenberg 2015; Turner et al. 2013). While it is difficult to pinpoint the origins of conservation knowledge, Berkes and Turner (2006) argued that it might have evolved through mechanisms that overlap both resource depression scenarios (a depletion crisis model) and traditional ecological knowledge frameworks (an ecological understanding model).

Central Place Storage, Territorialism, and Complexity

Why do hunter-gatherers engage in storage and how are central place storage decisions made? A number of scholars who have recognized storage as critical to understanding the behavior and cultural evolution of hunter-gatherers have addressed these questions (Binford 1990; Cannon and Yang 2006; Chatters 1995; Morgan 2012; Rowley-Conwy and Zvelebil 1989; Soffer 1989; Testart 1982; Woodburn 1980). Storage features prominently in archaeological models of hunter-gatherer settlement and subsistence that locate groups that store and groups that do not at opposing ends of the foraging continuum: for example, foragers versus collectors (Binford 1980), terrestrial versus aquatic foragers (Binford 1990), delayed- versus immediate-return economies (Woodburn 1980), or storing versus nonstoring economies (Testart 1982).

Delayed-return economies use complex strategies that can be a powerful way to buffer against environmental shortfalls. In recent studies, models that expand on the optimal foraging theory concept of central place provide a framework for understanding why storage develops and how foragers decide what resources to store. This approach offers a framework for evaluating how aquatic hunter-gatherers in the northeast Pacific Rim dealt with time, mobility, and environmental constraints (Bettinger et al. 2015; Tushingham and Bettinger 2013, 2019). Much of this research draws on the logic of the front-back-loading model (Bettinger 2009:47–55) and the observation that much of the Pacific Northwest has a storage economy that is rich with front-loaded foods (e.g., dried fish, meat) that require significant costs up front. In contrast, back-loaded foods (e.g., nuts, seeds) generally take more time to process but can be laid up for storage rather quickly and processing can be delayed on the back end. Acorns, a prime example of a back-loaded resource, were a vital commodity throughout California. Given the high economic potential of salmon, it might seem surprising that acorns were the focus of economic intensification prior to salmon in places where both were abundant. But the front-back-loading model explains a forager preference for the less risky and more flexible back-loaded acorns (despite higher overall costs) over front-loaded salmon (Tushingham and Bettinger 2013). Additional advancements in the application of the optimal foraging theory concept of central place to questions of storage have incorporated key insights into the sexual division of labor, provisioning, and childcare opportunity costs. One advance considers how women might have weighed the costs and benefits of storage under variable conditions (Fulkerson and Tushingham 2021; Tushingham 2019; Whelan et al. 2013).

A similar logic is used in the storage defense model of hunter-gatherer territorialism (Tushingham and Bettinger 2019). This model posits that storage defense territoriality occurs when the cost of defending stores is less than the cost of losing them. The basic cost-benefit dynamics of defending stored food is fundamentally connected to seasonality and storage (front-back loading) timing. For instance, stored resources that are front loaded are more subject to seizure and therefore have higher defense costs than stored resources that are back loaded. Ethnohistoric data that includes 47 northeast Pacific Rim groups suggests that much of western North America developed along two fundamentally different territorialism strategies, one expansive and the other intensive. These strategies profoundly influenced diet choice and defensive behavior (Jorgenson 1980). Intensive territorialism, a strategy that was commonly practiced in California and much of the Pacific Northwest Coast, involved local, insular strategies that emphasized increasing diet breadth by focusing on back-loaded plant resources and individual ownership as populations become more packed. In contrast, extensive territorialism, which was practiced by some Pacific Northwest groups, involved outward expansion strategies that emphasized reliance on front-loaded food stores, corporate group ownership, greater degrees of sociopolitical complexity, and raiding and defense of territories (Tushingham and Bettinger 2019:Table 2).

Codding and colleagues (2019) also explored the evolution of territorial strategies among western North American hunter-gatherers. They observed that such behavior tends to be greater among larger corporate groups. Building on ideal distribution models, the authors hypothesized that when groups get larger, Allee's principle might apply, where individuals are incentivized to participate in larger cooperative groups and in group-level exclusionary and defensive tactics. They predicted that these dynamics would have been most important in local ecologies that were more clumped (for instance in places where groups focused on aquatic foods in aggregated or defendable patches). Their evaluation of 157 ethnohistoric groups established that groups in the Pacific Northwest Coast with the largest cooperative group sizes had the highest levels of ownership and intergroup violence, likely due to incentives associated with clumped resource productivity (Codding et al. 2019). Notably, the largest of these corporate groups were aquatically focused groups that used expansive territorialism as outlined by Tushingham and Bettinger (2019).

Evolutionary principles also help articulate the development of hereditary inequality in the northeast Pacific Rim (Bird and O'Connell 2006:168; Fitzhugh 2003). There is an ongoing interest in the development of inequality in the Pacific Northwest Coast (e.g., Ames 1994; Hayden 2001; Moss 2011; Testart 1982). As Codding and colleagues (2019:38) noted, corporate-level territorialism and sociopolitical complexity might have developed to "despotic" conditions where leaders emerge and inequalities and hierarchal leadership might develop. Fitzhugh and Kennett (2010) have argued that ideal despotic distribution conditions might have evolved among seafaring communities in the northeast Pacific Rim under ecological conditions where competition for spatiotemporally limited and productive resource habitats was high. Individuals (despots) might have benefited from controlling access to these circumscribed resources, as likely occurred at different points in time in a region that stretches from the Kodiak archipelago (Alaska) to Haida Gwaii (Queen Charlotte Islands, British Columbia) and the Northern Channel Islands (California). Similarly, in an examination of ecological and cultural data from 89 Pacific Northwest Coast and California hunter-gatherer societies, Smith and Codding (2021) found that the presence of clumped, defensible resources was the most parsimonious explanation for the evolution of institutionalized hierarchy and patron-client systems compared to other explanatory frameworks (e.g., population pressure, population density or polity size, or intergroup conflict).

The Sexual Division of Labor: Risk and Variation in Reproductive Goals

Studies of modern foragers suggest that men and women have different fitness-related foraging goals and constraints. For instance, women tend to be more focused on childcare provisioning and thus pursue more stable or reliable resources—e.g., plants, small game, shellfish—compared to men, who generally target more unpredictable resources with large potential payoffs (e.g., large game; Bird 1999; Hawkes 1996; Panter-Brick 2002). Although complicated by the fact that all of this work has been based in studies of mobile foraging communities, there have been some interesting applications of models that apply this basic logic.

Certainly, a great deal of regional research has focused on male sociopolitical leadership and explanatory frameworks that see status-seeking "big men" or "aggrandizers" as being major forces in cultural change and drivers of institutionalized inequality and sociopolitical complexity among some northern Pacific Northwest societies (e.g., Hayden 1998). Though not always explicitly laid out as in a fitness-enhancing framework, such models—which highlight male status-seeking behavior in the development—affiliate well with costly signaling explanations. Fitzhugh's study, however, does draw on evolutionary notions of "show-off" behavior to explain evidence of feasting and the development of complex hunter-gatherers and sociopolitical stratification in the Kodiak archipelago (Fitzhugh 2003:121–129).

Women's Decision-Making, Storage, and Household Production

An emphasis on "higher-level" sociopolitical leadership in the literature has biased scholarship toward analysis of men's decision-making. This has impeded our understanding of household and family leadership, which is often associated with women's decision-making. A shift in research emphasis might reveal that "a greater proportion of women than men might occupy leadership roles" (Garfield et al. 2019:74). Since the household was the main unit of production throughout the northeast Pacific Rim, this is a vital point. Full evaluation of women's contributions in the development of storage-based communities, in particular the evolution of women's decision-making and leadership, is critical for the future development of human behavioral ecology theory. This theory has the potential to help us develop new frameworks for understanding how the gender division of labor and women's decision-making relates to intensification and storage trajectories in the Pacific Rim region.

Central place storage models are poised to contribute to our understanding of how women's decision-making related to childcare opportunity costs in past societies. While research demonstrates that childcare needs do not typically pose a significant conflict with processing activities, childcare is likely one of the most significant activities hunter-gatherer women engaged in outside of foraging or collecting (e.g., see Hawkes et al. 1997; Hurtado et al. 1985; Hurtado and Hill 1987; Gurven et al. 2009:163; Whelan et al. 2013:665–666). Behavioral ecology studies suggest that the time required to harvest and process surplus foods for storage had the potential to create an opportunity cost vis-à-vis other activities (Morgan 2012; Whelan et al. 2013).

The high cost and greater time expenditures associated with laborious work are central components of intensification arguments. Women, who are assumed to have borne the burden of plant intensification and the preparation of fish and food for storage, are often cast as the losers who had to endure high levels of drudgery. Costly signaling theory takes for granted that women's labor and contributions provided the economic foundation for society so that men would be able to engage in prestige hunting, and some researchers posit that women's work became more valuable over time (e.g., Bettinger 2015). Why did women engage in more costly processing? Evolutionary theory suggests that women's decisions might have been influenced by childcare and family responsibilities and by the desire to ensure steady provisioning for dependent offspring. Plant intensification might have offered more reliable access to food and thus enhanced provisioning for offspring.

However, for women there were advantages that extended beyond reducing risk and provisioning. For instance, there were strategic advantages to the intensification of back-loaded plants. Examples include acorns, which reduced childcare opportunity costs, reduced risk of storage loss, and improved household autonomy and efficiency (e.g., Whelan et al. 2013; Tushingham and Bettinger 2013; Tushingham 2020). There were likely also power and status advantages (Ackerman 2003; Frink 2007; Klein and Ackerman 2000). There is no question that women played a critical role in storage-based hunting and gathering societies, not just as producers but also as keepers of stores. In much of western North America, women commonly kept track of stored food, directed decisions about gathered and hunted resources, and controlled (and often owned) processed food (plants, fish, and meat; Ackerman 2003; Tushingham 2019). Under these circumstances it seems likely that women would have chosen alternatives that enhanced and/or maintained their control over the fruits of their labor and provided alternatives that reduced the opportunity costs of childcare (Fulkerson and Tushingham 2021; Tushingham 2019, 2020; Whelan et al. 2013). Understanding these gender-based dynamics has implications for our understanding of how people positioned themselves on the landscape, which foods they chose to store, and other issues.

Discussion: Human Behavioral Ecology Challenges and Opportunities

This review demonstrates that many archaeological studies of northeast Pacific Rim societies have found human behavioral ecology approaches and models to be useful. However, application of human behavioral ecology in studies of the Pacific Rim continues to lag behind other parts of western North America. Recent reviews illustrate the general skepticism regional archaeologists express about human behavioral ecology (e.g., Campbell and Butler 2010a; Fitzhugh et al. 2019; Grier et al. 2017; Moss 2011). A major objection is that the model cannot possibly capture the environmental and cultural diversity of the region or complex social dynamics and processes involving resource management and stewardship practices. Many critiques have centered on setting human behavioral ecology (in particular resource depression models) in opposition to the traditional ecological knowledge paradigm, which includes ideas about sustainability and stewardship of pooled resources. Such critiques point to numerous cases in the ethnohistoric literature of coastal hunter-gatherers who built sustainable fisheries through cooperative efforts (Campbell and Butler 2010a). These important critiques have led to healthy debate, pushed scientific boundaries, and "stimulated considerable empirical research, resulting in cases supporting both positions" (Campbell and Butler 2010a:3; see also recent discussions in Fitzhugh et al. 2019 and Moss and Wellman 2017).

Yet the dichotomy between human behavioral ecology and traditional ecological knowledge is often a false one: human behavioral ecology frameworks can and do address similar socioeconomic processes, although they do so using formal models (e.g., niche construction). Indeed, many criticisms of human behavioral ecology involve misconceptions about the approach (it is often equated with simple diet choice models) and general discomfort with the focus on optimality ("humans don't always behave optimally," Smith et al. [1983] noted) and contingency models. General critiques highlight, for example, that human behavioral ecology models are too simple and too unsophisticated and that while they might hold value for analysis of mobile foragers, they are less useful in contexts involving more sedentary groups, highly productive environments, sociopolitical complexity, and storage.

Other challenges specific to the Pacific Rim center on problems with currencies (i.e., it's not just about kilocalories) and discomfort about modeling decisions for groups that have delayed-return economies.

There are also general challenges that relate to cultural and natural taphonomy; namely that working in the dynamic coastal environments of the northeastern Pacific Rim, a region with a great deal of tectonic activity and natural erosion can significantly alter the archaeological record and thus our understanding of past developments (Losey 2005). Although such problems are not specific to human behavioral ecology, they can and should be carefully considered.

To be successful, foraging models must be realistic. Numerous studies demonstrate the importance of considering alternative rankings, constraints, and currencies in diet breadth models (see discussions in Bettinger et al. 2015:118–120 and Lupo 2007:153–158). Human behavioral ecology models force us to break down the logic of basic assumptions about how decisions were made in the past (Fitzhugh 2003:153–155; Fitzhugh and Habu 2002). Such simplicity can be quite powerful, although the nature of the aquatic resource base and highly seasonal environments of the northeast Pacific can certainly complicate matters. This is particularly true when considering the myriad ways that people pursued, processed, stored, defended, and managed resources and impacted landscapes.

Archaeologists are taking materialist and evolutionary approaches in exciting directions. Fitzhugh and colleagues (2019:1079) advocate for a "human ecodynamics" approach, or one that combines human behavioral ecology and traditional ecological knowledge and other complementary approaches (see also Berkes and Turner 2006). Evolutionary frameworks are also being expanded to include better models that incorporate Indigenous voices and expand work on women's decision-making strategies and the development of storage. This approach is exemplified by a study by Fulkerson and Tushingham (2021) that employs both human behavioral ecology approaches and feminist theory to articulate geophyte field processing and women's decision-making dynamics. They argue that while women were both producers and drivers of geophyte-related economies, Indigenous women have been erased from archaeological narratives. Their geophyte field-processing model provides a predictive framework for understanding when women would decide to process food at upland root camps or in home base villages. Economically, key variables are transport time, processing time, and utility (value of a load of food stated in weight or other currency) at different processing stages. However, the model expands on social elements that are often neglected in standard field-processing models, including how decision-making may have been influenced by childcare needs and family group activities that often involved bulk processing events (baking and drying multiple loads of roots at the same time). Furthermore, collaboration with Indigenous communities in such work is an ideal means of ensuring that models are within the bounds of reality. The responsibility archaeologists have to communicate their ideas with descendant communities can also be an opportunity. In the Northwest, for example, many Native practitioners have an intimate knowledge of the procurement, processing, and storage activities that are the subject of human behavioral ecology models. Consulting (and, if possible, coauthoring) with these experts is an ideal situation as it can help archaeologists establish more realistic models. For instance, testing models through collaborative field research and experimental research, exploring varied currencies and values, and similar activities that center on traditional ecological knowledge are potentially powerful means of improving cost-benefit data and logical arguments.

Conclusion

Almost forty years ago, Binford (1990:134) noted that understanding when and why aquatic resources were intensified might be "one of the major problems archaeologists have yet to address realistically in terms of the issues of complexity and human evolution." While human behavioral ecology models are not without challenges, if they are applied realistically, they can offer a framework for understanding aquatic adaptations. While human behavioral ecology has been used in many interesting ways in the northeast Pacific Rim, many opportunities to advance research and to incorporate Indigenous knowledge in model building remain. Such research might help us expand our understanding of archaeology of the region, from the initial colonization of the region to the evolution of mass harvesting techniques, the dynamics of humans and fisheries, sedentism, storage, women's decision-making, and the opportunity costs of childcare.

Acknowledgments

An earlier version of this work was presented at the 2019 Society for American Archaeology annual meeting in the symposium "Human Behavioral Ecology at the Coastal Margins: Global Perspectives on Coastal and Maritime Adaptations."

References Cited

Ackerman, Lillian Alice. 2003. *A Necessary Balance: Gender and Power among Indians of the Columbia Plateau*. University of Oklahoma Press, Norman.

Ames, Kenneth M. 1994. The Northwest Coast: Complex Hunter-Gatherers, Ecology, and Social Evolution. *Annual Review of Anthropology* 23:209–229.

———. 2002. Going by Boat: The Forager-Collector Continuum at Sea. In *Beyond Foraging and Collecting: Evolutionary Change in Hunter-Gatherer Settlement Systems*, edited by Ben Fitzhugh, and Junko Habu, pp. 19–52. Kluwer/Plenum, New York.

Berkes, Fikret, and Nancy J. Turner. 2006. Knowledge, Learning and the Evolution of Conservation Practice for Social-Ecological System Resilience. *Human Ecology* 34(4):479–494.

Bettinger, Robert L. 2009. Hunter-Gatherer Foraging: Five Simple Models. Eliot Werner, Clinton Corners, New York.

———. 2015. *Orderly Anarchy: Sociopolitical Evolution in Aboriginal California*. University of California Press, Oakland.

Bettinger, Robert L., Raven Garvey, and Shannon Tushingham. 2015. *Hunter-Gatherers: Archaeological and Evolutionary Theory*. Springer, London.

Binford, Lewis R. 1980. Willow Smoke and Dog's Tails: Hunter-Gatherer Settlement Systems and Archaeological Site Formation. *American Antiquity* 45(1):4–20.

———. 1990. Mobility, Housing, and Environment: A Comparative Study. *Journal of Anthropological Research* 46(2):119–152.

Bird, Douglas W., and James F. O'Connell. 2006. Behavioral Ecology and Archaeology. *Journal of Archaeological Research* 14(2):143–188.

Bird, Rebecca. 1999. Cooperation and Conflict: The Behavioral Ecology of the Sexual Division of Labor. *Evolutionary Anthropology* 8(2):65–75.

Butler, Virginia L. 2000. Resource Depression on the Northwest Coast of North America. *Antiquity* 74(285):649.

Butler, Virginia L., and Sarah K. Campbell. 2004. Resource Intensification and Resource Depression in the Pacific Northwest of North America: A Zooarchaeological Review. *Journal of World Prehistory* 18(4):327–405.

Campbell, Sarah, and Virginia Butler. 2010a. Archaeological Evidence for Resilience of Pacific Northwest Salmon Populations and the Socioecological System over the Last ~7,500 Years. *Ecology and Society* 15(1):17. http://www.ecologyandsociety.org/vol15/iss1/art17/.

———. 2010b. Fishes and Loaves? Explaining Sustainable, Long-Term Animal Harvesting on the Northwest Coast Using the Plant Paradigm. In *The Archaeology of Anthropogenic Environments*, edited by Rebecca M. Dean, pp. 175–203. Center for Archaeological Investigations Occasional Paper 37. Southern Illinois University, Carbondale.

Cannon, Aubrey, and Dongya Y. Yang. 2006. Early Storage and Sedentism on the Pacific Northwest Coast: Ancient DNA Analysis of Salmon Remains from Namu, British Columbia. *American Antiquity* 79(1):123–140.

Charnov, Eric L. 1976. Optimal Foraging, the Marginal Value Theorem. *Theoretical Population Biology* 9(2):129–136.

Chatters, James C. 1995. Population Growth, Climatic Cooling, and the Development of

Collector Strategies on the Southern Plateau, Western North America. *Journal of World Prehistory* 9(3):341–400.

Codding, Brian F., and Terry L. Jones. 2013. Environmental Productivity Predicts Migration, Demographic, and Linguistic Patterns in Prehistoric California. *Proceedings of the National Academy of Sciences* 110(36):14569–14573.

Codding, Brian F., Ashley K. Parker, and Terry L. Jones. 2019. Territorial Behavior among Western North American Foragers: Allee Effects, within Group Cooperation, and between Group Conflict. *Quaternary International* 518:31–40.

Cordain, Loren, Janette Brand Miller, S. Boyd Eaton, Neil Mann, Susanne H. A. Holt, and John D. Speth. 2000. Plant-Animal Subsistence Ratios and Macronutrient Energy Estimations in Worldwide Hunter-Gatherer Diets. *American Journal of Clinical Nutrition* 71(3):682–692.

Erlandson, Jon M. 2001. The Archaeology of Aquatic Adaptations: Paradigms for a New Millennium. *Journal of Archaeological Research* 9(4):287–350.

Etnier, Michael A. 2007. Defining and Identifying Sustainable Harvests of Resources: Archaeological Examples of Pinniped Harvests in the Eastern North Pacific. *Journal for Nature Conservation* 15(3):196–207.

Fitzhugh, Ben. 2001. Risk and Invention in Human Technological Evolution. *Journal of Anthropological Archaeology* 20(2):125–167.

———. 2003. *The Evolution of Complex Hunter-Gatherers: Archaeological Evidence from the North Pacific.* Kluwer Academic, New York.

Fitzhugh, Ben, Virginia L. Butler, Kristine M. Bovy, and Michael A. Etnier. 2019. Human Ecodynamics: A Perspective for the Study of Long-Term Change in Socioecological Systems. *Journal of Archaeological Science: Reports* 23:1077–1094.

Fitzhugh, Ben, and Junko Habu (editors). 2002. *Beyond Foraging and Collecting: Evolutionary Change in Hunter-Gatherer Settlement Systems.* Springer Science & Business Media, New York.

Fitzhugh, Ben, and Douglas J. Kennett. 2010. Seafaring Intensity and Island–Mainland Interaction along the Pacific Coast of North America. In *The Global Origins and Development of Seafaring*, edited by Atholl Anderson, James H. Barrett, and Katherine V. Boyle, pp. 69–80. McDonald Institute for Archaeological Research, Cambridge.

Fretwell, Stephen D., and Henry L. Lucas. 1970. On Territorial Behavior and Other Factors Influencing Habitat Distribution in Birds, 1: Theoretical Development. *Acta Biotheoretica* 19(1):16–36.

Frink, Lisa. 2007. Storage and Status in Precolonial and Colonial Coastal Western Alaska. *Current Anthropology* 48(3):349–374.

Fulkerson, Tiffany J., and Shannon Tushingham. 2021. Geophyte Field Processing, Storage, and Women's Decision Making in Hunter-Gatherer Societies: An Archaeological Case Study from Western North America. *Journal of Anthropological Archaeology* 62:101299.

Garfield, Zachary H., Christopher von Rueden, and Edward H. Hagen. 2019. The Evolutionary Anthropology of Political Leadership. *Leadership Quarterly* 30(1):59–80.

Grier, Colin. 2014. Landscape Construction, Ownership and Social Change in the Southern Gulf Islands of British Columbia. *Canadian Journal of Archaeology* 38(1):211–249.

Grier, Colin, Lilian Alessa, and Andrew Kliskey. 2017. Looking to the Past to Shape the

Future: Addressing Social-Ecological Change and Adaptive Trade-Offs. *Regional Environmental Change* 17(4):1205–1215.

Groesbeck, Amy S., Kirsten Rowell, Dana Lepofsky, and Anne K. Salomon. 2014. Ancient Clam Gardens Increased Shellfish Production: Adaptive Strategies from the Past Can Inform Food Security Today. *PLOS ONE* 9(3):e91235.

Gurven, Michael, Jeffrey Winking, Hillard Kaplan, Christopher von Rueden, and Lisa McAllister. 2009. A Bioeconomic Approach to Marriage and the Sexual Division of Labor. *Human Nature* 20:151–183.

Hawkes, Kristen. 1996. Foraging Differences between Men and Women: Behavioral Ecology of the Sexual Division of Labor. In *Power, Sex and Tradition: The Archaeology of Human Ancestry*, edited by James Steele and Stephen Shennan, pp. 283–305. Routledge, New York.

Hayden, Brian. 1998. Practical and Prestige Technologies: The Evolution of Material Systems. *Journal of Archaeological Method and Theory* 5(1):1–55.

———. 2001. Richman, Poorman, Beggarman, Chief: The Dynamics of Social Inequality. In *Archaeology at the Millennium: A Sourcebook*, edited by T. Douglas Price and Gary M. Feinman, pp. 231–272. Springer, Boston.

Hewes, Gordon Winant. 1947. Aboriginal Use of Fishery Resources in Northwestern North America. PhD dissertation, University of California, Berkeley.

Hildebrandt, William R., and Terry L. Jones. 1992. Evolution of Marine Mammal Hunting: A View from the California and Oregon Coasts. *Journal of Anthropological Archaeology* 11(4):360–401.

———. 2002. Depletion of Prehistoric Pinniped Populations along the California and Oregon Coasts: Were Humans the Cause? In *Wilderness and Political Ecology: Aboriginal Influences and the Original State of Nature*, edited by C. E. Kay, and R. T. Simmons, pp. 72–110. University of Utah Press, Salt Lake City.

Hoffmann, Tanja, Natasha Lyons, Debbie Miller, Alejandra Diaz, Amy Homan, Stephanie Huddlestan, and Roma Leon. 2016. Engineered Feature Used to Enhance Gardening at a 3800-Year-Old Site on the Pacific Northwest Coast. *Science Advances* 2(12):e1601282.

Hurtado, A. Magdalena, and Kim R. Hill. 1987. Early Dry Season Subsistence Ecology of Cuiva (Hiwi) Foragers of Venezuela. *Human Ecology* 15(2):163–187.

Jones, Terry L., William R. Hildebrandt, Douglas J. Kennett, and Judith F. Porcasi. 2002. Prehistoric Marine Mammal Overkill in the Northeastern Pacific: A Review of New Evidence. *Journal of California and Great Basin Anthropology* 24:2002–2004.

Jorgensen, Joseph G. 1980. *Western Indians: Comparative Environments, Languages, and Cultures of 172 Western American Indian Tribes*. W. H. Freeman, San Francisco.

Kennett, Douglas J., Atholl Anderson, and Bruce Winterhalder. 2006. The Ideal Free Distribution, Food Production, and the Colonization of Oceania. In *Behavioral Ecology and the Transition to Agriculture*, pp. 265–288. University of California Press, Berkeley.

Klein, Laura F., and Lillian A. Ackerman. 2000. *Women and Power in Native North America*. University of Oklahoma Press, Norman.

Kroeber, Alfred Louis. 1939. *Cultural and Natural Areas of Native North America*. University of California Press, Berkeley.

Kroeber, A. L., and S. A. Barrett. 1960. *Fishing among the Indians of Northwestern Cali-*

fornia. University of California Anthropological Records 21. California Indian Library Collections, Berkeley.

Kuhnlein, Harriet V., Alvin C. Chan, J. Neville Thompson, and Shuryo Nakai. 1982. Ooligan Grease: A Nutritious Fat Used by Native People of Coastal British Columbia. *Journal of Ethnobiology* 2(2):154–161.

Losey, Robert J. 2005. Earthquakes and Tsunami as Elements of Environmental Disturbance on the Northwest Coast of North America. *Journal of Anthropological Archaeology* 24(2):101–116.

Lupo, Karen D. 2007. Evolutionary Foraging Models in Zooarchaeological Analysis: Recent Applications and Future Challenges. *Journal of Archaeological Research* 15:143–189.

Lyman, R. Lee. 2003. Pinniped Behavior, Foraging Theory, and the Depression of Metapopulations and Nondepression of a Local Population on the Southern Northwest Coast of North America. *Journal of Anthropological Archaeology* 22(4):376–388.

McKechnie, Iain, Dana Lepofsky, Madonna L. Moss, Virginia L. Butler, Trevor J. Orchard, Gary Coupland, Fredrick Foster, Megan Caldwell, and Ken Lertzman. 2014. Archaeological Data Provide Alternative Hypotheses on Pacific Herring (*Clupea pallasii*) Distribution, Abundance, and Variability. *Proceedings of the National Academy of Sciences* 111(9):E807–E816.

McLaren, Duncan, Daryl Fedje, Angela Dyck, Quentin Mackie, Alisha Gauvreau, and Jenny Cohen. 2018. Terminal Pleistocene Epoch Human Footprints from the Pacific Coast of Canada. *PLOS ONE* 13(3):e0193522.

Mohlenhoff, Kathryn A., and Brian F. Codding. 2017. When Does It Pay to Invest in a Patch? The Evolution of Intentional Niche Construction. *Evolutionary Anthropology: Issues, News, and Reviews* 26(5):218–227.

Monks, Gregory G. 1987. Prey as Bait: The Deep Bay Example. *Canadian Journal of Archaeology* 11:119–142.

Morgan, Christopher. 2012. Modeling Modes of Hunter-Gatherer Food Storage. *American Antiquity* 77(4):714–736.

Moss, Madonna. 2011. *Northwest Coast: Archaeology as Deep History*. Society for American Archaeology, Washington, DC.

Moss, Madonna L., and Hannah P. Wellman. 2017. The Magoun Clam Garden near Sitka, Alaska: Niche Construction Theory Meets Traditional Ecological Knowledge, but What about the Risks of Shellfish Toxicity? *Alaska Journal of Anthropology* 15(1–2):7–24.

Panter-Brick, Catherine. 2002. Sexual Division of Labor: Energetic and Evolutionary Scenarios. *American Journal of Human Biology* 14(5):627–640.

Potter, Ben A., James F. Baichtal, Alwynne B. Beaudoin, Lars Fehren-Schmitz, C. Vance Haynes, Vance T. Holliday, Charles E. Holmes, John W. Ives, Robert L. Kelly, Bastien Llamas, Ripan S. Malhi, D. Shane Miller, David Reich, Joshua D. Reuther, Stephan Schiffels, and Todd A. Surovell. 2018. Current Evidence Allows Multiple Models for the Peopling of the Americas. *Science Advances* 4(8). DOI: 10.1126/sciadv.aat5473

Rosenberg, J. Shoshana. 2015. Study of Prestige and Resource Control Using Fish Remains from Cathlapotle, a Plankhouse Village on the Lower Columbia River. MA thesis, Department of Anthropology, Portland State University.

Rowley-Conwy, Peter, and Marek Zvelebil. 1989. Saving It for Later: Storage by Prehistoric Hunter-Gatherers in Europe. In *Bad Year Economics: Cultural Responses to Risk and*

Uncertainty, edited by Paul Halstead and John O'Shea, pp. 40–56. Cambridge University Press, Cambridge.

Schalk, Randall F. 1977. The Structure of an Anadromous Fish Resource. In *For Theory Building in Archaeology: Essays on Faunal Remains, Aquatic Resources, Spatial Analysis, and Systemic Modeling*, edited by Lewis R. Binford, pp. 207–249. Academic Press, New York.

———. 1981. Land Use and Organizational Complexity among Foragers of Northwestern North America. In *Affluent Foragers*, edited by S. Koyama and D. Thomas, pp. 53–76. Senri Ethnological Studies 9. National Museum of Ethnology, Osaka, Japan.

Smith, Bruce D. 2011. General Patterns of Niche Construction and the Management of "Wild" Plant and Animal Resources by Small-Scale Pre-industrial Societies. *Philosophical Transactions of the Royal Society B: Biological Sciences* 366(1566):836–848.

Smith, Eric Alden, Robert L. Bettinger, Charles A. Bishop, Valda Blundell, Elizabeth Cashdan, Michael J. Casimir, Andrew L. Christenson, Bruce Cox, Rada Dyson-Hudson, and Brian Hayden. 1983. Anthropological Applications of Optimal Foraging Theory: A Critical Review. *Current Anthropology* 24(5):625–651.

Smith, Eric Alden, and Brian F. Codding. 2021. Ecological Variation and Institutionalized Inequality in Hunter-Gatherer Societies. *Proceedings of the National Academy of Sciences* 118(13):e2016134118.

Soffer, Olga. 1989. Storage, Sedentism and the Eurasian Palaeolithic Record. *Antiquity* 63(241):719.

Speth, John D. 1989. Early Hominid Hunting and Scavenging: The Role of Meat as an Energy Source. *Journal of Human Evolution* 18(4):329–343.

———. 2010. Big-Game Hunting: Protein, Fat, or Politics? In *The Paleoanthropology and Archaeology of Big-Game Hunting: Protein, Fat, or Politics?* by John D. Speth, pp. 149–161. Springer, New York.

Speth, John D., and Katherine A. Spielmann. 1983. Energy Source, Protein Metabolism, and Hunter-Gatherer Subsistence Strategies. *Journal of Anthropological Archaeology* 2:1–31.

Suttles, Wayne. 1968. Coping with Abundance: Subsistence on the Northwest Coast. In *Man the Hunter*, edited by R. B. Lee, and I. Devore, pp. 56–68. Aldine Press, Chicago.

Testart, Alain. 1982. The Significance of Food Storage among Hunter-Gatherers: Residence Patterns, Population Densities, and Social Inequities. *Current Anthropology* 23:523–537.

Thornton, Thomas F., Madonna L. Moss, Virginia L. Butler, Jamie Hebert, and Fritz Funk. 2010. Local and Traditional Knowledge and the Historical Ecology of Pacific Herring in Alaska. *Journal of Ecological Anthropology* 14(1):81–88.

Tremayne, Andrew H., and Bruce Winterhalder. 2017. Large Mammal Biomass Predicts the Changing Distribution of Hunter-Gatherer Settlements in Mid-Late Holocene Alaska. *Journal of Anthropological Archaeology* 45:81–97.

Turner, Nancy J., Douglas Deur, and Dana Lepofsky. 2013. Plant Management Systems of British Columbia's First Peoples. *BC Studies: The British Columbian Quarterly* 179:107–133.

Tushingham, Shannon. 2019. Why Women Store: Risk Minimizing Strategies, Provisioning, and the Evolution of Hunter-Gatherer-Fisher Delayed Return Economies. Paper presented at the Northwest Evolution, Ecology, and Human Behavior Annual Symposium, Boise, Idaho.

———. 2020. The Ordered Anarchy Frontier: Storage, Sedentism, and the Evolution of Plank House Villages in the Southern Pacific Northwest Coast. In *Cowboy Ecology: Essays in Honor of R. L Bettinger*, edited by Michael G. Delacorte, Terry L. Jones, and Roshanne S. Bakhtiary, pp. 49–69. Monograph 19. Center for Archaeological Research, University of California, at Davis.

Tushingham, Shannon, Loukas Barton, and R. L. Bettinger. 2021. How Ancestral Subsistence Strategies Solve Salmon Starvation and the "Protein Problem" of Pacific Rim Resources. *American Journal of Physical Anthropology* 2021:1–21. https://doi.org/10.1002/ajpa.24281.

Tushingham, Shannon, and Robert L. Bettinger. 2013. Why Foragers Choose Acorns before Salmon: Storage, Mobility, and Risk in Aboriginal California. *Journal of Anthropological Archaeology* 32(4):527–537.

———. 2019. Storage Defense: Expansive and Intensive Territorialism in Hunter-Gatherer Delayed Return Economies. *Quaternary International* 518:21–30.

Tushingham, Shannon, Amy Spurling, and Timothy R. Carpenter. 2013. The Sweetwater Site: Archaeological Recognition of Surf Fishing and Temporary Smelt Camps on the North Coast of California. *Journal of California and Great Basin Anthropology* 33(1):25–37.

Ugan, Andrew. 2005. Does Size Matter? Body Size, Mass Collecting, and Their Implications for Understanding Prehistoric Foraging Behavior. *American Antiquity* 70(1):75–89.

Ugan, Andrew, Jason Bright, and Alan Rogers. 2003. When Is Technology Worth the Trouble? *Journal of Archaeological Science* 30(10):1315–1329.

Whelan, Carly S., Adrian R. Whitaker, Jeffrey S. Rosenthal, and Eric Wohlgemuth. 2013. Hunter-Gatherer Storage, Settlement, and the Opportunity Costs of Women's Foraging. *American Antiquity* 78(4):662–678.

Winterhalder, Bruce, Douglas J. Kennett, Mark N. Grote, and Jacob Bartruff. 2010. Ideal Free Settlement of California's Northern Channel Islands. *Journal of Anthropological Archaeology* 29(4):469–490.

Woodburn, James. 1980. Hunters and Gatherers Today and Reconstruction of the Past. In *Soviet and Western Anthropology*, edited by Ernest Gellner, pp. 95–117. Duckworth, London.

3

Potential Applications of Human Behavioral Ecology in the Prehistoric Mediterranean

DANIEL PLEKHOV, EVAN LEVINE,
AND THOMAS P. LEPPARD

Predictive models derived from behavioral ecology have proved useful for understanding past human behavior (Bird and O'Connell 2006; Codding and Bird 2015; Winterhalder and Smith 2000). The application of human behavioral ecology models has enabled archaeologists to evaluate the impacts of environmental and social constraints on human behavior by measuring dissonances between reconstructed behavior and modeled predictions. This approach has great potential for collaborative and synthetic research, particularly in contexts where robust spatial and temporal datasets are available. The Holocene record of the Mediterranean basin's coasts and islands is one such context; it is one of the most minutely studied archaeological regions on the planet. Artifact chronotypologies based on increasingly tight radiometric chronologies are accurate on subcentennial scales (e.g., Davis 2001:417–418; Gregory 2004), while regional settlement data are expansive and indicate diachronic human occupation of highly diverse landscapes at multiscale resolutions (e.g., Alcock and Cherry 2004). This extensive corpus of archaeological data documents long-term processes such as the relatively early neolithicization of the Mediterranean basin and the diverse trajectories of social organization that followed it. Moreover, the Mediterranean is insular and coastal (Figure 3.1). The study of human behavior in insular and coastal environments is a good topic for insights derived from behavioral ecology (see, e.g., DiNapoli and Morrison 2016). Within this unique research context, human behavioral ecology offers powerful tools for enriching our understanding of Mediterranean prehistory.

Yet human behavioral ecology has had only a minimal impact on the study of human settlement dynamics and the attendant social processes in

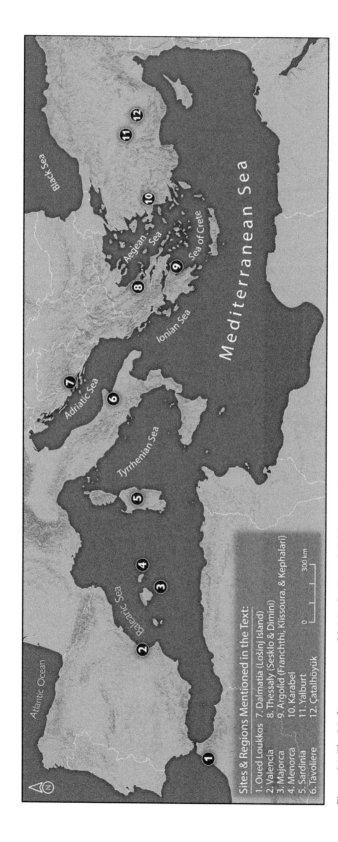

Figure 3.1. The Mediterranean world. Map by Daniel Plekhov and Thomas P. Leppard.

the Holocene Mediterranean. While exceptions exist, human behavioral ecology studies in the Mediterranean have tended to focus on hunter-gatherer-foragers and on Pleistocene periods of Mediterranean history (e.g., Brantingham 2006; Starkovich 2017; Stiner and Kuhn 1992). These research trends reflect the historical emphasis of human behavioral ecology research on hunter-gatherer-forager societies and the common perception that those societies were absent in later periods (see, e.g., Vigne et al. 2016).

The rarity of human behavioral ecology approaches to the postglacial Mediterranean presents an opportunity for future research. We begin with a brief review of studies of Holocene Mediterranean human ecodynamics and explore why Mediterranean prehistorians have been disinclined to borrow conceptual frameworks from behavioral ecology. We then draw attention to fruitful avenues for research agendas in Mediterranean prehistory (i.e., until about 1200 BCE) that use human behavioral ecology. Although we emphasize the value of human behavioral ecology for understanding prehistoric human ecodynamics, human behavioral ecology models can be usefully applied in the study of other time periods in the region, including the Roman, Byzantine, Ottoman, Venetian, or even modern-day Mediterranean.

The Absence of Human Behavioral Ecology in Studies of the Mediterranean

A small number of archaeological researchers have used ecological approaches in the study of the Mediterranean. The earliest is a study of island biogeography that is itself an intellectual antecedent of population ecology (Cherry 1981). Some studies have borrowed or adopted principles from community and population ecology (e.g., Cherry and Leppard 2018; Vandam et al. 2013), and recent work has combined ecological principles with environmental and demographic modeling (Roberts et al. 2019). However, very few studies use predictive models derived from human behavioral ecology. The value of human behavioral ecology models and frameworks for understanding behavior in a wider array of economies has been amply demonstrated in other regions (e.g., Kennett and Winterhalder 2006). The gap in the research on the Mediterranean Holocene, then, requires explanation. Why are human behavioral ecology studies so rare in Mediterranean prehistory?

Part of the answer lies in the North American disciplinary traditions and academic structures that separated classical archaeology (and thereby, to an extent, Mediterranean prehistory) from anthropological archaeology in the 1970s (Renfrew 1980, 2003; Snodgrass 1985). While much has been done to span the "great divide," disciplinary biases remain hard to overcome. Human behavioral ecology applications in archaeology have a decidedly anthropological pedigree. Early examples include Bruce Winterhalder's (1981) and James F. O'Connell's (1987) research, concerned with small-scale societies such as the Cree and Alyawarre. This focus on small-scale societies in the Western hemisphere is a defining feature of more recent research, such as Douglas J. Kennett's (2005) work on the Island Chumash of the California Channel Islands. Thus, it is unsurprising that graduate training of Mediterranean archaeologists rarely includes exposure to these foundational works; Mediterraneanists are not often exposed to currents in anthropological archaeology that draw on ecological and evolutionary models, particularly when they have little perceived geographic, cultural, or thematic relevance.

Relatedly, there is a perception that human behavioral ecology approaches are quantitative because of the frequent inclusion of mathematical notation and statistical modeling in the presentation of human behavioral ecology studies. We would certainly not argue that Mediterranean archaeologists are, in general, any better or worse trained in quantitative approaches than their colleagues working in other regions of the world, but coursework in such subjects is not often intrinsic to Mediterranean graduate programs. More to the point, within Mediterranean archaeology, there is arguably a historical aversion to assumptions regarding optimality, the validity of abstraction, and the modeling of past human behaviors—concepts that are fundamental to human behavioral ecology studies. This aversion is perhaps attributable to the availability of data that often makes it possible to tell more specific stories. Long-term projects at Neolithic sites such as Çatalhöyük, Göbekli Tepe, Sesklo, Dimini, and Valencina de la Concepción and those in the Tavoliere delle Puglie provide deep histories of social organization and cultural practice over millennia, while written administrative records appeared as early as the second millennium BCE. Put another way, there is a particularism to Mediterranean archaeology that arises as much from the region's extreme ecological fragmentation (Horden and Purcell 2000) as it does from the modern-day legacies of nationalism and the reification of borders (Hamilakis and Momigliano 2006; Seretis 2005).

In contrast, definitions of culture within human behavioral ecology as "the outcome of dynamic interactions between socially shared intent[,] . . . behavior, and the environment" position culture as a phenomenon to be explained rather than a unit of study itself (Codding and Bird 2015:10–11). Such cultural abstractions of the Mediterranean archaeological record can seem insensitive to the stories and lived experiences of ancient people, particularly those groups that have traditionally been marginalized and left out of historical narratives (Colwell-Chanthaphonh et al. 2010; van Dommelen 2011).

Yet in particularism is central to human behavioral ecology. While Mediterranean archaeology is somewhat lacking in ethnographic or ethnohistorical models for small-scale or pre-state societies (except, notably, Annis 1985; Forbes 2007; and Halstead 2014), such models have been key in applying human behavioral ecology and testing its predictions (O'Connell 1995).

We also speculate that the Mediterraneanist postdegree career structure is organized in a way that does not immediately reward attempts to contextualize the Holocene Mediterranean more broadly within anthropological archaeology. Whatever the precise reasons, it is clear that structural constraints have limited the applications of human behavioral ecology in a postglacial Mediterranean context. However, we suggest that this gap in the literature is a substantial missed opportunity.

Optimal Foraging Theory and the Aegean Mesolithic

Optimal foraging theory is a collection of principles and models that predict how individuals select, pursue, and consume resources within their habitats. It makes predictions about individuals based on the assumption that they always act in ways that maximize their survival and reproductive success (Stephens and Krebs 1986). Such success is evaluated through proxies that are presumed to be correlates of fitness, such as the net rate of return (of energy or nutrients) per unit of foraging time (Smith 1983). Quantifying fitness in these ways enables researchers to rank the costs and benefits of different foraging decisions on the same scale and predict which decisions individuals should make. The diet breadth model, the most common analytical approach derived from optimal foraging theory, concerns prey choice and the range of resources an individual consumed. According to this model, individuals will preferentially pursue high-ranked resources that are likely to give them the highest net return of energy or nutrients per unit of foraging time (Charnov 1976; MacArthur and Pianka 1966). In an environment where encounters with the highest-ranked prey types are common, the diet breadth of an individual should be narrow because it consists entirely of high-ranked resources. In a resource-depleted environment where this encounter rate is reduced, diet breadth increases to include more low-ranked resources.

The archaeological correlates of these predictions are clear and have been explored by zooarchaeologists and archaeobotanists (e.g., Bayham 1979; Broughton 1994; Hollenbach 2009). The ability to reconstruct environmental pressures such as habitat degradation and resource stress from faunal and botanical remains enables researchers to examine how changes in climate, technology, social structure, demography, and settlement correspond to these pressures. Although optimal foraging theory and the diet breadth model have predominantly been applied to hunter-gatherer studies, they can also be used in the study of agricultural or pastoral subsistence economies. Indeed, recent applications (from outside the Mediterranean) have sought to do that, applying optimal foraging theory principles, for example, to the study of irrigation systems (Boomgarden et al. 2019). More broadly, optimal foraging theory or the diet breadth model are convincingly being used to argue for periods of scarcity and resource stress immediately before the development of agriculture in various parts of the world, as evidenced by progressive additions of wild resources to diets (e.g., Diehl and Waters 2006; Weitzel 2019). These findings challenge interpretations that early agriculture emerged in the context of prosperity and abundance and provide fruitful ground for regional comparison.

Such comparisons have thus far been largely absent from the Mediterranean. One context in which optimal foraging theory has been productively applied is changes in Aegean subsistence in the transition from the Paleolithic to the Neolithic. Franchthi Cave, located in the Argolid of southern Greece, preserves an exceptional sequence of subsistence change (Jacobsen 1981). Stratified deposits record histories of occupation from the late Pleistocene through the early Holocene, during which period climate change caused marine transgression and significant changes in the landscape that presented new challenges and opportunities for resource exploitation. The study of faunal and botanical remains from this site has provided rare insight into the transition from foraging to agriculture and pastoralism and made possible detailed investigations of the relative effects of climate change, population growth, and landscape change on human subsistence economies (Stiner and Munro 2011). Results indicate that diet breadth expanded twice. First, it expanded terrestrially as increasing population and consequent hunting pressure at Franchthi Cave and inland sites led to progressive exploitation of lower-ranked resources such as tortoises, hares, and birds. Second, as sea levels rose, foragers at sites such as Franchthi Cave gradually turned to exploiting marine resources, beginning with low-cost resources such as land snails and then shifting to costlier littoral and deep-water fish (Munro and Stiner 2015).

The use of optimal foraging theory as a unifying analytic framework has permitted researchers to compare these processes at regional scales. Applying human behavioral ecology models and approaches to faunal datasets from multiple sites in the southern Argolid has made possible further investigation of these processes and the identification of broader patterns and differences. For example, sites such as Klissoura Cave (Starkovich 2014, 2017) and Kephalari Cave (Starkovich et al. 2018), both within 45 km of Franchthi

Cave, have been studied using optimal foraging theory. Results from these studies are comparable and match those of other contemporary sites in the Aegean, showing that the overall transition to a wider diet breadth was regional during the late Paleolithic and that there was a shift within the region to greater exploitation of marine resources during the Mesolithic. That this pattern is seen at inland sites and coastal and now-inundated sites like Franchthi shows that this subsistence shift was not entirely the result of marine transgression (Starkovich et al. 2018).

These examples come from a constrained geographic area and a particular period. We emphasize them not because they are the only examples of such approaches in the Mediterranean (e.g., Stiner 2006; Stiner and Kuhn 1992) but because they highlight opportunities to synthesize data from multiple sites that could contribute to regional interpretations. The density of sites in the Mediterranean, the duration of their occupations, and the long-term study of the data calls for a more synthetic and unified investigation of subsistence practices that can provide important contributions to our understanding of human behaviors and population dynamics.

Ideal Distribution Models and Neolithic Agricultural Landscapes

Ideal distribution models—of which the ideal free distribution and ideal despotic distribution models are the most notable variants—predict the distribution of individuals across a range of habitats based on the suitability of those habitats and their changing population densities (Fretwell and Lucas 1969; see Jazwa et al. 2019 for a review of ideal distribution models). These models predict that individuals with assumed perfect knowledge of a region and its habitats will occupy the most suitable habitats first, as those habitats are most likely to maximize their survival and reproductive fitness (Winterhalder et al. 2010). The suitability of habitats is dynamic and sensitive to environmental factors such as drought or to the effects of population increases or lifeway changes (Collins-Elliott and Jazwa 2020; Vernon et al. 2020). As more individuals occupy the most ideal habitats, the suitability of these habitats will decrease because of competition for limited resources. As a result, people will occupy less suitable habitats. In some cases, however, the suitability of habitats may increase due to Allee effects as greater populations afford benefits such as greater defense or more available labor resources (Kramer et al. 2009).

The application of ideal distribution models is becoming increasingly attractive due to their relative simplicity and ease of analysis. Habitat suitability can be calculated in a range of ways, many of which use publicly available data and tools common to all GIS programs. Most popular are net primary productivity values derived from satellite remote sensing (Codding and Jones 2013), and other comparable environmental or climatological proxies (Giovas and Fitzpatrick 2014; Tremayne and Winterhalder 2017). Weighted sets of topographical and hydrological values are also frequently used. These data define habitats as watersheds and help researchers estimate suitability based on variables such as distance to coastline, area of the watershed, and distance to centers of political or economic importance (Jazwa and Jazwa 2017; Winterhalder et al. 2010).

The other necessary component is a distributional dataset (i.e., of places and attributes) pertaining to chronology and, ideally, population. Few places in the world have an archaeological record as intensely surveyed, studied, and published as the Mediterranean. We have highly detailed distribution datasets for the region that in many cases cover extensive and contiguous areas (Alcock and Cherry 2004; Barker and Mattingly 1999–2001). The Mediterranean is also comparatively rich in radiocarbon dates (Chaput and Gajewski 2016), which have been used to evaluate population change through summed calibrated radiocarbon date distributions (e.g., Roberts et al. 2019). Combining these robust distribution and demographic datasets, as is already occurring in North America (Robinson et al. 2019), should make applications of ideal distribution models attractive in Mediterranean contexts.

Few prehistoric studies in the Mediterranean have used ideal distribution models. However, Jazwa and Jazwa (2017) have demonstrated its efficacy in more recent periods through their study of diachronic settlement patterns in the Greek Peloponnese. Their findings broadly approximate the expectations of ideal free distribution. Jazwa and Jazwa integrated sociocultural and political factors with environmental factors in their modeling of settlement suitability, demonstrating the flexibility of ideal distribution models and their potential to be applied in a wide range of contexts. This flexibility is also illustrated in a recent study by Collins-Elliott and Jazwa (2020) that focused on the Oued Loukkos valley of northern Morocco, where the authors modeled long-term settlement patterns in response to changing environmental and demographic conditions. This work offers preliminary insights into the history of the region from the Roman period to the Middle Ages. Both of these examples demonstrate the applicability of ideal distribution models to relatively recent periods of Mediterranean history.

Focusing on earlier periods, research by McClure and colleagues (2006, 2009) in Valencia, Spain, is one of the earliest applications of ideal distribution models in the region. Their work interprets changes in habitat occupation during the Neolithic transition to agriculture as a result of intensive farming and grazing that overexploited valley bottoms. As a result, the previously low-ranked valley margins became increasingly suitable, particularly as forest clearance and the advent of ox-drawn plows made them more accessible for farming. Further investment in these new valley margin habitats, such as by terracing, ensured that they remained occupied even as population increased in these areas and valley bottom habitats became more suitable.

These studies target a critical moment in the transition to agriculture in Europe. Analysis of this process is somewhat contentious (Robb 2013). This work suggests the potential for insightful comparisons to other regions of Europe that experienced early neolithicization. The Thessalian plain of northern Greece and the Tavoliere plain in southern Italy, to take two examples, also experienced pronounced transitions to agriculture with consequent changes in settlement pattern and organization (Figure 3.2). Although each region has received substantial scholarly analysis of settlement patterns and subsistence economies (Thessaly: Perlès 2001; van Andel and Runnels 1995; Tavoliere: Brown 1997; Jones 1987; Sargent 2001), no work has synthesized research from these two regions or compared them with other regions such as eastern Spain to consider the specificities of the emergent settlement patterns. The ideal distribution model, for example, would provide a unifying theoretical framework for predicting how past settlement developed in response to demographic and environmental values, based on general principles and models rather than on inductively formed interpretations of local contexts. The early pattern in both regions of numerous dispersed settlements suggests that Allee effects are not present and that people had the ability to freely occupy new habitats of higher suitability as the suitability of occupied sites declined with increasing population growth (Halstead 2008). The appearance of relatively large sites in later phases of the Neolithic in both regions such as Sesklo (Kotsakis 1996) and Passo di Corvo (Tiné 1983) suggests that at this time the benefits of aggregation outweighed the suitability of whatever habitats remained unoccupied, perhaps indicating some despotic activity or the emergence of Allee effects due to new technologies or climatic changes (Bell and Winterhalder 2014).

This large-scale comparative work can be difficult or unattractive for a variety of reasons, such as environmental differences, seemingly incomparable scales of phenomena, varying resolutions of detail in publication, or resistance to what are perceived as universalist explanations (Gremillion et al. 2014). However, using ideal distribution models as a unifying framework of analysis for these regions can facilitate and encourage comparison because

Figure 3.2. Views of the Thessalian plain of northern Greece (*left*) and the Tavoliere plain in southern Italy (*right*). *Left:* Photo provided by Evan I. Levine; *right:* photo by Giovanni Zagaria, distributed under a CC BY 3.0 license.

of the simplicity of the model. While it abstracts particular circumstances or dimensions of each dataset, it places them on equal terms. Thus, while Passo di Corvo is larger than Sesklo by more than 100 ha, both can be discussed as functioning in fundamentally similar roles in response to similar constraints, namely relative metrics of suitability and population density. We can then begin to inquire whether the trajectories of land use and settlement in eastern Spain, Thessaly, or Tavoliere are due to local effects and circumstances or whether there was a more general pattern of behavior during the agricultural transition.

Costly Signaling and West Mediterranean Megalithicism

Costly signaling theory aims to explain the benefits of seemingly wasteful or excessive behavior in both human and nonhuman agents or groups (Salahshour 2019; see especially Quinn 2019 for a review of costly signaling theory studies in New World anthropology and archaeology). This theory developed from the handicap principle in evolutionary biology (Zahavi 1975; Zahavi and Zahavi 1999), which notes that members of one or more species communicate through a series of apparently wasteful symbols of conspicuous consumption. For example, the tail of a male peacock, which requires an enormous metabolic load, limits flight, and increases predatory risk, would conventionally be considered a handicap. However, when interpreted by females of the same species as a metric of health quality or resource availability, this characteristic leads to higher reproductive fitness and is therefore evolutionarily beneficial. The handicap principle and other forms of biological signaling are also tied to the concept of honest signaling, as dishonest signals have been shown to be intrinsically unsustainable (Grafen 1990; Számadó 2011). Salahshour (2019) has theorized that the high cost of honest signals limits opportunities for wasteful dishonesty. Costly signaling theory has been adopted to interpret conspicuous consumption, lavish spending, risky behavior, and resource extraction strategies among human actors on a diachronic scope, from the use of ochre by early Paleolithic communities (Power 2014; Watts 2009) to contemporary examples of sports cars or designer clothes (Nelissen and Meijers 2011; Sundie et al. 2011).

Costly signaling theory was first deployed archaeologically in Neiman's (1997) evolution-based investigation of the spatial distribution of monumental construction in the Terminal Classic Maya. Neiman explored correlations of this activity with ecological factors as a way of understanding subsequent widespread societal collapse in the transition to the Postclassic period. Since then, archaeological approaches to costly signaling theory have been used to explore topics such as dangerous game hunting (Lupo and Schmitt 2016) or religious activity (Sosis and Bressler 2003) as examples of behavior that offer benefits beyond those that are immediately evident. Most archaeological applications of costly signaling theory (e.g., Aldenderfer 2006; Bliege Bird and Smith 2005; Bliege Bird et al. 2001; Hawkes and Bliege Bird 2002) have been undertaken in places far from the Mediterranean. However, costly signaling theory has been sporadically applied to case studies in Mediterranean contexts or associated regions. Focusing on Bronze Age Anatolia, Glatz and Plourde (2011) explored the spatial distribution of rock-cut and constructed monuments in the Hittite heartland and its periphery, arguing that these costly interventions allowed Hittite kings, princes, and other administrative officials to claim contested territories. Taking the implications of this analysis further, Glatz and Plourde (2011:362) proposed that in this context "the mere fact that monument construction occurs indicates an unsettled political landscape in which reaffirmative statements of strength are required." Beyond its immediate relevance to the understanding of the politics of Late Bronze Age Anatolia and the dynamics of noteworthy sites such as Karabel and Yalburt, this approach illustrates that the most effective examples of research that uses costly signaling theory push their analyses past the exploration of costly signaling itself, highlighting the social, political, or economic drivers behind costly signals.

Of particular relevance to this volume, Čučković (2017) used costly signaling theory to explore the prolific construction of hillforts in coastal and island Dalmatia during the Bronze Age. To our knowledge, this study is the only application of costly signaling theory to a coastal or island landscape in the Mediterranean. Čučković highlighted several categories of social benefit when these enormous earthworks were constructed at a relatively high density in the landscape. While more than 1,000 such sites are known in the northeast Adriatic, the island of Lošinj in Kvarner Bay contains 30 Bronze Age hillfort constructions within an area of 74 square km. This density is unique in the Adriatic. The site is thus a clear example of the potential for costly signaling theory approaches on the islands and coasts of the Mediterranean. Čučković argued that these hillforts simultaneously served as symbols of community strength, defensive preparedness, and re-source availability, and—when viewed as a collective, especially from the sea—offer an image of an undeniably fortified seascape. These conclusions are drawn solely from data collected through visibility analysis, and in-deed the visibility of costly signals has been demonstrated to be a major factor in ensuring the social benefits of both ephemeral (e.g., a religious ceremony or feast) and more durable (e.g., a project of monumental con-struction) signals (Ames 2010; Kantner and Vaughn 2012; Munson et al. 2014). However, in the case of Lošinj island and the hillforts of the Bronze Age Adriatic, relying solely on viewing these features—instead of a mul-tifaceted approach that ties this key variable to other aspects of the local archaeological record—limits the potential for costly signaling theory to inform our understanding of, for example, the broader pattern of Adriatic settlement in the Bronze Age or the subsequent transition to new ways of living in the early Iron Age.

Potential applications for research based on costly signaling theory abound in the Mediterranean. The traditions of monumental megalithic construction on the Balearic Islands are good candidates for such research. Majorca and Minorca, which were first colonized in the later third millen-nium, much more recently than other Mediterranean islands (Micó 2006), both feature traditions of conspicuous megalithic monumentality during the Bronze and Iron Ages. Micó (2006) segmented pre- and protohistoric occupation into six main phases based on changes in monumental archi-tecture, settlement patterning, burial rites, and portable material culture. Gili and colleagues (2006:838), who charted developments in monumen-tal funerary architecture on Menorca based on Micó's categories, described

Figure 3.3. Talatí de Dalt, Minorca, Spain. Photo by Paul Stephenson, distributed under a CC BY 2.0 license.

"uninterrupted development of above-ground funerary structures, between at least *c.* 1800 and 850 BC . . . [with an] overall tendency towards larger and higher burial chambers, which in general also demanded the construction of bigger and more complex constructions." The pattern is also present in the domestic architectural sphere on both Majorca and Minorca, which transitioned from ephemeral villages around the turn of the second millennium to the more durable naviforme domestic and production spaces in the middle of the second millennium and finally to the proliferation of monumental talayots in the early Iron Age (Figure 3.3).

How can costly signaling theory inform our understanding of Balearic megaliths? De Cet's (2017) substantial study of settlement and landscape exploitation on a diachronic scale in Menorca highlighted periods of particularly intense megalithic construction. Costly signaling theory could be used with this dataset to explore the behavioral ecodynamics behind these traditions and the potential material consequences and benefits of such energetically intensive construction methodologies in Menorca and elsewhere in the prehistoric and protohistoric coastal and island Mediterranean.

Discussion and Conclusion

While we have highlighted the disciplinary-driven reasons for the paucity of human behavioral ecology research in the Mediterranean basin, it is important to note that this is in no way related to the peculiar environmental and topographic characteristics of the region. Broodbank (2013:61) contextualizes the Mediterranean as an ecological space comparable to a small handful of "mediterraneoid" areas that have similar semiarid climates, coastal weather patterns, and flora and fauna. It is perhaps surprising that the Mediterranean-like environment of coastal California is one of the most richly explored areas of human behavioral ecology research. For example, several researchers have conducted studies guided by ideal distribution models in the Channel Islands off the coast of Southern California (Jazwa et al. 2019; Winterhalder et al. 2010) and in parts of mainland California (Broughton 1994; Codding and Jones 2013). Research that uses human behavioral ecology models might offer the opportunity to bridge the gap between scholarship in these two areas of prehistoric studies. At a more general level, we might expect environmental organization to constrain the range of adaptations adopted by colonizing or growing populations. This is especially the case with patterns of precocious urbanism and polity formation in the Mediterranean, compared to the absence of urban forms in California, central Chile, the Cape, and Western Australia. Human behavioral ecology surely has a role in elucidating very different long-term sociopolitical outcomes in comparable environments.

In the past, Mediterranean archaeology has been somewhat resistant to the mode of inquiry that human behavioral ecology represents. This is for disciplinary reasons. We have attempted to demonstrate that the few archaeological studies of the Mediterranean that have used human behavioral ecology models show the way to broader vistas of application. The richness of the data in the prehistoric Mediterranean and the extent to which the region provides a broad geographic sweep whose constituent components are united in their heterogeneity offer promising opportunities for research that uses human behavioral ecology methods. Dispersed Mediterranean microecologies are environmentally similar. Because of this, we should be able to test case studies against the expectations of human behavioral ecology models and against one another. Such research should enable us to understand the local specifics that helped generate the particular social forms that emerged in the Mediterranean from the middle Holocene onward. Mediterranean archaeological datasets are an excellent ground for testing anthropological theory more broadly, for exploring processes of growth, diversity, and interconnection elsewhere (e.g., Broodbank 2018). That is why it is so vital to include the Mediterranean in global and comparative archaeologies.

Acknowledgments

We thank the editors for their patience in awaiting this chapter and for their kind invitation to contribute to this volume. We would also like to thank John F. Cherry and Elic Weitzel for their helpful comments and close readings of a draft of this text.

References Cited

Alcock, Susan E., and John F. Cherry (editors). 2004. *Side-by-Side Survey: Comparative Regional Studies in the Mediterranean World.* Oxbow, Oxford.

Aldenderfer, Mark. 2006. Costly Signaling, the Sexual Division of Labor, and Animal Domestication in the Andean Highlands. In *Behavioral Ecology and the Transition to Agriculture*, edited by Douglas J. Kennett and Bruce Winterhalder, pp. 167–196. University of California Press, Berkeley.

Ames, Kenneth M. 2010. On the Evolution of the Human Capacity for Inequality and/or Egalitarianism. In *Pathways to Power: New Perspectives on the Emergence of Social Inequality*, edited by T. Douglas Price and Gary Feinman, pp. 15–44. Springer, New York.

Annis, M. Beatrice. 1985. Resistance and Change: Pottery Manufacture in Sardinia. *World Archaeology* 17(2):240–255.

Barker, Graeme, and David Mattingly (editors). 1999–2001. *The Archaeology of Mediterranean Landscapes.* 5 vols. Oxbow, Oxford.

Bayham, Frank. 1979. Factors Influencing the Archaic Pattern of Animal Exploitation. *Kiva* 44:219–235.

Bell, Adrian Viliami, and Bruce Winterhalder. 2014. The Population Ecology of Despotism: Concessions and Migration between Central and Peripheral Habitats. *Human Nature* 25(1):121–135.

Bird, Douglas W., and James F. O'Connell. 2006. Behavioral Ecology and Archaeology. *Journal of Archaeological Research* 14(2):143–188.

Bliege Bird, Rebecca, and Eric Alden Smith. 2005. Signaling Theory, Strategic Interaction, and Symbolic Capital. *Current Anthropology* 46(2):221–248.

Bliege Bird, Rebecca, Eric Alden Smith, and Douglas Bird. 2001. The Hunting Handicap: Costly Signaling in Human Foraging Strategies. *Behavioral Ecology and Sociobiology* 50(1):9–19.

Boomgarden, Shannon A., Duncan Metcalfe, and Ellyse T. Simons. 2019. An Optimal Irrigation Model: Theory, Experimental Results, and Implications for Future Research. *American Antiquity* 84(2):252–273.

Brantingham, P. Jeffrey. 2006. Measuring Forager Mobility. *Current Anthropology* 47(3): 435–459.

Broodbank, Cyprian. 2013. *The Making of the Middle Sea.* Thames & Hudson, London.

———. 2018. Does Island Archaeology Matter? In *Regional Approaches to Social Complexity*, edited by Alex Knodell and Thomas Leppard, pp. 188–206. Equinox, Sheffield.

Broughton, Jack M. 1994. Declines in Mammalian Foraging Efficiency during the Late Holocene, San Francisco Bay. *Journal of Anthropological Archaeology* 13:371–401.

Brown, Keri A. 1997. Domestic Settlement and the Landscape during the Neolithic of the Tavoliere, S.E. Italy. In *Neolithic Landscapes*, edited by Peter Topping, pp. 125–138. Oxbow, Oxford.

Chaput, Michelle A., and Konrad Gajewski. 2016. Radiocarbon Dates as Estimates of Ancient Human Population Size. *Anthropocene* 15:3–12.

Charnov, Eric L. 1976. Optimal Foraging, the Marginal Value Theorem. *Theoretical Population Biology* 9(2):129–136.

Cherry, John F. 1981. Pattern and Process in the Earliest Colonization of the Mediterranean Islands. *Proceedings of the Prehistoric Society* 47:41–68.

Cherry, John F., and Thomas P. Leppard. 2018. Patterning and Its Causation in the Pre-Neolithic Colonization of the Mediterranean Islands (Late Pleistocene to Early Holocene). *Journal of Island and Coastal Archaeology* 13(2):191–205.

Codding, Brian F., and Douglas W. Bird. 2015. Behavioral Ecology and the Future of Archaeological Science. *Journal of Archaeological Science* 56:9–20.

Codding, Brian F., and Terry L. Jones. 2013. Environmental Productivity Predicts Migration, Demographic, and Linguistic Patterns in Prehistoric California. *Proceedings of the National Academy of Sciences* 110(11):14569–14573.

Collins-Elliott, Stephen A., and Christopher S Jazwa. 2020. Dynamic Modeling of the Effects of Site Placement on Environmental Suitability: A Theoretical Example from Northwest Morocco. *Environmental Archaeology* 27(4):447–460.

Colwell-Chanthaphonh, Chip, T. J. Ferguson, Dorothy Lippert, Randall H. McGuire, George P. Nicholas, Joe E. Watkins, and Larry J. Zimmerman. 2010. The Premise and Promise of Indigenous Archaeology. *American Antiquity* 75(2):228–238.

Čučković, Zoran. 2017. Claiming the Sea: Bronze Age Fortified Sites of the North-Eastern Adriatic Sea (Cres and Lošinj Islands, Croatia). *World Archaeology* 49(4):526–546.

Davis, Jack L. 2001. Classical Archaeology and Anthropological Archaeology in North America: A Meeting of Minds at the Millennium? In *Archaeology at the Millennium: A Sourcebook*, edited by Gary Feinman and T. Douglas Price, pp. 415–438. Springer, New York.

de Cet, Monica. 2017. *Long-Term Social Development on a Mediterranean Island: Menorca between 1600BCE and 1900CE*. Bonn: Dr. Rudolf Habelt GmbH.

Diehl, Mike W., and Jennifer A. Waters. 2006. Aspects of Optimization and Risk during the Early Agricultural Period in Southeastern Arizona. In *Behavioral Ecology and the Transition to Agriculture*, edited by Douglas J. Kennett and Bruce Winterhalder, pp. 63–86. University of California Press, Berkeley.

DiNapoli, Robert J., and Alex E. Morrison. 2016. Human Behavioural Ecology and Pacific Archaeology. *Archaeology in Oceania* 52(1):1–12.

Forbes, Hamish. 2007. *Meaning and Identity in a Greek Landscape: An Archaeological Ethnography*. Cambridge University Press, Cambridge.

Fretwell, Stephen Dewitt, and Henry L. Lucas Jr. 1969. On Territorial Behaviour and Other Factors Influencing Habitat Distribution in Birds. *Acta Biotheoretica* 19(1):16–36.

Gili, Sylvia, Vicente Lull, Rafael Micó, Cristina Rihuete, and Roberto Risch. 2006. An Island Decides: Megalithic Burial Rites on Menorca. *Antiquity* 80(310):829–842.

Giovas, Christina M., and Scott M. Fitzpatrick. 2014. Prehistoric Migration in the Caribbean: Past Perspectives, New Models and the Ideal Free Distribution of West Indian Colonization. *World Archaeology* 46(4):569–589.

Glatz, Claudia, and Aimée M. Plourde. 2011. Landscape Monuments and Political Competition in Late Bronze Age Anatolia: An Investigation of Costly Signaling Theory. *Bulletin of the American Schools of Oriental Research* 361:33–66.

Grafen, Alan. 1990. Biological Signals as Handicaps. *Journal of Theoretical Biology* 144(4):517–546.

Gregory, Timothy E. 2004. Less Is Better: The Quality of Ceramic Evidence from Archaeological Survey and Practical Proposals for Low-Impact Survey in a Mediterranean Context. In *Mediterranean Archaeological Landscapes: Current Issues*, edited by Effie F. Athanassopoulos and LuAnn Wandsnider, pp. 15–36. University of Pennsylvania Press, Philadelphia.

Gremillion, K. J., L. Barton, and D. R. Piperno. 2014. Particularism and the Retreat from Theory in the Archaeology of Agricultural Origins. *Proceedings of the National Academy of Sciences* 111(17):6171–6177.

Halstead, Paul. 2008. Between a Rock and a Hard Place: Coping with Marginal Colonisation in the Later Neolithic and Early Bronze Age of Crete and the Aegean. In *Escaping the Labyrinth: Cretan Neolithic in Context*, edited by Valasia Isaakidou and Peter Tomkins, pp. 229–257. Oxbow, Oxford.

———. 2014. *Two Oxen Ahead: Pre-mechanized Farming in the Mediterranean*. Wiley-Blackwell, Hoboken, New Jersey.

Hamilakis, Yannis, and Nicoletta Momigliano (editors). 2006. *Archaeology and European Modernity: Producing and Consuming the "Minoans."* Bottega d'Erasmo, Padua.

Hawkes, Kristen, and Rebecca Bliege Bird. 2002. Showing Off, Handicap Signaling, and the Evolution of Men's Work. *Evolutionary Anthropology* 11(2):58–67.

Hollenbach, Kandace D. 2009. *Foraging in the Tennessee River Valley, 12,500 to 8,000 Years Ago*. University of Alabama Press, Tuscaloosa.

Horden, Peregrine, and Nicholas Purcell. 2000. *The Corrupting Sea: A Study of Mediterranean History*. Blackwell, Malden.

Jacobsen, Thomas W. 1981. Franchthi Cave and the Beginning of Settled Village Life in Greece. *Hesperia* 50(4):303–319.

Jazwa, Christopher S., and Kyle A. Jazwa. 2017. Settlement Ecology in Bronze Age Messenia. *Journal of Anthropological Archaeology* 45:157–169.

Jazwa, Christopher S., Douglas J. Kennett, Bruce Winterhalder, and Terry L. Joslin. 2019. Territoriality and the Rise of Despotic Social Organization on Western Santa Rosa Island, California. *Quaternary International* 518:41–56.

Jones, G. D. B. 1987. *Apulia*. Vol. 1, *Neolithic Settlement in the Tavoliere*. Thames & Hudson, London.

Kantner, John, and Kevin J. Vaughn. 2012. Pilgrimage as Costly Signal: Religiously Motivated Cooperation in Chaco and Nasca. *Journal of Anthropological Archaeology* 31(1):66–82.

Kennett, Douglas J. 2005. *The Island Chumash: Behavioral Ecology of a Maritime Society*. University of California Press, Berkeley.

Kennett, Douglas J., and Bruce Winterhalder (editors). 2006. *Behavioral Ecology and the Transition to Agriculture.* University of California Press, Berkeley.

Kotsakis, Kostas. 1996. The Coastal Settlements of Thessaly. In *Neolithic Culture in Greece,* edited by George A. Papathanassopoulos, pp. 49–57. Museum of Cycladic Art, Athens.

Kramer, Andrew M., Brian Dennis, Andrew M. Liebhold, and John M. Drake. 2009. The Evidence for Allee Effects. *Population Ecology* 51(3):341–354.

Lupo, Karen D., and Dave N. Schmitt. 2016. When Bigger Is Not Better: The Economics of Hunting Megafauna and Its Implications for Plio-Pleistocene Hunter-Gatherers. *Journal of Anthropological Archaeology* 44:185–197.

MacArthur, Robert H., and Eric R. Pianka. 1966. On Optimal Use of a Patchy Environment. *American Naturalist* 100:603–609.

McClure, Sarah B., C. Michael Barton, and Michael A. Jochim. 2009. Human Behavioral Ecology, Domestic Animals, and Land Use during the Transition to Agriculture in Valencia, Eastern Spain. *Journal of Anthropological Research* 65(2):253–269.

McClure, Sarah B., Michael A. Jochim, and C. Michael Barton. 2006. Human Behavioral Ecology, Domestic Animals, and Land Use during the Transition to Agriculture in Valencia, Eastern Spain. In *Behavioral Ecology and the Transition to Agriculture,* edited by Douglas J. Kennett and Bruce Winterhalder, pp. 197–216. University of California Press, Los Angeles.

Micó, Rafael. 2006. Radiocarbon Dating and Balearic Prehistory: Reviewing the Periodization of the Prehistoric Sequence. *Radiocarbon* 48(3):421–434.

Munro, Natalie D., and Mary C. Stiner. 2015. Zooarchaeological Evidence for Early Neolithic Colonization at Franchthi Cave (Peloponnese, Greece). *Current Anthropology* 56(4):596–603.

Munson, Jessica, Viviana Amati, Mark Collard, and Martha J. Macri. 2014. Classic Maya Bloodletting and the Cultural Evolution of Religious Rituals: Quantifying Patterns of Variation in Hieroglyphic Texts. *PLoS ONE* 9(9):e107982.

Neiman, Fraser D. 1997. Conspicuous Consumption as Wasteful Advertising: A Darwinian Perspective on Spatial Patterns in Classic Maya Terminal Monument Dates. In *Rediscovering Darwin: Evolutionary Theory and Archeological Explanation,* edited by C. Michael Burton, Geoffrey Clark, and Douglas Bamforth, pp. 267–290. American Anthropological Association, Arlington, Virginia.

Nelissen, Rob M. A., and Marijn H. C. Meijers. 2011. Social Benefits of Luxury Brands as Costly Signals of Wealth and Status. *Evolution and Human Behavior* 32(5):343–355.

O'Connell, James F. 1987. Alyawara Site Structure and Its Archaeological Implications. *American Antiquity* 52(1):74–108.

———. 1995. Ethnoarchaeology Needs a General Theory of Behavior. *Journal of Archaeological Research* 3(3):205–255.

Perlès, Catherine. 2001. *The Early Neolithic in Greece.* Cambridge University Press, Cambridge.

Power, Camilla. 2014. The Evolution of Ritual as a Process of Sexual Selection. In *The Social Origins of Language,* edited by Jerome Lewis, Danny Dor, Chris Knight, and Daniel Dor, pp. 196–207. Oxford University Press, Oxford.

Quinn, Colin P. 2019. Costly Signaling Theory in Archaeology. In *Handbook of Evolution-*

ary Research in Archaeology, edited by Anna Marie Prentiss, pp. 275–294. Springer International, New York.

Renfrew, Colin. 1980. The Great Tradition versus the Great Divide: Archaeology as Anthropology? *American Journal of Archaeology* 84(3):287–298.

———. 2003. Retrospect and Prospect: Mediterranean Archaeology in a New Millennium. In *Theory and Practice in Mediterranean Archaeology: Old and New World Perspectives*, edited by John Papadopoulous and Richard M. Leventhal, pp. 311–318. Cotsen Institute of Archaeology, Los Angeles.

Robb, John. 2013. Material Culture, Landscapes of Action, and Emergent Causation: A New Model for the Origins of the European Neolithic. *Current Anthropology* 54(6):657–683.

Roberts, C. Neil, Jessie Woodbridge, Alessio Palmisano, Andrew Bevan, Ralph Fyfe, and Stephen Shennan. 2019. Mediterranean Landscape Change during the Holocene: Synthesis, Comparison and Regional Trends in Population, Land Cover and Climate. *Holocene* 29(5):923–937.

Robinson, Erick, H. Jabran Zahid, Brian F. Codding, Randall Haas, and Robert L. Kelly. 2019. Spatiotemporal Dynamics of Prehistoric Human Population Growth: Radiocarbon 'Dates as Data' and Population Ecology Models. *Journal of Archaeological Science* 101 (January): 63–71.

Salahshour, Mohammad. 2019. Evolution of Costly Signaling and Partial Cooperation. *Scientific Reports* 9(1):1–7.

Sargent, Andrew. 2001. Changing Settlement Location and Subsistence in Later Prehistoric Apulia, Italy. *Origini* 23:145–167.

Seretis, Kylie. 2005. An Island Divided: Politicised Landscapes, Modern Borders, and Shifting Identities. *Journal of Conflict Archaeology* 1(1):215–233.

Smith, Eric Alden. 1983. Anthropological Applications of Optimal Foraging Theory: A Critical Review with Comment. *Current Anthropology* 24(5):625–651.

Snodgrass, Anthony M. 1985. The New Archaeology and the Classical Archaeologist. *American Journal of Archaeology* 89(1):31–37.

Sosis, Richard and Eric Bressler. 2003. Cooperation and Commune Longevity: A Test of the Costly Signaling Theory of Religion. *Cross-Cultural Research* 37(2):211–239.

Starkovich, Britt M. 2014. Optimal Foraging, Dietary Change, and Site Use during the Paleolithic at Klissoura Cave 1 (Southern Greece). *Journal of Archaeological Science* 52:39–55.

———. 2017. Paleolithic Subsistence Strategies and Changes in Site Use at Klissoura Cave 1 (Peloponnese, Greece). *Journal of Human Evolution* 111:63–84.

Starkovich, Britt M., Natalie D. Munro, and Mary C. Stiner. 2018. Terminal Pleistocene Subsistence Strategies and Aquatic Resource Use in Southern Greece. *Quaternary International* 465:162–176.

Stephens, David W., and John R. Krebs. 1986. *Foraging Theory*. Princeton University Press, Princeton, New Jersey.

Stiner, Mary C. 2006. *The Faunas of Hayonim Cave, Israel: A 200,000-Year Record of Paleolithic Diet, Demography, and Society*. Peabody Museum of Archaeology and Ethnology, Cambridge, MA.

Stiner, Mary C., and Steven L. Kuhn. 1992. Subsistence, Technology, and Adaptive Variation in Middle Paleolithic Italy. *American Anthropologist* 94(2):306–339.

Stiner, Mary C., and Natalie D. Munro. 2011. On the Evolution of Diet and Landscape during the Upper Paleolithic through Mesolithic at Franchthi Cave (Peloponnese, Greece). *Journal of Human Evolution* 60(5):618–636.

Sundie, Jill M., Douglas T. Kenrick, Vladas Griskevicius, Joshua M. Tybur, Kathleen D. Vohs, and Daniel Beal. 2011. Peacocks, Porsches, and Thorstein Veblen: Conspicuous Consumption as a Sexual Signaling System. *Journal of Personality and Social Psychology* 100(4):664–680.

Számadó, Szabolcs. 2011 The Cost of Honesty and the Fallacy of the Handicap Principle. *Animal Behaviour* 81(1):3–10.

Tiné, A. 1983. *Passo di Corvo e la civiltà neolitica del Tavoliere*. Sagep, Genova.

Tremayne, Andrew H., and Bruce Winterhalder. 2017. Large Mammal Biomass Predicts the Changing Distribution of Hunter-Gatherer Settlements in Mid-Late Holocene Alaska. *Journal of Anthropological Archaeology* 45:81–97.

van Andel, Tjeerd H., and Curtis N. Runnels. 1995. The Earliest Farmers in Europe. *Antiquity* 69(264):481–500.

Vandam, Ralf, Eva Kaptijn, and Bram Vanschoenwinkel. 2013. Disentangling the Spatio-Environmental Drivers of Human Settlement: An Eigenvector Based Variation Decomposition. *PLoS ONE* 8(7): e67726.

van Dommelen, Peter. 2011. Postcolonial Archaeologies between Discourse and Practice. *World Archaeology* 43(1):1–6.

Vernon, Kenneth B., Peter M. Yaworsky, Jerry Spangler, Simon Brewer, and Brian F. Codding. 2020. Decomposing Habitat Suitability across the Forager to Farmer Transition. *Environmental Archaeology* 27(4): 420–433.

Vigne, Jean Denis, Julie Daujat, and Hervé Monchot. 2016. First Introduction and Early Exploitation of the Persian Fallow Deer on Cyprus (8000–6000 cal. BC). *International Journal of Osteoarchaeology* 26(5):853–866.

Watts, Ian. 2009. Red Ochre, Body Painting, and Language: Interpreting the Blombos Ochre. In *The Cradle of Language*, edited by Rudolph Botha and Chris Knight, pp. 93–129. Oxford University Press, Oxford.

Weitzel, Elic M. 2019. Declining Foraging Efficiency in the Middle Tennessee River Valley Prior to Initial Domestication. *American Antiquity* 84(2):191–214.

Winterhalder, Bruce. 1981. Foraging Strategies in the Boreal Forest: An Analysis of Cree Hunting and Gathering. In *Hunter-Gatherer Foraging Strategies: Ethnographic and Archaeological Analyses*, edited by Bruce Winterhalder and Eric Alden Smith, pp. 66–98. University of Chicago Press, Chicago.

Winterhalder, Bruce, Douglas J. Kennett, Mark N. Grote, and Jacob Bartruff. 2010. Ideal Free Settlement of California's Northern Channel Islands. *Journal of Anthropological Archaeology* 29(4):469–490.

Winterhalder, Bruce, and Eric Alden Smith. 2000. Analyzing Adaptive Strategies: Human Behavioral Ecology at Twenty-Five Years. *Evolutionary Anthropology* 9(2):51–72.

Zahavi, Amotz. 1975. Mate Selection—A Selection for a Handicap. *Journal of Theoretical Biology* 53(1):205–214.

Zahavi, Amotz, and Avishag Zahavi. 1999. *The Handicap Principle: A Missing Piece of Darwin's Puzzle*. Oxford University Press, Oxford.

II

Local Case Studies

4

Human Niche Construction and Shifts in Subsistence and Settlement during the Early Formative in the Eastern Soconusco Mangrove Zone

JAMES T. DANIELS JR., HEATHER B. THAKAR, AND HECTOR NEFF

The factors that led to the shift from highly mobile egalitarian hunter-gatherers to sedentary ranked societies have been the subject of many debates. Residential mobility is closely tied to human adaptations to environmental pressures. The environmental responses to those adaptations may then affect the persistence of sedentariness. It is unlikely that a single causal factor is the linchpin of the emergence of sedentariness. Earlier theoretical approaches to understanding sedentariness have been abandoned because they relied heavily on essentialist and commonsense-based ideas instead of on examinations of the ecological contingencies that affect human settlement and how humans interact with the landscape that surrounds them.

The Soconusco, located between the Sierra Madre and the Pacific Ocean along Mexico's southeastern coast, is an ideal place to examine shifts in residential mobility. In the Archaic (5500–1900 BC), it was home to the Chantuto, who were relatively mobile egalitarian hunters, gatherers, fishers, and foragers (Voorhies 1976). Their archaeological footprint is primarily associated with large, mounded shell middens such as Cerro de las Conchas, which lies on the edge of El Hueyate, a freshwater marsh (Clark 1994; Voorhies et al. 2002). In the Early Formative (1900–1000 BC), the Mokaya, who were sedentary, village-dwelling people, lived there (Voorhies 1976; Figure 4.1). They are associated with the manufacture and use of high-quality pottery with elaborate surface treatments. The predominant vessel forms were *tecomates* with a globular shape, a narrow neckless opening, and deep flat-bottomed bowls. The changes seen in the archaeological record between the Archaic and Early Formative suggest a regional increase in population. Clark and Blake (1994)

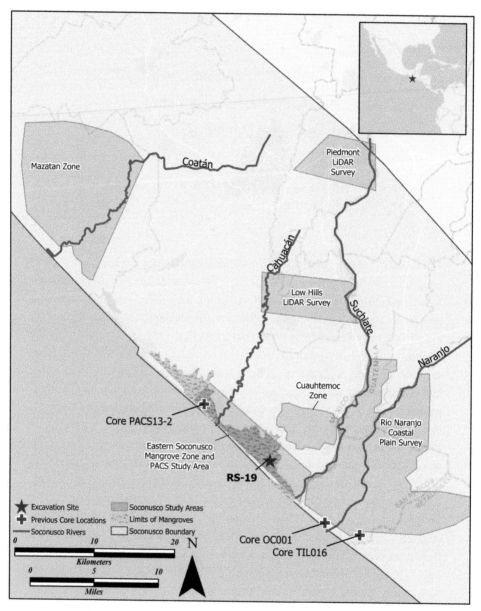

Figure 4.1. Map of eastern Soconusco showing the study area of the Proyecto Arqueológico Costa del Soconusco and features and survey areas mentioned in this chapter. Figure by Hector Neff and James T. Daniels Jr.

have argued that by 1700 BC, the Mokaya had made the transition from an egalitarian society to simple chiefdoms. They were the first people in the region to do so.

These changes in human culture during the Archaic and the Early Formative undoubtedly impacted the landscape and environment. Phytolith and charcoal evidence from sediment cores near the Mexico-Guatemala border suggest that people were clearing inland forests and growing maize as early as the Archaic (Kennett et al. 2010; Neff et al. 2006a). These practices during the Archaic (Chantuto) and the Early Formative (Mokaya) may have had unintended impacts on the landscape that changed the environmental constraints and selective pressures for future generations. We examine archaeological and paleoenvironmental evidence from the mangrove estuary of southern Pacific Chiapas, Mexico, through the theoretical lenses of niche construction theory and human behavioral ecology to reconstruct the evolving relationship between humans and the environment. Specifically, we assess the impact of the subsistence strategies of the Archaic period Chantuto and the Early Formative Mokaya cultures on the ecology of the region, including the availability and diversity of resources and how those factors influenced decisions regarding subsistence and settlement (Figure 4.1).

Niche Construction and Human Behavioral Ecology

Niche construction theory is a valuable theoretical framework for examining changes in residential mobility because it focuses on how dynamic feedbacks between ecological and evolutionary processes shape human behavior even as human behavior shapes the environment (Laland et al. 2016). The theory, which draws on expectations derived from human behavioral ecology (Codding and Bird 2015; Mohlenhoff and Codding 2017), provides a framework for archaeologists to assess the coevolution of ecosystems and human societies. Similar to natural selection, these forces shape the pool of cultural variation that gets transmitted to future generations (Constant et al. 2018), thus influencing the evolutionary trajectory of human societies that occupy a modified ecosystem (Ellis 2015; Laland et al. 2015). For example, Freeman and colleagues (2015) have suggested that the development of disparate investments in emerging food production systems is a consequence of the different ways early foraging and cultivating modified ecosystems and the net benefits of different behaviors. Decades of clearing land to plant crops might positively or negatively change selection pressures on wild resources. This interaction effect determines how people allocate effort in subsistence pursuits. In this way, eco-evolutionary feedback between optimal behavior in the present, the structure of an ecosystem, and optimal behavior in the future creates interdependencies between foraging, farming, and ecosystems.

Because local environmental and adaptive contexts differ, it is not possible to assume that niche construction had systematic or orderly effects (Constant et al. 2018). The central insight of the niche construction framework is the recognition that the way that organisms modify their environment becomes an "ecological inheritance" that changes the selective pressures their descendants will face (Ellis 2015; Laland and O'Brien 2010; Laland et al. 2016; Matthews et al. 2014; O'Brien and Laland 2012; Odling-Smee et al. 2013). By changing the selective environment so that it generates an evolutionary trajectory different from what would otherwise have been the case, the organisms play a role in their own evolution. However, while agents (organisms) are part of the process, selection, not agency, is the mechanism that generates change. From this perspective, niche construction theory complements other evolutionary approaches by highlighting feedbacks and historical dynamics (Gremillion et al. 2014:6175; Piperno 2017:219).

The general processes of human niche construction are illustrated in Figure 4.2. The horizontal arrows labeled "niche construction" represent the effects of human activity that modify the interior and coastal environments. For example, forest clearance increases sediment loads in rivers and streams, which reconfigures stream channels and floodplains and increases chances of downstream flooding. Increased sediment loads can also lead to the creation of new barrier beaches and lagoons, which then become more productive coastal habitats. The horizontal arrows labeled "selection" represent categories of human exploitation, such as planting gardens, hunting, shellfish collecting, fishing, salt production, harvesting fuel wood, and ceramic production, all of which could have been pursued from Archaic times on. The effects of niche construction, including canals and lagoons, become a part of the ecological inheritance that also facilitate commercial interaction and population dispersal. For example, lagoon fisheries and interior farmlands benefited from the buffering effect of mangrove forests during storms and tsunamis. In addition to providing enhanced opportunities, selection has included constraints for coastal populations, such as the difficulties of fishing on exposed coasts, fluctuations in prey abundance and crop yields, and flooding.

We see human sociocultural niche construction as discussed by Ellis (2015) as an important aspect of how humans transform the environment and the organization of their societies. Such activity produced adaptive consequences that required increasing dependence on cultural traits for survival and reproduction. The transformation of both the biosphere and the social

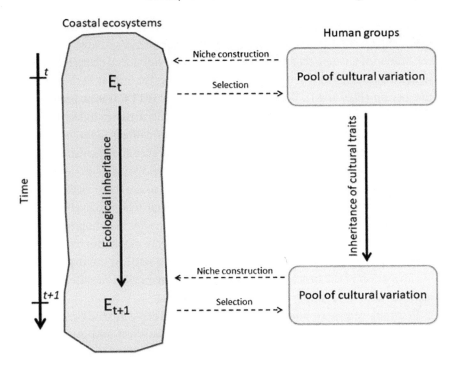

Figure 4.2. Diagram of the niche construction evolutionary process that shapes coastal ecosystems and resident human groups. Modified from Laland and O'Brien (2012:Fig. 1b).

organization created by the feedback inherent in niche construction would have generated an increase in social complexity much like we see during the transition from the Archaic to the Early Formative period in Mesoamerica. As Archaic and Early Formative populations transitioned from mobile subsistence strategies to more sedentary ones, they likely became more invested in the productivity of the ecosystems in which they lived and relied more heavily on engineering cooperative ecosystems. Communal cooperation and social cohesion would have been selected as an adaptive response to the intended and unintended consequences of ecosystem engineering.

A Case Study from the Eastern Soconusco Mangrove Zone

Since 2011, the Proyecto Arqueológico Costa del Soconusco (PACS) has focused on archaeological and paleoenvironmental data from the eastern Soconusco mangrove zone in the southeasternmost corner of Chiapas, Mexico, between the Río Cahuacán and the Río Suchiate. During the 2017 field season, archaeological excavations at the Early Formative archaeological site of Rancho Soledad-19 (RS-19), which is located in the mangrove estuary near the border of Guatemala and Mexico, produced evidence of changes in subsistence strategies and settlement patterns during the initial Early Formative period (Figure 4.1). The local name for RS-19 is El Castaño, but in this chapter we refer to the site by its PACS site name in order to follow the site naming and numbering conventions for all sites previously identified in the study area. Sediment coring was conducted on the barrier beach and within the mangrove estuary during the 2018 and 2019 field seasons to determine the timing of the formation of the beach in relation to Early Formative settlement in the mangrove estuary. The combined data from excavations and sediment cores provided data to help us determine whether abundance and diversity of resources in the mangrove estuary were stable during the Archaic and Early Formative, thus drawing people to settle in the region, or if the formation of the beach and expansion of the mangrove was the result of niche construction following inland land clearance.

Previous sediment coring within and near the PACS study area have identified phytoliths and charcoal that suggest that slash-and-burn horticulture began in the region as early as 4550 cal BC (Kennett et al. 2010; Neff et al. 2006a). Cores TIL016, located east of the Rio Naranjo, and PACS13-2, located in the northeastern limits of the PACS study area (see Figure 4.1), contain maize pollen and increasing numbers of charcoal and open-habitat pollen in sediments dated to 3000–1600 cal BC (Neff et al. 2006a; Neff et al. 2018). In central Pacific Guatemala, cores SIP001 and SIP014 show charcoal spikes and maize pollen in sediments that date around 3500 cal BC (Neff et al. 2006a). In the Chantuto zone, 50 km north of the PACS study area, five shell mound sites located in the Acapetahua Estuary northwest of El Hueyate demonstrate evidence of more intensive extraction of estuarine resources, specifically marsh clams (*Polymesoda radiata*) and small fish species in the period 3000–1800 BC (Kennett et al. 2010; Voorhies 2004). The evidence for Archaic period land clearance and horticulture and subsequent increases in reliance on estuarine resources suggests that anthropogenic impacts during the middle Holocene may have accelerated the formation of productive lower coastal environments. These new environments would have offered more resources and opportunities to develop technological innovations.

The PACS study aims to address several hypotheses related to the previous core data. The primary hypothesis we evaluated is that increased land clearance on the coastal plain during the Archaic and initial Early Formative periods may have contributed to the expansion of the mangrove estuary.

Increased sediment loads in the eastern Soconusco mangrove zone would have resulted in barrier beaches that formed more rapidly than usual, lagoons filled with fine sediment, and an expansion of the mangrove estuary. This would have created an opportunity for Early Formative people to exploit the increasingly abundant resources and would have resulted in selection for sedentary subsistence strategies. We also hypothesize that increased sedentism in the mangroves resulted in larger populations and an increased demand for subsistence resources. Overexploitation of resources altered the landscape and the ecosystem of the mangroves in ways that led to decline of the diversified subsistence strategy the initial Early Formative inhabitants used. As a result, by the end of the Early Formative, people moved inland to gain greater access to agricultural land, and the mangrove estuaries became specialized areas for salt production.

We recognize that the barrier beach may have formed in another way and that sedentary village life may have emerged for different reasons. The barrier beach may have formed and the mangrove estuaries may have expanded because of natural processes before population expansion in the late Archaic and initial Early Formative. If that was the case, human settlement in the region would have been a result of the presence of a resource-abundant habitat that already existed. Or perhaps human occupation in the region during the Archaic accelerated changes that were already under way in the estuarine environment. However, whether the barrier beach formed as a direct result of anthropogenic processes or whether its formation was simply accelerated by anthropogenic activities, the formation process still qualifies as niche construction.

Methods

Fieldwork during the 2017 through 2019 field seasons included deep-pit excavations, sediment coring, extraction of shell samples from deeply buried shell lenses on the barrier beach, and ground-penetrating radar (GPR) surveys of RS-19 and the barrier beach. Excavation methods were designed to obtain stratigraphic data for the entire sequence of occupation at RS-19 and to optimize retrieval of invertebrate and vertebrate remains to identify changes in the types and amounts of species exploited. Sediment cores from the mangroves were extracted at the interface between the mangrove and barrier beach to obtain information regarding siltation rates in the mangrove and to determine when and how the barrier beach may have begun forming. We extracted deeply buried shell from shell lenses that represent late Holocene shallow open waters beneath the barrier beach to determine the growth rate of the beach and date its formation. We conducted GPR surveys at RS-19 to detect locations of archaeological features and changes in subsurface stratigraphy. We conducted GPR surveys on the barrier beach to investigate the mode of beach progradation. Our hypothesis was that riverine sediment supply was the main mechanism by which the barrier beach formed rather than storm surges and deposits from overwash.

Archaeological Excavations

RS-19 is a seven-meter-high mound roughly 400 m inland from the current beach. The site is surrounded on all sides by mangroves. The vegetation surrounding the site consists of red mangroves (*Rhizophora mangle*), water lettuce (*Pistia stratiotes*), and cogongrass (*Imperata cylindrica*). The vegetation on the site consists of coconut palms (*Cocos nucifera*), cabbage palms (*Sabal palmetto*), gumbo-limbo trees (*Bursera simaruba*), sapodilla trees (*Manilkara zapota*), and kapok trees (*Ceiba pentandra*). We made decisions about placement of excavation units at RS-19 partly on the basis of anomalies that GPR revealed and partly because of our need to obtain a lengthy stratigraphic profile (Figure 4.3). Thus, we began one 2-by-4-m unit near the top of the mound over a large GPR anomaly. We excavated these units as two separate 2-by-2-m units, Units 1 and 2. We placed a third unit of 2-by-2-m at the base of the mound on the eastern side over a circular anomaly. Units 1 and 2 reached an excavated depth of 7 m before we encountered the water table. We used an auger with a PVC mold to sample sediments below the water table to a depth of 9 m. We recovered artifacts and shell to a depth of 8 m; sediments between 8 and 9 m consisted of a sterile gray clay.

Sediment Cores

Our extraction of deeply buried shell associated with past open-ocean environments within the barrier beach relied on a technique local well diggers use. We probed six locations using this method, but only three yielded shell samples for radiocarbon dating. At these three locations, we encountered a shell lens containing predominately a bean clam species of shell (*Donax kindermanni*) between 8 and 9 m below the surface. We extracted two sediment cores from the mangrove estuary near site mounds BER-19 and RS-7. We used a vibracore sampler to extract sediments from the mangrove bottom. The core from near RS-7 returned 270 cm of sediment before failure and the core from near BER-19 returned 180 cm.

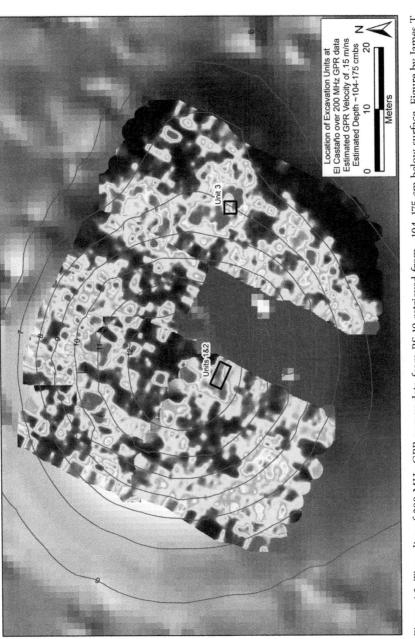

Figure 4.3. Time slice of 200 MHz GPR survey data from RS-19 retrieved from ~104–175 cm below surface. Figure by James T. Daniels Jr.

PACS Project Results, 2017–2019

RS-19

The GPR survey at RS-19 revealed a number of subsurface anomalies. While we identified multiple features and floors in Units 1 and 2 that could have caused the anomalies identified in the GPR data, there were no obvious features in Unit 3 that could explain the curvilinear anomaly our excavation targeted.

Twelve of 16 radiocarbon dates from charcoal samples that we collected from RS-19 Units 1 and 2 calibrate to between 1600 and 1400 cal BC (Table 4.1), which would place the primary occupation of the site in the initial Early Formative period. The initial Early Formative period has been divided into three ceramic phases (Barra, Locona, and Ocós) that begin as early as 1800 cal BC and extend to roughly 1400 cal BC (Blake et al. 1995). The ceramic assemblage recovered from RS-19 dates primarily to the Locona and Ocós phases. The twelve samples that date from 1600 BC to 1400 BC were recovered from deposits 170–760 cm below surface. This suggests that the mound was constructed within about 200 years.

Two dates from the upper strata of Units 1 and 3 indicate that the site was last occupied during the Late Postclassic period. The site was intensively occupied during the Terminal Classic period, as evidenced by the facts that level 7 of Unit 1 yielded a single date and that level had a high density of ceramics. A charred seed from level 22 of Unit 2 returned a date range of 2290–1635 cal BC. The error range for this sample was extremely high due to its small sample weight, so it is not adequate for pinning down the precise occupation span at RS-19 (see Table 4.1).

The rapid accumulation of deposits within the initial Early Formative period argues against interpreting RS-19 as purely a tell-like accumulation of domestic debris. Rather, it is likely that Early Formative colonizers of the RS-19 wetlands deliberately raised an elevated island in the swamp that provided a dry surface for human activities. Since artificially elevated platforms would have provided new opportunities for Early Formative inhabitants, they qualify as examples of niche construction.

Constructing elevated platforms in the intertidal coastal wetlands may have entailed making innovations in construction technology. In the levels dominated by *tecomates* in Units 1 and 2, we encountered multiple clusters of shallow, circular, and oblong features at 170–680 cm below surface. Most were shallow circular pits lined with packed clay, and the bottoms of some were coated with calcareous material. Some were fire reddened; some were not. A few of the features resemble the salt-evaporating ponds Williams (2010) described for several areas of Mexico. Tentatively, therefore, we interpret these

Table 4.1. AMS radiocarbon dates for shell and charcoal samples recovered from RS-19 grouped by unit of recovery and in order of depth

UCI Sample Number and Material Dated	Unit/Level/Feature	Depth (cmbs)	Conventional Radiocarbon Date[a] (yr BP)	Calibrated age[b] (95% confidence)
206544 (charcoal)	Unit 1 L3	20–30	415 ± 20	cal AD 1435–1610
206547 (charcoal)	Unit 1 L7	60–70	1315 ± 15	cal AD 655–775
206561 (charcoal)	Unit 1 L18	170–180	3220 ± 15	1510–1440 cal BC
206550 (charcoal)	Unit 1 L32	320	3270 ± 15	1610–1495 cal BC
206545 (charcoal)	Unit 1 L36A	350	3210 ± 20	1510–1430 cal BC
215286 (charred seed)	Unit 2 L22 Feature 17C	220	3600 ± 110	2290–1635 cal BC
206546 (charcoal)	Unit 2 L44 Feature 42A	430–440	3240 ± 20	1535–1445 cal BC
206551 (charcoal)	Unit 2 L45 Feature 45A	450	3230 ± 15	1520–1445 cal BC
206562 (charcoal)	Unit 2 L52	520	3195 ± 15	1505–1425 cal BC
206557 (charcoal)	Unit 2 L56 Feature 55A	550–560	3185 ± 15	1500–1425 cal BC
206556 (charcoal)	Unit 2 L64 Feature 64C	635	3235 ± 20	1535–1445 cal BC
206558 (charcoal)	Unit 2 L65 Feature 64B	650	3155 ± 15	1500–1400 cal BC
206555 (charcoal)	Unit 2 L66 Feature 66A	660	3225 ± 25	1535–1435 cal BC
206553 (charcoal)	Unit 2 L67 Feature 65D	666	3185 ± 15	1500–1425 cal BC
206572 (shell)	Unit 2 L70	690–700	3575 ± 20	1445–1055 cal BC
206559 (charcoal)	Unit 2 L73	730–760	3225 ± 15	1515–1440 cal BC
206560 (charcoal)	Unit 3 L10	90–100	485 ± 15	cal AD 1415–1450

Note: AMS ages were provided by Keck Carbon Cycle AMS Facility at University of California–Irvine.
[a] Conventional radiocarbon age date was calculated using the Libby half-life of 5,568 years and is corrected for total isotopic fraction. Radiocarbon concentrations are given as fractions of the Modern standard, D14C, and conventional radiocarbon age, following the conventions of Stuiver and Polach (1977:355).
[b] Calibrated age was calculated using OxCal v. 4.4 (Bronk Ramsey 2021) with the IntCal20 (Reimer et al. 2020) or Marine20 calibration curve (Heaton et al. 2013). Local Marine Delta R (76,50).

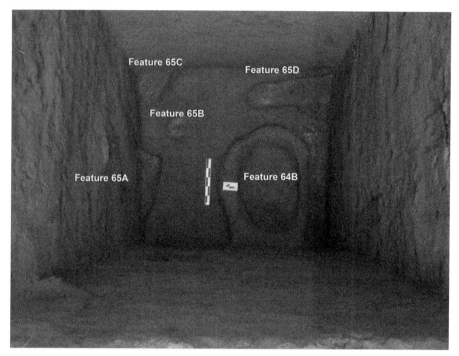

Figure 4.4. Level 65 in Unit 2, with concrete features. Basin Feature 64B is clay, but Features 65A–65D consist of hydraulic concrete. Photo by James T. Daniels Jr.

features as basins for evaporating saline water to produce salt using the *sal solar* technique. In addition to the clay-lined basins, we encountered several concrete features (Figure 4.4). We have found such concretions in other contexts within the PACS study area, including contexts where ceramics and salt were produced (e.g., Neff et al. 2016), but these other examples are amorphous and smaller than the features at RS-19. In the other cases, we have interpreted the concretions as hydraulic cement created by the accidental mixing of wood ash, silicates in soil, and water, but the regular forms at RS-19 suggest deliberate manipulation of the hydraulic concrete medium, perhaps as floors, piers for wooden platforms, or retaining walls for dredged sediments.

The subsistence activities made possible by constructing the elevated platform at RS-19 focused on procuring fish and shellfish. The first meter of deposits in Units 1 and 2 yielded almost no faunal remains. The amount of vertebrate remains by weight increased gradually. The highest concentrations were located at 4.5–6.0 m and in sediments from beneath the water table. Invertebrate remains did not show up in abundance until a depth of

3 m. One peak in abundance was located 330–370 cm below surface and another peak was at 590–610 cm below surface.

Shifts in the ratios of species of shellfish in Units 1 and 2 appear to track changes in the lagoon-estuary environment (Figure 4.5). The presence of *Polymesoda radiata* corresponds with spikes in *Cerithidia* spp. and dips in *Lliochione subrugosa* and *Leukoma metodon*. The *Polymesoda radiata* and *Cerithidia* spp. gastropods are indicative of a marsh environment. The other two species are predominantly found in environments with higher salinity, usually beyond the influence of environments with seasonal freshwater inputs such as the mouth of an estuary or an ocean beach (Lesure 2009:83).

The vertical fluctuations in faunal remains suggest that the intertidal

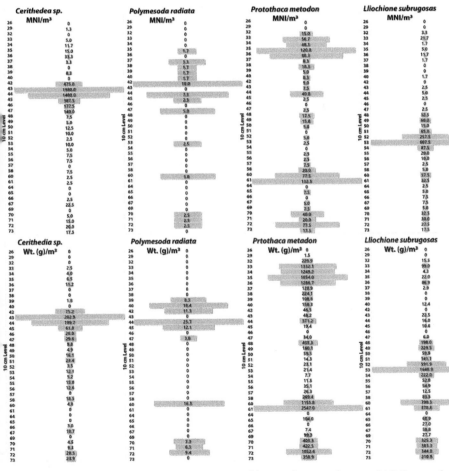

Figure 4.5. Distribution of shell species represented by weight per volume and MNI per volume in Units 1 and 2 (2 by 4 m). Figure by James T. Daniels Jr.

coastal wetlands remained dynamic during the Early Formative occupation. The quantities of vertebrate and invertebrate remains are greatest in the deepest deposits, below the water table. At 610–690 cm below surface, there is a dramatic decrease in the amount of faunal remains. This corresponds with the highest number of hydraulic cement features and clay basins, which may suggest a shift in function for this precise location of the site through time. It is possible that salt production was the primary focus during earlier occupations and that inhabitants shifted to cooking shellfish and other animals later. The concrete features may be the result of wood-ash calcite from burning mangrove wood that was unintentionally mixed with silicates in the soil and water (as discussed by Neff et al. 2016) to form a natural concrete, but their size and relatively regular circular and oblong shapes may suggest an intentional use of hydraulic cement. The exact purpose or cause of these concrete features is still unclear, but one interpretation is that they were the result of burning mangrove wood to produce salt through a technique called *sal cocida*, as discussed later in this chapter. The clay basin features may have also been used to produce salt by filling them with brine and allowing the water to evaporate (*sal solar*).

In levels that have clay basin features, there is an uptick in the number of *Cerithidia* spp. snails. The snails may have been used to make a broth or they may be a by-product of dredging the mangrove swamp for clay to make the basins. In either case, the fluctuations in depth suggest seasonal changes in the types of subsistence strategies people used, presumably to optimize their use of resources that were available during dry months and wet months. Another interesting observation is that ocean beach invertebrate remains, including *Tagelus affinis*, *Anadara grandis*, and *Lliochione subrugosa*, are larger in deposits below about 600 cm. This may suggest that these species were overharvested during initial occupation of the area. Faunal analysis is ongoing, but the preliminary data indicate that the dominant fauna represented are fish and crab. These data seem to show more fish and crab than mollusks than are found in late Archaic shell deposits. This would suggest that the environment was richer in fish and crab or that technological innovations had improved the harvesting returns from fishing. Most likely, both changes happened. At RS-19, *Polymesoda radiata* and *Cerithidia* spp., which are commonly found in a closed marsh environment, were most prevalent at 400–470 cm below surface. At these levels, we found a significant reduction in the amount of the ocean beach species. We will need further assessment to determine whether this represents seasonal inundation of the mangrove estuary or an expansion of the estuary and progradation of the barrier beach. In deposits at 300–400 cm below surface, we found an absence of clay basin features. Instead, we found hardened floors. The most prominent were at 360 cm below surface. This feature coincided with the highest density of *Leukoma metodon* shell of any level. This pattern suggests a return to a predominant reliance on shell gathering along the beach.

Subsurface Coring Results

The shell samples from the barrier beach and the charcoal from the mangrove cores were radiocarbon dated to help determine when the barrier beach may have started to form (Table 4.2 and Figure 4.6). We used the distance between the current coastline, the locations of barrier beach samples, and a possible relic beach edge that was visible in the lidar data and the dates returned from those locations to calculate a minimum and maximum rate of growth using a least-squares regression. The present-day barrier beach narrows considerably from southeast to northwest. Because the innermost edge of the beach near Jaime 2018 Core-4 connects with relict beaches 3 to 4 km farther northwest, near the mouth of the Río Cahuacán, we suggest that a wider beach once existed at the location of Silviano 2019 Core-2 but that its inner edge was scoured away by a flood or tsunami. The minimum and maximum rates of beach growth calculated using the least-squares method for the distances between Silviano 2018 Core-6, Silviano 2019 Core-2, and the current beach edge would place the initial barrier beach shoreline between 1945 and 1380 cal BC. Another possibility is that the beach at the Silviano locations did not close until 1040–605 cal BC based on minimum and maximum rates of growth and extrapolating 50 m inland from Silviano 2019 Core-2 to the current inner edge of the beach. If that was the case, rates of beach growth at the Jaime 2018 Core-4 location yield estimates of 2390–1590 cal BC for the initial formation of the wider beach. The basal date range from mangrove core RS7 2018 Core-5 is 2195–1985 cal BC. The sample that returned this date range was extracted from sediments that represent an open lagoon or wetland environment. This combined with the dates from the barrier beach suggest that based on several assumptions, the wide beach that extends south from the Jaime 2018 Core-4 location to the Río Suchiate may have been established just prior to the initial Early Formative period.

The GPR data from the beach surveys show beach progradation and linear dips that represent foreshore and backshore deposits from previous locations of the beach edge (Figure 4.7). Multiple signs of progradation are visible in the GPR radargrams. Other GPR studies of beaches show similar signs and have used the spacing between these anomalies to calculate rates of beach growth (see Brooke et al. 2008; Nooren et al. 2017). The position of the water table in

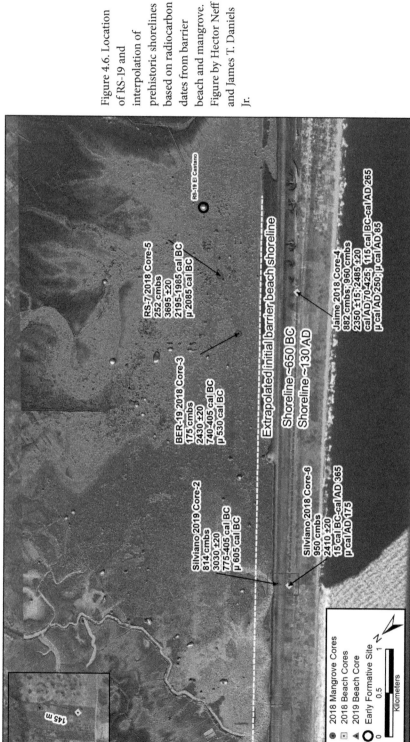

Figure 4.6. Location of RS-19 and interpolation of prehistoric shorelines based on radiocarbon dates from barrier beach and mangrove. Figure by Hector Neff and James T. Daniels Jr.

Table 4.2. AMS radiocarbon dates for shell and charcoal samples recovered from barrier beach and mangrove cores

UCI Sample Number and Material Type	Core ID and Provenience	Depth (cmbs)	Conventional Radiocarbon Date[a] (yr BP)	Calibrated age[b] (95% confidence)
206548 (charcoal)	BER-19-Core-3 Mangrove	175	2430 ± 20	740–405 cal BC
206549 (charcoal)	RS-7-Core-5 Mangrove	252	3695 ± 20	2195–1985 cal BC
206569 (shell)	Silviano-Core-6 Beach	950	2410 ± 20	15 cal BC–cal AD 365
206570 (shell)	Jaime-Core-4 Beach	960	2485 ± 20	115 cal BC–cal AD 265
206571 (shell)	Jaime-Core-4 Beach	784–882	2350 ± 15	cal AD 70–425
215292 (shell)	Silviano-Core-2 Beach	814	3030 ± 20	775–405 cal BC

Note: AMS ages were provided by Keck Carbon Cycle AMS Facility at University of California–Irvine.

[a] Conventional radiocarbon age date was calculated using the Libby half-life of 5,568 years and is corrected for total isotopic fraction. Radiocarbon concentrations are given as fractions of the Modern standard, D14C, and conventional radiocarbon age, following the conventions of Stuiver and Polach (1977:355).

[b] Calibrated age was calculated using OxCal 4.4 (Bronk Ramsey 2021) with the IntCal20 (Reimer et al. 2020) or Marine20 calibration curve (Heaton et al. 2013). Local Marine Delta R (76,50).

the PACS study area beach was at approximately 2.5 m below the surface and can be seen in the reflection characteristics visible in the radargram. Using the hyperbola search function in the GPR-SPLICE software, we calculated a time-to-depth conversion for deposits above and below the groundwater table with velocities of 0.15 m/nanosecond above the table and 0.08 m/nanosecond below the groundwater table. This depth was confirmed at Jaime Beach Core-4. The relic foreshore identified in the GPR data and targeted at Jaime Beach Core-4 returned a date range of cal AD 70–425 ($p = 0.95$) from shell recovered from sand at 784–882 cm below surface. A shell sample from 960 cm below surface returned a date of 115 cal BC–cal AD 265 ($p = 0.95$). These data indicate that at this time the beach edge was approximately 430 m inland from its current position today.

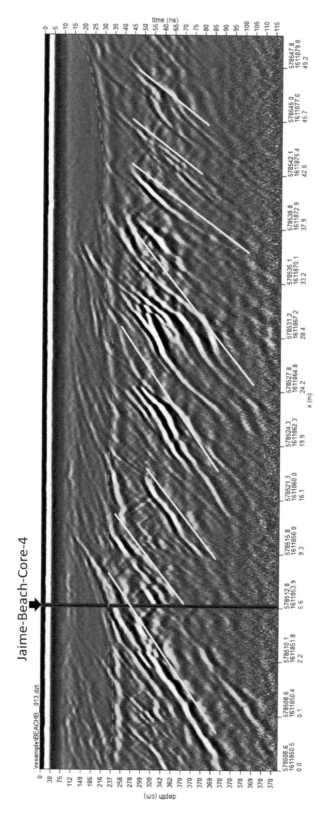

Figure 4.7. White lines in this GPR radargram of the barrier beach at Rancho Soledad-19 highlight reflections of relic foreshores associated with beach progradation. Figure by James T. Daniels Jr.

Discussion

Early Formative Settlement Patterns

The results from the 2017–2019 PACS field seasons provide promising evidence that supports our hypothesis that the barrier beach started to form just prior to or coinciding with the earliest evidence of sedentary settlements in the eastern Soconusco mangrove zone. Our calculated date for the formation of the barrier beach is also consistent with the hypothesis that Archaic period slash-and-burn agriculture began as early as 4550 cal BC (Kennett et al. 2010; Neff et al. 2006a; Neff et al. 2018), which increased sediment loads in rivers in the region and led to the formation of barrier beaches and an expansion of intertidal coastal wetlands by around 2000 cal BC.

The eastern Soconusco mangrove zone is not the only coastal region with evidence that supports the hypothesis that human niche construction occurred in the middle Holocene. Other locations in Mesoamerica that have anthropogenic impacts in the sedimentary record invariably also have clusters of Early Formative settlements. The best documented are the lower Río Naranjo drainage and the central Guatemalan coast (Neff et al. 2006a; Neff et al. 2018). While the data are not yet complete, initial Early Formative settlement clusters are strongly associated with niche-constructed lower coastal wetlands.

Adaptation to expanded subsistence opportunities in niche-constructed lower coastal wetlands in the PACS study area began shortly after 2000 cal BC. Initial Early Formative settlements are located around what would have been open lagoons interspersed with patches of mangrove forest behind a barrier beach. Early Formative villagers would likely have preferred settlement locations near the ecotone between wetlands and cultivable coastal plain land.

A similar pattern focused on an ecotone characterizes initial Early Formative settlement in the lower Río Naranjo drainage (Coe and Flannery 1967), the lower Río Jesus drainage (near El Mesak in Figure 1; Pye 1995), and the Sipacate region of the central Guatemalan coast (Arroyo 2000, 2004; Arroyo et al. 2002). Where initial Early Formative sites are present on the coastal plain, such as in the Mazatán zone (Clark 1991, 1994; Lesure 2009) and the Cuauhtémoc zone (Rosenswig 2008, 2011, 2015), they are located just inland from productive wetlands. Evidence from this broad area, which stretches from the Isthmus of Tehuantepec (Paillés 1980) to western El Salvador (Arroyo 1994), shows that in the Early Formative period, subsistence depended on a combination of horticulture on the coastal plain and efficient exploitation of estuarine resources from the mangrove zone (e.g., Lesure 2009; Lesure and Wake 2011; Rosenswig 2015).

A rapid shift from Archaic to Early Formative subsistence and settlement patterns accords with expectations for sociocultural niche construction. In that theory, feedback between ecological inheritances and cultural inheritances greatly accelerate changes in the ecosystem (Ellis 2015). In the eastern Soconusco mangrove zone, the ecosystem was rapidly changing as the barrier beach formed and the mangrove estuary expanded during the late Archaic and initial Early Formative periods. The abundance of resources the expanded mangrove estuary offered would have influenced the Chantuto and Mokaya to invest more in the local environment, including constructing mounded surfaces as a base for harvesting the resources available in the surrounding estuary, thus reducing residential mobility.

We theorize that the mound sites in the mangrove estuary served as more than special-purpose sites but were rather long-term habitation sites, where Early Formative peoples lived through much of the year. The evidence of possibly intentional use of hydraulic cement in combination with storage features, water basins, evidence of food processing, prepared floors, and the use of ceramic vessels for cooking provide support for interpreting RS-19 as a residential site. While the GPR evidence from RS-19 is presently inconclusive, the circular anomalies identified around the base of the mound could represent some type of site planning if they represent structures or larger clay pits. Additional excavations are needed to collect more data about the anomalies and determine whether they are caused by archaeological features.

Early Formative Cultural Innovations

Innovations such as mounded sites are not the only adaptations that correlate with the selective pressures of the expanded wetland environment of the Archaic. Lesure and Wake (2011:88) have suggested that the adaptive shift of the initial Early Formative also involved innovations in processing technology. They focus on the *tecomate*, the predominant vessel form at RS-19 and throughout the Early Formative, arguing that it made possible intensified and diversified production of estuary resources. They theorize that the *tecomate* was a generalized tool that could have been used to process a variety of resources, including boiling fish, crab, and shellfish and boiling shrimp before drying them. The *tecomate* could also have been used to quickly reduce brine to salt, which could then be used to preserve foods. Many of the bases of the *tecomates* recovered from RS-19 showed signs of being burned, suggesting that they were used for cooking food or boiling brine.

Lesure and Wake's (2011) argument for salt production via brine boiling (*sal cocida*) pertains to the end of the Early Formative (1300–1000 cal BC, the Cuadros and Jocotal phases, or Late Conquista in the PACS terminology) as defined by Burger (2015; see also Pye 1995). At RS-19, the evidence suggests that initial Early Formative (Early Conquista, 1560–1350 cal BC) salt production relied on the *sal solar* technique; that is, evaporating brine in the shallow clay-walled features we encountered in our excavations of Units 1 and 2 and possibly *sal cocida* evidenced by the burned *tecomates* and concrete features. Salt produced on site may have been used to preserve fish, shellfish, crabs, and shrimp. It could also have been carried to interior sites on the coastal plain. Salt production appears to have been a key component of the initial Early Formative adaptation, from 1600 cal BC on through to the Terminal Formative period (roughly cal AD 100–250), when populations in the region began to decline (Neff et al. 2018). Salt production met the need for salt supplements in diets increasingly based on maize and made it possible to preserve, store, and transport inland fish, shellfish, and other products of the lagoon-estuary zone. Evidence from Mazatán (Lesure 2009), the El Mesak region of Guatemala (Pye 1995), the Suchitepéquez coast of Guatemala (Arroyo 2000, 2004), and the PACS study area (Neff et al. 2018) confirms that by the end of the Early Formative period, 1300–1000 cal BC, salt production had shifted to the brine-boiling (*sal cocida*) technique.

The shift sometime between 1500 and 1200 cal BC from *sal solar* to *sal cocida* makes sense in the context of the continuing effects of human niche construction. *Sal solar* would have been a dry-season activity because a rainstorm would have ruined an evaporation pond. An expanding Early Formative farming population, however, would have created a selective pressure that favored year-round salt production to meet increased demand. This would have created pressure to shift to *sal cocida*, a practice that could be done all year, even indoors (McKillop 2002, 2005). An expanding coastal plain population also would have further deforested the interior, continuing the delivery of sediment to the wetlands that would have filled lagoons and further expanded mangrove forests. Larger stands of mangrove forest would have reduced the cost of procuring wood for fuel, thus also favoring a shift to *sal cocida*. An additional contributing factor in the shift to *sal cocida* may have been the fact that a wetter climate with longer wet seasons appears in the sedimentary record in the period 1300–1000 cal BC (Neff et al. 2006b).

Comparison to other Relevant Case Studies

We hypothesize that a crucial threshold of wetland productivity was crossed sometime between 2000 and 1600 cal BC. This is supported by the increase in the variety of resources harvested from the ecosystem during the Early Formative compared to the resources harvested in the Archaic. Greater productivity favored rapid evolution of an adaptation that combined interior cultivation with the harvesting of estuarine resources within the expanded, niche-constructed wetlands. A crucial geomorphological element of this framework is the establishment of a barrier beach, which would have sheltered low-lying areas immediately behind it from wave action so that the lagoon-estuary system could become established. Our chronological evidence from the beach, from wetland sediments, and from the cultural deposit at RS-19 demonstrates that, as predicted, the initial Early Formative settlement followed soon after this protected lower coastal environment was established.

Similar effects of anthropogenic land clearance on coastal environments have been documented in other regions of Mesoamerica. In Oaxaca, Mexico, research in the Río Verde drainage basin has provided geomorphological and pedological evidence that land clearance contributed to upstream erosion and that subsequent increased sediment loads had significant effects on the coastline (Joyce and Goman 2012; Joyce and Mueller 1992, 1997; Mueller et al. 2013). Sediment cores from Laguna Pastoría indicate that by 350 cal BC, a bay barrier formed by sand discharged from the Río Verde had closed a previously open bay, creating the rich estuarine system that persists today (Joyce and Goman 2012:14). Populations in the lower Río Verde Valley during the Middle Formative (805–400 cal BC) increased following the ecological changes triggered by highland erosion. Joyce and Goman (2012) argue that the increased sediment loads along the Río Verde and the subsequent expansion of the floodplain and formation of estuaries increased the productivity of both maize agriculture and estuarine resources such as fish, shellfish, and waterfowl. Evidence of this increase in productivity was recovered from sediment cores and auger drives in the estuaries. Macroscopic charcoal and carbon isotopic data show increased maize cultivation. Archaeofaunal analyses from the region demonstrate an increase in the proportion of estuarine shellfish in midden deposits from the Middle Formative to the Early Classic period.

As in the case study from Oaxaca, evidence from eastern Soconusco suggests that inland land clearance in the period 3000–1600 cal BC preceded rapid colonization of the lower coast by Early Formative villagers (Neff et al. 2006a; Neff et al. 2018). Our dates from the barrier beach add another piece to this picture; they demonstrate that it formed immediately before and perhaps during the initial Early Formative colonization of lower coastal wetlands. The results of the GPR surveys along the beach identify relic foreshores

Figure 4.8. Satellite imagery from July 2003 showing the mouth of the Suchiate River with a sand plume moving northwest along longshore currents. Google Earth. Image © Maxar Technologies.

created by riverine sediment supply from Ríos Suchiate and Cahuacán. An analysis of satellite imagery of the region confirms that sediment flows from the Suchiate River are carried northwest along the shoreline of PACS study area (Figure 4.8). Evidence from excavations shows that soon after the beach was established, the variety of estuarine resources harvested by coastal dwellers increased. These resources were not present in the archaeological record of the Archaic. In addition, the rate of local resource investment increased, as did sedentary subsistence strategies.

Conclusion

The niche construction framework has much to offer archaeology because it integrates anthropogenic impacts and takes into account that they become an ecological inheritance that changes the selective environment future generations face (Gremillion et al. 2014; Piperno 2017). Sociocultural niche construction is an evolutionary theory that helps explain that the ultimate causes of human transformation of the biosphere are inherently social and cultural (Ellis 2015). In the eastern Soconusco mangrove zone, inland forest clearance was the main niche construction effect detectable in the sedimentary record. Clearing forests modified the inland environment and the environment and ecosystem of the coast. During the Early Formative, those inadvertent modifications of the coast became the ecological inheritance that selected for a variety of innovations, including reduced residential mobility, colonization of the wetlands, and innovations in resource procurement and processing technology.

The theoretical framework of niche construction focuses attention on how early inhabitants of the eastern Soconusco mangrove zone coevolved with their surrounding environment. At around 3000 cal BC, late Archaic foragers were storing food resources and exploiting particular sites for extracting estuarine resources, suggesting a logistically organized subsistence strategy and, as Kennett and Voorhies (1996) have argued, that horticultural gardens were increasingly important. Sedimentary sequences from various cores in the region show evidence of forest clearance by burning together with evidence of domesticates such as maize by the third millennium BC. These activities increased sediment delivery to the coast, and around 2000 BC, a barrier beach began forming that offered opportunities for increased returns from wetland exploitation. This is the context for the emergence of the Barra phase, which is characterized by sedentary residence, ceramics, and increased wetland returns. Continued deforestation during the initial Early Formative period further expanded wetlands, creating protected lagoons and expanded mangrove forests. By the Locona phase, selection for settlement at lagoon edges and construction of raised platforms led to a shift in settlement patterns. Locona and Ocós phase villagers rapidly colonized multiple lower coastal wetland locations and innovations such as the *tecomate* and *sal solar* salt production became prominent features of the new adaptive strategy. The initial expansion into the littoral zone and construction of raised platforms provided easily accessible bases of operation for low-cost exploitation of wetlands. At the same time, continued expansion of the mangrove forest created an abundance of fuel wood, which offered opportunities for new pyrotechnological activities, such as salt production by *sal cocida*. As a result, by the beginning of the Middle Formative, specialized salt production based on *sal cocida* had begun. This became the dominant activity of littoral zone occupants for more than the next 1,000 years (Neff et al. 2018).

Typically, when anthropogenic deforestation and subsequent erosion are discussed, the negative effects of those actions come to mind. However, we have examined the seemingly positive effects for continued extraction of resources and maintenance of the environment. The results of our study provide data for better understanding both the intentional and unintentional consequences of human modification of the environment and how such modifications may alter selective pressures on and the behavior of future generations. Human settlement and subsistence practices have lasting and broader impacts on both local and neighboring ecosystems. Nowhere is this effect clearer than in the dynamic environments produced where land meets ocean water, where geomorphological effects such as sea-level rise, sediment discharge, longshore currents, and wave action interact with human niche construction activities. In the eastern Soconusco mangrove zone, these dynamic processes were creating a new coastal landscape with new opportunities for human adaptation before 4,000 years ago.

References Cited

Arroyo, Bárbara. 1994. The Early Formative in Southern Mesoamerica: An Explanation for the Origins of Sedentary Villages. PhD dissertation, Vanderbilt University, Nashville, Tennessee.

———. 2000. Informe preliminar del proyecto de medioambiente y recursos antiguos en la Costa del Pacífico. Manuscript prepared for Instituto de Atropología e Historia de Guatemala.

———. 2004. Of Salt and Water: Ancient Commoners on the Pacific Coast of Guatemala. In *Ancient Maya Commoners*, edited by John Lohse and Fred Valdez, pp. 73–94. University of Texas Press, Austin.

Arroyo, Bárbara, Hector Neff, and James Features. 2002. The Early Formative Sequence of Pacific Coastal Guatemala. In *Incidents of Archaeology in Central America and Yucatán: Essays in Honor of Edwin M. Shook*, edited by Michael Love, Marion Popenoe de Hatch, and Hector L. Escobedo, pp. 35–50. University Press of America, Lanham, Maryland.

Blake, Michael, John E. Clark, Barbara Voorhies, George Michaels, Michael W. Love, Mary E. Pye, Arthur A. Demarest, and Bárbara Arroyo. 1995. Radiocarbon Chronology for the Late Archaic and Formative Periods on the Pacific Coast of Southeastern Mesoamerica. *Ancient Mesoamerica* 6:161–183.

Bronk Ramsey, Christopher. 2020. OxCal, v. 4.4. Electronic resource, https://c14.arch.ox.ac.uk/oxcal.html, accessed January 20, 2021.

Brooke, Brendan, Roland Lee, Malcolm Cox, Jon Olley, and Tim Pietsch. 2008. Rates of Shoreline Progradation during the Last 1700 Years at Beachmere, Southeastern Queensland, Australia, Based on Optically Stimulated Luminescence Dating of Beach Ridges. *Journal of Coastal Research* 24(3):640–648.

Burger, Paul Henry. 2015. A Formative Ceramic Sequence of Coastal Socunusco. MA thesis, California State University, Long Beach.

Clark, John E. 1991. The Beginnings of Mesoamerica: Apologia for the Soconusco Early Formative. In *The Formation of Complex Society in Southeastern Mesoamerica*, edited by William R. Fowler, pp. 13–26. CRC Press, Boca Raton, Florida.

———. 1994. The Development of Early Formative Rank Societies in the Soconusco, Chiapas, Mexico. PhD dissertation, University of Michigan, Ann Arbor.

Clark, John E., and Michael Blake. 1994. The Power of Prestige: Competitive Generosity and the Emergence of Rank Societies in Lowland Mesoamerica. In *Factional Competition and Political Development in the New World*, edited by Elizabeth M. Brumfiel and John W. Fox, pp. 17–30. Cambridge University Press, Cambridge.

Codding, Brian F., and Douglas W. Bird. 2015. Behavioral Ecology and the Future of Archaeological Science. *Journal of Archaeological Science* 56:9–20.

Coe, Michael D., and Kent Flannery. 1963. Cultural Development in Southeastern Mesoamerica. In *Aboriginal Cultural Development in Latin America: An Interpretative Review*, edited by Betty J. Meggers and Clifford Evans, pp. 27–44. Smithsonian Institution, Washington, DC.

———. 1967. *Early Cultures and Human Ecology in South Coastal Guatemala.* Smithsonian Contributions to Anthropology 3. Smithsonian Institution, Washington, DC.

Constant, Axel, Maxwell J. D. Ramstead, Samuel P. L. Veissière, John O. Campbell, and Karl J. Friston. 2018. A Variational Approach to Niche Construction. *Journal of the Royal Society Interface* 15(141):20170685.

Cooke, R. G., D. W. Steadman, Máximo Jiménez, and Ilean Isaza Aizpurúa. 2013. Pre-Columbian Exploitation of Birds around Panama Bay. In *The Archaeology of Mesoamerican Animals*, edited by Christopher Markus Götz and Kitty F. Emery, pp. 479–530. Lockwood Press, Atlanta.

Cooke, Richard. 2005. Prehistory of Native Americans on the Central American Land Bridge: Colonization, Dispersal, and Divergence. *Journal of Archaeological Research* 13(2):129–187.

Ellis, Erle C. 2015. Ecology in an Anthropogenic Biosphere. *Ecological Monographs* 85(3):287–331.

Freeman, Jacob, Matthew A. Peeples, and John M. Anderies. 2015. Toward a Theory of Non-linear Transitions from Foraging to Farming. *Journal of Anthropological Archaeology* 40:109–122.

Gremillion, Kristen J., Loukas Barton, and Dolores R. Piperno. 2014. Particularism and the Retreat from Theory in the Archaeology of Agricultural Origins. *Proceedings of the National Academy of Sciences* 111(17):6171–6177.

Heaton, Timothy J., Peter Köhler, Martin Butzin, Edouard Bard, Ron W. Reimer, William E. N. Austin, Christopher Bronk Ramsey, Pieter M. Grootes, Konrad A. Hughen, Bernd Kromer, Paula J. Reimer, Jess Adkins, Andrea Burke, Mea S. Cook, Jesper Olsen, and Luke C. Skinner. 2020. Marine20—The Marine Radiocarbon Age Calibration Curve (0–55,000 cal BP). *Radiocarbon* 62(4):779–820.

Joyce, Arthur A., and Michelle Goman. 2012. Bridging the Theoretical Divide in Holocene Landscape Studies: Social and Ecological Approaches to Ancient Oaxacan Landscapes. *Quaternary Science Reviews* 55:1–22.

Joyce, Arthur A., and Raymond G. Mueller. 1992. The Social Impact of Anthropogenic

Landscape Modification in the Río Verde Drainage Basin, Oaxaca, Mexico. *Geoarchaeology* 7(6):503–526.

———. 1997. Prehispanic Human Ecology of the Río Verde Drainage Basin, Mexico. *World Archaeology* 29(1):75–94.

Kennett, Douglas J., Dolores R. Piperno, John G. Jones, Hector Neff, Barbara Voorhies, Megan K. Walsh, and Brendan J. Culleton. 2010. Pre-pottery Farmers on the Pacific Coast of Southern Mexico. *Journal of Archaeological Science* 37(12):3401–3411.

Kennett, Douglas J., and Barbara Voorhies. 1996. Oxygen Isotopic Analysis of Archaeological Shells to Detect Seasonal Use of Wetlands on the Southern Pacific Coast of Mexico. *Journal of Archaeological Science* 23(5):689–704.

Kluiving, Sjoerd J. 2015. How Geoarchaeology and Landscape Archaeology Contribute to Niche Construction Theory (NCT). *Water History* 7(4):557–571.

Laland, Kevin, Blake Matthews, and Marcus W. Feldman. 2016. An Introduction to Niche Construction Theory. *Evolutionary Ecology* 30(2):191–202.

Laland, Kevin N., and Michael J. O'Brien. 2010. Niche Construction Theory and Archaeology. *Journal of Archaeological Method and Theory* 17(4):303–322.

Laland, Kevin N., Tobias Uller, Marcus W. Feldman, Kim Sterelny, Gerd B. Müller, Armin Moczek, Eva Jablonka, and John Odling-Smee. 2015. The Extended Evolutionary Synthesis: Its Structure, Assumptions and Predictions. *Proceedings of the Royal Society B: Biological Sciences* 282(1813):20151019.

Lesure, Richard G. 2009. *Settlement and Subsistence in Early Formative Soconusco: El Varal and the Problem of Inter-site Assemblage Variation.* Cotsen Institute of Archaeology Press, Los Angeles.

Lesure, Richard G., and Thomas A. Wake. 2011. Archaic to Formative in Soconusco. In *Early Mesoamerican Social Transformations: Archaic and Formative Lifeways in the Soconusco Region,* edited by Richard G. Lesure, pp. 67–93. University of California Press, Berkeley.

Matthews, Blake, Luc De Meester, Clive G. Jones, Bas W. Ibelings, Tjeerd J. Bouma, Visa Nuutinen, Johan van de Koppel, and John Odling-Smee. 2014. Under Niche Construction: An Operational Bridge between Ecology, Evolution, and Ecosystem Science. *Ecological Monographs* 84(2):245–263.

McGimsey, Charles R. 1956. Cerro Mangote: A Preceramic Site in Panama. *American Antiquity* 22(2, Part 1):151–161.

McKillop, Heather. 2002. *Salt: White Gold of the Ancient Maya.* University Press of Florida, Gainesville.

———. 2005. Finds in Belize Document Late Classic Maya Salt Making and Canoe Transport. *PNAS* 102(5):5630–5634.

Mohlenhoff, Kathryn A., and Brian F. Codding. 2017. When Does It Pay to Invest in a Patch? The Evolution of Intentional Niche Construction. *Evolutionary Anthropology: Issues, News, and Reviews* 26(5):218–227.

Mueller, Raymond G., Arthur A Joyce, Aleksander Borejsza, and Michelle Goman. 2013. Anthropogenic Landscape Change and the Human Ecology of the Lower Río Verde Valley. In *Polity and Ecology in Formative Period Coastal Oaxaca,* edited by Arthur A. Joyce, pp. 65–96. University Press of Colorado, Boulder.

Neff, Hector, Scott J. Bigney, Sachiko Sakai, Paul R. Burger, Timothy Garfin, Richard G. George, Brendan J. Culleton, and Douglas J. Kennett. 2016. Characterization of Archaeological Sediments Using Fourier Transform Infrared (FT-IR) and Portable X-Ray Fluorescence (pXRF): An Application to Formative Period Pyro-Industrial Sites in Pacific Coastal Southern Chiapas, Mexico. *Applied Spectroscopy* 70(1):110–127.

Neff, Hector, Paul H. Burger, Brendan J. Culleton, Douglas J. Kennett, and John G. Jones. 2018. Izapa's Industrial Hinterland: The Eastern Soconusco Mangrove Zone during Archaic and Formative Times. *Ancient Mesoamerica* 29(2):395–411.

Neff, Hector, Deborah M. Pearsall, John G. Jones, Bárbara Arroyo, Shawn K. Collins, and Dorothy E. Freidel. 2006a. Early Maya Adaptive Patterns: Mid-Late Holocene Paleoenvironmental Evidence from Pacific Guatemala. *Latin American Antiquity* 17(3):287–315.

Neff, Hector, Deborah M. Pearsall, John G. Jones, Bárbara Arroyo de Pieters, and Dorothy E. Freidel. 2006b. Climate Change and Population History in the Pacific Lowlands of Southern Mesoamerica. *Quaternary Research* 65(3):390–400.

Nooren, C. A. M., Wim Z. Hoek, T. G. Winkels, Annika Huizinga, J. van der Plicht, R. Van Dam, Sytze Van Heteren, Manfred J. Van Bergen, Maarten A. Prins, and Tony Reimann. 2017. The Usumacinta-Grijalva Beach-Ridge Plain in Southern Mexico: A High-Resolution Archive of River Discharge and Precipitation. *Earth Surface Dynamics* 5(3):529–556.

O'Brien, Michael J., and Kevin N. Laland. 2012. Genes, Culture, and Agriculture: An Example of Human Niche Construction. *Current Anthropology* 53(4):434–470.

Odling-Smee, John, Douglas H. Erwin, Eric P. Palkovacs, Marcus W. Feldman, and Kevin N. Laland. 2013. Niche Construction Theory: A Practical Guide for Ecologists. *Quarterly Review of Biology* 88(1):3–28.

Odling-Smee, John, and Kevin N. Laland. 2011. Ecological Inheritance and Cultural Inheritance: What Are They and How Do They Differ? *Biological Theory* 6(3):220–230.

Paillés, H., Maricruz. 1980. *Pampa el Pajón: An Early Estuarine Site, Chiapas, Mexico.* New World Archaeological Foundation Papers 44. Brigham Young University, Provo, Utah.

Piperno, Dolores R. 2017. Assessing Elements of an Extended Evolutionary Synthesis for Plant Domestication and Agricultural Origin Research. *Proceedings of the National Academy of Sciences* 114(25):6429–6437.

Pye, Mary E. 1995. Settlement, Specialization, and Adaptation in the Rio Jesus Drainage, Retalhuleu, Guatemala. PhD dissertation, Vanderbilt University, Nashville, Tennessee.

Reimer, P. J., W. E. Austin, E. Bard, A. Bayliss, P. G. Blackwell, C. B. Ramsey, M. Butzin, H. Cheng, R. L. Edwards, M. Friedrich, and P. M. Grootes. 2020. The IntCal20 Northern Hemisphere Radiocarbon Age Calibration Curve (0–55 cal kBP). *Radiocarbon* 62(4):725–757.

Rosenswig, Robert M. 2008. Prehispanic Settlement in the Cuauhtémoc Region of the Soconusco, Chiapas, Mexico. *Journal of Field Archaeology* 33(4):389–411.

———. 2011. An Early Mesoamerican Archipelago of Complexity. In *Early Mesoamerican Social Transformations: Archaic and Formative Lifeways in the Soconusco Region*, edited by Richard G. Lesure, pp. 242–271. University of California Press, Berkeley.

———. 2015. A Mosaic of Adaptation: The Archaeological Record for Mesoamerica's Archaic Period. *Journal of Archaeological Research* 23(2):115–162.

Stuiver, M., and H. Polach. 1977. Discussion Reporting of 14C Data. *Radiocarbon* 19(3):355–363. doi:10.1017/S0033822200003672

Voorhies, Barbara. 1976. *The Chantuto People: An Archaic Period Society of the Chiapas Littoral, Mexico*. Papers of the New World Archaeological Foundation 41. New World Archaeological Foundation, Brigham Young University, Provo, Utah.

———. 2004. *Coastal Collectors in the Holocene: The Chantuto People of Southwest Mexico*. University Press of Florida, Gainesville.

Voorhies, Barbara, Douglas J. Kennett, John G. Jones, and Thomas A. Wake. 2002. A Middle Archaic Archaeological Site on the West Coast of Mexico. *Latin American Antiquity* 13(2):179–200.

Williams, Eduardo. 2010. Salt Production and Trade in Ancient Mesoamerica. In *Pre-Columbian Foodways: Interdisciplinary Approaches to Food, Culture, and Markets in Ancient Mesoamerica*, edited by John Staller, and Michael Carrasco, pp. 175–190. Springer, New York.

5

Swordfish Hunting as Prestige Signaling?

A Case Study from Middle Holocene Fishing Communities of the Atacama Desert Coast

CAROLA FLORES FERNANDEZ AND LAURA OLGUÍN

Fishing communities are complex socioecological systems. Obtaining the catch implies an intricate web of social relationships with organized activities related to manufacturing fishing technology and managing fishing activities (Cornejo 2020; Escobar 2017; Rubio Munita et al. in press). These dynamics were likely the same in the past, but the archaeological record of mobile fishers, which includes debris related to food and fishing technology, sometimes makes it difficult to know about the complex social aspects of the activities that produced those artifacts. Despite these limitations, some vestiges are left in archaeological deposits that allow the study of aspects of fishing community culture that go beyond food consumption, such as social prestige (Hildebrandt and McGuire 2002).

The Atacama Desert coast, located on the Pacific coast of Chile, has been inhabited by humans since at least 12000 cal BP (Castelleti 2007; Llagostera et al. 2000; Salazar et al. 2018; Santoro et al. 2017). It is a location where a continuous and intimate relationship between humans and the sea has shaped people's whole spectrum of life (Ballester 2018a; Disspain et al. 2017; Monroy et al. 2016).

By the beginning of middle Holocene, around 8500 years cal BP, studies in the area of Taltal (lat. 25° S), the southernmost part of the Atacama Desert, show evidence of an increase in the number of residential sites such as denser and more complex shell midden deposits and a high diversity and abundance of cultural and faunal remains. This pattern has been interpreted as an indication of growing population density and decreasing residential mobility in the area (Salazar et al. 2015, 2020). This area also shows evidence of maritime specialization, including shellfish hooks, fishing weights, hooks,

and harpoons (Alcalde and Flores 2020; Ballester 2018b). A pronounced increase in the abundance and richness of these fish assemblages also characterizes the area (Béarez et al. 2016; Olguín et al. 2014; Rebolledo et al. 2016;
Salazar et al. 2015).

The diet of middle Holocene fishing communities was based almost ex-
clusively on the consumption of marine protein (Andrade et al. 2014, 2015).
Although jack mackerel (*Trachurus murphyi*) dominates faunal assemblages
in all the archaeological sites of Taltal during this period, representing up
to 80% of the minimum number of individuals and number of individual
specimens of fish, offshore species such as sharks (*Notorynchus cepedianus*),
marlins (*Kajikia audax*), and (most notably) swordfish (*Xiphias gladius*) have
also been recovered (Béarez et al. 2016; Olguín et al. 2014; Rebolledo et al.
2016). The presence of these large pelagic fish has been interpreted as indirect evidence of the use of specialized navigation technology for hunting
or fishing on the open sea (Béarez et al. 2016; Olguín et al. 2014). A deep
knowledge of prey behavior and oceanographic conditions is required to
navigate and acquire offshore prey, as is knowledge about producing highly
specialized artifacts such as rafts and harpoons (Arnold 1995; Arnold and
Bernard 2005; Ballester 2017, 2018a). These activities represent high-risk and
high-energy practices that may have conferred prestige to persons or groups
involved in a successful hunt (Alvard and Gillespie 2004; Arnold 1995; Arnold and Bernard 2005; Davenport et al. 1993).

Within this context, can swordfish hunting be considered a mechanism of
prestige signaling in middle Holocene fishing communities of the Atacama
Desert coast? In this chapter, we evaluate whether the application of costly
signaling theory can enrich our interpretations of the sociopolitical context
of middle Holocene fishing communities from the southern coast of the Atacama Desert using archaeological information already available from the
literature.

Costly Signaling Theory

Costly signaling theory provides an evolutionary explanation for investments in activities that require a high expenditure of energy that do not
have a clear utilitarian function. It has been used in anthropology and archaeology derived from human behavioral ecology theory (Bettinger et al.
2015). It is often linked to the production or obtaining of complex prestige
goods that seem to have been used to legitimate authority through the act
of signaling competition and social consolidation (Bliege Bird and Smith
2005). Costly signaling theory proposes that some energetically expensive

behaviors are adaptive in socioenvironmental contexts because they signal information about unobservable qualities of one or more individuals, such as reproductive fitness or potential as an ally. In order to correspond with the predictions of costly signaling theory, the behavior under study should "(1) signal a particular hidden attribute, (2) provide benefits to both signaler and observers, and (3) demonstrate how signals of attribute quality remain credible" (Bliege Bird and Smith 2005:225). In addition, costly signaling theory is an explanation for why people share behaviors that benefit both givers and receivers. The display must meet the following characteristics: "(1) the extension of consumption rights to multiple others regardless of their exchange relationship to the 'giver,' (2) distribution or consumption in a social arena in which knowledge of the distribution is transmitted to multiple others, and (3) the dependence of the ability to produce the display upon some hidden attribute of the donor in which observers (who may or may not be recipients of the material donation) have a significant interest" (226).

Several studies have proposed that hunting difficult prey may be a costly signaling behavior, since it was part of the whole spectrum of subsistence activities such as acquiring raw material for manufacturing tools, fishing, and gathering food (i.e., Hawkes and Bliege Bird 2002). These activities may also involve public forums for successful hunters that involved political prestige within the community and benefits related to mate selection (Smith et al. 2003; Sosis 2000).

Other studies have referred to sea hunting as costly signaling behavior based on the fact that in most of the ethnographic cases, these practices follow predictions that hunting is costly to the hunters in terms of time, material investment, risk to life, and the loss of opportunities to engage in other, more efficient activities. They also correlate with predictions about hunting success as an honest signal and about social opportunities to share large game prey and effectively broadcast the honest and costly signal (e.g., Alvard and Gillespie 2004; Bliege Bird and Smith 2005; Smith et al. 2003; Sosis 2000). Sea hunting seems to provide a way for individuals to assess the competitive capabilities of potential political rivals or allies, for example. Some of these ethnographic studies focus on turtle hunting among the Meriam people of Torres Strait, Australia (Smith et al. 2003); torch fishing for dog-toothed tuna in Ifaluk in Micronesia (Sosis 2000); and hunting for whales in Lamalera, Indonesia (Alvard and Gillespie 2004). In the first example, the extensive sharing of turtle meat that was acquired by an economically costly activity put Meriam hunters in a better position in terms of competing for status, mates, food, or territory (Smith and Bliege Bird 2000; Smith et al. 2003). In the case of Ifaluk, because researchers consider fishing for dog-toothed tuna to be the most ritualized fishing method and see it as energetically costly in terms of preparation, they have interpreted it as playing the role of advertising human productivity (Sosis 2000). Finally, as whale hunting in Lamalera is considered to be a costly activity in terms of risk to life because of the size and strength of the prey, whale hunters gain substantial benefits in terms of nutrition (large shares of meat) and reproduction (an early age of marriage and a large number of offspring; Alvard and Gillespie 2004).

Environmental Setting

To contextualize swordfish hunting during the middle Holocene, we will first briefly describe the environment where it took place. Taltal is located in Chile on the southernmost part of the coast of the Atacama Desert (Figure 5.1). The terrestrial environment is a hyperarid desert (Marquet et al. 1998) with no permanent sources of freshwater except for small springs, or *aguadas*, that are fed by torrential and occasional coastal rains linked to El Niño Southern Oscillation events (Herrera et al. 2018).

In contrast with the productivity of the hyperarid desert, biological productivity along the shoreline is extremely high. Semi-permanent winds along the shore that move toward the equator bring deeper waters that are cold and high in nutrients to the surface. As these recently upwelled waters come into

Figure 5.1. The arid northern coast of Chile near Taltal and a map showing the location of Taltal. Figure by Carola Flores Fernandez.

contact with sunlight near the shore, they fuel the enormous productivity that characterizes the Humboldt Current System (Chavez and Messié 2009). The pelagic fisheries of the Humboldt Current, particularly along the coasts of southern Peru and northern Chile, are dominated by small, planktivorous fish such as anchovy and sardine that are foraged by fishes of higher trophic levels, such as the south Pacific jack mackerel and hake, which in turn are preyed upon by larger species such as bonito and marine mammals (Alegre et al. 2015).

Records from isotopic analyses of archaeological shell carbonates for the area of Taltal show that sea surface temperatures at the beginning of the middle Holocene (~8500–6900 cal BP) were as warm as they are now and suggest that coastal upwelling was weaker than it is today (Flores and Broitman 2021). This implies a possible contraction of the upwelling region along the shore that would have brought the coastal front close to the shoreline (Hormazabal et al. 2004). The data also implies an associated increase in the abundance of oceanic and neritic fish taxa such as swordfish (*Xiphias gladius*) and jack mackerel (*Trachurus murphy*) (Yáñez et al. 2008). These conditions imply a possibly decreased intensity of coastal fog and therefore a decrease in overall humidity along the coast because of the effects of the combination of warmer waters and weak upwelling on the terrestrial environment (Cereceda et al. 2008). This oceanographic scenario supports previous reconstructions of hyperarid terrestrial coastal conditions during the middle Holocene (Barberena et al. 2016). It is not until around 5800–5000 cal BP that an increase in the intensity and frequency of El Niño Southern Oscillation events is recorded for the area (Vargas et al. 2006). This implies that the region had occasional but torrential rains that may have recharged the small *aguadas* available for human use (Herrera et al. 2018).

Modern Swordfish Hunting on the Atacama Desert

Despite the fact that modern swordfish hunting is fueled by the market economy, the hunting technique using a harpoon, or hunting "by stick," still survives along the coast of the Atacama Desert as a traditional practice. Recent ethnographic studies of local fishermen and specialists on swordfish hunting in the small fishing towns of Taltal and Caldera show that even thousands of years later, this activity is alive and is regarded as a tradition that reflects the expertise of humans on the sea (Cornejo 2020; Escobar 2017). The stories Escobar (2017) gathered from modern sea hunters in Taltal highlight the fact that the way swordfish is hunted is even more important than the fact of catching it. As swordfish hunting is considered to be a true battle between the hunter and the prey, when a hunter kills the fish with a single harpoon shot, their social prestige and recognition increases (Escobar 2017). The average length of a swordfish is 3 m, and they can weigh between 200 and 300 kg (Nakamura 1985). Descriptions of swordfish hunting in other parts of the world highlight the strong fights this fish can give; they are even able to attack boats (Ellis 2013; Gudger 1940). As swordfish are not easy to catch, hunters must be skilled, physically strong, and knowledgeable about fish behavior and optimal marine conditions (Cornejo 2020; Escobar 2017).

The technological implements modern hunters in Taltal use include motorboats, or *faluchos*, which have a metal structure that extends from the bow of the boat and enables hunters to stand above the water and see the fish from a higher location. The other main tool is a metal harpoon around 3 m long that has a shaft and a head made of stainless steel (Escobar 2017). The shape of modern and archaeological harpoons are similar; the difference is that modern harpoons are made of metal and archaeological ones are made of *guanaco* (*Lama guanicoe*) or sea lion (Otariidae family) bones (Ballester 2017, 2018b; Cornejo 2020; Escobar 2017). Modern hunting excursions are organized from the end of February through May (the end of austral summer and the middle of fall; Cornejo 2020; Escobar 2017). During this time, warmer ocean currents come closer to the shore, bringing schools of anchovy, sardines, and jack mackerel, prey that swordfish follows (Nakamura 1985). The rest of the year, swordfish migrate to other latitudes because conditions in Taltal and Caldera are not good for them due to strong swells and winds (Nakamura 1985).

Interviews and observations done in fishing communities in Taltal and Caldera revealed that initiations in offshore hunting begin at an early age (10–12 years) and are generally conducted by a relative. The arrival at the wharf of sea hunters with swordfish specimens generates great admiration and recognition. Everyone knows who the swordfish hunters are (Cornejo 2020; Escobar 2017). Nowadays, hunting feats and people's talent in harpoon throwing is perpetuated through cellphone video recordings shared within the community through social media. Likes on social media platforms are one of the mechanisms that socially validate hunters and increase their status and prestige above the rest of other fisher groups (Escobar 2017).

Local communities from both Taltal and Caldera recognize swordfish hunting as an important element of their identity that reinforces their socio-territorial heritage (Cornejo 2020; Escobar 2017). In fact, in Taltal, modern hunters identify themselves with sea-hunting scenes depicted in El Médano rock art along the southern coast of the Atacama Desert (Ballester 2018a; Berenguer 2009; Monroy et al. 2016). This link between modern sea-hunting practices and rock art scenes seems to bring the symbolic meaning of sword-fish hunting with harpoons into the present.

Despite the enormous differences between the social, economic, and cultural contexts of communities along coastal settlements of the Atacama Desert today and those in the middle Holocene, modern records of sword-fish hunting may be a valuable frame to consider when exploring the social implications of offshore hunting in prehistory. However, we cannot system-atically evaluate whether modern swordfish hunting is a costly signaling behavior using the information provided by the two ethnographic studies available for the area (Cornejo 2020; Escobar 2017). There is no quantita-tive data about how often hunters go out in a certain period of time, how frequently they are successful, or swordfish's relative proportion of the diet compared to everyday foods, but the potential for investigations to explore these questions is promising.

Presenting and Discussing the Archaeological Case Study

Archaeological research in the Taltal-Paposo area indicates that this coast has been inhabited since at least the Pleistocene-Holocene transition. Oc-cupations date to 12500–10000 cal BP (Castelleti 2007; Llagostera et al. 2000; Salazar et al. 2018). Sites of this period are characterized by small rock shel-ters and a broad spectrum of subsistence strategies around nearshore and in-land resources (Salazar et al. 2015, 2018). The archaeological evidence shows that after a chronological gap of nearly two millennia, the first open-air resi-dential site in Taltal developed around 8500 cal BP (Andrade and Salazar 2011). The stratigraphic sequence of this site shows a gradual change toward a more dense and stable occupation around 7500 cal BP, a time when other sites of the same type also appeared in the area. These sites were inhabited until around 4500 cal BP (Salazar et al. 2015). All of these sites conform to the middle Holocene archaeological record, which shows a process toward a more specialized maritime economy, a semi-sedentary settlement system, and signs of growing social complexity (Olguín et al. 2014; Rebolledo et al. 2016; Salazar et al. 2015, 2020). This is the context in which the first evidence of swordfish hunting appeared in the area of Taltal (Béarez et al. 2016; Olguín et al. 2014; Rebolledo et al. 2016).

A process of increasing social complexity has been interpreted during this time. The combination of an increase in the number and size of open-air shell midden sites, the presence of faunal remains from all of the resources locally available, and artifacts linked to diverse activities suggests a decreased residential mobility and an increase in the number of people inhabiting the area (Salazar et al. 2015, 2020). This implies possibly longer times of cohabitation at the sites, a settlement system centered on coastal shell midden sites, and more intensive social interactions (Salazar et al. 2020).

During the middle Holocene, the abundance of bone technology increased, as evidenced by a great variety of harpoon types. This suggests a greater emphasis on sea hunting (Ballester 2017, 2018b; Salazar et al. 2015, 2020). Manufacturing, using, and maintaining hunting toolkits must have been critical for pursuing offshore hunting. Harpoons and watercraft surely imply deep knowledge among the skilled people who manufactured them (Arnold 1995; Arnold and Bernard 2005; Ballester 2017, 2018b). Archaeological harpoons found around the southern coast of the Atacama Desert were mainly made of guanaco bones, and watercraft made with the skin of sea lions have been described for historic times (Álvarez 2013; Ballester 2017, 2018b; Niemeyer 1965–1966; Páez 1986). The frequency of guanaco and sea lion bones at Taltal archaeological sites from the middle Holocene is proportionally higher than from the early Holocene (Salazar et al. 2015). This may indicate an elaborate chain of activities related to offshore hunting that included hunting to obtain the raw material to make tools, manufacturing specialized tools, going offshore, and coming back with the precious prey. Based on the ethnographic descriptions of swordfish hunting on the northern coast of Chile, we consider all of these activities to entail expensive practices in terms of energy and time invested and reckless and dangerous behavior (Cornejo 2020; Escobar 2017). As we have mentioned in previous work (Salazar et al. 2020), successful hunters may have acquired prestige and status because of the difficulties and danger associated with offshore hunting and because of their contributions of meat to community gatherings (Wiessner 1996).

What about the social context of swordfish hunting and its role in the symbolic sphere of fishing communities of the Atacama Desert? El Médano rock art is a pictorial expression that is conspicuously present along the southern coast of the Atacama Desert (Ballester 2018a; Berenguer 2009; Monroy et al. 2016). These representations of sea-hunting scenes in red paint include boats and lines connected to whales, turtles, and swordfish, among other animal figures (Figure 5.2; Ballester 2018a; Berenguer 2009; Monroy et al. 2016). Their abundance and distribution along the coast, in ravines, and in inland locations may imply a public and symbolic context of this art and the practices depicted. Some studies suggest that this rock art did not appear until around 1000 years cal BP, based on characteristics of the motifs and dates from associated archaeological deposits (Ballester 2018a; Berenguer 2009; Gallardo et al. 2012). Alternatively, other investigations have proposed

Figure 5.2. (*a*) Example of Médano rock art located in the area of Taltal, inland in the desert, 37 km from the coast. (*b*) Scene portraying offshore hunting of swordfish and two sea lions in a vertical position (Monroy et al. 2016). (*c*) Scenes portraying offshore cetacean hunting with boats and two possible hunters (Monroy et al. 2016). Photos courtesy of Ignacio Monroy.

an early date of around 7000 years BP (not calibrated) based on accelerator mass spectrometry and archaeomagnetic dating on the red paint of some motifs (Castelleti et al. 2015; Goguitchaichvili et al. 2016). Despite the fact that the chronological definition of El Médano rock art is still under debate, this early date suggests that offshore hunting was relevant at the beginning of the middle Holocene. In addition, offshore fish remains and hunting technology in archaeological contexts of the Taltal area have been proposed as indirect evidence that watercraft use began around 7000 years cal BP (Béarez et al. 2016; Olguín et al. 2014). Future research will contribute to more precise dating of the El Médano paintings. Nevertheless, their possible middle Holocene age provides an interesting reference to the social context of swordfish hunting and its role in the symbolic sphere of fishing communities of the Atacama Desert coast during this time.

Other references to prestige-garnering behaviors associated with swordfish hunting in prehispanic time come from Southern California, where several archaeological sites have evidence of swordfish bones, offshore hunting technology, and rock art with swordfish pictographs (Bernard 2004; Lebow et al. 2005; Rick et al. 2019). In addition, one funerary context includes an elaborate swordfish mask that refers to a swordfish dancer (Davenport et al. 1993). This collection of evidence illustrates the ceremonial and mythological value of offshore hunting for the Chumash people of the Santa Barbara and Channel Islands region (Bernard 2004; Hildebrandt and McGuire 2012).

Within this context, we examined whether middle Holocene swordfish hunting in Taltal supports key predictions of costly signaling theory. First, we began with the assumption that the main benefit of offshore hunting was something other than nutrition. Despite the fact that a single swordfish can provide large pieces of meat, zooarchaeological data from shell midden sites in Taltal suggest that it was not strictly necessary for feeding the community. Eighty to ninety percent of Middle Holocene shell midden sites consist of jack mackerel; offshore species are represented in very low percentages (Béarez et al. 2016; Olguín et al. 2014, 2015; Rebolledo et al. 2016; Salazar et al. 2020). The low abundance of offshore species such as sharks, dolphins, marlins, and swordfish in the archaeological record raises the possibility that they were acquired opportunistically when they came close to the shore due to changes in ocean currents or because they became beached. Nevertheless, the absence of several oceanic fish species in early Holocene deposits and the consistent presence of these species throughout the middle Holocene together with increased evidence of hunting technology such as harpoons suggests that by around 7000 years cal BP, fishing communities in Taltal were hunting large fish prey (Olguín et al. 2014).

In addition, the increase in human demography that archaeologists infer for the middle Holocene archaeological context implies potentially more pressure on local resources to feed larger populations. This may have driven the need for risky offshore hunting. However, archaeologists interpret the increase in the number of exploited habitats and fish species, together with the dominance of jack mackerel, as the development of a combined strategy of intensified and specialized fishing (Béarez et al. 2016; Olguín et al. 2014,

2015; Rebolledo et al. 2016; Salazar et al. 2020). As the available fish data do not show a decline in the abundance of high-ranked fish species or in the abundance of easy prey, a context of marine resource depression to explain the choice of going offshore to hunt swordfish or other billfishes is not supported by the archaeological data.

Ethnographic and archaeological information about swordfish hunting in Taltal suggest that the hidden attribute was the power of going out to the sea and hunting a large, strong, and dangerous fish prey. We believe that this act signaled hidden attributes such as physical endurance, technical expertise, and ecological knowledge. Unfortunately, the high degree of disturbance of archaeological burial contexts in the area precludes exploration of the relationship between swordfish hunting and social prestige in funerary offerings and evaluation of reproductive fitness through bioarchaeological analysis. Thus, we do not know whether the social and reproductive benefits that costly signaling theory suggests were obtained in the context of past swordfish hunting. Nevertheless, the overall context of decreased mobility and growing population in the middle Holocene make it feasible to posit that certain members of the community developed strategies to thwart competitors or to defend potential allies and mates, especially because of a need for social organization and differentiation. The combination of the presence of swordfish bones in archaeological deposits at Taltal and the synchronic increase in harpoon remains can be considered as the material evidence of a behavior that signaled attributes that were impossible to fake: hunters manufactured sophisticated technology and went offshore to hunt swordfish and other big prey.

How did the signal of swordfish hunting mediate social relationships during the middle Holocene in Taltal? We do not have enough information to provide an answer, but El Médano rock art shows that it had an important place in the sea-hunting world. Even though we do not know the social context of distribution and consumption of swordfish meat, we believe that, as it is in present times, the arrival of hunters on the beach with swordfish specimens, probably on rafts made with the skins of sea lions, did not go unnoticed—especially when it implied that hunters had survived and succeeded despite the risk of offshore conditions.

Conclusions

Offshore hunting during the middle Holocene in the Taltal region was part of the maritime specialization process local communities undertook, but it may also have originated as an activity whose goal was more than just solving economic needs. Although swordfish hunting offered the reward of large pieces of meat, it is a costly large-scale investment activity that does not appear to have been strictly necessary to feed the community. During the middle Holocene, great quantities of other fish and mollusk species that had lower procurement costs were clearly abundant and contributed heavily to people's diet. Thus, we posit that the specialized technology required for swordfish capture functioned as both utilitarian and prestige goods that successful swordfish hunters depended on to gain personal prestige as worthy leaders, as competitive allies, or as mates. This interpretation may be supported by the fact that images of swordfish and other offshore animals are depicted in rock art of the study area in prominent marine hunting scenes.

Thousands of years ago, swordfish hunting was developed in the context of the contrasting environments of the Atacama Desert: rich marine and coastal ecosystems at the edge of hyperarid terrestrial landscapes. We believe that what motivated people to go offshore was not a need for marine proteins but rather a social context of growing social complexity, a need for social differentiation, and ritual and religious beliefs related to the power of sea creatures and peoples' strength. Ethnographic examples from Chile and the Pacific Islands suggest that the social relevance of offshore hunting may go beyond certain environmental conditions or types of societies. Further comparative studies may help us better understand evolutionary explanations for costly and apparently wasteful practices.

The archaeological literature from the southern coast of the Atacama Desert, especially from Taltal, indicates that the practice of swordfish hunting was in place from the beginning of the middle Holocene. The activity entailed high energy investment, high risk, and a public role, as demonstrated in the rock art distributed along the coast. We propose that swordfish hunting was a prestige-signaling behavior. The knowledge and skills required to manufacture harpoons, build boats, and use them in offshore hunting gave certain members high prestige that was derived from their hunting skill and generosity in sharing meat.

Can a costly signaling approach enrich our interpretations of the sociopolitical context of fishing communities from the southern coast of the Atacama Desert? It provides a valuable and alternative way to understand the phenomenon of swordfish hunting during the middle Holocene on the northern coast of Chile. Nevertheless, concepts such as the context for sharing hunting kills, the benefits that accrued to hunters, the inefficiency of the hunting behavior, and the underlying qualities hunters broadcast are difficult to identify or evaluate in the archaeological record. We believe that costly signaling theory opens interesting questions about collective actions and social prestige among coastal hunter-gatherer and fishing communities and that future research designed to evaluate the predictions of costly signaling theory will contribute significantly to interpretations of past human behavior in the study area.

Acknowledgments

This work was supported by the National Fund for Scientific and Technological Development (FONDECYT 11200953, 1151203) and the National Agency of Research and Development's Millennium Science Initiative (UPWELL-NCN19_153). Special thanks to Ignacio Monroy for providing pictures of El Médano rock art used in Figure 5.2.

References Cited

Alcalde, Verónica, and Carola Flores. 2020. Variabilidad morfológica de anzuelos en concha de Choromytilus chorus (8500–4500 cal aP), costa sur del desierto de Atacama, Taltal, Chile. *Latin American Antiquity* 31(4):664–682.

Alegre, Ana, Arnaud Bertrand, Marco Espino, Pepe Espinoza, Teobaldo Dioses, Miguel Ñiquen, Ivan Navarro, Monique Simier, and Fédéric Ménard. 2015. Diet Diversity of Jack and Chub Mackerels and Ecosystem Changes in the Northern Humboldt Current System: A Long-Term Study. *Progress in Oceanography* 137(Part A): 299–313.

Alvard, Michael S., and Allen Gillespie. 2004. Good Lamalera Whale Hunters Accrue Reproductive Benefits. *Research in Economic Anthropology* 23:225–247.

Álvarez, Oriel. 2013. *El último constructor de balsas de cuero de lobo.* Ediciones Mediodía en Punto, Vallenar.

Andrade, Pedro, Ricardo Fernandez, Katia Codjambassis, Josefina Urrea, Laura Olguín, Sandra Rebolledo, Francisca Lira, Christian Aravena, and Mauricio Berríos. 2015. Subsistence Continuity Linked to Consumption of Marine Protein in the Formative Period in the Interfluvic Coast of Northern Chile: Re-assessing Contacts with Agropastoral Groups from Highlands. *Radiocarbon* 57(4):679–688.

Andrade, Pedro, and Diego Salazar. 2011. Revisitando Morro Colorado: Comparaciones y propuestas preliminares en torno a un conchal arcaico en las costas de Taltal. *Taltalia* 4:63–83.

Andrade, Pedro, Diego Salazar, Josefina Urrea, and Victoria Castro. 2014. Modos de vida de los cazadores-recolectores de la Costa Arreica del Norte Grande Chile: Una aproximación bioarqueológica a las poblaciones prehistóricas de Taltal. *Chungara* 46(3):467–492.

Arnold, Jeanne E. 1995. Transportation Innovation and Social Complexity among Maritime Hunter-Gatherer Societies. *American Anthropologist* 97(4):733–747.

Arnold, Jeanne E., and Julienne Bernard. 2005. Negotiating the Coasts: Status and the Evolution of Boat Technology in California. *World Archaeology* 37(1):109–131.

Ballester, Benjamín. 2017. La delgada línea roja: Sogas de arpón de los últimos cazadores marinos del norte de Chile (1000–1500 dc). *Revista Chilena de Antropología* 35:45–71.

——. 2018a. El Médano Rock Art Style: Izcuña Paintings and the Marine Hunter-Gatherers of the Atacama Desert. *Antiquity* 92(361):132–148.

——. 2018b. Tecnología de arponaje en la costa del desierto de Atacama, norte de Chile TT / Harpoon Technology in the Atacama Desert Coast, Northern Chile. *Estudios atacameños* 57:65–950.

Barberena, Ramiro, César Méndez, and María Eugenia de Porras. 2016. Zooming Out from Archaeological Discontinuities: The Meaning of Mid-Holocene Temporal Troughs in South American Deserts. *Journal of Anthropological Archaeology* 46:68–81.

Béarez, Philippe, Felipe Fuentes-Mucherl, Sandra Rebolledo, Diego Salazar, and Laura Olguín. 2016. Billfish Foraging along the Northern Coast of Chile during the Middle Holocene (7400–5900 cal BP). *Journal of Anthropological Archaeology* 41:185–195.

Berenguer, José. 2009. Las pinturas de El Médano, norte de Chile: 25 años después de Mostny y Niemeyer. *Boletín del Museo Chileno de Arte Precolombino* 14(2):57–95.

Bernard, Julienne. 2004. Status and the Swordfish: The Origins of Large-Species Fishing among the Chumash. In *Foundation of Chumash Complexity, Perspectives in California Archaeology*, edited by Jean Arnol, pp. 25–52. Los Angeles: Cotsen Institute of Archaeology, University of California, Los Angeles.

Bettinger, Robert, Garvey Raven, and Shannon Tushingham. 2015. *Hunter-Gatherers: Archaeological and Evolutionary Theory.* 2nd ed. Springer, New York.

Bliege Bird, Rebecca, and Eric Alden Smith. 2005. Signaling Theory, Strategic Interaction, and Symbolic Capital. *Current Anthropology* 46(2):221–248.

Castelleti, José. 2007. Patrón de asentamiento y uso de recursos a través de la secuencia ocupacional prehispánica de la costa de Taltal. Master's thesis, Universidad Católica del Norte, Universidad de Tarapacá.

Castelleti, José, Avto Goguitchaichvili, Carolina Solís, María Rodríguez Ceja, and Juan Morales. 2015. Evidencia de tempranas manifestaciones rupestres en la costa del desierto de Atacama (25°S). *Arqueología Iberoamericana* 28:16–21.

Cereceda, Pilar, Horacio Larrain, Paulina Osses, Martín Farías, and Isolina Egaña. 2008. The Climate of the Coast and Fog Zone in the Tarapacá Region, Atacama Desert, Chile. *Atmospheric Research* 87(3):301–311.

Chavez, Francisco P., and Monique Messié. 2009. A Comparison of Eastern Boundary Upwelling Ecosystems. *Progress in Oceanography* 83(1–4):80–96.

Cornejo, María Gloria. 2020. *La pesca patrimonial de la albacora al palo.* Sociedad Atacama Visión 360 Press, Caldera, Chile.

Davenport, Demorest, John R. Johnson, and Jan Timbrook. 1993. The Chumash and the Swordfish. *Antiquity* 67(255):257–272.

Disspain, Morgan C. F., Sean Ulm, Calogero M. Santoro, Chris Carter, and Bronwyn M. Gillanders. 2017. Pre-Columbian Fishing on the Coast of the Atacama Desert, Northern Chile: An Investigation of Fish Size and Species Distribution Using Otoliths from Camarones Punta Norte and Caleta Vitor. *Journal of Island and Coastal Archaeology* 12(3):428–450.

Ellis, Richard. 2013. *Swordfish: A Biography of the Ocean Gladiator.* University of Chicago Press, Chicago.

Escobar, Javier. 2017. Caza tradicional de la albacora: Imaginario y patrimonio intangible de los pescadores de Taltal. *Taltalia* 10:69–85.

Flores, Carola, and Bernardo R. Broitman. 2021. Nearshore Paleoceanogaphic Conditions through the Holocene: Shell Carbonate from Archaeological Sites of the Atacama Desert Coast. *Palaeogeography, Palaeoclimatology, Palaeoecology* 562:110090.

Gallardo, Francisco, Gloria Cabello, Gonsalo Pimentel, Marcela Sepúlveda, and Luis Cornejo. 2012. Flujos de información visual, interacción social y pinturas rupestres en el desierto de Atacama (norte de Chile). *Estudios Atacameños* 43:35–52.

Goguitchaichvili, Avto, Juan Morales, Jaime Urrutia-Fucugauchi, Ana María Soler Arechalde, Guillermo Acosta, and José Castelleti. 2016. The Use of Pictorial Remanent Magnetization as a Dating Tool: State of the Art and Perspectives. *Journal of Archaeological Science Reports* 8:15–21.

Gudger, Eugene Willis. 1940. The Alleged Pugnacity of the Swordfish and the Spearfishes as Shown by Their Attacks on Vessels. *Royal Asiatic Society of Bengal* 12(2):215–315.

Hawkes, Kristen, and Rebecca Bliege Bird. 2002. Showing Off, Handicap Signaling, and the Evolution of Men's Work. *Evolutionary Anthropology* 11(2):58–67.

Herrera, Christian, Carolina Gamboa, Emilio Custodio, Teresa Jordan, Linda Godfrey, Jorge Jódar, José A. Luque, Jimmy Vargas, and Alberto Sáez. 2018. Groundwater Origin and Recharge in the Hyperarid Cordillera de la Costa, Atacama Desert, Northern Chile. *Science of the Total Environment* 624(2):114–132.

Hildebrandt, William R., and Kelly McGuire. 2002. The Ascendance of Hunting during the California Middle Archaic: An Evolutionary Perspective. *American Antiquity* 67(2):231–256.

Hildebrandt, William R., and Kelly McGuire. 2012. The Land of Prestige. In *Contemporary Issues in California Archaeology*, edited by Terry L. Jones and Jennifer E. Perry, pp. 133–151. Left Coast Press, Walnut Creek, California.

Hormazabal, Samuel, Gary Shaffer, Ole Leth. 2004. Coastal Transition Zone off Chile. *Journal of Geophysical Research: Oceans* 109(C1):1–13.

Lebow, Clayton G., Douglas R. Harro, Rebecca L. McKim, Ann M. Munns, Carole Denardo, Jill Onken, and Rick Bury. 2005. *The Archaeology and Rock Art of Swordfish Cave (CA-SBA-503), Vandenberg Air Force Base, Santa Barbara County, California*. Volume I. Submitted to 30 CES/CEVPC. Vandenberg Air Force Base, California. MS on file at the California Historic Resources Information System, Central Coast Information Center, University of California, Santa Barbara.

Llagostera, Agustín, Rodolfo Weisner, Gastón Castillo, Miguel Cervellino, and María Antonietta Costa-Junqueira. 2000. El complejo Huentelauquén bajo una perspectiva macro-espacial y multidisciplinaria. *Contribuciones Arqueológicas* 5:461–480.

Marquet, Pablo, Francisco Bozinovic, Gay A. Bradshaw, Cintia Cornelius, Héctor Gonzalez, Julio R. Gutierrez, Ernst R. Hajek, Jorge A. Lagos, Francisco López-Cortés, Lautaro Nuñez, Eugenia Rosello, Calogero Santoro, Horacio Samaniego, Vivian Standen, Juan C. Torres-Mura, and Fabián M. Jaksic. 1998. Los ecosistemas del desierto de Atacama y área Andina adyacente. *Revista Chilena de Historia Natural* 71:593–617.

Monroy, Ignacio, César Borie, Andrés Troncoso, Ximena Power, Sonia Parra, Patricio Galarce, and Mariela Pino. 2016. Navegantes del desierto: Un nuevo sitio con arte rupestre estilo el Médano en la depresión intermedia de Taltal. *Revista Taltalia* 9:27–47.

Nakamura, Izumi. 1985. *Billfishes of the World: An Annotated and Illustrated Catalogue of Marlins, Sailfishes, Spearfishes and Swordfishes Known to Date.* FAO Fisheries Synopsis 125(5):1–65.

Niemeyer, Hans. 1965–1966. Una balsa de cueros de lobo de la caleta de Chañaral de Aceituno (Prov. de Atacama, Chile). *Revista Universitaria* 50–51:257–269.

Olguín, Laura, Victoria Castro, Isaac Peña-Villalobos, Jimena Ruz, and Boris Santander. 2015. Exploitation of Faunal Resources by Marine Hunter-Gatherer Groups during the Middle Holocene at the Copaca 1 site, Atacama Desert Coast. *Quaternary International* 373:4–16.

Olguín, Laura, Diego Salazar, and Donald Jackson. 2014. Tempranas evidencias de navegación y caza de especies oceánicas en la costa Pacífica de Sudamérica (Taltal, ~7.000 Años Cal. a.P.). *Chungara* 46(2):177–192.

Páez, Roberto. 1985. Balsas de cuero de lobo en Chañaral de Aceituno (Norte Chico): Un antiguo constructor revisitado. *Proceedings of Primer Congreso Chileno de Antropología* 1:474–490.

Rebolledo, Sandra, Philippe Béarez, Diego Salazar, and Felipe Fuentes. 2016. Maritime Fishing during the Middle Holocene in the Hyperarid Coast of the Atacama Desert. *Quaternary International* 391:3–11.

Rick, Torben, Virginia L. Harvey, and Michael Buckley. 2019. Collagen Fingerprinting and the Chumash Billfish Fishery, Santa Barbara Channel, California, USA. *Archaeological and Anthropological Sciences* 11:6639–6648.

Rubio Munita, Felipe, Nicolás Lira San Martín, and Victoria Castro Rojas. 2023. Balsa Rafts and Chinchorro Fishing: A Maritime Ethnoarchaeology Approach to the Study of Miniature Rafts from Arica, Chile (AD 1000–1400). In *Underwater and Coastal Archaeology in Latin America*, edited by Dolores Elkin and Christophe Delaere. University Press of Florida, Gainesville.

Salazar, Diego, Camila Arenas, Pedro Andrade, Laura Olguín, Jimena Torres, Carola Flores, Gabriel Vargas, Sandra Rebolledo, César Borie, Consuelo Sandoval, Claudia Silva, Ayelén Delgado, Nicolás Lira, and Camilo Robles. 2018. From the Use of Space to Territorialisation during the Early Holocene in Taltal, Coastal Atacama Desert, Chile. *Quaternary International* 473(Part B):225–241.

Salazar, Diego, Valentina Figueroa, Pedro Andrade, Hernán Salinas, Laura Olguín, Ximena Power, Sandra Rebolledo, Sonia Parra, Héctor Orellana, and Josefina Urrea. 2015. Cronología y organización económica de las poblaciones arcaicas de la costa de Taltal. *Estudios Atacameños* 50:7–46.

Salazar, Diego, Carola Flores, César Borie, Laura Olguín, Sandra Rebolledo, Manuel Escobar, and Ariadna Cifuentes. 2020. Economic Organization and Social Dynamics of Middle-Holocene Hunter-Gatherer-Fisher Communities on the Coast of the Atacama Desert (Taltal, Northern Chile). In *Maritime Communities of the Ancient Andes*, edited by Gabriel Prieto and Daniel H. Sandweiss, pp. 74–100. University Press of Florida, Gainesville.

Santoro, Calogero, José M. Capriles, Eugenia M. Gayo, María Eugenia de Porras, Antonio Maldonado, Vivien G. Standen, Claudio Latorre, Victoria Castro, Dante Angelo, Virginia McRostie, Mauricio Uribe, Daniela Valenzuela, Paula C. Ugalde, and Pablo A. Marquet. 2017. Continuities and Discontinuities in the Socio-environmental Systems of the Atacama Desert during the Last 13,000 Years. *Journal of Anthropological Archaeology* 46:28–39.

Smith, Eric Alden, and Rebecca Bliege Bird. 2000. Turtle Hunting and Tombstone Opening: Public Generosity as Costly Signaling. *Evolution Human Behavior* 21(4):245–261.

Smith, Eric Alden, Rebecca Bliege Bird, and Douglas W. Bird. 2003. The Benefits of Costly Signaling: Meriam Turtle Hunters. *Behavioral Ecology* 14(6):116–126.

Sosis, Richard. 2000. Costly Signaling and Torch Fishing on Ifaluk Atoll. *Evolution and Human Behavior* 21(4):223–244.

Vargas, Gabriel, José Rutllant, and Luc Ortlieb. 2006. ENSO Tropical-Extratropical Climate Teleconnections and Mechanisms for Holocene Debris Flows along the Hyperarid Coast of Western South America (17°–24°S). *Earth and Planetary Science Letters* 249(3–4):467–483.

Wiessner, Polly. 1996. Leveling the Hunter: Constraints on the Status Quest in Foraging Societies. In *Food and the Status Quest: An Interdisciplinary Perspective*, edited by Polly Wiessner and Wulf Schiefenhövel, pp. 171–192. Berghahn, Providence, Rhode Island.

Yáñez, Eleuterio, Rodrigo Vega, Claudio Silva, Jaime Letelier, María Ángela Barbieri, and Fernando Espíndola. 2008. An Integrated Conceptual Approach to Study the Swordfish (Xiphias gladius Linnaeus, 1758) Fishery in the Eastern South Pacific. *Revista de biología marina y oceanografía* 43(3):641–652.

6

Eighteenth-Century Shipbuilding and Forestry Management

Assessing the Impacts of Resource Intensification in Southwestern France

MARIJO GAUTHIER-BÉRUBÉ AND HEATHER B. THAKAR

Human behavioral ecology provides powerful models for understanding interactions between humans and their environment. Archaeologists traditionally apply human behavioral ecology models to foraging groups or early agriculturalists and use other theoretical models to analyze preindustrial societies. However, human behavioral ecology is sufficiently robust and flexible to address human decision-making and behavior in a wide range of social and cultural contexts (Winterhalder and Smith 2000). Human behavioral ecology models are well suited to and highly beneficial for the exploration of historical ships due to the critical importance of raw material extraction and exploitation of forests.

Drawing on the well-established prey choice model, we have developed a framework for interpreting resource use in wooden shipbuilding industries. This framework provides answers to important questions, such as the environmental and socioeconomic factors that influenced tree selection during the construction of a ship and how these factors interacted with one another. We also explore the methods used to document timber characteristics and highlight their selection process. The last section, a case study of the *Machault*, a 1757 French frigate discovered in Chaleur Bay, Quebec, Canada (Figure 6.1), focuses on prey choice models for analyzing how wooden remains indicate behaviors and decisions associated with timber acquisition.

Shipbuilding and Human Behavioral Ecological Models

Models derived from human behavioral ecology assume that human behavior tends toward optimization, although trade-offs and temporal lags in

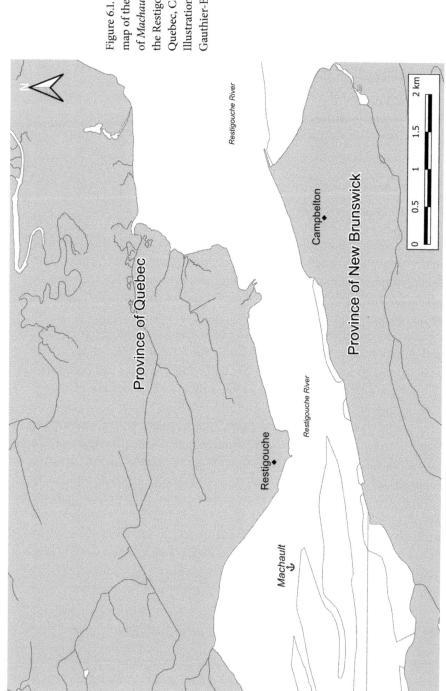

Figure 6.1. Regional map of the location of *Machault* wreck in the Restigouche River, Quebec, Canada. Illustration by Marijo Gauthier-Bérubé.

adaptation might contribute to deviation from expectations based on optimality models (Winterhalder and Kennett 2006). The prey choice model is a useful tool for identifying the economic, social, environmental, and technological factors in the complex relationship between shipbuilding and forestry practices. This model also provides a first step toward integrating shipbuilding practices into a larger discussion on resource management and selection as part of the behaviors and decisions of humans.

The prey choice model supports robust predictions about what resources an efficient individual would select under a specific environmental setting. This model enables researchers to identify changes that might be associated with cultural and economic decisions (Winterhalder 2001). An effective application of the prey choice model requires the researcher to identify a goal, a currency, a set of constraints, and what the alternative resources were (Winterhalder and Smith 2000).

The goal of acquiring timber resources for shipbuilding is to harvest the highest-quality timber that is best suited to the purpose of a vessel. For example, the tree species selected must adapt to fluctuations between wet and dry environments, resist insects and rot, and provide great physical strength. For hulls, early modern northern European countries relied mostly on oak (Gardiner 1994), a high-quality timber whose natural growth pattern provides great physical strength. Moreover, oak is a robust species that is resistant to insects, rot, and fluctuations between wet and dry environments. Its wide distribution throughout the European temperate forests also facilitated local access for people involved in shipbuilding.

Currency, the second element of the prey choice model, is the proxy metric that measures foraging efficiency. For timber resource acquisition, the primary currency that must be maximized is the financial investment needed to cover human labor, tools, and any timber resources that had to be imported. The detailed cost of a ship is sometimes available in historical records, but it is usually difficult to precisely quantify each individual category. The financial investment is an underlying element of every step of the construction process. From extraction of forest resources to the transport of wood to shipyards, investment needs to be optimized in terms of the time required and the cost of each task and the number of men employed. In eighteenth-century France, every step that could be taken to reduce both financial and human costs was attempted. The methods tried included issuing decrees and regulations, appointing officers to surveil forest lands, and reducing wood importation (Ballu 2014; Plouviez 2014; Service historique de la Marine 1997).

The third element in the prey choice model is the set of constraints that play a role in resource selection (Winterhalder and Smith 2000). In ship-building, four sets of constraints interact and impact decision-making: 1) vessel purpose, 2) available capital, 3) resource suitability, and 4) available technology. The essential purposes of a vessel include at a minimum the abil-ity to float on water, navigate a specific waterway, carry individuals or goods or both, and (most of the time) make multiple voyages. Beyond these basic criteria, the specific design of a vessel is shaped by its intended use. Differ-ences in optimal capacity, size, quality, significance, and intended longevity influence the resources invested in vessel construction. The environmen-tal constraints of different maritime environments such as lakes, rivers, the open ocean, and coastlines also influence vessel shape. For example, seven-teenth-century Dutch ships had fairly flat bottoms because of the shallow-water ports located throughout the Netherlands (Unger 1978). Flat-bottom forms in turn influenced the required shape of timber. Thus, consideration of a vessel's purpose and intended use provides an opportunity to explore the trade-offs imposed on available resources for ship construction, since they can determine which timber is appropriate.

The second constraint that can impact shipbuilding is available capital. Differential access to money, human labor, and mechanical resources (tools, cranes, etc.) translates into different forestry practices regardless of how available other resources are. For example, in the eighteenth century, the French navy had the first choice of natural resources, including wood. En-tire forests were reserved for shipbuilding, and not even locals were allowed to extract oak timbers without permission (Herbin de Halle 1813; Plouviez 2014). Private shipyards had second access to available resources, and private harvests were generally restricted to lower-quality timbers.

The third constraint is the suitability of available resources. In this case, suitability relates to environmental constraints on the growth of certain spe-cies. In early modern Europe, firs were considered the best resource for masts since they grow tall and straight and are flexible. Countries such as France or England, which had limited ecological zones for fir growth, quickly overex-ploited their own resources and had to use other species that were less suit-able or import masts from Finland, Norway, and Sweden (Plouviez 2014). A ship's point of origin offers important information about the potential range of locally available resources and the potential need for costly importation due to local resource depletion or the absence of desirable tree types. Suitable resources are directly tied to both the purposes of vessels and the availability of capital, as their abundance and accessibility define both resource selection and the most appropriate building strategy.

Available resources also relate to technology, the fourth and last constraint. Shipwrights used a variety of types of tools to extract, transport, and transform trees into ship timbers. These tools evolved and required variable amounts of time and human capital, factors that impacted the types of resources that could be harvested or how they could be transformed. For example, the use of explosives in the nineteenth century to create pathways in mountains or alter riverbeds to make them more navigable are examples of technological improvement that impacted which forests the French navy could exploit and how quickly timbers could be transported to shipyards (Service historique de la Marine 1997).

The prey choice model also includes alternative sets of behaviors and resources (Winterhalder and Smith 2000). In the case of shipbuilding, lower-quality timbers are the alternative to the higher-quality ones, particularly when multiple species are exploited for timber. When it was not possible for modern European navies to access or pay for oak, they used other wood species such as elm or beech (Ballu 2014). Other trade-off behaviors could be adopted, such as using numerous smaller timbers instead of a larger one or using lower-quality timber when higher-quality timbers were unavailable or deemed unworthy of the investment.

The prey choice model helps identify which factors need to be considered and understood when interpreting timber acquisition behaviors. It highlights goals and constraints that can influence which resources were deemed adequate for ship construction. In the following sections, we explore the methods of analysis that provide the necessary insight into shipbuilding practices.

Methods of Analysis

Evaluation of ship construction reveals lasting traces of human behaviors and decisions. Analyzing shipwreck timbers to reconstruct forest characteristics has become increasingly common over the past decade. Such analyses are useful for documenting species selection, patterns of overexploitation, and forestry management practices (Creasman 2010). Identifying wood species, assessing tree-age clusters, and assessing tree shape are the three main methods used to assess the quality of ship timber.

These methods require a basic understanding of the architectural features of ships. The main structures of a ship can be divided into two broad categories: planking timbers and curved timbers. Planking timbers are long, wide, straight pieces. Hull planking and ceiling planking use straight timbers (Figure 6.2). Framing timbers are generally curved; their angles and other variable dimensions depend on their role and the size of the ship. The floor

Figure 6.2. The hull planks cover the exterior of the hull and are examples of the use of straight timbers. Illustration from Diderot and d'Alembert, *Encyclopédie ou Dictionnaire raisonné des sciences, des arts et des métiers* (1769), vol. 7, Marine section, plate 15, figure 2. Courtesy of gallica.bnf.fr / Bibliothèque nationale de France.

timbers that form the base of the ship and the futtocks that extend the frame of the ship upward use curved wood (Figure 6.3). Because of their shape, the curved timbers had to come from trees or large branches that grew curved, just as straight planking timbers had to come from trees that grew straight. By acknowledging the variety of shapes present in a ship and the differences in terms of roles and required features, nautical archaeologists attempt to determine how shipwrights worked with natural resources and if shipwrights adopted specific forestry practices to increase the efficiency with which they exploited forest resources.

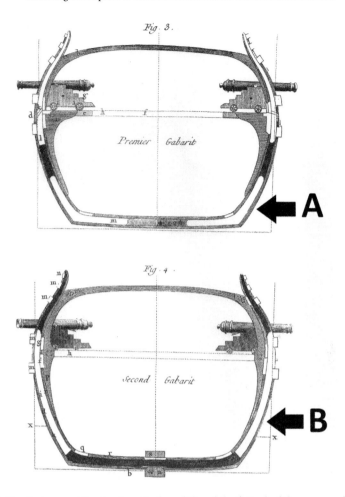

Figure 6.3. The timber used for the floor timbers (*A*) and the futtocks (*B*) are examples of curved timbers. Illustration from Diderot and d'Alembert, *Encyclopédie ou Dictionnaire raisonné des sciences, des arts et des métiers* (1769), volume 7, Marine section, plate 16, figures 3 and 4. Courtesy of gallica.bnf.fr / Bibliothèque nationale de France.

Assessment of Species

Identifying the species of wood used in a ship provides interesting information about resource availability and selection. An example is the work of Frédéric Guibal and Patrice Pomey (2002), who created a dendrochronological sequence based on the analysis of twenty-eight Mediterranean shipwrecks from the first half of the first century to the end of the fourth century AD. Pomey and Guibal's research determined that tree species were preferentially selected for certain architectural features within the construction of a single ship. Species selection also appeared to be informed by the availability of local timber resources. Homogeneity in species used can indicate good access to resources, while heterogeneity might indicate more opportunistic acquisition methods. Species use also must be analyzed in relation to how adequate a species is for its purpose. For example, fir was excellent for masts, but it was not seen to be as appropriate for planking as oak.

Assessments of Clusters in Tree Age

Because several factors can impact the selection of timbers, archaeologists also assess tree-age clusters and the shape of timbers. Analysis of tree rings provides useful cultural information about timber selection. Dendrochronology also documents whether the ages when trees were cut created distinct age groups among specific architectural features. Planking and framing require distinctive shapes that were usually acquired from differently shaped trees. Archaeologists can evaluate whether trees selected for the hull and ceiling planking were generally younger or older than trees selected for the frame. Evidence of homogeneity or heterogeneity within and between categories of architectural features can provide information about resource availability and the selection process. Homogeneity in age clusters within categories of architectural features is an indication of a higher investment in timber quality or of greater resource availability or both. Heterogeneity in age clusters is an indication of opportunistic harvesting that can be attributable to a lack of capital or to difficulty accessing appropriate timbers or both.

Assessments of Timber Quality

Another approach to the study of ship construction is evaluating the concordance between the original shape of the tree and the shape of the architectural structure of a ship. The underlying logic is that greater similarity between the two variables would have resulted in superior timber strength (e.g., Guibal and Pomey 2002). Higher-quality timbers have visible pith that is relatively centered at each end of the timber. This characteristic indicates that the timber was cut following the natural growth pattern of the tree, or, in other words, that there is a high concordance between the shape of the cut timber and the shape of the tree it was cut from (Loewen 2007a). This harvesting pattern produces stronger timbers that are less likely to crack or twist under pressure. On the other hand, lower-quality timbers might have visible pith at only one end of the timber, the pith might be uncentered, or they might exhibit a combination of these characteristics. These characteristics suggest that the timber did not follow the natural growth pattern of the tree, resulting in a low concordance between the shape of the cut and the shape of the original tree. This harvesting pattern can result in weaker timbers that are more likely to crack or twist.

Identifying the grain on the timber also provides information about the original shape. Wood grain that follows the same shape as the timber is an indication of a high-quality tree that had the same shape. Wood grain that does not follow the same shape as the timber is an indication of a lower-quality timber that came from a tree that did not have the same natural growth pattern.

The similarity between finished timber dimensions and the original tree diameter is also relevant to assessments of timber quality (Creasman 2010). Shipwrights generally removed the cambium (the layer between the rings and the bark) and most of the sapwood (the outer tree rings) because these porous, sap-filled portions of the timber were likely to rot and were vulnerable to insect infestation and consumption by marine organisms (Figure 6.4). In an optimal setting, shipwrights conserved only the heartwood rings (the inner tree rings). The presence of cambium and porous outer tree rings on a finished timber are an indication of lower timber quality. However, the presence of a small portion of cambium might also suggest highly selective harvest patterns. When cambium is detected only at the edge of a timber, the width of the

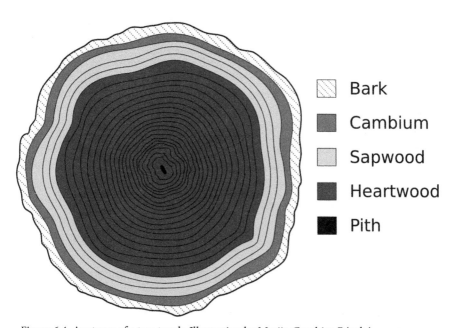

Figure 6.4. Anatomy of a tree trunk. Illustration by Marijo Gauthier-Bérubé.

timber is similar to the original diameter of the tree. This indicates that the entire tree was used to produce the timber (e.g., Loewen 2007a). This pattern suggests that either larger trees were not available or that smaller trees were purposely selected to increase harvest efficiency or to minimize waste. The relative percentage of timbers with cambium and porous outer rings provides a measure of timber quality and tree selection.

These three metrics have proved useful in the analysis of timber quality and decisions regarding resource selection or management in historical shipbuilding practices. For example, investigation of the fifteenth-century *Cavalaire I* wreck along the Mediterranean coast of France concluded that the first and second futtocks, which required curved timbers, were each cut from a separate single section of a tree whose curved shape was closely related to the final shape of the timbers. Tree-age cluster analysis revealed that the trees used to create the highly specialized framing futtock timber were uniformly about 65 years old (± 5 years) when they were harvested (Loewen and Delhaye 2003). The homogeneity in the tree-age distribution of the futtock timbers is interpreted as the result of some degree of purposive cultivation designed to produce high-quality ship timbers. Although the floor timbers of *Cavalaire I* (which required less curvature) were similarly cut from individual trees whose shape closely matched the final shape of the timber, this wood was harvested from trees that ranged from 80 to 140 years old. Greater heterogeneity in the tree-age distribution of the flooring timbers suggests that the trees selected for this architectural feature might have been harvested more opportunistically (Loewen and Delhaye 2003).

Similarly, tree-age cluster analysis of the timbers from the sixteenth-century *Red Bay* wreck, a Basque whaler found in Labrador, Canada, revealed that the frame timbers were clustered from 36 to 40 years. The age of the planking timbers varied from 80 to 150 years. Most of the frame components (such as futtocks and floor timbers) had a curved shape closely related to the final shape of the timber. Moreover, the diameter of the trees these timbers were harvested from was close to their final dimensions (Loewen 2007a). Cambium was sometimes visible, confirming that the timber width was similar to the original tree diameter and that entire trees were used to produce elements of the frame. Planks and frames were free of branches and knots, which was interpreted as evidence for pruning practices. Pruning prevents weakening of the main trunk and decreases irregularities in the wood grain (Shmulsky and Jones 2019). The homogeneity in the age distribution of the frames, the similarity between the tree diameter and the final dimensions of timber, the presence of cambium, and evidence of pruning led Loewen (2007b) to suggest that trees selected for the construction might have been purposefully cultivated.

Case Study: The Frigate *Machault*

In 1757 Louis XV formally sanctioned privateers (privately owned ships engaged in warfare) as part of the Seven Years' War with Britain. Only a few months after this proclamation, the frigate *Machault* was launched in Bayonne, France. King Louis had promised to buy ships built and operated privately during the war effort as long as the vessels were constructed according to the French navy's specifications. Subsequently, Jean-Baptiste de Machault d'Arnouville (1701–1794), the secretary of state for the navy, wrote to the Bayonne Chamber of Commerce that the city would serve as the first port privateering ships would depart from (Croizier 1905). Although historical records do not document that the *Machault* was built in the official naval yard at Bayonne, there is no doubt that it was built according to the plans of the royal architect Geoffroy and that it was built by shipwright Jean Hargous. However, there was a private shipyard adjacent to the official naval yard, and shipwrights were known to move from one shipyard to the next (Plouviez 2017). It is likely that Hargous built this vessel in the adjacent private shipyard, especially since the *Machault* was privately owned. The *Machault* was dispatched in 1760 as the flagship of a small fleet dedicated to the rescue of the New France colony. After a series of misfortunes, the French scuttled the *Machault* on July 8, 1760.

In 1968 employees of Parks Canada discovered the wreck of the *Machault* in Chaleur Bay, Quebec. Parks Canada conducted excavations at the site from 1969 to 1971. Analysis of the timbers of the *Machault* through the lens of the prey choice model offers novel insights into forestry practices and the decisions historical shipbuilders made in eighteenth-century France. It also demonstrates the utility and importance of using a larger theoretical framework that can be expanded to accommodate a larger number of ships in order to exploit the full potential of human behavioral ecology models for shipbuilding research.

Environmental and Historical Context

Situated at the confluence of two major waterways (the Nive and the Ardour) in southwestern France, Bayonne served for many centuries as a central place for shipbuilding (Figure 6.5). Fishing and whaling vessels were built and launched beginning in AD 1311 from this important port. From AD 1664, Bayonne had a shipyard that provided military vessels for the navy

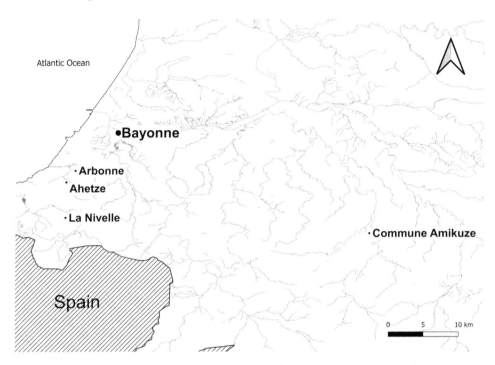

Figure 6.5. Map of Bayonne and surrounding area showing its network of rivers and nearby forest locations. Illustration by Marijo Gauthier-Bérubé.

and for smaller private shipyards (Goyhenetche 1998). Shipbuilders sourced timber from forests upstream in the Commune of Amikuze (50 km west of Bayonne) and from the regions of La Nivelle, Arbonne, and Ahetze—all located less than 20 km to the south. The regions supplied Bayonne's shipbuilding industry (Goyhenetche 1998) and the Rochefort royal shipyard (Plouviez 2014). High-quality oak resources from these regions came under increasing pressure in the early eighteenth century as production of frigates brought notoriety to Bayonne's shipwrights (Croizier 1905).

Predictions of the Prey Choice Model

Based on consideration of the set of constraints and alternative behaviors of prey choice model explored earlier, it is possible to make predictions about the choices shipbuilder made about the timbers of the *Machault*. *Prediction 1:* The frigate was built by privateers who did not have access to the navy's shipyard or timber resources. This limited the capital available for construction and therefore constrained resource suitability. *Prediction 2:* However, since the *Machault* was constructed under King Louis's promise to buy ships built according to the French navy's specifications, the potential for capital returns might have positively influenced the quality of the material used for its construction. *Prediction 3:* Trade-offs are still expected because of the limited capital available to privateers and their limited access to high-quality resources.

It is unlikely that the timbers used to build the *Machault* were of the same quality as the timbers used to build official navy vessels. Historical documents indicate that the French navy rejected any timber below 1.63 m in diameter, which could be roughly estimated as 80- to 100-year-old trees (Boudriot 1999). Given that parameter, we would expect to see alternative behaviors such as selecting smaller timber than the navy's standard. Timber selection could be the result of opportunistic harvesting. Evidence of this would be the absence of tree-age clusters and a lower concordance between the original tree shape and the shape of the timbers. We can also expect to see other alternative behaviors. Lower-quality timber could be of the same species as those the navy required but with less desirable characteristics. Lower-quality timbers show a greater degree of deviation between the shape of the tree and the final shape of the timber (e.g., a curved timber could come from a tree whose curvature angle is not the same). Similarly, lower-quality timbers have a higher number of structural anomalies produced by surficial knots or scarring from growth problems. These structural weaknesses reduce the resistance of timber to physical pressure.

Many of the timber characteristics, including the species used, the ages and dimensions of the trees, and the concordance between the original shape of the tree and the final shape of the timber are all expected to fall below the optimal range. Data acquired from dendrochronology analyses, species identification, tree-age clusters, and assessments of the quality of the *Machault*'s timbers provide the opportunity to evaluate the predictions of the prey choice model.

Results of Timber Quality Assessments

Catherine Lavier of the Laboratoire d'archéologie moléculaire et structurale de l'Université Pierre et Marie-Curie in Paris conducted the dendrochronological analysis of timbers from the *Machault*. She dated a subsample of eleven timbers to the period 1715–1753 (Lavier 2014). However, no bark or cambium was present, which means that these dates do not represent the exact year the timbers were cut. All of the timbers were oak, and since we know that the *Machault* was built in 1757, Lavier proposed that timbers were cut in the period 1754–1757. This analysis suggests that timbers used to build the *Machault* were cut specifically for this vessel and were not surpluses from previous harvests or recycled resources from older ships. Moreover, the timber was likely from sources that were local to Bayonne (Lavier 2014).

Assessments of Clusters in Tree Age

Significant quantities of cambium and sapwood were missing from *Machault* timbers (Lavier 2014). Investing in timber preparation by removing these parts of the wood enhanced its quality, but it affects archaeological tree-age assessments. Studies of the number of sapwood rings produced by oak trees in France indicate that 95% of oak trees aged 40 to 140 years old have from 2 to 38 sapwood rings (Lambert 2012). Szepertyski (1999) suggests that in optimal conditions, shipwrights used timbers with dimensions similar to their final shape to reduce the workload. Based on this observation, she posits that no more than ten heartwood rings should have been removed in addition to the sapwood (Szepertyski 1999). Gauthier-Bérubé's analysis of 45 frames and 49 planks from the *Machault* revealed that the last observable ring represents a period approximately 2 to 48 years before the oak tree was felled for ship construction.

In addition to identifying whether rings are missing toward the outer section, it is also important to evaluate if any heartwood rings could be missing toward the pith. It is possible to estimate how many rings could be missing based on the way the tree was converted into timber. The closer the timber was to the pith, the fewer heartwood rings it is missing. In order to estimate these missing heartwood rings in *Machault* timbers, Gauthier-Bérubé looked at 37 frames and 29 planks.

One tree provides one frame, but the frame can be cut in different ways based on the morphology of the tree or the required timber dimensions. Each of these cuts has a different name based on its position. Gauthier-Bérubé observed three types of cuts: pith, false-quarter, and outboard (Figure 6.6). Because the pith is present on all these types of cuts, no inner heartwood rings are missing in the *Machault* frames.

Tangential cuts make it possible for one tree to provide multiple planks. Like the frames, the cuts are given names based on where the planks are extracted. On the *Machault*, Gauthier-Bérubé observed three different types of cuts: quarter, false-quarter and outboard cuts (Figure 6.7). Since one tree could provide multiple individual planks, planks tend to be missing multiple inner heartwood rings. The proximity to the pith provides information for evaluating how many rings might be missing.

A plank that was quarter cut was originally located right next to the pith

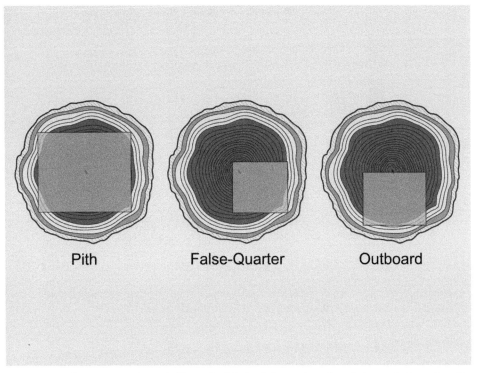

Figure 6.6. Different types of cuts visible on the *Machault* frames based on their proximity to the pith. Illustration by Marijo Gauthier-Bérubé.

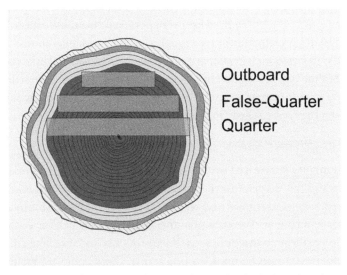

Figure 6.7. Different types of cuts on the *Machault* planking based on their proximity to the pith. Illustration by Marijo Gauthier-Bérubé.

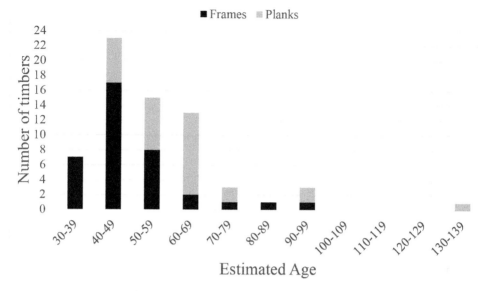

Figure 6.8. Estimated age of planks and frames once the missing rings are evaluated and added to the visible rings. Illustration by Marijo Gauthier-Bérubé.

and had no missing rings. The missing rings of the false quarter, which was located farther away from the pith, can be estimated to be at least equal to half of the number of observable rings (n + 50%). The estimate of the number of missing rings for an outboard cut is at least equal to the number of observable rings (n + 100%; Brad Loewen, personal communication 2015).

Thus, based on estimates of tree age, including estimated counts for the inner and outer missing rings, it appears that the *Machault* planks were cut from trees that were 67 years old (± 19.5 years) when they were felled and that the *Machault* frames were cut from trees that were 50 years old (± 12 years) when they were felled (Figure 6.8).

Assessments of Timber Quality

As timber quality is assessed by the relationship between the original shape of the tree and the shape of the architectural feature constructed, Gauthier-Bérubé first evaluated frames and planks for the position of the pith at both extremities of a timber. The quality of the frame timbers can be assessed by noting the position of the pith at each extremity based on their cut. Even though one tree would be used for one frame, there could be variation at both extremities due to a morphological deviation of the pith, the dimensions required, cutting to avoid weakness, and so forth. The frame timbers that have a pith cut at each extremity were considered to be high quality, since they benefitted from strength of the hardest section of the tree. False-quarter and outboard timbers still benefitted from the robustness of heart-wood but were not as strong as the pith-cut timbers. Table 6.1 reports the type of cut visible at both extremities of the timbers. At least 36 timbers (76.6%) had a pith cut on at least one extremity.

The quality of planks can also be assessed by looking at the position of the pith at both extremities of a timber based on their cut. While one entire tree section was used for one frame, one tree could provide multiple planks. Because of this, a greater variation in the types of cuts on planks is expected. Quality is assessed in a similar manner, with the exception that the presence of the pith at the center is not desirable because it can create greater torsion on both sides. The high-quality timber was quarter sawn close to the pith. Lower-quality timber had pith present. The quality of timber cut as false quarters or with outboard cuts was adequate. The planks observed (n = 26; 68.4%) were mostly quarter sawn, and none had pith present (Table 6.2).

Table 6.1. Types of cuts visible at the extremities of frame timbers

Pith at both extremities		Pith/outboard frame timbers		Pith/false quarter frame timbers		False quarter frame timbers at both extremities		Outboard frame timbers at both extremities		Total	
N	%	N	%	N	%	N	%	N	%	N	%
11	23.4	6	12.8	19	40.4	6	12.8	5	10.6	47	100.0

Note: Frames with pith present in at least at one extremity are considered to be of higher quality than timbers that have no pith.

Table 6.2. Types of cuts visible at both extremities of plank timbers

Outboard		False quarter		Quarter		Total	
N	%	N	%	N	%	N	%
7	18.4	5	13.2	26	68.4	38	100.0

Note: In contrast to frames, planks that have pith are considered to be of lower quality. A high-quality plank would have a quarter cut at each extremity.

Gauthier-Bérubé also assessed timber quality by looking at the wood grain and the original shape of the tree. Only the curved timbers were considered, since curved trees were more difficult to obtain with the adequate shape. She rated timbers as A, B, or C, depending on how close the shape of the timber was to the tree (Dagneau 2004). Grade A was for the timbers with a perfect relation between the original shape of the tree and the shape of the architectural feature. These timbers had no deviation, knots, or weaknesses at the surface. Grade B was for timbers that had a slight deviation between the original shape of the tree and the finished timber, but nothing that could impede its physical strength. Grade C was assigned to timbers that had an important divergence between the original shape of the tree and the finished timber. It was also given to timbers that had multiple knots and other weaknesses at its surface. This examination revealed that 42.2% were Grade A, 51.1% were Grade B, and only 6.7% were Grade C.

Discussion

Dendrochronology showed that the oak timbers used to construct the hull of the *Machault* were not salvaged from older vessels and reused. High-quality timber with few structural irregularities in the wood grain (e.g., knots) were used. The presence of pith in most timbers also indicates good concordance between the original tree shape and the final shape of the timber. Despite this significant investment in timber quality, it is also clear that the *Machault*'s ship builders did not choose or did not have access to the highest-quality timber. The French navy's specifications for shipbuilding in the late eighteenth century required the use of oak that was 80 to 100 years old (Boudriot 1999), but the *Machault* was built using much younger (and therefore smaller) trees.

We expected to see constraints on the building of the *Machault* that would predict a lower-quality vessel because it was built from a private shipyard. Nevertheless, analyses show that there was no trade-off in terms of quality other than the younger age of the timbers. It is possible to state that while private shipbuilders had access to somewhat optimal resources for building their ships, they adopted the alternative resource of younger trees.

Interpretation of forestry practice through study of the timber acquisition process for shipbuilding often addresses the question of forestry management and to what extent forests could be tailored for ship timbers. However, there is not enough evidence from the *Machault* to distinguish between a managed environment or opportunistic harvesting in an unmanaged forest. Pruning and pollarding are two historically documented methods of forestry management that are known to indicate human involvement in the natural growth process and that contributed to anthropogenically managed forests. Pruning can be seen through the removal of branches and knots and the scarring process of the tree (Nayling and Jones 2014). Pollarding refers to the removal of the top of a tree in variable ways that can encourage branch growth from the tree's main trunk (Petit and Watkins 2003). It is much more difficult to assess the practice of pollarding, as it leaves no trace except a certain homogeneity in the shape and age of its branches. Welmoed and colleagues (2013, 2018) have demonstrated that the same distribution of diameter and age can occur in both managed and unmanaged trees. Therefore, these characteristics cannot be assumed to be useful in identifying woodland management.

A third method is mentioned in historical documents but has not yet been proven with evidence: artificial tree bending. According to thirteenth-century documents, the Genoese standardized their timber measurements, including the precise angle of curvature required to provide the shipyard with the right shape. Branches resulting from pollarding would have been forced to adopt a certain shape (Ciciliot 2002). Historian Robert G. Albion briefly mentioned the use of cultivated fields of curved trees for the frames but did not provide sources or evidence (Albion 1926). Nineteenth-century French theoreticians also discussed silviculture based on the best way to bend trees to force a certain angle, but it is almost certain that this manipulation in the forest never went beyond small-scale experimentation (Ballu 2014). It is also difficult to assess the traces these bending methods would have left in the wood and the possibility of identifying such practices in archaeological contexts. Studies have proven that it is possible to document age clusters and assess the shape of trees, but it is still difficult to say to what extent human actions led to specific shapes.

Despite these references to artificial tree bending, ships require thousands of trees for their construction, and in addition to logistical issues inherent in bending thousands of trees at once, there is no historical documentation to support the practice to such a wide extent. Moreover, the idea of artificial bending implies significant investment not only in bending the trees but also in protecting them from accidental harvest for decades. Preservation of these trees would almost certainly have required restrictive laws and constant vigilance. Perhaps more important, artificial bending also implies significant conservatism in design and construction technique. A tree might take many decades, and therefore generations, before it was ready to harvest (Ciciliot 2002; Loewen 2007b). Significant investment in artificial bending assumes that the timber shape created during one generation would still be desired decades later by another generation. Given the development of nautical technology, this assumption is questionable at the very least.

Finally, the simple division between managed and natural forest does not leave enough room for variation in terms of optimization of resource harvesting and the different choices that could have been made. As seen with the application of the prey choice model to shipwreck analysis and the discussion of constraints, shipwrights did not always build ships to be optimal in terms of resistance and durability. Ships could be disposable units with a very limited purpose. Such vessels (and their builders) would not have benefited from a large investment in resources or human labor. This means that a ship could have included timbers with low-quality features even if high-quality timbers were generally available. Thus, it is important to be careful when interpreting homogeneity in timber resources as evidence of woodland management and to acknowledge that multiple factors influenced the available supply for ship construction. Considering resource acquisition in just two categories—managed forests and natural forests—oversimplifies a complex reality in which multiple possibilities existed and overlapped. Archaeologists have provided interpretations of timber acquisition strategy before, but the application of the prey choice model to the data allows us to explore the trade-offs and explore the impact of the different set of constraints and how they interacted with one another. The prey choice model provides adequate tools for multisite investigations and can support a large corpus of archaeological data.

Further work could also include field-processing models that could explore the trade-off in timber choice and the efficiency of transportation between the extraction site and shipyards. Despite the fact that processing sites were never documented and were probably too ephemeral to survive in the archaeological record, processing can be inferred from the shape of finished timber and archival documents can be used to help distinguish between processing done in the forest and processing done on site at shipyards. The question of multigenerational investment in forestry management could also be investigated to explore if there could have been any optimality and rationality to it from a human behavioral ecology perspective, not only from a shipbuilding perspective but also a larger sociological perspective of how and when societies would decide to invest into large projects that transcended generations.

Using a high-level theoretical framework such as human behavioral ecology could improve our understanding of the interactions between ship construction and resource acquisition strategies by reframing our analysis in a broader perspective of human behavior. This could help us better understand human influence on woodland exploitation within the context of shipbuilding. It would also allow researchers to interpret shipwrecks within larger archaeological ecological paradigms.

Conclusion

This chapter evaluated the utility of human behavioral ecology models for the study of wooden remains from shipwrecks in order to reconstruct and interpret past behaviors linked to wood acquisition. Methods that nautical archaeologists developed in the last decades have made it possible to evaluate the environmental characteristics of the wood used for shipbuilding, but high-level theoretical applications and models are still needed. This study contributes to that effort and shows that human behavioral ecology models provide new tools that enable us to better understand shipbuilders' decisions and wood acquisition strategies as part of a wider human behavioral context. Additional shipwreck data will enrich the study of larger patterns of the relationships between human societies, their environments, and their resource acquisition patterns over time and space.

References Cited

Albion, Robert. 1926. *Forest and Sea Power: The Timber Problem of the Royal Navy 1652–1862*. Harvard University Press, Cambridge, Massachusetts.

Ballu, Jean-Marie. 2014. *Bois de marine, Les bateaux naissent en forêt*. 3rd ed. Gerfaut, Paris.

Boudriot, Jean. 1999. Chênes et vaisseaux. In *Forêt et Marine*, edited by Andrée Corvol, pp. 339–347. L'Harmattan, Paris.

Ciciliot, F. 2002. Garbo Timber. In *Tropis VII: Seventh International Symposium on Ship Construction in Antiquity Proceedings*, edited by Harry Tzalas, pp. 255–264. Hellenic Institution for the Preservation of Nautical Tradition, Athens.

Creasman, Pearce Paul. 2010. Extracting Cultural Information from Ship Timber. PhD dissertation, Texas A&M University, College Station.

Croizier, Jean. 1905. *Histoire du port de Bayonne*. Imprimerie Y. Cadoret, Bordeaux, France.

Dagneau, Charles. 2004. The Batteaux Plats of New France. *International Journal of Nautical Archaeology* 33(2):281–296.

Gardiner, Robert. 1994. *Cogs, Caravels and Galleons: The Sailing Ship, 1000–1650*. U.S. Naval Institute Press, Annapolis, Maryland.

Goyhenetche, Manex. 1998. La construction navale en Pays Basque Nord: État de la recherche et portrait chronologique. In *Itsas Memoria: Revista de Estudios Maritimos del Pais Vasco*, vol. 2, 147–168. Untzi Museoa–Museo Nava, Donostia-San Sebastián.

Guibal, Frédéric, and Patrice Pomey. 2002. Essences et qualité des bois dans la construction navale antique: L'apport de l'étude anatomique et dendrochronologique. *Forêt méditerranéenne* 23(2):91–104.

Herbin de Halle, P. Etienne. 1813. *Des bois propres au service des arsenaux de la marine et de la guerre: Ou developpement et rapprochement de lois, reglemens et instructions concernant la recherche, le martelage et lexploitation des arbres propres aux constructions navales, des lartillerie, etc.* S. C. L'Huillier, Paris.

Lambert, George. 2012. Datation précise des charpentes par la dendrochronologie: Nouveau cadre méthodologique. In *Les charpentes du XIe Au XIXe, grand ouest de la France: Typologie et évolution, analyse de la documentation de la Médiathèque de l'architecture et du patrimoine*, edited by Patrick Hoffsummer, pp. 3–18. Brepols N.V., Turnhour, Belgium.

Lavier, Catherine. 2014. *Compte-rendu, CRI 2014-03-27.* Laboratoire d'archéologie moléculaire et structurale, Paris.

Loewen, Brad. 2007a. The Frames: Atlantic Design Principles and Basque Fabrication Methods. In *The Underwater Archaeology of Red Bay*, vol. 3, edited by Robert Grenier, Marc-André Bernier, and Willis Stevens, pp. 53–101. Parcs Canada, Ottawa.

———. 2007b. The Basque Shipbuilding Trades: Design, Forestry and Carpentry. In *The Underwater Archaeology of Red Bay*, vol. 3, edited by Robert Grenier, Marc-André Bernier, and Willis Stevens, pp. 253–298. Parcs Canada, Ottawa.

Loewen, Brad, and Marion Delhaye. 2003. Oak Growing, Hull Design and Framing Style: The Cavalaire-sur-Mer Wreck, c. 1470. In *Connected by the Sea: Proceedings of the Tenth International Symposium on Boat and Ship Archaeology*, edited by Lucy Blue, Frederick Hockers, and Anton Englert, pp. 99–104. Roskilde, Denmark.

Nayling, Nigel, and Toby Jones. 2014. The Newport Medieval Ship, Wales, United Kingdom. *International Journal of Nautical Archaeology* 43(2):239–278.

Petit, Sandrine, and Charles Watkins. 2003. Pollarding Trees: Changing Attitudes to a Traditional Land Management Practice in Britain, 1600–1900. *Rural History* 14(2):157–176.

Plouviez, David. 2014. *La Marine française et ses réseaux économiques au XVIIIe siècle.* Paris: Indes savantes.

———. 2017. Un ingénieur de la marine à l'école des constructeurs du "commerce": Chevillart le cadet à Saint-Malo pendant la guerre d'Indépendance américaine. In *Mobilités d'ingénieurs en Europe, XVe–XVIIIe siècle*, edited by Stéphane Blond, Hilaire-Pérez Liliane, and Virol Michèle, pp. 101–127. Presses Universitaires de Rennes, France.

Service historique de la Marine. 1997. *Du bois dont on fait les vaisseaux . . . de l'arbre en sa futaie à la figure de proue sculptée: Catalogue de l'exposition du 10 septembre au 12 décembre 1997, Château de Vincennes.* Service historique de la Marine, Paris.

Shmulsky, Rubin, and P. David Jones. 2019. *Forest Products and Wood Science: An Introduction.* 7th ed. John Wiley & Sons, West Sussex, UK.

Szepertyski, Béatrice. 1999. *Datations en dendrochronologie «La Belle», Vaisseau de René Robert Cavelier de La Salle.* Laboratoire d'Analyses et d'Expertises en Archéologie et Œuvres d'arts, Bordeaux, France.

Unger, Richard W. 1978. *Dutch Shipbuilding before 1800: Ships and Guilds.* Van Gorcum, Amsterdam.

Welmoed, A. Out, Kirsti Hänninen, and Caroline Vermeeren. 2018. Using Branch Age and Diameter to Identify Woodland Management: New Developments. *Environmental Archaeology* 23(3):254–266.

Welmoed, A. Out, Caroline Vermeeren, and Kirsti Hänninen. 2013. Branch Age and Diameter: Useful Criteria for Recognising Woodland Management in the Present and Past? *Journal of Archaeological Science* 40(11):4083–4097.

Winterhalder, Bruce. 2001. The Behavioral Ecology of Hunter-Gatherers. In *Hunter-Gatherers: An Interdisciplinary Perspective*, edited by Catherine Panter-Brick, Robert Layton, and Peter Rowley-Conry, pp. 12–38. Cambridge University Press, Cambridge.

Winterhalder, Bruce, and Douglas Kennett. 2006. Behavioral Ecology and the Transition from Hunting and Gathering to Agriculture. In *Behavioral Ecology and the Transition to Agriculture*, edited by Bruce Winterhalder and Douglas Kennett, pp. 1–21. University of California Press, Berkeley.

Winterhalder, Bruce, and Eric Alden Smith. 2000. Analyzing Adaptive Strategies: Human Behavioral Ecology at Twenty-Five. *Evolutionary Anthropology: Issues, News, and Reviews* 9(2):51–72.

7

What Makes a Forager Turn Coastal?

An Agent-Based Approach to Coastal Foraging on the Paleoscape of South Africa

COLIN D. WREN, MARCO A. JANSSEN,
KIM HILL, AND CURTIS W. MAREAN

At the fine scale, a foraging pattern that includes intertidal resources is quite simple to understand. Optimal foraging theory predicts that if the benefits of foraging for shellfish are greater than the benefits of hunting for a certain species of animal or gathering a certain plant, shellfish will be included in the diet (Stephens and Krebs 1986). This of-the-moment choice focused on individual caloric return rate maximization is readily modeled. However, a long-term and broad-scale landscape perspective on foraging behavior across a spatially and temporally heterogeneous landscape is considerably more difficult to model. Modeling behavior is also more complex when groups of foragers optimize total harvest rather than individual caloric return rates. For example, Hawkes and colleagues (1995) suggested that Hadza women prefer to visit fruit patches with lower returns where their children could also collect food efficiently instead of exploiting root patches with higher returns where their children were not able to obtain food efficiently.

We use an agent-based modeling approach, which we call the Paleoscape-ABM, to simulate the aggregated effects of optimal foraging theory logic within a dynamic and heterogeneous reconstructed landscape set on the Cape South Coast of South Africa. Our goal is to better understand the sustainable human population size in the Later (~40,000–10,000 years ago) and Middle Stone Age (~300,000–40,000 years ago) of coastal South Africa, the specifics of diet and landscape use, and the factors that may have motivated populations to include coastal foods in their diet. The Middle Stone Age sites we consider in this chapter figure prominently in our understanding of the origins of modern humans. We have investigated which features of human cognition and of the changing environment might have influenced Middle Stone Age foragers to include shellfish in their diet as early as ~160,000 years ago, the time period of the earliest evidence for coastal foraging (Jacobs 2010; Marean et al. 2007). Since we base our approach on generalized models of optimal foraging theory, the PaleoscapeABM is designed to be applied to any foraging environment made up of any number of animal, plant, and intertidal resources.

Background

Agent-based modeling is a form of computer simulation that focuses on heterogeneous and autonomous decision-making units referred to as agents (Railsback and Grimm 2011). Agent-based models use sequences of computer-programmed actions of agents to determine how they will interact with each other and with their simulated environment. In our case, the modeled agents represent individual foragers and foraging groups. This bottom-up approach is compatible with optimal foraging theory models, which are similarly designed to understand fine-scale foraging and mobility decisions. However, our agent-based modeling approach expands on the results of optimal foraging theory by aggregating those fine-scale decisions over the long term and on a broad scale into a form that is more directly comparable to the cumulative record of human activity—that is, the archaeological record (Lake 2000, 2001; Mithen 1990). Agent-based modeling also enables us to examine the cumulative impacts of foraging at the landscape scale, as the location of current foraging will impact where food is likely to be available in the immediate future (e.g., in one day) and the more distant future (e.g., in one month).

In the agent-based modeling literature, the concept of emergence refers to the often-unexpected dynamics that arise from the aggregated interaction of fine-scale behavior (Axelrod 1997; Berry et al. 2002). Emergence is particularly relevant to the complex interactions between humans and their environments because the decisions an individual makes do not directly predict the long-term effect of the behavior of a population. For example, classic optimal foraging theory models ask whether or not an individual forager will stop for an encountered food item but do not address the long-term sustainability of a region's resource base for 100 people who are each making their own decisions.

We argue that increasing the breadth of a diet to include shellfish, which first appeared in a human population during marine isotope stage 6 (124,000–161,000 years ago) in the Middle Stone Age, is an emergent effect that arose in a complex foraging system within a dynamic and heterogeneous landscape. The context and causes of this dietary shift are relevant to understanding how the population responded to significant climatological and ecological changes in the landscape (Cawthra et al. 2020; Cowling et al. 2020; De Vynck et al. 2020; Esteban et al. 2020; Venter et al. 2020). They are also relevant to the broader discussion about the origins of key human characteristics, including an increase in brain size (Marean 2015).

Since 2010, the members of the Paleoscape Project, an international and interdisciplinary team of researchers from Arizona State University and Nelson Mandela University, among others, funded by the Templeton Foundation, have systematically been building a framework for understanding these changes using an interdisciplinary and multifaceted approach to reconstructing the climate, ecology, forageable resources, and archaeological record of the Cape South Coast of South Africa (Figure 7.1; Franklin et al. 2015). The results of these studies have been assembled into the PaleoscapeABM, an agent-based model that forms a human behavioral testbed for evaluating our hypotheses related to human behavior and the reconstructed habitat landscape. A key issue for the Paleoscape Project was understanding the role of shellfish within the broader foraging system and the impacts of changes in human behavior on the benefits of including shellfish in the diet. Marean (2010) hypothesized that a human population with the cognitive capacity to predict low spring tides based on the phases of the moon would be able to target intertidal foraging more efficiently. This population would have higher caloric return rates than a population that encountered shellfish only by chance. This is particularly relevant for human societies with very large home ranges, since they are not able to monitor the tides directly. De Vynck, Anderson, and colleagues (2016) added support for this hypothesis when they demonstrated very high caloric returns from shellfish during spring low tides (the highest recorded was 3,400 kcal/hour) and negligible returns when the tides were high or during non-spring-tide days (10 out of every 14 days).

Previous papers on the PaleoscapeABM demonstrate the potential of our approach through examinations of population density, diet, and the possible effects of anticipating the tides (Wren et al. 2018, 2020). In this chapter, we describe the integration of optimal foraging theory logic in the PaleoscapeABM computer simulation in detail and examine the impact of various assumptions we make about behavior within the program code of the agent-based model.

Translating Optimal Foraging Theory into Agent-Based Model Code

One challenge of the application of optimal foraging theory to archaeology has been coping with the differences in temporal scale between archaeological

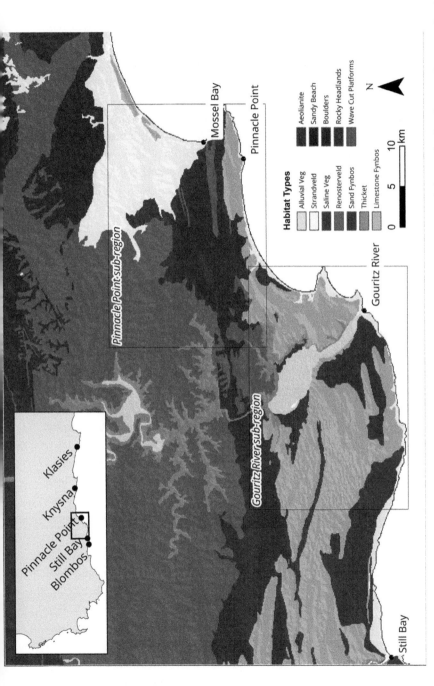

Figure 7.1. Paleoscape study region and subregions in the Cape South Coast, South Africa. The legend depicts the distribution of terrestrial and coastal habitat types that impact resource availability. Labeled points highlight landscape features and archaeological sites mentioned in the text. Vegetation data from Mucina and Rutherford's (2006) map projected in the UTM Zone 34 (geographic coordinate system). Figure by Colin Wren.

and ethnographic data. Archaeological data typically reflects very long-term sequences of human activity, often at the scale of a whole population's behavior during a particular temporal phase (Perreault 2019). This contrasts with the shorter time scales for foraging decisions recorded by ethnographers and evolutionary anthropologists studying hunter-gatherer behavior in the field. Optimal foraging theory is designed to address these shorter time scales.

Agent-based modeling provides a bridge between scales. Like optimal foraging theory, agent-based models are built from a bottom-up perspective. Instead of imposing an overarching subsistence system, we think about individual human actions on the local scale. We then observe the impact of these small actions as they aggregate into a broader pattern of subsistence that we can compare to an archaeological record. In other words, while we design the programming around the local scale, the resulting model outputs represent broader temporal and spatial scales. In this case, we apply optimal foraging theory principles one by one to the behaviors of the forager agents and then run simulations of their behavior on a reconstructed resource landscape. To stay as true as possible to optimal foraging theory principles, we coded applications for each of the core models of optimal foraging theory into agent behaviors. We think that the combination of optimal foraging theory and agent-based modeling will overcome many of the obstacles to applying optimal foraging theory to archaeology.

The PaleoscapeABM code and a full description of the model dynamics are available online at the Computational Modeling in Social and Ecological Sciences (CoMSES) OpenABM Model Library.[1] In the following sections, we describe how we implemented the patch choice model, the marginal value theorem, and the prey choice model.

At the beginning of each day, camp agents, who represent the collective decision-making of a small group of forager agents, select a raster cell based on expected gathering returns (described later) that will be the forager agents' meeting place at the end of the day. This acts as a directional goal for foragers to travel toward as they begin to run out of foraging time and acts as a location for food sharing at the end of each modeled day. The model's gatherer and hunter agents follow different daily routines, described in the following sections.

The Patch Choice Model of Gathering

Our patch choice model assumes homogeneous distribution of resources within specific cells and systematic harvest until the cell is empty. This implies a constant return rate within a given patch or cell because the forager has (on average) a constant probability of locating specific resources. The forager chooses which cell they expect to be most productive and moves through the landscape to maximize their time in those cells (MacArthur and Pianka 1966). The model assumes no decreasing return rate until the cell is completely depleted.

The PaleoscapeABM imports a GIS raster map of 1-ha cells, each of which has a number that represents specific habitat types. This resourcescape is 20 × 30 km and includes 8 terrestrial vegetation types for plant gathering and 5 coastal habitat types for shellfish gathering (Table 7.1). Since a raster map is a continuous surface of adjacent cells, there is effectively no in-between patch space within our model where foraging cannot occur. Gatherers select a sequence of cells by calculating the net caloric intake for every cell within a 2-km search radius (1,257 cells) and then choosing to move to the one with the most promising returns given the foraging time they have left that day. This is represented in Equation 1:

$$C = R \, (T - Tc \cdot D)$$

where C is the net return in calories, R is the return rate per hour for a given habitat type, T is the foraging time left in the day, Tc is the time it takes to walk across a single cell, and D is the distance to that cell. Tc is determined by the cell size (100 m) and the default walking speed of 2 km per hour. This means that foragers use only 3 minutes (0.05 hours) of foraging time to walk across a single cell to reach a more highly valued cell. After the best cell is completely exploited, they continue to travel to, and exploit, other cells if there is still foraging time left in that day.

The gatherers therefore assume there will be other neighboring cells of the same habitat type if the cell they're considering becomes depleted before the end of their foraging day. Agents may decide to pass over several cells in order to reach a cell of a higher-valued habitat type. In these cases, the agent loses time due to travel (i.e., agents do not stop to consume slightly lower-ranked resources along the way) but this may be worthwhile depending on the expected net return over the combined time that travel and exploitation require. Camp movement decisions at the start of each foraging day follow the same logic and assumptions but always include a full foraging day.

The model assigns caloric return rates (kilocalories/hour) according to the habitat type of the cell. We calculated these rates from experimental foraging data collected in previous studies (Table 7.1; Botha et al. 2020; see also De Vynck, Anderson, et al. 2016; De Vynck, Cowling, et al. 2016; De Vynck, Van Wyk, et al. 2016). We also used a daily and bimonthly tidal cycle to limit the availability of shellfish to the first two hours of each day (followed by terrestrial gathering nearby) and to only five days of each 15-day cycle, as shellfish have negligible return rates outside spring low tides.

The model replenishes the shellfish with the start of each spring low tide based on experimental data (De Vynck et al. 2020). We modeled plant seasonality by cycling the assigned caloric return rates of each habitat type every 91–92 days. We replenished previously harvested plant resources at the start of each season. Botha and colleagues (2020) found that many plants, especially the high-calorie tubers, had variable growth cycles such that repeated years of harvesting the same patch did not have reduced yields until the third year of intensive harvest in the same experimental plot.

Our agent-based model simplifies foraging within cells by assuming that a constant return rate is available to the agents until they have used up the cell's total harvestable time and that foragers recognize when depletion is complete. Several of the key plant resources are tubers that must be dug out of the ground, which would leave obvious signs of recent foraging. This means that the caloric return rate within the cell would remain approximately constant for some period of time and then drop to zero when the forager has completed searching and digging in all areas within the cell. Given the variability in harvesting times for different plant species (e.g., berries versus tubers) and within different soil types (e.g., rocky versus sandy soils), the amount of time needed to harvest the same percentage of a cell also varies by habitat type (Table 7.1). The model assumes that a constant 100-by-20-m strip of a cell is harvested each time a forager extracts resources (i.e., 20% of the cell). Each time a forager acquires resources in a cell, they reduce the cell's total-harvest-time variable by 20%, such that after 5 passes the cell is depleted (Table 7.1). Intertidal shellfish and plant foraging are treated the same way, except that a single pass of a coastal cell takes 33% of that harvestable time (i.e., 3 passes to deplete the cell). We derived both of these values from observations during repeated timed experimental foraging bouts for edible plants or shellfish in each habitat type (De Vynck, Anderson, et al. 2016; De Vynck et al. 2020). The model also totals the time spent and the calories earned by the forager after each pass of a cell.

In our model, the gatherer agents constantly compare their current harvesting potential to the potential in all other cells. Often gatherers will harvest many contiguous cells of a single habitat type since the travel time will be minimal between those cells. However, foragers can abandon a cell before it is fully depleted if they are running out of time or coming in range of a better habitat or if they are foraging the end of low tide. An alternative model design, which we did not choose, would assume that foragers could not recognize earlier foraging. This design alternative would decrease the caloric return rate incrementally and each subsequent turn at the cell would effectively simulate the increased difficulty of locating unexploited plants.

Prey Choice Model of Hunting

The prey choice model determines which prey species should be included in the diet of the foragers to maximize caloric return rates. The hunter agents in the Paleoscape follow the logic of the prey choice model. When agents are in a given habitat type, they encounter different mammalian prey species at specific rates. These rates are programmed as probabilities calculated from estimated species densities assuming 100% detection within a relatively narrow 20-m swath (Buckland et al. 2015). As with gathering, we predetermined which species would be available to the hunter agents (i.e., were within the possible diet breadth). However, the result of the daily hunt reflects the dynamics of the model's programming. This works well for an archaeological model, since we have good data on which species are represented within the assemblages of excavated sites but less data about daily hunting returns. This approach enables us to better understand the daily contribution of meat to the diet, where hunters acquire most of that meat, and what effect access to meat has on the distribution of hunting-related artifacts (Gravel-Miguel et al. 2021).

The program uses a random draw weighted to the probability that each species will be encountered to select which prey hunter agents will encounter. Other model parameters determine the pursuit time per species, probability of a successful kill per species, and caloric return per species if a hunt is successful. The model records the caloric returns per hunter and per camp both daily and over the duration of the simulation.

While we have limited the simulation to include only species that are present in the archaeological and paleontological record, it is possible to add other species and allow the model to produce their presence or absence. For example, in an unpublished experiment, we added eland (*Taurotragus oryx*) to see if it would increase the daily hunting returns, since the species was noted to be present in the region but was largely absent from the archaeological record of the period. It did not improve returns, so we felt justified in running our final model without that species.

The prey choice model as classically defined (MacArthur and Pianka 1966; Pulliam 1974) was not designed to operate on complex spatially and temporally heterogeneous resource landscapes or with the complex cooperative social behavior of multiple hunters. In the Paleoscape model, we used an initially coordinated search where a randomly chosen lead hunter agent picks a target direction based on a habitat type that is nearby and profitable. The other hunter agents then face that direction and adjust their travel direction using small random turns. This helps avoid multiple agents searching in the same cell. As their daily foraging time begins to run out, each agent shifts their direction back toward their end-of-day camp location, which results in a flower-petal-like search pattern (Pacheco-Cobos et al. 2019; Yellen 1972).

In the following sections, we first describe our use of a simplified toy landscape to illustrate the model dynamics and the interdependence of foraging in the terrestrial and coastal habitats. We then present our reconstructed paleoscape and compare simulated foraging on two segments of the South African Cape South Coast. This final iteration demonstrates how the fine-scale model dynamics derived from optimal foraging theory interact with different resource landscapes to produce a broader-scale simulated archaeological record.

Toy Landscape Examples

We created a simple landscape of 100 by 100 cells, 1 ha each, to demonstrate the model dynamics piece by piece. The landscape has three rows of ocean cells across the bottom and one row of intertidal shellfish habitat. The rest of the map consists of a single habitat type (Figure 7.2). On the map, we created a single camp with fifteen individual gatherers. The location of the camp moves at the beginning of each day as a target goal for the foragers at the end of the day. The individual gatherers use their allotted foraging time while walking to gather resources.

For this simple example, we disabled plant seasonality, but tidal cycling still means that shellfish give high net caloric returns for only 5 days of each 15-day cycle (i.e., during the spring tide) and only for the first 2 hours of each day (low tide). Each of the scenarios below were run for a simulated 10-year period with modeled daily time intervals and were repeated 30 times to find an average. Other default parameter settings and the full code description are available with the code at the CoMSES OpenABM site.

A key aspect of these four scenarios is that the net caloric return from shellfish gathering is much higher than the caloric return for gathering plants (a maximum of ~2,000 kcal per hour on aeolionite coastline versus a maximum of ~350 kcal per hour in sand fynbos). However, shellfish are spatially bounded to the narrow band of intertidal cells and are temporally bounded by the bimonthly and daily tidal cycles.

In the following comparisons, the actual estimated quantity of daily

Figure 7.2. The toy landscape has a uniform terrestrial habitat (dark gray cells) and a higher-caloric-return coastal strip for the first several scenarios (white cells). The house represents the position of the gatherers' campsite. Figure by Colin Wren.

kilocalories is not important. Instead, we demonstrate the relative improvement in caloric returns when certain behaviors are added to the model. Figure 7.3 compiles the results for all four toy landscape experiments.

Experiment 1: Random Walk Baseline

For the first experiment, we used a random walk both for the gatherers and the location of the camp. This means that the camp moves to a random non-ocean cell within the landscape and then the gatherers randomly move to neighboring cells and gather throughout the landscape until their time begins to run

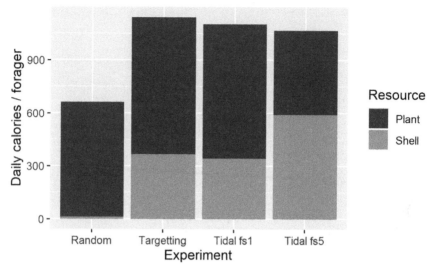

Figure 7.3. Combined results of the first four toy landscape experiments showing the kilocalories from plant and shellfish gathering. Tidal fs1 and Tidal fs5 show the experiments with tidal knowledge and differing number of days of foresight (one versus five). Figure by Colin Wren.

out and they head for their camp. This establishes a baseline for comparison to the more complex behaviors of the gatherer agents (cf. Brantingham 2003).

Unsurprisingly, the average daily kilocalories per forager is quite low (mean 670) in this model. This is both because the number of foraging hours per day is low (six hours) due to the small size of the toy landscape (Wren et al. 2020) and because random movement means that agents frequently traverse cells they have already harvested. The diet also consists almost entirely of terrestrial plant resources (97.5% of diet by calories) with only a few chance occurrences of shellfish (see Figure 7.4a).

Experiment 2: Targeted Search

In the second experiment, the gatherers and the camp location specifically target the highest net caloric returns within a given search radius. This means that when gatherers choose a camp location, they calculate the tradeoff between travel time and caloric return and choose a cell in the landscape that will optimize their net caloric return (see Equation 1). Since there are only two habitat types, this will mean either a coastal or a terrestrial cell. The gatherers repeatedly make decisions about mobility and gathering as their time is incrementally used up through their foraging day. This ensures they

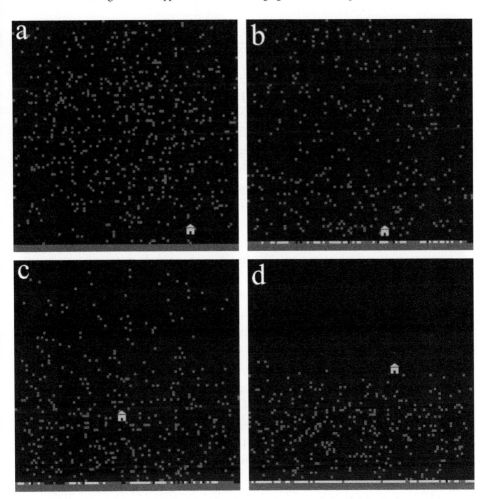

Figure 7.4. These maps illustrate the cumulative pattern of campsite occupation during single runs of each scenario: (a) random walk; (b) targeted search; (c) tidal knowledge, one day of foresight; and (d) tidal knowledge, five days of foresight. In each map, gray cells were chosen more than once, white cells were chosen many times (only along the coast), and black cells were chosen once or never. Note that the white coastal strip in all but the random walk shows that it is a frequent target for occupation. Figure by Colin Wren.

are able to keep their caloric returns high and that they will not cross cells they or other gatherers have already depleted.

The average daily kilocalories per forager is much higher in this scenario (1,090; 63% higher than the random walk baseline). The percentage of shellfish in the diet also increases (27% of gathered calories), but shellfish are only exploited when they are within the perceptual range of the gatherers (set to 2 km for this experiment). This means that there are low spring tides when the gatherers do not consume any shellfish since they are too far inland to perceive that shellfish are available (Figure 7.4b).

Experiments 3 and 4: Tidal Knowledge

To better allow gatherer agents to forage for shellfish, we simulated tidal knowledge by having agents always be able to perceive the current state of the coastal cells, even when they are far inland, where the coast is beyond their perceptual range. Agents used the same algorithm to calculate net caloric returns after travel time, but with the knowledge that shellfish would be available only for the first two hours of the day. We also programmed an option that enabled agents to anticipate the arrival of the spring tides by a specific number of days (parameter days of foresight). This enabled agents to arrive for the start of the spring tide or perhaps the day before instead of noticing that shellfish were available after the spring tide had arrived. Ideally, this enabled the gatherers to maximize their shellfish gathering time and the corresponding caloric returns by not missing the first day due to travel.

The results of these experiments show that for one day of foresight (Tidal fs1) the caloric returns decrease slightly compared to the returns in the targeted search (an average of 30 runs, 1,142 versus 1,104 daily kcal per forager) and decrease more for five days of foresight (Tidal fs 5) (1,069 daily kcal per forager). Both are much higher than the random baseline run (66% and 61% higher, respectively). The proportion of the diet from shellfish increases to its highest levels (56% of gathered calories) when agents anticipate the arrival of the spring tide by five days (Figure 7.4c and d).

If we compare the spatial distribution of camp locations among these four scenarios, we see the clear interdependence between terrestrial and coastal foraged resources (Figure 7.4a and b). In the random and targeted maps, camp locations are scattered across the landscape. However, when agents have knowledge of the tides, camps cluster more heavily along the coast (during spring tides) and in the terrestrial strip next to the coast (during non-spring tides). The cells that are farthest in the interior remain unexploited, since camps can only get so far from the coast during non-spring days before they are called back down for the next spring tide. Anticipating the spring tides by five days increases this effect, further concentrating gatherers near the coast and making a wider unexploited swath in the far interior.

Experiment 5: Hunting Search

Ethnographic descriptions of decisions about moving camp (e.g., Marlowe 2010) suggest that decisions about when to move are largely based on the availability of plants for foraging. Thus, our modeled camps moved when

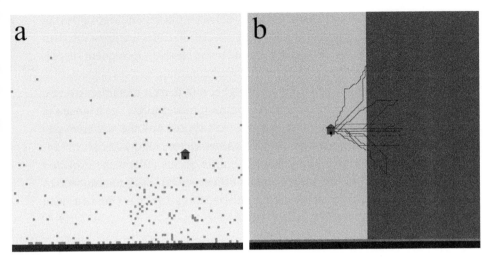

Figure 7.5. Maps on the toy landscape where the left side has a relatively low caloric return compared to the right. (*a*) The small squares show locations where agents successfully killed a prey mammal over a 10-year period of the simulation. Hunters preferentially target the right side if they are close enough to make the trip worthwhile. (*b*) Out-and-back movement patterns of hunters over a single simulated day. This illustrates the hunters moving toward the right and fanning out. Figure by Colin Wren.

their seven-day average daily return dropped below 2,000 kcal per forager and their decisions about where to move were based on optimizing gathering returns (with tidal knowledge, as in Experiment 4). Our previous analyses showed that the majority of calories come from plant foraging (Wren et al. 2020). For these reasons, our modeled hunters followed the lead of gatherers and ended their daily forays at the same camp agent location as the gatherers.

Within their day, hunters chose their own path through the landscape, searching for game. In a final experiment (Figure 7.5a and b) we illustrated how hunters targeted high-probability habitats for their day's searching (note that Figure 7.5a represents the kills for a full 10-year run, whereas Figure 7.5b shows just a single day for illustrative purposes). We split the toy landscape such that the left side has a lower average caloric return from hunting than the right side. Equation 2 calculates this as a best estimate for the hunters:

$$E = \sum_{i}^{n} \frac{s_i\, e_i}{t_i} \varepsilon_i$$

In this equation, i is each of the n number of prey species, s_i is probability of successful pursuit, e_i is the kilocalories, t_i is the pursuit time, and ε_i is the probability of encounter in each habitat type.

In Figure 7.5a, the spatial difference (between the left and right sides) of cumulative kilocalories hunted during a simulation run is less apparent than the difference in gathered kilocalories due to the relatively infrequent success of hunting on these resourcescapes. However, hunting success is greater on the right in the higher-probability habitat because there is more prey overall. In addition, hunting success is more common nearer to the coast since the hunters' days start at the camp the gatherers choose and the gatherers frequently return to the coast for shellfish gathering (see Figure 7.5d).

The daily movement pattern of the hunter agents reflects the expected pattern (Figure 7.5b). Agents followed the flower-petal search pattern seen in previous studies that tracked hunter-gatherer foraging walks (Binford 1980; Pacheco-Cobos et al. 2019; Yellen 1972).

Cape South Coast Terrestrial Coastal Foraging

Interregional Comparison

In this section, our model incorporates the resourcescapes of two small areas of the Cape South Coast region. The first is located along the coastal strip near Pinnacle Point and the second near Vleesbaai and the mouth of the Gouritz River (Oestmo et al. 2014). For both regions, habitat type locations and expected return rates from those habitats (including differences in shellfish based on tidal patterns and differences in plants based on season) were determined by experimental foraging and transect field work that has been described in previous publications (Botha et al. 2020; De Vynck, Anderson, et al. 2016; De Vynck, Cowling, et al. 2016; De Vynck, Van Wyk, et al. 2016; De Vynck et al. 2020).

The Cape South Coast region is in the Cape Floristic Region, a Mediterranean vegetation zone. It includes a significant number of well-known archaeological sites that date to the origins of modern humans. Pinnacle Point, Blombos Cave (Henshilwood et al. 2009; Jacobs et al. 2020), and Klasies River Mouth (Grine et al. 2017) are some of the key coastal sites that date to ~160,000–50,000 calendar years ago. Pinnacle Point is well known for containing the earliest evidence of humans' systematic exploitation of shellfish (Marean et al. 2007).

As part of the Paleoscape Project, we have reconstructed resourcescapes of this region representing the availability and caloric return of heterogeneous plant, mammal, and shellfish resources (Botha et al. 2020; De Vynck, Anderson, et al. 2016; De Vynck, Cowling, et al. 2016; De Vynck, Van Wyk, et al. 2016; Venter et al. 2020). In this experiment, shellfish availability varies with bimonthly and daily tidal cycles as before, and now plant resources vary seasonally as well. This resourcescape represents an interglacial preagricultural landscape with a modern sea level that is seen both in the late Later Stone Age in the Holocene and during the much older marine isotope stage 5e (~125,000 years ago), part of the Middle Stone Age (Mucina and Rutherford, 2006; Wren et al. 2020).

For this experiment, we segmented the larger study area into two subregions for comparison, each which was 20 by 30 km. The first is centered on the Gouritz River valley and has a long stretch of diverse coastal habitats running from Vleesbaai in the east almost to Stillbaai in the west (Figure 7.6a). Two patches of sand fynbos are near the coastline, but much of the landscape is dominated by limestone fynbos that has about a third of the

Table 7.1. Key foraging values for terrestrial and coastal habitats

Habitat	Caloric return (kcal/hr in summer or spring lows)	Harvestable time before depletion (hr/ha in summer or spring lows)
TERRESTRIAL		
Sand fynbos	354	1.88
Freshwater wetlands	270	1.54
Albany thicket	241	0.58
Strandveld	219	0.62
Alluvial vegetation	179	2.18
Limestone fynbos	130	1.60
Renosterveld	63	1.51
Saline vegetation	0	0.00
COASTAL		
Aeolianite reefs	2,019	1.50
Table-mountain sandstone (TMS) wave-cut platforms	1,867	1.50
TMS boulders	1,799	1.50
TMS rocky headlands	1,203	1.50
Sandy beaches	87	1.50

Note: Values cycle due to seasonality (terrestrial habitats) or bimonthly and daily tides (coastal habitats). Only summer or spring low values are included here.

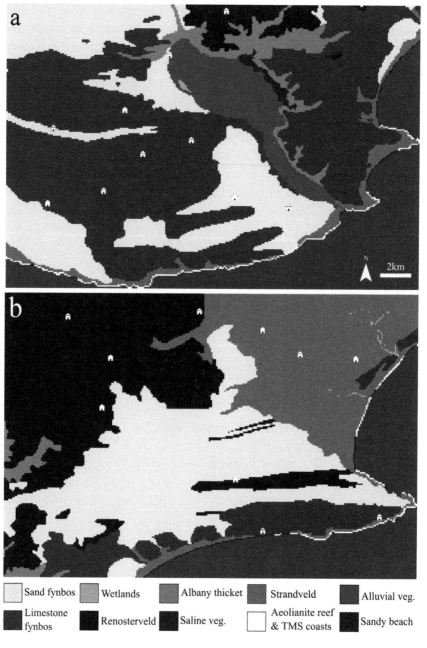

| Sand fynbos | Wetlands | Albany thicket | Strandveld | Alluvial veg. |
| Limestone fynbos | Renosterveld | Saline veg. | Aeolianite reef & TMS coasts | Sandy beach |

Figure 7.6. The two subregional resourcescapes with shades representing the caloric return rate of different habitat types (lighter shades have higher returns). Gathering plants and shellfish for (*a*) Gourtiz River valley and (*b*) Pinnacle Point. Figure by Colin Wren.

caloric return rate of sand fynbos. Intermediate-quality freshwater wetlands run up the Gouritz River valley to more patches of sand fynbos, and the western and northern sides of the valley have stands of Albany thicket. See Table 7.1 for the caloric return rates of these terrestrial habitats.

The second subregion centers on the Pinnacle Point site and contains parts of Mossel Bay to the east and Vleesbaai to the west (Figure 7.6b). A large area of sand fynbos habitat is nearly adjacent to the coastline. The renosterveld habitat, which has a lower return rate, dominates much of the far western interior, and an intermediate strandveld is next to the eastern coast and extends inland in the east. This subregion is nearly the same as the one published recently by Wren and colleagues (2020) but has been shifted southward slightly to include a greater stretch of coastline and to exclude a small patch of sand fynbos in the northeast. Hunting returns are far lower on average and much higher in variance than gathering returns.

To summarize the resource distribution of these two subregions (Figure 7.6a and b), the Gouritz landscape has smaller patches of high-return habitats near the coast and far into the interior and the river valley acts as a corridor. In the Pinnacle Point landscape, the majority of the high-return habitat is nearly adjacent to the coast and areas far in the interior have little of value.

We ran identical simulations with 30 gatherers and 30 hunters divided equally into 10 camps and with 12-hour foraging days on these two distinct resourcescapes. Assuming an equal number of juveniles and adults, this result implies a human population density of 0.2 persons per square kilometer in our model on these two landscapes. These simulations show that the average amount of shellfish included in the diet is higher in the Pinnacle Point landscape (6.0% for Pinnacle Point versus 3.3% for Gouritz) even as the average caloric intake is approximately equal (2,300 daily kcal per forager for Pinnacle Point versus 2,270 for Gouritz). This result is striking because the number of kilometers of rocky coast with shellfish returns in the Gouritz landscape is much higher than in the Pinnacle Point landscape (35.9 km versus 21.6 km measured as counts of 100-by-100-m cells). The difference appears to be due to the fact that there are more aeolianite reefs along the shores east of Pinnacle Point, leading to a higher average return rate for coastal foraging (1,618 kcal per hour for Pinnacle Point versus 1,412 kcal per hour for Gouritz).

Figure 7.7 shows that the pattern of locations camp agents chose (which are based on the algorithms described above) is fairly similar for the two landscapes. Both are clustered in the sand fynbos terrestrial habitat next to the coast or on high-valued coastal cells. Northeast of Pinnacle Point, a number of coastal cells with aeolianite reef habitat in Mossel Bay have a

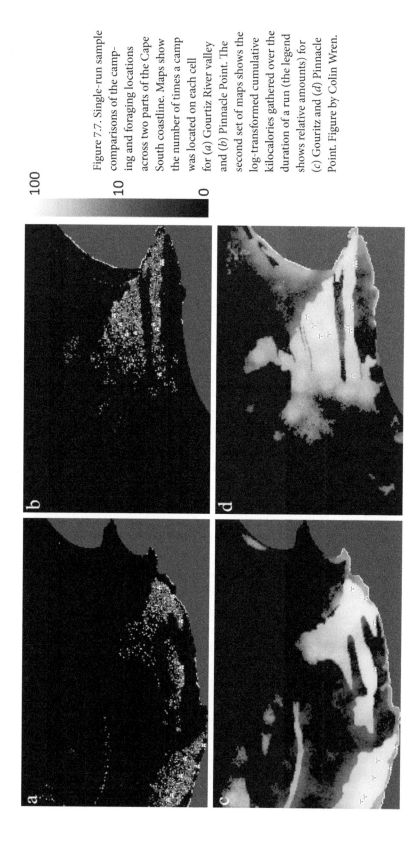

Figure 7.7. Single-run sample comparisons of the camping and foraging locations across two parts of the Cape South coastline. Maps show the number of times a camp was located on each cell for (*a*) Gourtiz River valley and (*b*) Pinnacle Point. The second set of maps shows the log-transformed cumulative kilocalories gathered over the duration of a run (the legend shows relative amounts) for (*c*) Gouritz and (*d*) Pinnacle Point. Figure by Colin Wren.

100

10

0

high frequency of camp occupations even though they are not next to high-valued terrestrial habitats. In both regions, the depletion of plant resources in the sand fynbos closest to the coast forces camps to gradually move farther inland, at least until the start of the next season, when the plant resources are replenished according to the model. Approximately 8% of the kilocalories on both landscapes comes from mammal hunting. This is consistent with our previous findings (Wren et al. 2020), but, as noted, anticipated hunting returns do not factor into camp mobility decisions.

When we compare the positions of camps to the pattern of logged total kilocalories gathered per cell there are noticeable differences (Figure 7.7). For example, while terrestrial habitats that are not optimal are rarely selected for campsites, significant foraging occurs in areas adjacent to good stretches of coastline even when their foraging returns are not high. The agents go for the shellfish, but once the tides have come back in, they gather whatever is close at hand. This includes the site of Pinnacle Point, which was not often selected as a camp location. But it was chosen for foraging at relatively high frequency, both on the rocky shores in front of the site and in the surrounding terrestrial habitats. The camps often remained in the sand fynbos habitat while foragers traveled to the coast for shellfish during spring tides. The model does not factor in the shelter that caves provide or any transport costs. When meat from shellfish has not been extracted, the shells add considerable carrying weight. That may favor a closer camp location. Extracting the meat on the coast before continued foraging would reduce daily foraging time but increase the likelihood of spoilage.

Population Density Effects

The effects of increased population density can be unintuitive. Here we compare the runs we describe above with 60 foragers to runs with 40, 80, and 100 foragers divided across the same 10 camps. The proportion of shellfish included in the diets of these 4 population sizes varies substantially (Figure 7.8).

Several trade-offs determine the degree to which a population relies on shellfish for their caloric needs. On the one hand, shellfish have higher return rates and are replenished more frequently than terrestrial plant resources. The supply of shellfish is replenished twice a month with the spring tide (De Vynck et al. 2020), while plants in coastal South Africa regrow seasonally every three months (Botha et al. 2020). However, coastal cells occupy less than 1% of each resourcescape. In addition, greater population sizes meant that the foragers moved farther inland to pursue unexploited plant resources. This made their return to the coast less worthwhile because of increased

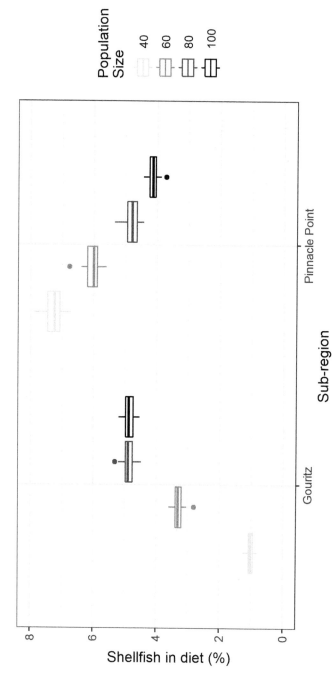

Figure 7.8. The boxplots for different population sizes show that the percentage of shellfish harvested varies depending on population density and on the study areas. The variance comes from running 30 replicate trials for each population size and landscape.

travel time. The spatial distribution of high-return terrestrial resources has a large and unpredictable effect on where a population of any given size will be when the spring tide arrives.

On the Gouritz resourcescape, as larger populations overexploited the terrestrial sand fynbos habitat across the map, they increased their reliance on shellfish by ~4% to compensate for the lack of high-return plant habitats (Figure 7.8). Near Pinnacle Point, the sand fynbos habitat is much larger and continues westward away from the coast and especially away from the highest-return aeolianite coasts. In this case, as the population increased, the distance from the coast increased as the populations harvested farther inland, so the proportion of shellfish decreased by ~3%. As population density got closer to carrying capacity, populations on both landscapes converged toward a similar value for shellfish consumption, ~4–5% of all harvested calories (Figure 7.8). Increasing the population density beyond this point would have resulted in a population that was not capable of supplying enough daily calories to the group (Wren et al. 2020).

Summary of Results

The aggregated individual choices of a population produces unexpected effects that classic optimal foraging theory models do not anticipate. Otherwise equal populations (in size, foraging strategy, mobility behavior, etc.) on different resourcescapes can have different dietary compositions even when the same resources are available in the landscape as a whole. The PaleoscapeABM simulations show that the proximity of higher-return terrestrial plant resources to the coastline can increase the proportion of shellfish in the diet and that lower-return plant resources directly adjacent to the coastline may be more common in the diet than expected. The toy landscape experiments showed that while an understanding of the tides increased the proportion of shellfish in the diet, it did not necessarily increase caloric intake. In the Cape South Coast, this suggests more foraging along coastal and nonoptimal terrestrial habitats near the site of Pinnacle Point, even when camps were located farther inland.

Conclusions

Classic optimal foraging theory models focus on minute choices rather than the long-term patterns of resource availability and regrowth or replenishment. The highest proportion of shellfish in the diet of our simulated South African foragers occurs with low population density, the ability to anticipate the tides using detailed knowledge of the tidal system, and a specific distribution of terrestrial and coastal habitats in the subregion around the Pinnacle Point site. Coastal adaptations appear relatively late in human evolution, and so far the evidence suggests that only modern humans chose a true coastal adaptation (Marean 2014). We have previously argued that the ability to use abstract knowledge of lunar phases as a way to predict tidal conditions is a requirement for a coastal adaptation and that this requires the enhanced working memory and executive function characteristic of human cognitive evolution. The hypothesis is that this cognitive ability appeared only after the origin of the modern human lineage and is unique to it (Marean 2011). While other species such as long-tailed macaques (*Macaca fascicularis*; Haslam et al. 2016; Luncz et al. 2017), Neanderthals (Cortés-Sánchez et al. 2011), and chacma baboons (*Papio ursinus*) in the Cape are known to consume shellfish (Hall 1962), even regularly, the volume and intensity of *Homo sapiens'* shellfish harvests are unique. In future work, we will adapt the model for lower sea levels to experiment with the impact on the diet when the grasslands of the Palaeo-Agulhas Plain were exposed and the coastline was farther from the current coastal sites (Marean et al. 2020). We will also add a submodel that explores the impact of foraging patterns on the distribution of lithic artifacts on the landscape (Gravel-Miguel et al. 2021).

Our agent-based modeling approach forms a conceptual bridge between the local-scale understanding of human decision-making from optimal foraging theory and the longer-term and broader-scale patterns that are more directly comparable to the archaeological record. In so doing, we highlight that the spatial and temporal variability in resources means that human foraging is a complex system with unexpected emergent effects (Downey 2018). The application of optimal foraging theory to human foraging provides a highly successful framework for understanding human decision-making in the present and in the past (Bettinger et al. 2015; Kaplan and Hill 1992; Kelly 2013; Smith 1983, 1987; Winterhalder 1981, 1986), often with unintuitive conclusions (e.g., Hawkes et al. 1982). We argue that agent-based modeling has a similar potential because it expands the logic of optimal foraging theory to a broader range of research questions. While traditional optimal foraging theory asks which resources might be included in the diet and when a forager might move on to a new patch, an agent-based model can address the sustainable population size of a given resource landscape, the overall composition of the diet, or even the response of past populations to specific climatological and ecological changes.

Intertidal foraging is known in the archaeological record as early as 162,000 years ago. Many hypotheses have been published regarding the significance of including shellfish in the human diet. Many shellfish have high protein, fat, and caloric content to support the larger and more complex brain of early *Homo sapiens*, and, at least along the South African coast, exploiting them effectively requires a detailed understanding of the tidal system. Intertidal caloric returns are negligible during non-spring low tides, which means that traveling the distance to the coast only to find the resources unavailable would be a potentially costly mistake. This is compounded by our finding that the terrestrial habitats next to the coast may become rapidly depleted of plant resources, depending on the density of a population. This makes the net benefit of trips to the coast contingent on a wide array of variables. In other words, a chance encounter of shellfish would be an easy foraging decision, but the existence of a coastal adaptation on the Cape South Coast represents a much more complex interplay of human behavior, population density, and the availability of terrestrial and intertidal resources.

Note

1. Colin Wren, "The Foraging Potential of the Holocene Cape South Coast of South Africa without the Palaeo-Agulhas Plain," CoMSES OpenABM, https://www.comses.net/codebases/2d6a597a-76af-4ee8-bf90-0ba8c531b686/releases/1.0.0/.

References Cited

Axelrod, R. 1997. Advancing the Art of Simulation in the Social Sciences. *Complexity* 3(2):16–22.

Berry, B. J. L., L. D. Kiel, and E. Elliott. 2002. Adaptive Agents, Intelligence, and Emergent Human Organization: Capturing Complexity through Agent-Based Modeling. *PNAS* 99:7187–7188.

Bettinger, R. L., R. Garvey, and S. Tushingham. 2015. *Hunter-Gatherers: Archaeological and Evolutionary Theory*. 2nd ed. Springer, Boston.

Binford, L. R. 1980. Willow Smoke and Dogs' Tails: Hunter-Gatherer Settlement Systems and Archaeological Site Formation. *American Antiquity* 45(1):4–20.

Botha, M. S., R. M. Cowling, K. J. Esler, J. C. De Vynck, N. E. Cleghorn, and A. J. Potts. 2020. Return Rates from Plant Foraging on the Cape South Coast: Understanding Early Human Economies. *Quaternary Science Reviews* 235:106129.

Brantingham, P. J. 2003. A Neutral Model of Stone Raw Material Procurement. *American Antiquity* 68(3):487–510.

Buckland, S. T., E. A. Rexstad, T. A. Marques, and C. S. Oedekoven. 2015. *Distance Sampling: Methods and Applications*. Springer International, Cham, Switzerland.

Cawthra, H. C., R. J. Anderson, J. C. De Vynck, Z. Jacobs, A. Jerardino, K. Kyriacou, and C. W. Marean. 2020. Migration of Pleistocene Shorelines across the Palaeo-Agulhas Plain:

Evidence from Dated Sub-Bottom Profiles and Archaeological Shellfish Assemblages. *Quaternary Science Reviews* 235:106107.

Cortés-Sánchez, M., A. Morales-Muñiz, M. D. Simón-Vallejo, M. C. Lozano-Francisco, J. L. Vera-Peláez, C. Finlayson, J. Rodríguez-Vidal, A. Delgado-Huertas, F. J. Jiménez-Espejo, F. Martínez-Ruiz, M. A. Martínez-Aguirre, A. J. Pascual-Granged, M. M. Bergadà-Zapata, J. F. Gibaja-Bao, J. A. Riquelme-Cantal, J. A. López-Sáez, M. Rodrigo-Gámiz, S. Sakai, S. Sugisaki, G. Finlayson, D. A. Fa, and N. F. Bicho. 2011. Earliest Known Use of Marine Resources by Neanderthals. *PLOS ONE* 6:e24026.

Cowling, R. M., A. J. Potts, J. Franklin, G. F. Midgley, F. Engelbrecht, and C. W. Marean. 2020. Describing a Drowned Pleistocene Ecosystem: Last Glacial Maximum Vegetation Reconstruction of the Palaeo-Agulhas Plain. *Quaternary Science Reviews* 235:105866.

De Vynck, J. C., R. Anderson, C. Atwater, R. M. Cowling, E. C. Fisher, C. W. Marean, R. S. Walker, and K. Hill. 2016. Return Rates from Intertidal Foraging from Blombos Cave to Pinnacle Point: Understanding Early Human Economies. *Journal of Human Evolution* 92:101–115.

De Vynck, J. C., R. M. Cowling, A. J. Potts, C. W. Marean. 2016. Seasonal Availability of Edible Underground and Aboveground Carbohydrate Resources to Human Foragers on the Cape South Coast, South Africa. *PeerJ* 4:e1679.

De Vynck, J. C., M. Difford, R. Anderson, C. W. Marean, R. M. Cowling, K. Hill. 2020. The Resilience to Human Foraging of Intertidal Resources on the South Cape Coast of South Africa and the Implications for Pre-Historic Foragers. *Quaternary Science Reviews* 235:106041.

De Vynck, J. C., B.-E. Van Wyk, and R. M. Cowling. 2016. Indigenous Edible Plant Use by Contemporary Khoe-San Descendants of South Africa's Cape South Coast. *South African Journal of Botany* 102:60–69.

Downey, A. 2018. *Think Complexity: Complexity Science and Computational Modeling.* 2nd ed. O'Reilly Media, Boston.

Esteban, I., C. W. Marean, R. M. Cowling, E. C. Fisher, D. Cabanes, and R. M. Albert. 2020. Palaeoenvironments and Plant Availability during MIS 6 to MIS 3 on the Edge of the Palaeo-Agulhas Plain (South Coast, South Africa) as Indicated by Phytolith Analysis at Pinnacle Point. *Quaternary Science Reviews* 235:105667.

Franklin, J., A. J. Potts, E. C. Fisher, R. M. Cowling, and C. W. Marean. 2015. Paleodistribution Modeling in Archaeology and Paleoanthropology. *Quaternary Science Reviews* 110:1–14.

Gravel-Miguel, C., J. Murray, B. J. Schoville, C. D. Wren, and C. W. Marean. 2021. Exploring the Variability in Lithic Armature Discard in the Archaeological Record. *Journal of Human Evolution* 155:102981.

Grine, F. E., S. Wurz, and C. W. Marean. 2017. The Middle Stone Age Human Fossil Record from Klasies River Main Site. *Journal of Human Evolution* 103:53–78.

Hall, K. R. L. 1962. Numerical Data, Maintenance Activities and Locomotion of the Wild Chacma Baboon, Papio Ursinus. *Proceedings of the Zoological Society of London* 139(2):181–220.

Haslam, M., L. Luncz, A. Pascual-Garrido, T. Falótico, S. Malaivijitnond, and M. Gumert. 2016. Archaeological Excavation of Wild Macaque Stone Tools. *Journal of Human Evolution* 96:134–138.

Hawkes, K., K. Hill, and J. F. O'Connell. 1982. Why Hunters Gather: Optimal Foraging and the Aće of Eastern Paraguay. *American Ethnologist* 9(2):379–398.

Hawkes, K., F. O'Connell, and N. G. B. Jones. 1995. Hadza Children's Foraging: Juvenile Dependency, Social Arrangements, and Mobility among Hunter-Gatherers. *Current Anthropology* 36(4):688–700.

Jacobs, Z. 2010. An OSL Chronology for the Sedimentary Deposits from Pinnacle Point Cave 13B: A Punctuated Presence. *Journal of Human Evolution* 59:289–305.

Jacobs, Z., B. G. Jones, H. C. Cawthra, C. S. Henshilwood, and R. G. Roberts. 2020. The Chronological, Sedimentary and Environmental Context for the Archaeological Deposits at Blombos Cave, South Africa. *Quaternary Science Reviews* 235:105850.

Kaplan, H., and K. Hill. 1992. Evolutionary Ecology of Food Acquisition. In *Evolutionary Ecology and Human Behavior*, edited by E. A. Smith and B. Winderhalder, pp. 167–202. Aldine, Chicago.

Kelly, R. L. 2013. *The Lifeways of Hunter-Gatherers: The Foraging Spectrum*. 2nd ed. Cambridge University Press, Cambridge.

Lake, M. W. 2000. MAGICAL Computer Simulation of Mesolithic Foraging. In *Dynamics in Human and Primate Societies: Agent-Based Modeling of Social and Spatial Processes*, edited by T. A. Kohler and G. J. Gumerman, pp. 107–143. Oxford University Press, New York.

———. 2001. The Use of Pedestrian Modelling in Archaeology, with an Example from the Study of Cultural Learning. *Environment and Planning B* 28(3):385–404.

Luncz, L. V., A. Tan, M. Haslam, L. Kulik, T. Proffitt, S. Malaivijitnond, and M. Gumert. 2017. Resource Depletion through Primate Stone Technology. *eLife* 6:e23647.

MacArthur, R. H., and E. R. Pianka. 1966. On Optimal Use of a Patchy Environment. *American Naturalist* 100(916):603–609.

Marean, Curtis W. 2010. Pinnacle Point Cave 13B (Western Cape Province, South Africa) in Context: The Cape Floral Kingdom, Shellfish, and Modern Human Origins. *Journal of Human Evolution* 59(3–4):425–443.

———. 2011. Coastal South Africa and the Coevolution of the Modern Human Lineage and the Coastal Adaptation. In *Trekking the Shore: Changing Coastlines and the Antiquity of Coastal Settlement*, edited by N. F. Bicho, J. A. Haws, and L. G. Davis, pp. 421–440. Springer, New York.

———. 2014. The Origins and Significance of Coastal Resource Use in Africa and Western Eurasia. *Journal of Human Evolution* 77:17–40.

———. 2015. An Evolutionary Anthropological Perspective on Modern Human Origins. *Annual Review of Anthropology* 44:533–556.

Marean, C. W., M. Bar-Matthews, J. Bernatchez, E. Fisher, P. Goldberg, A. I. R. Herries, Z. Jacobs, A. Jerardino, P. Karkanas, T. Minichillo, P. J. Nilssen, E. Thompson, I. Watts, and H. M. Williams. 2007. Early Human Use of Marine Resources and Pigment in South Africa during the Middle Pleistocene. *Nature* 449(7164):905–908.

Marean, C. W., R. M. Cowling, and J. Franklin. 2020. The Palaeo-Agulhas Plain: Temporal and Spatial Variation in an Extraordinary Extinct Ecosystem of the Pleistocene of the Cape Floristic Region. *Quaternary Science Reviews* 235:106161.

Marlowe, F. 2010. *The Hadza: Hunter-Gatherers of Tanzania*. University of California Press, Berkeley.

Mithen, S. J. 1990. *Thoughtful Foragers: A Study of Prehistoric Decision Making.* Cambridge University Press, Cambridge.

Mucina, L., and M. C. Rutherford (editors). 2006. *The Vegetation of South Africa, Lesoto and Swaziland, Strelitzia.* South African National Biodiversity Institute, Pretoria.

Oestmo, S., B. J. Schoville, J. Wilkins, and C. W. Marean. 2014. A Middle Stone Age Paleoscape near the Pinnacle Point Caves, Vleesbaai, South Africa. *Quaternary International* 350:147–168.

Pacheco-Cobos, L., B. Winterhalder, C. Cuatianquiz-Lima, M. F. Rosetti, R. Hudson, and C. T. Ross. 2019. Nahua Mushroom Gatherers Use Area-Restricted Search Strategies that Conform to Marginal Value Theorem Predictions. *Proceedings of the National Academy of Sciences of the United States of America* 116(21):10339–10347.

Perreault, C. 2019. *The Quality of the Archaeological Record.* University of Chicago Press, Chicago.

Pulliam, H. R. 1974. On the Theory of Optimal Diets. *American Naturalist* 108(959):59–74.

Railsback, S. F., and V. Grimm. 2011. *Agent-Based and Individual-Based Modeling: A Practical Introduction.* Princeton University Press, Princeton, New Jersey.

Smith, E. A. 1983. Anthropological Applications of Optimal Foraging Theory: A Critical Review. *Current Anthropology* 24(5):625–651.

———. 1987. Optimization Theory in Anthropology: Applications and Critiques. In *The Latest on the Best: Essays on Evolution and Optimality,* edited by J. Dupré, pp. 201–240. MIT Press, Cambridge, Massachusetts.

Stephens, D. W., and J. R. Krebs. 1986. *Foraging Theory.* Princeton University Press, Princeton, New Jersey.

Venter, J. A., C. F. Brooke, C. W. Marean, H. Fritz, and C. W. Helm. 2020. Large Mammals of the Palaeo-Agulhas Plain Showed Resilience to Extreme Climate Change but Vulnerability to Modern Human Impacts. *Quaternary Science Reviews* 235:106050.

Winterhalder, B. 1981. Optimal Foraging Strategies and Hunter-Gatherer Research in Anthropology: Theory and Methods. In *Hunter-Gatherer Foraging Strategies: Ethnographic and Archaeological Analyses,* edited by B. Winterhalder and E. A. Smith, pp. 13–35. University of Chicago Press, Chicago.

———. 1986. Optimal Foraging: Simulation Studies of Diet Choice in a Stochastic Environment. *Journal of Ethnobiology* 6(1):205–223.

Wren, C. D., C. Atwater, K. Hill, M. A. Janssen, J. C. De Vynck, and C. W. Marean. 2018. An Agent-Based Approach to Weighted Decision Making in the Spatially and Temporally Variable South African Paleoscape. In *Oceans of Data: Proceedings of the 44th Computer Applications and Quantitative Methods in Archaeology Conference,* edited by Mieko Matsumoto and Espen Uleberg, pp. 507–522. Archaeopress, Oxford.

Wren, C. D., S. Botha, J. C. De Vynck, M. A. Janssen, K. Hill, E. Shook, J. Harris, B. M. Wood, J. Venter, J. Franklin, R. M. Cowling, A. J. Potts, E. C. Fisher, and C. W. Marean. 2020. The Foraging Potential of the Holocene Cape South Coast of South Africa without the Palaeo-Agulhas Plain. *Quaternary Science Reviews* 235:105789.

Yellen, J. E. 1972. Trip V Itinerary, May 24–June 9, 1968. In *Exploring Human Nature,* pp. 1–17. Educational Development Center, Cambridge, Massachusetts.

8

Evaluating Mid- to Late Holocene Economic Intensification through Analysis of a Mollusk Assemblage on the Tropical North Australian Coast

MARTIN WRIGHT, PATRICK FAULKNER,
AND MICHAEL WESTAWAY

This chapter presents a method for identifying population pressure based on the analysis of zooarchaeological assemblages and site occupation data. Estimating the size and distribution of past populations using archaeological data is problematic for archaeologists because of the incomplete nature of archaeological assemblages and the complex interactions between landscape, climate, and environmental change. A number of methods have been presented in recent years using site- or regional-based approaches. At the site level, deposition and accumulation rates and indices of small to large prey have been used as proxies for population density (Jerardino 2010; Stiner et al. 2000). At the regional level, the summed probabilities of radiocarbon dates have been used as proxies for population change (Tallavaara et al. 2010; Torfing 2015; Williams 2013). Complex assessments of climate and ethnographic data have also been used to estimate past population sizes (Bocquet-Appel et al. 2005). Instead of quantifying population size or density, in this chapter we present a model derived from optimal foraging theory and Boserupian economic intensification to identify signals that are indicative of population pressure.

Population change is one of a number of drivers used to explain variation in the intensity and timing of Holocene occupation in Australia's Great Barrier Reef region (Attenbrow 2004:13; Hiscock 2008:184–186; Lourandos 1997:21–23; Lourandos and Ross 1994). The evidence for Great Barrier Reef coastal occupation suggests sparse and sporadic early Holocene occupation, followed by increased establishment of sites and increased intensity of site use in later periods. Very few sites have been found that date to before 4000 cal BP; the oldest, from the Whitsunday Islands, dates to 9000 cal BP

(Barker 1991). Two pulses of site establishment within the Great Barrier Reef have been noted; the first dates from 3500 BP to 2400 BP and the second from 1000 BP onward (Ulm 2011:450). Explanation for these patterns include changes in population size and structure (Beaton 1985), climate and environmental change (Rowland et al. 2015), and changes in social complexity and exchange systems (Barker 2004). These explanations have been partisan; researchers have argued for one explanation to the exclusion of all others (Hiscock 2008:162). It is more parsimonious to suggest that there is a complex interaction between climate, environment, culture, and demography and that at best we can identify the primary driver at any given time and place. Our approach focuses on arguments that relate to population and climate or environmental change. We do not attempt to discount the effect of social or cultural change on foraging behavior; instead, we seek only to identify where population, climate, or environmental explanations provide a good fit with the available evidence.

This chapter outlines a model for identifying the presence of Boserupian economic intensification and applies that model to shell midden material from the Yindayin rock shelter. While the role of mollusks has been minimized in the past, there is now greater recognition of their importance to human development and to our understanding of coastal colonization (Braje and Erlandson 2009:270; O'Connell and Allen 2012). Because mollusks are often static and predictable resources, they are regularly a staple in coastal diets. Thus, changes in mollusk consumption may be indicative of changes in the broader dietary structure (Erlandson 1988; Whitaker 2008:1115). Work from South Africa (Jerardino 2010) and California (Braje and Erlandson 2009; Braje et al. 2012) has demonstrated how data from shell middens can be used to identify settlement and subsistence patterns and to understand the drivers behind foraging behavior. Despite this, some caution should be used when focusing on mollusks, as variation in foraging patterns can be the result of unseen changes in other areas of the economy. Importantly, the model presented in this chapter is not limited to mollusks and can be applied across broader zooarchaeological assemblages.

Economic Intensification Model

In this study, economic intensification refers to an increase in total economic production with an accompanying decrease in productivity per unit of input. This interpretation is based on the work of Boserup (2003) and assumes that population growth causes increased demand for subsistence. If other factors remain stable (e.g., distribution and density of resources, environment, and climate), this pattern of increased abundance and decreased efficiency provides a method of testing for population-driven resource pressure. Some authors conflate economic intensification with any change that results in the increased use of a resource (Arnold et al. 2004:15; Morgan 2015:165). These observations describe an increase in resource production but not necessarily an increase in foraging effort (Arnold et al. 2004:15). We argue that it is necessary to identify increasing production in conjunction with decreasing productivity in order to detect population-driven resource pressure.

Changes in relative economic production can be measured through the assessment of site occupation and deposition and the quantification of food resources over time. Measuring productivity requires an assessment of foraging efficiency over time. Optimal foraging theory suggests that when demand for high-ranked prey outstrips supply, lower-ranked prey or patches will be exploited (Kelly 2013:50). This is detectable in the archaeological record as a pattern of increasing specialization followed by periods of diversification (Butler and Campbell 2004; Munro and Atici 2009; Thakar 2011). Combining ecological measures of richness and diversity with an assessment of patch and prey choices provides a method for assessing these changes.

The criteria we used to test for the presence of economic intensification are outlined in Table 8.1. Changes in economic production and productivity can also be the result of drivers related to environment and climate. When the economic intensification criteria are met during a period when the effects of changing climate and environment are negligible, that may be a signal that population is driving pressure on resources.

Table 8.1. Economic intensification criteria and measures

Criterion	Criterion	Measure
Economic Intensification Criterion 1	Evidence of increased intensity of site occupation and deposition of cultural material (site occupation).	Accumulation and deposition rates
Economic Intensification Criterion 2	Evidence of increased quantities of subsistence material being deposited (deposition).	Accumulation and deposition rates
Economic Intensification Criterion 3	Evidence of increased diversity in both taxa and patches being exploited (diversity).	Ecological measures of richness and diversity
Economic Intensification Criterion 4	Evidence for a decline in foraging efficiency (foraging efficiency).	Prey or patch ranking

Excavation and Analytical Methods at Yindayin Rock Shelter

The Yindayin rock shelter (formerly known as Endaen) is situated in the northwest of Stanley Island in Princess Charlotte Bay, North Queensland (Figure 8.1). The rock shelter is a long, wide overhang of sandstone facing north; several large boulders enclose the front of the shelter. Intertidal habitats are located within a kilometer radius of the site: mangroves to the north, reef flats to the north and northwest, and a long white sandy beach to the northwest.

Despite Beaton's (1985) previous excavation in 1979–80, very little has been published about this midden deposit. In the research discussed here, the data have been derived from a 1-by-1-m excavation undertaken in August 2016. The excavation was conducted in arbitrary spits to an approximate depth of 1 m, after which a probe to 1.5 m revealed limited anthropogenic material. Anthropogenic shell was obtained from the first 12 spits. All excavated sediment was weighed and sieved through nested 3 mm and 6 mm mesh; the sieved portions were retained for analysis.

The midden material data was collected and calculated as follows. Standard zooarchaeological techniques were used to identify taxa to the lowest possible taxonomic level based on visible diagnostic elements. Identifications were made with reference to published literature such as Eichhorst (2016) and Wilson and colleagues (1993) and the University of Sydney molluscan reference collection.

Minimum number of individuals (MNI) was calculated using the procedures laid out by Harris and colleagues (2015). The number of identified specimens (NISP) and weight were also used to quantify the relative frequencies of taxa. Volume correction for NISP and MNI (by cubic centimeters) was applied to adjust for changes in spit volume following Bailey and Craighead (2003) and Faulkner and colleagues (2018). The data have been presented as grams per liter for easier interpretation of the data.

We assessed the changing dominance and evenness of taxa using number of taxa identified (NTAXA), Simpson's Diversity Index (Simpson 1-D), and the Shannon-Wiener Diversity Index (Shannon-Wiener [H']). We used the PAST (PAleontological STatistics) version 3.15 analysis package to calculate results (Hammer et al. 2001). We selected these indices because they provide statistically representative results and are simple to calculate and interpret (Hammer et al. 2006; Magurran 1988:80).

We identified patches according to the preferences of taxa for different coastal zones and substrate composition as specified in published literature (e.g., Eichhorst 2016). The identified patches are mangroves, intertidal sand/mud, hard substrates in supralittoral and intertidal zones, and reef flats.

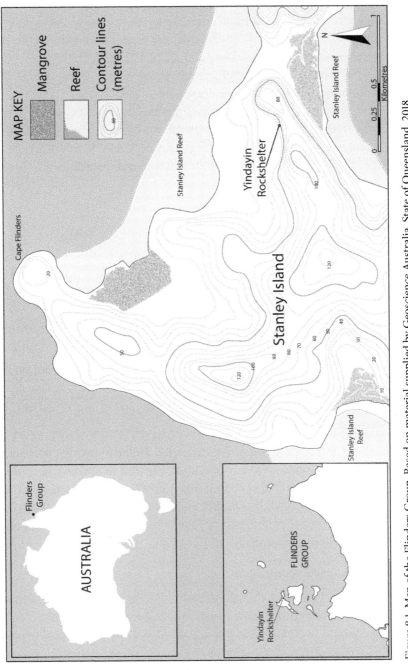

Figure 8.1. Map of the Flinders Group. Based on material supplied by Geoscience Australia, State of Queensland, 2018.

Accumulation rates were calculated by correlating the depth of material recovered with the age of dated materials. Deposition rates were calculated as the quantity of material deposited relative to the volume of the analytical unit. Radiocarbon dating was conducted by the Australian National University (ANU) Radiocarbon Laboratory and calibrated using OxCal 4.4 (build 132) and the Marine20 radiocarbon age calibration curve using a ΔR of 12±10 (Bronk Ramsey 2009; Heaton et al. 2020; Ulm 2006).

Where possible, climatic and environmental data specific to the Great Barrier Reef region or Princess Charlotte Bay has been sourced. The collated data includes sea-level variations, effective precipitation, temperature, fluctuations in the El Niño Southern Oscillation, and reef formation.

Results

Radiocarbon Dating

The 95.4% confidence interval calibrated radiocarbon dates (Table 8.2) reveal three distinct chronological phases:

Phase I: a single date in the period 5930–6255 cal BP (Spit 11). Dating for Spit 12 was not possible due to a lack of viable samples.

Phase II: seven dates, the oldest of which is in the period 2945–2670 cal BP (Spit 10) and the most recent of which is in the period 2070–1745 cal BP (Spit 4).

Phase III: two dates between 120 and 0 cal BP (Spits 1 and 2) and one between 155 and 0 cal BP (Spit 3).

The number and consistency of the calibrated radiocarbon ages provide a relatively robust sequence for the deposit. The inversion of the radiocarbon age obtained for Spit 6 (2055–1735 cal BP) is possibly the result of a pit that cuts through Spits 4 (2070–1745 cal BP) and 5 (2305–1985 cal BP), but any effect on the sequence is minimal as the calibrated ages fall within the broadly defined upper limit of this phase.

Accumulation and Deposition Rates

Accumulation rates and the age-depth plot (Figure 8.2) illustrate the grouping of spits into the three phases highlighted above. Accumulation rates between Spits 3 (155–0 cal BP) and 4 (2070–1745 cal BP) and Spits 10 (2945–2670 cal BP) and 11 (6255–5930 cal BP) are indicative of a potential hiatus in occupation. Declining accumulation rates are also recorded between Spits 4 and 5 and again between Spits 8 (2490–2145 cal BP) and

Table 8.2. Radiocarbon dates and 95.4% confidence calibrated ages for Spits 1–12 from Yindayin rock shelter midden

Phase	Spit	Depth (cm)	Lab code	Sample type	^{14}C age ± error	95.4% confidence calibrated range
III	1	0–5	ANU-55227	Shell: *Conomurex luhuanus*	475 ± 25	120–0 BP
	2	6–10	ANU-55230	Shell: *C. luhuanus*	456 ± 26	120–0 BP
	3	11–15	ANU-55229	Shell: *C. luhuanus*	549 ± 26	155–0 BP
II	4	16–20	ANU-55231	Shell: *C. luhuanus*	2455 ± 28	2070–1745 BP
	5	21–25	ANU-55232	Shell: *C. luhuanus*	2636 ± 29	2305–1985 BP
	6	26–30	ANU-55318	Shell: *C. luhuanus*	2446 ± 28	2055–1735 BP
	7	31–35	ANU-55319	Shell: *C. luhuanus*	2705 ± 28	2355–2055 BP
	8	36–40	ANU-55320	Shell: *C. luhuanus*	2783 ± 28	2490–2145 BP
	9	41–50	ANU-55321	Shell: *C. luhuanus*	3076 ± 26	2830–2520 BP
	10	51–60	ANU-55323	Shell: *C. luhuanus*	3167 ± 27	2945–2670 BP
I	11	61–70	ANU-55324	Shell: *Pinctada* sp.	5881 ± 31	6255–5930 BP
	12	70–80	n/a		n/a	n/a

Note: ANU-55227 (Spit 1), ANU-55230 (Spit 2), and ANU-55229 (Spit 3) may be out of range for this calibration curve.

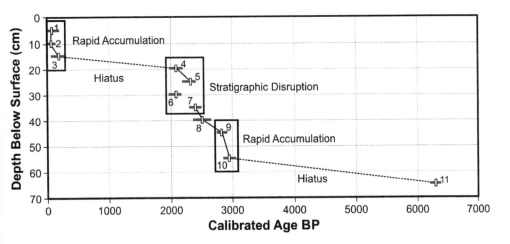

Figure 8.2. Age-depth plot and interpretation. Calibrated radiocarbon ages (BP) are indicated per spit (gray bars = 95.4% confidence interval; boxes = median calibrated age). Figure by the authors.

9 (2830–2520 cal BP). Peak periods of accumulation occur between Spits 9 (2830–2520 cal BP) and 10 (2945–2670 cal BP) and across Spits 1 (120–0 cal BP) to 3 (155–0 cal BP).

Table 8.3 displays volume-corrected (grams per liter) weights for each spit by excavated component. Shell (67.3%) and stone (29.15%) dominate the deposit, and charcoal, bone, coral, pumice, and organic material contribute minor amounts. Apart from stone, the data shows trends for increasing accumulation and deposition across the assemblage. The quantity of material for Spits 1–3 (Phase III) is the most notable; Spit 1 (120–0 cal BP) contained the highest concentration of all components except stone.

Molluscan Quantification Data

Measures of MNI, NISP, and weight provide slightly differing perspectives on the composition of the Yindayin midden. Summary data for raw and volume-corrected measures are displayed in Table 8.4 and a comparison of the volume-corrected NISP and MNI is shown in Figure 8.3.

The direction of patterns in volume-corrected MNI and NISP is broadly consistent, although there is some variation in amplitude. Table 8.5 displays volume-corrected MNI by patch type and spit. Low values for volume-corrected MNI and NISP in Spits 11 (6255–5930 cal BP) and 12 suggest limited activity in Phase I. A significant peak in volume-corrected MNI in Spit 10

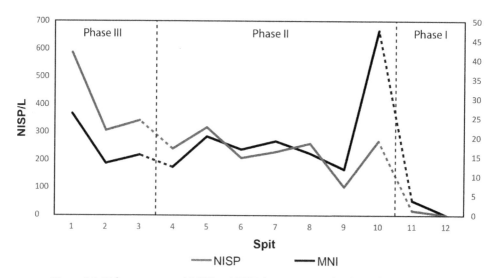

Figure 8.3. Volume-corrected MNI and NISP by spit. Figure by the authors.

Table 8.3. Volume-corrected weights (in grams/liter) for all material recovered from 5 mm mesh

Phase	Spit	Depth (cm)	Bone	Organic	Coral and pumice	Stone	Charcoal	Shell	Spit totals
III (0–155 cal BP)	1	0–5	6.00	2.90	1.70	71.50	21.50	417.40	522.20
	2	6–10	3.40	0.90	0.50	30.70	14.30	274.90	326.70
	3	11–15	2.10	0.50	0.50	42.10	12.60	298.80	359.60
II (1745–2945 cal BP)	4	16–20	1.40	0.07	0.30	52.70	11.40	213.10	300.97
	5	21–25	3.20	0.20	0.70	96.40	17.80	262.70	386.00
	6	26–30	2.10	0.03	1.10	115.30	5.20	136.20	265.93
	7	31–35	2.00	0.02	0.50	85.80	1.50	143.90	240.72
	8	36–40	0.90	0.02	0.40	89.00	1.10	188.90	288.32
	9	41–50	0.70	0.01	0.40	25.10	1.70	104.00	140.91
	10	51–60	3.40	0.01	0.40	160.40	1.00	188.80	364.01
I (5930–6255 cal BP)	11	61–70	0.90	—	0.04	229.90	0.10	28.20	270.14
	12	70–80	2.90	—	—	127.40	0.01	1.00	143.31
	Totals		29.00	4.66	6.54	1,126.30	88.20	2,275.90	3,608.61

Table 8.4. Summary of raw and volume-corrected quantification data for identified shell by spit

Spit	Phase III (5930–6255 cal BP)					Phase II (1745–2945 cal BP)					Phase I (0–155 cal BP)		Total
	1	2	3	4	5	6	7	8	9	10	11	12	
MNI	1,310	670	784	621	1012	847	959	802	1,186	4,761	150	5	13,107
NISP	29,421	15,324	17,109	12,026	15,864	10,332	11,484	12,969	10,288	26,745	743	39	162,344
Grams	20,385	13,386	14,595	10,408	12,560	6375	6745	9,028	10,068	17,837	440	18	121,845
MNI/liter	26.2	13.4	15.7	12.4	20.2	16.9	19.2	16	11.9	47.6	7.5	0.3	—
NISP/liter	588.4	306.5	342.2	240.5	317.3	206.6	229.7	259.4	102.9	267.5	37.2	2	—
Grams/liter	407.7	267.7	291.9	208.2	251.2	127.5	134.9	180.6	100.7	178.4	22	0.9	—

(2945–2670 cal BP) is driven by large quantities of the small-bodied *Nerita* spp. This peak in volume-corrected MNI is substantial and indicative of mass harvesting. However, due to low fragmentation rates, this peak is less prominent in the NISP data (Figure 8.3). In Spit 9 (2830–2520 cal BP), a steep decline in volume-corrected MNI and NISP correlates with similar observations of accumulation and deposition rates for other materials (Table 8.3). After Spit 9 (2830–2520 cal BP), volume-corrected MNI and NISP are relatively stable; the trend for NISP increases slightly and the trend for MNI is flat. The exception is a substantial increase in both MNI and NISP for Spit 1.

Neritidae and Potamididae dominate the MNI and NISP count (Table 8.5). Neritidae account for approximately 50% of all MNI, and Potamididae contribute just over 18%. Conversely, Potamididae contribute 58.4% of NISP while Neritidae contribute 13%. For volume-corrected MNI, Neritidae dominate earlier spits (5–12) and Potamididae dominate later spits (1–4). For volume-corrected NISP, this change in dominance occurs from Spit 9 (2830–2520 cal BP): Neritidae dominate Spits 10–12. Potamididae dominate the NISP count because of their larger size and increased potential for fragmentation. Because NISP trends are linked to increasing Potamididae deposition and postdepositional fragmentation, MNI is more likely to be representative of the real abundances at Yindayin. Contributions by other common taxa are highest in Spit 10 (2945–2670 cal BP) and mostly decline over time (Table 8.5).

The quantification measures for mollusks provide data for assessing Economic Intensification Criterion 1 (site intensity) and Economic Intensification Criterion 2 (deposition). Volume-corrected MNI does not display the increasing trend seen in site occupation data. This metric does not display the same intensity noted in the NISP, weight, and deposition rates for Phase III (Figure 8.2 and Table 8.3). The MNI data for Spit 10 (2945–2670 cal BP) is important because of the dominance of Neritidae and significant numbers of other small taxa found in hard substrate intertidal areas (Table 8.5a). This is meaningful for Economic Intensification Criterion 3 (diversity) and Economic Intensification Criterion 4 (foraging efficiency).

Diversity Indices

Table 8.6 displays the NTAXA and the Simpson 1-*D* and Shannon-Wiener (*H*′) diversity indices. We have used NISP for NTAXA and MNI for the Simpson 1-*D* and Shannon-Wiener (*H*′) indices.

The indices in Table 8.6 suggest stability and moderate diversity across the sequence. This stability reflects the dominance of a core group of taxa

Table 8.5. MNI/liter by patch type and spit

Family	Taxa	Phase III (0–155 cal BP)				Phase II (1745–2945 cal BP)						Phase I (5930–6255 cal BP)		Total
		1	2	3	4	5	6	7	8	9	10	11	12	
A. SUPRALITTORAL AND INTERTIDAL HARD														
Neritidae	*Nerita undata*	1.70	2.10	2.50	2.30	4.20	3.80	4.90	3.00	2.40	14.20	1.50	0.00	42.60
Neritidae	*Nerita* spp.	2.60	1.30	1.20	1.40	3.10	3.00	3.60	3.10	2.40	10.40	1.40	0.10	33.60
Neritidae	*Nerita polita*	0.90	0.40	0.50	0.20	0.60	1.40	1.20	1.1	0.90	5.00	0.40	0.10	12.70
Neritidae	*Nerita costata*	0.90	0.40	0.60	0.30	0.40	0.10	0.04	0.02	0.01	0.01	0.00	0.00	2.78
Neritidae	*Nerita albicilla*	0.00	0.04	0.00	0.00	0.04	0.04	0.02	0.04	0.01	0.10	0.10	0.00	0.39
-	*Polyplacophora* sp.	1.90	0.80	0.80	0.90	0.70	0.40	0.50	0.90	0.50	1.80	0.50	0.00	9.70
Turbinidae	*Lunella cinerea*	0.30	0.10	0.10	0.20	0.50	1.10	1.60	1.40	0.80	2.70	0.50	0.00	9.30
Trochidae	*Monodonta labio*	0.50	0.40	0.60	0.20	0.50	0.40	0.80	0.70	0.70	2.90	1.10	0.00	8.80
Ostreidae	*Saccostrea cucullata*	0.04	0.04	0.10	0.10	0.30	0.04	0.10	0.02	0.10	0.50	0.80	0.00	2.14
	Other taxa	0.10	0.02	0.20	0.04	0.10	0.20	0.10	0.10	0.10	0.10	0.00	0.00	1.06
TOTAL		8.94	5.60	6.60	5.64	10.44	10.48	12.86	10.38	7.92	37.71	6.30	0.2	123.07
B. MANGROVE														
Potamididae	*Terebralia* spp.	6.00	2.90	3.80	2.60	3.00	1.00	0.60	1.20	0.60	0.40	0.00	0.10	22.20
Potamididae	*Terebralia palustris*	1.80	1.80	2.50	1.80	2.60	0.20	0.10	0.60	0.70	0.70	0.10	0.00	12.90
Potamididae	Potamididae spp.	1.90	1.00	1.20	0.90	1.00	0.50	0.20	0.10	0.10	0.00	0.00	0.00	6.90
Potamididae	*Telescopium telescopium*	0.40	0.20	0.20	0.10	0.10	0.30	0.30	0.10	0.04	0.20	0.10	0.00	2.04
Potamididae	*Terebralia sulcata*	0.04	0.02	0.00	0.10	0.10	0.20	0.10	0.10	0.03	0.10	0.10	0.00	0.89

Neritidae	Nerita planospira	0.5	0.1	0.10	0.20	0.60	0.20	0.10	0.20	0.50	2.10	0.30	0.10	5.00
	Other taxa	0.02	0.00	0.02	0.00	0.00	0.04	0.10	0.10	0.01	0.01	0.00	0.00	0.30
Total		10.66	8.0	7.82	5.70	7.40	2.44	1.50	2.40	1.98	3.51	0.60	0.20	52.21
C. INTERTIDAL SAND														
Mesodesmatidae	Atactodea striata	5.5	1.3	0.6	0.2	0.1	0.1	0.1	0.3	0.4	1.8	0.1	0.0	10.5
Psammobiidae	Asaphis violascens	0.2	0.1	0.1	0.1	0.7	1.1	1.7	0.8	0.2	1.4	0.5	0.0	6.9
Veneridae	Gafrarium pectinatum	0.02	0.0	0.02	0.1	0.1	0.2	0.3	0.3	0.5	0.8	0.2	0.0	2.54
	Other taxa	0.2	0.04	0.1	0.1	0.3	0.2	0.2	0.1	0.1	0.3	0.1	0.0	1.74
Total		5.9	1.4	0.8	0.5	1.2	1.6	2.3	1.5	1.2	4.4	0.9	0.0	21.68
D. REEF FLAT														
Margaritidae	Pinctada sp.	0.02	0.0	0.1	0.1	0.5	1.7	1.7	0.9	0.3	0.9	0.1	0.0	6.32
Strombidae	Conomurex luhuanus	0.2	0.1	0.1	0.1	0.2	0.4	0.2	0.5	0.4	0.9	0.0	0.0	3.10
Strombidae	Lambis lambis	0.2	0.1	0.1	0.2	0.2	0.3	0.5	0.2	0.1	0.2	0.1	0.0	2.20
Trochidae	Tectus niloticus	0.3	0.2	0.02	0.1	0.04	0.0	0.0	0.0	0.0	0.01	0.1	0.0	0.77
Echinoidea		0.0	0.1	0.04	0.04	0.1	0.0	0.02	0.0	0.0	0.0	0.0	0.0	0.30
Cardiidae	Tridacna crocea	0.0	0.04	0.1	0.0	0.0	0.02	0.02	0.02	0.02	0.02	0.0	0.0	0.24
Cardiidae	Tridacna spp.	0.04	0.02	0.0	0.1	0.0	0.0	0.0	0.0	0.01	0.0	0.0	0.0	0.17
	Other taxa	0.04	0.04	0.0	0.02	0.02	0.02	0.1	0.1	0.0	0.1	0.0	0.0	0.44
Total		0.80	0.60	0.46	0.66	1.06	2.44	2.54	1.72	0.83	2.13	0.03	0.0	13.54
ALL PATCHES														
Total		26.32	15.64	15.70	12.50	20.10	16.96	19.20	16.00	11.93	47.65	8.10	0.4	210.5

Table 8.6. Diversity indices: family level or higher

Spit	Phase III (0–155 cal BP)				Phase II (1745–2945 cal BP)						Phase I (5930–6255 cal BP)	
	1	2	3	4	5	6	7	8	9	10	11	12
Number of taxa	27	20	24	21	28	27	27	27	25	36	16	9
Simpson 1-D	0.74	0.69	0.65	0.68	0.68	0.71	0.70	0.75	0.70	0.54	0.73	0.32
Shannon H'	1.60	1.52	1.47	1.54	1.58	1.78	1.78	1.90	1.76	1.42	1.77	0.50

(Neritidae and Potamididae), albeit in changing proportions (Table 8.5). The Simpson 1-D index indicates that after an initial reduction in diversity in Spits 10 (2945–2670 cal BP) and 12, there is moderate diversity across the rest of the sequence. The Shannon H' index displays a similar trend within a lower diversity range. Similarly, NTAXA (richness) is mostly stable following a peak in Spit 10 (2945–2670 cal BP). Data for Spit 10 (2945–2670 cal BP) indicates a broadening of diet (richness) but also a narrowing of focus onto a smaller group of taxa (1-D and H'). In Spit 10 (2945–2670 cal BP), foragers were consuming a wide range of taxa but were also harvesting Neritidae in greater numbers (which suppressed 1-D and H'). While a broadening diet implies decreasing foraging efficiency, the dominance of a small group of taxa suggests a narrowing of foraging preference. Diversity and richness increased during Phase III and peak in Spit 1 (155–0 cal BP). During this same period, the contribution of lower-ranked patches increased (discussed later). This increase in diversity accompanied by a decrease in productivity may represent a period of economic intensification for Spit 1 (155–0 cal BP).

Patch Preferences

We have based our definition of patches on zonation and the substrate preferences of the Yindayin taxa. Habitat preferences for taxa have been identified and aggregated to create five patches plus a miscellaneous category. Table 8.7 lists the patches, common taxa, and patch characteristics.

We have used a simplified system for ranking patches that assumes that processing costs are similar across taxa and that accessibility and visibility within a patch was constant over time. According to the marginal value theorem, if movement costs are not prohibitive, foragers will move out of a patch when the net return rate decreases below the average return rates for all other patches (Kelly 2013; Nagaoka 2002). Return rates are determined by the interaction of resource productivity and the search and handling times for those resources. Relative to other patches, high-ranking patches will contain prey that is abundant (high productivity), visible and easily accessed (low search time), and easily processed (low handling time). If we assume that visibility, access, and processing times are constant within a patch, the main variable becomes productivity. Productivity has been assessed by identifying the size and abundance (MNI) of the dominant taxa within each patch.

During Phases I and II, the supralittoral and intertidal hard patch was ranked the highest because of the high number of taxa taken from it, likely because ranked prey was highly visible and accessible (Figure 8.4). This patch is dominated by the small-bodied, motile *Nerita* (Table 8.5a) species, particularly *Nerita undata* and *Nerita polita*. While *N. undata* has an approximate

Table 8.7. Substrate types, inundation levels, foraging methods, and prevalent taxa in patches

Patch	Patch description	Substrate	Inundation	Foraging method	Prevalent taxa
Supralittoral and intertidal hard	Hard substrate in the splash zone (above the spring high-tide line) and intertidal	Rock	Very low to low	Surface collection	*Nerita* spp., *Lunella cinerea*, *Monodonta labio*, Polyplacophora
Mangrove	Mangrove forest split between three zones: landward (closest to shore), seaward (closest to the sea), and a middle zone between the landward and seaward zones	Mangrove roots, mud	Low to high	Surface collection	*Terebralia* spp., *Telescopium telescopium*, *Nerita planospira*, *Geloina coaxans*
Intertidal sand/mud	Soft or firm sand or mud substrates in the intertidal	Sand, mud	Low	Digging	*Asaphis violascens*, *Atactodea striata*, *Gafrarium pectinatum*
Reef flat	Horizontal section of the fringing reef that grows directly from the shoreline	Seagrass, coral sands, sand flats, pavement	Moderate to high	Surface collection, wading, diving	*Pinctada* sp., *Conomurex luhuanus*, *Lambis lambis*, *Tectus niloticus*, *Tridacna* spp.
Terrestrial	Nonaquatic areas	Varied	N/A	Surface collection	Camaenidae spp., *Sigmurethra*
Varied	—	—	—	—	May be used for patches where taxonomic identification is to genus/family level and subcategories of taxa occupy multiple patches

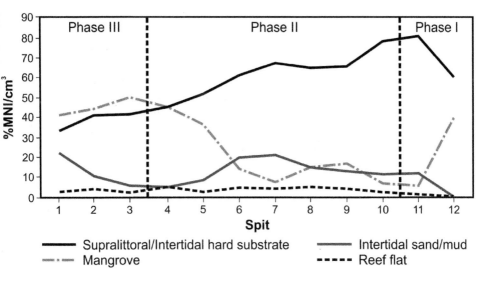

Figure 8.4. Aggregated patch preference: percentage of volume-corrected MNI for the four dominant patches. Figure by the authors.

meat weight of only 1–2 g (Barker 2004:88; Bird and Bliege 1997), their high abundance offsets their small size. The motility of *Nerita* spp. enables them to adapt to changing sea levels and this, coupled with rapid maturation rates, provides it with protection from overexploitation and changing environmental conditions (Codding et al. 2014; Giovas et al. 2013).

By the end of Phase II, the level of foraging in the mangrove patch meant that the supralittoral and intertidal hard patch was no longer ranked highest. The dominance of the mangrove patch continued throughout Phase III (Figure 8.4). This change in patch preference does not signify economic intensification in the Boserupian sense. Because the difference in search and handling costs for hard substrates and mangroves is not substantial, the change in dominance shown in the data represents a change in productivity. The size and fecundity of mangrove taxa would have made mangroves increasingly attractive as they became established across the island. Most mangrove taxa in the assemblage were *Terebralia* spp. and *Terebralia palustris* (Table 8.5b). *T. palustris* can accumulate in great numbers with adults occupying the landward section or the midtidal flat of mangroves (Houbrick 1991:310; Willan 2013:74). *Terebralia* spp. grow up to 190 mm in length (Willan 2013:74). In one estimate, the average meat weight for *T. palustris* is 4.5 g (Smith 2013:170). *T. palustris* is resilient; it is able to withstand substantial desiccation and lack of sustenance for long periods (Soemodihardjo and

Kastoro 2008). Its resilience and large relative size may explain the growth of mangrove use during Phase II, when the volatility of environmental conditions increased (see "Environment and Climate Data").

The reduced visibility and increased effort required to dig prey out of the substrate relegated the intertidal sand/mud patch to third in the rankings. *Atactodea striata*, *Asaphis violascens*, and *Gafrarium pectinatum* (Table 8.5c) are the main species in the assemblage and occupy different depths within sandy substrates. *A. violascens* has a meat weight of approximately 9 g, while *A. striata* and *G. pectinatum* can average around 1 g (Bird and Bliege Bird 1997; Thomas 2001). Notably, high numbers of the shallow-burrowing *Atactodea striata* appear after Spit 3 (Table 8.5), suggesting an increase in the exploitation of the lower-ranked intertidal sand/mud patch.

We have ranked the reef flat patch lower than the intertidal sand/mud patch because of lower accessibility, lower visibility, and a low MNI count across all three phases of occupation. Reef flat taxa are dominated by *Pinctada* sp., *Conomurex luhuanus*, and *Lambis lambis* (Table 8.5d). Reef flat taxa can be substantially larger than taxa from other patches. The meat weight of specimens of *Hippopus hippopus* from the Torres Strait ranges from 50 g to 8.2 kg, while the meat weight of *Tridacna* spp. ranges from 45 g to 8.5 kg. The range for *Lambis lambis* is from 25 g to over 3 kg (Bird and Bliege Bird 1997). Despite the size of the taxa in this patch, MNI data suggests that it was low in importance to Yindayin's foragers. This may have been due to low productivity in the patch because of the low growth rate and low fecundity of these long-lived species. MNI counts may also have been depressed by the occurrence of field processing (Bird et al. 2002). Despite the potential for field processing, trends in abundance for both large (*L. lambis*) and small (*Pinctada* sp., *C. luhuanus*) reef taxa show a declining trend in MNI from Spit 6 onward. This trend suggests either decreasing productivity within the patch or a shift away from the reef to a foraging strategy that focused on upper intertidal zones.

The remaining two patches cover terrestrial gastropods (the terrestrial patch) and taxa that have only been classified to genus or family level and therefore cannot be precisely attributed to a patch (the varied patch). Because neither of these patches contributed significantly to the assemblage, data from them has been omitted from Table 8.5.

Environment and Climate Data

To confirm the presence of economic intensification, environmental and climate impacts must first be assessed to ensure that they do not provide a better explanation for the observed foraging patterns. Figure 8.5 compares data from Yindayin with environmental and climate data across the period of occupation. Sections a and b of Figure 8.5 represent depositions of material at Yindayin, while sections c–e relate to diversity measures that reflect the range of diet breadth in the assemblage. Section f shows mean sea levels from North Queensland and their 1σ and 2σ ranges (Khan et al 2015). Section g describes simulated sea surface temperatures and their relationship to El Niño frequency. Section h plots the frequency of the dry El Niño periods based on lake sediment sand content from El Junco Lagoon in the Galapagos and sediment deposition from Laguna Pallcacocha in Ecuador (Barr et al. 2019). The markers on sections a–e represent the spits where unequivocal radiocarbon dates are present. Spits 2 (120–0 cal BP) and 6 (2055–1735 cal BP) have been omitted because of dating ambiguities, while no date was obtained for Spit 12.

Phase I occurred during a period of high productivity in the Great Barrier Reef region. Precipitation during this period was approximately 50% higher than modern conditions and sea levels were 1.3–1.5 m higher than present (Lewis et al. 2013; Shulmeister and Lees 1995). Reef formation in the Great Barrier Reef region was initiated around 7100 BP and intensified vertical accretion peaked in the period 8000–5000 BP (Smithers et al. 2006). The peak reef accretion period overlaps with Phase I (6255–5930 cal BP), and it is likely that during this period reef formation at Stanley Island had not stabilized (Figure 8.5f). A microatoll between Stanley Island and nearby Flinders Island has been dated to 4100 cal BP, suggesting that local sea levels and reef formation continued to fluctuate well after Phase I (Chappell 1983; Hopley et al. 2007:78; Lewis et al. 2008; Lewis et al. 2013). Phase II (2945–1745 cal BP) occurred in a period of increasing environmental and climate variability (Figure 8.5g and h) and the occupation and subsequent abandonment of Yindayin may reflect changing resource patterns on the mainland. Increasing aridity may have forced foragers to seek new areas because of reduced productivity and may explain the timing of the initiation of Phase II. From 3700 BP, precipitation in Northern Australia declined markedly because of the onset of dominant El Niño Southern Oscillation weather patterns. This trend continued throughout Phase II (Barr et al. 2019; Shulmeister 1999:82; Shulmeister and Lees 1995:14–15). El Niño Southern Oscillation events became more common after 4000 BP. Peak frequency occurred around 1200 BP and amplitude peaked in 2000–1,000 cal BP (Barr et al. 2019; Moy et al. 2002). Sea-level instability has also been noted during Phase II; Lewis and colleagues recorded a 1-m oscillation for this part of the Great Barrier Reef in 3,000–2,700 BP (Lewis et al. 2008:79; Lewis et al. 2013:126). The dates of the oscillation correspond with the date range for Spit 10 (2945–2670 cal BP), and the likely habitat disruption may explain the diversification of foraging and the focus on motile Neritidae taxa. The rapid decline in sea level to

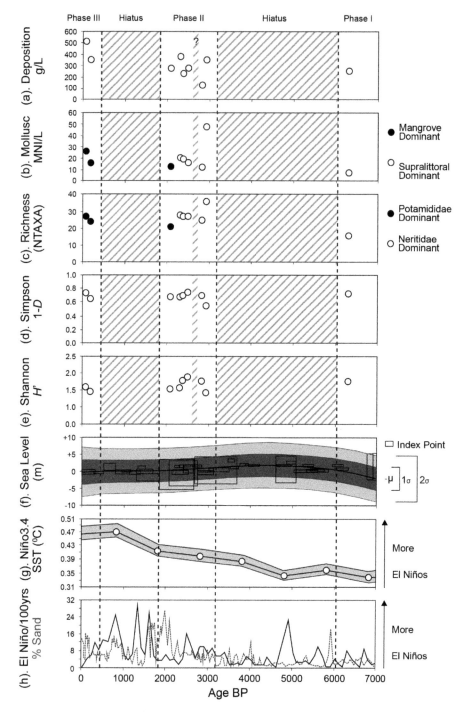

Figure 8.5. Comparison of Yindayin assemblage data to climate and environmental data. The sea-level data is adapted from Khan and colleagues (2015:Fig. 4). The simulated sea surface temperature and El Niño frequency is adapted from Barr and colleagues (2019:Fig. 3) and is based on sediment records from El Junco Lagoon in the Galapagos and Laguna Palcacocha in Ecuador. Figure by the authors.

modern levels that occurred from 2000 BP was contemporaneous with the abandonment at the end of Phase II and the occupation of the nearby chenier plains of Princess Charlotte Bay (Beaton 1985:9; Lewis et al. 2013:126). The final phase of occupation at Yindayin occurred during a more stable and biologically productive period. Sea levels and reef growth were stable, and higher-than-average precipitation in North Queensland created more productive environments. The increased quantities of molluscan material during Phase III (155–0 cal BP) support this idea (Burrows et al. 2014).

Synthesis and Discussion: Evaluating the Criteria for Economic Intensification

We use Butler and Campbell's (2004) definition of economic intensification as a sustained increase in the production/procurement of economic resources accompanied by a decrease in foraging efficiency. To assess the presence of economic intensification, it is necessary to compare the patterns of occupation and structure of the foraging economy to four economic intensification criteria. As each criterion builds on previous ones, only those portions of the deposit that meet all four criteria can be considered as meeting this definition of economic intensification.

Economic Intensification Criterion 1: Evidence for Increased Intensity of Site Occupation and Deposition of Cultural Material (Site Occupation)

We used accumulation and deposition rates as proxies for the intensity of site occupation and deposition. The data from Yindayin rock shelter indicates an increase in the intensity of site occupation in Spits 1 (120–0 cal BP) and 10 (2945–2670 cal BP; see Figure 8.2 and Table 8.3). Accumulation rates are highest across Spits 1–3 (120–0 cal BP to 155–0 cal BP) and within Spit 10 (2945–2670 cal BP). The deposition rates of all excavated components (excluding stone) were highest in Spit 1 (120–0 cal BP), while Spit 10 (2945–2670 cal BP) is notable for its high levels of shell, stone, and bone deposition relative to other spits in Phases I and II. No other spits exhibit occupation or deposition characteristics that suggest increased activity.

Economic Intensification Criterion 2: Evidence of Increased Quantities of Subsistence Material Being Deposited

There are two definite peaks in volume-corrected molluscan MNI (Figure 8.3). The first and most substantial increase is in Spit 10 (2945–2670 cal BP), and Spit 1 (120–0 cal BP) exhibits the second, smaller increase. Spit 10 (2945–2670 cal BP) is dominated by small-bodied taxa from hard substrates (Table 8.5a), while Spit 1 (120–0 cal BP) is dominated by the larger Potamididae, which dwell in mangroves (Table 8.5b). The data indicates that there was an increased discard of subsistence remains in Spits 1 (Phase III) and 10 (Phase II) and a general stability in all other spits. While there is no unidirectional trend, the peak in discard in Spits 1 (120–0 cal BP) and 10 (2945–2670 cal BP) suggest that this criterion has been met for these two spits. The results for Criteria 1 and 2 suggest that in Spits 1 (120–0 cal BP) and 10 (2945–2670 cal BP), there was an increase in the amount of subsistence and occupational material being deposited that may reflect increasing economic intensity. Because these signals can also be produced by standardization, diversification must also be assessed.

Economic Intensification Criterion 3: Evidence for Increased Diversity in Both Taxa and Environmental Patches Being Exploited

Diversity and patch preference data for Spits 1 (120–0 cal BP) and 10 (2945–2670 cal BP) indicate opposing trends (Table 8.5 and Figure 8.4). The data from Spit 10 (2945–2670 cal BP) suggests a generalized foraging strategy. Diversity indices demonstrate decreasing diversity coupled with increased richness. While decreased diversity suggests specialization, the increase in richness implies diversification and therefore a decrease in foraging efficiency. At the time that Spit 10 (2945–2670 cal BP) was deposited, Stanley Island was subject to the onset of increased El Niño Southern Oscillation fluctuations and the impact of oscillating sea levels. These variable environmental and climate conditions likely affected the foraging strategies used at this time (2945–2670 cal BP). A generalized foraging strategy that combines low diversity and wide diet breadth spreads risk, making it a sensible approach during periods of resource unpredictability. The foragers during this period were mostly taking small-bodied, hard substrate prey that are resilient to sea-level change, but they were also offsetting the risk of foraging failure by exploiting all patches. This pattern does not suggest that economic intensification was present during Spit 10 (2945–2670 cal BP).

The data for Spit 1 (120–0 cal BP) suggests an increasing overall diversity, and therefore it is more likely to meet this criterion. Diversity and richness data increased throughout Phase III and peaked in Spit 1 (120–0 cal BP), while at the same time taxa from a lower-ranked patch contributed to the assemblage in increasing numbers (Figure 8.4). While taxa from the mangrove patch and the hard substrate patch continued to dominate, there was an increase in the use of the intertidal sand/mud patch. The proportion of total MNI for the intertidal patch increased from 5.2% (Spit 3, 155–0 cal BP) to 22.3% (Spit 1, 120–0 cal BP). The diversity indices (Table 8.6) reflect this change. The Simpson 1-D index increased in Spit 3 (0.653) and Spit 2

(0.693) and peaked in Spit 1 (0.735). Richness (Table 8.6) is relatively stable after Spit 10 (2945–2670 cal BP) but fluctuates from Spit 4 (2070–1745 cal BP) onward, coinciding with the dominance of mangrove taxa. The average NTAXA dropped from 28.3 when the supralittoral and intertidal hard substrate patch was dominant (Spits 5–10) to 23.0 when the mangrove patch was dominant (Spits 1–4). Richness in Phase III fluctuated, starting at 24 in Spit 3 (155–0 cal BP), declining to 20 in Spit 2 (120–0 cal BP), and then peaking at 27 in Spit 1 (120–0 cal BP). When viewed against the average NTAXA for when the mangrove patch was dominant (Spits 1–4), Spit 1 (120–0 cal BP) represents an important increase in richness. This pattern of decreased dominance of previously productive patches, increasing evenness of patch contributions, and an increase in the use of more marginal patches fits with the patch-related signals for economic intensification.

Economic Intensification Criterion 4: Evidence for a Decline in Foraging Efficiency

Foraging efficiency decreased in Spit 10 (2945–2670 cal BP). However, this decrease represents a reaction to environmental instability rather than to economic intensification. The data for Phase III shows the greatest potential for decreased foraging efficiency. The abundance of *Atactodea striata* increased substantially in the spits following Spit 3 (155–0 cal BP; Table 8.5c), suggesting an increase in the exploitation of the lower-ranked intertidal sand/mud patch. The increased use of this lower-ranked patch coincides with an increase in overall mollusk abundance (Table 8.4) and may indicate the presence of economic intensification, particularly in Spit 1 (120–0 cal BP). That said, it has been noted elsewhere in the Pacific that despite its small size, *A. striata* is an attractive resource because of its occurrence in high densities and at depths of less than 5 cm in sandy substrates (Ash et al. 2013; Thomas et al. 2004). While it is likely that foragers would rank *A. striata* lower than Potamididae, if it were abundant enough to allow mass harvesting, its inclusion may represent a reorganization of foraging to incorporate a highly productive small prey rather than a decrease in foraging efficiency. While this may cast doubt on whether the inclusion of *A. striata* represents intensification, its limited presence prior to Spit 3 (155–0 cal BP) complicates this interpretation. The abundance of *A. striata* prior to Spit 3 (155–0 cal BP) occurs in significant numbers only in Spit 10 (2945–2670 cal BP), when a more generalized foraging strategy was likely in place. The absence of this taxon during the majority of Phase II is attributable to three possible factors: rate of preservation, environmental conditions, or a deliberate foraging decision. There is no evidence to suggest that preservation has been an issue, and while environmental conditions were changing during Phase II, the abundance of *Asaphis violascens* peaked during this period, suggesting that sandy substrates were productive and available for exploitation. It is likely that the limited contribution of *A. striata* is due to a conscious foraging decision about a resource that may have been viewed as less productive. However, the peak in abundance of *A. striata* in Spit 1 (120–0 cal BP) could have occurred as a single mass harvesting event; the absence of a peak in other sandy substrate taxa such as *Gafrarium pectinatum* and *A. violascens* may support this view.

Based on the assessment above, Spit 1 (120–0 cal BP) represents the only period when the criteria for economic intensification criteria were met. Phase III, and particularly Spit 1 (120–0 cal BP), demonstrates the following characteristics:

1. High relative levels of site occupation in terms of accumulation and deposition rates
2. High relative quantities of molluscan material
3. Increasing diversity and richness in the taxa being exploited after a period of more focused foraging
4. A possible decreasing trend in foraging efficiency

The combination of these four observations suggests that there was a narrow subsistence focus at the beginning of Phase III with high relative abundances of the dominant Potamididae and Neritidae taxa (Table 8.5a and 8.5b). In Spit 1 (120–0 cal BP), there is a relatively greater abundance of Potamididae and Neritidae complemented by the addition of *A. striata*, a much lower-ranked resource. The combination of high abundance of dominant taxa and the addition of lower-ranked taxa suggests that foragers produced less food relative to the amount of effort, resulting in decreased foraging efficiency. Over this same period (Phase III), there was an increase in accumulation and deposition rates, potentially indicating longer or more intense periods of occupation. However, the recent age of these deposits suggests that increased preservation may also have been a factor. The combination of wetter-than-average climate and environmental conditions and stable sea levels and reef growth suggests that declining environmental conditions were not responsible for the observed patterns.

Conclusions

The model presented in this chapter unites the predictions of the optimal foraging theory prey and patch choice models with the principles of Boserupian economic intensification to identify periods of population pressure within the

Yindayin assemblage. This analysis has shown that economic intensification, and therefore population pressure, did not become apparent until the last 150 years of occupation at Yindayin. For the time period before that, environmental and climate data provides a better explanation for changes in foraging behavior. The Yindayin data does not support simple, unidirectional models of development. Patterns in subsistence exemplify nondirectional foraging behavior, which is characterized by pulses of significant change and abandonment within periods of relative stability. Population pressure did not become a driver for subsistence patterns until the final phase of occupation at Yindayin. The mid- to late Holocene presents as a period of increasing environmental fluctuation with times of stability punctuated by pulses of rapid change, and subsistence at Yindayin reflects these patterns. Environmental change creates subsistence problems that foragers must respond to, and the alignment of environmental data with changes in subsistence behavior is unlikely to be a coincidence. It is important to note that Phase III overlaps with European contact; in calendar years, Phase III relates to the period 1795–1950. By the early to mid-nineteenth century, the region was frequented by explorers who were charting the Great Barrier Reef and whalers and guano miners who were exploiting natural resources. By the mid- to late nineteenth century, pearling, bêche-de-mer harvesting, and fishing had become important industries in the area (Bowen and Bowen 2002:119). The intensification signals identified in Phase III may have been directly or indirectly influenced by European contact.

Archaeomalacology provides valuable data for understanding past foraging behavior. Studies such as those by Faulkner and colleagues (2019), Jerardino (2010), and Thakar (2011) demonstrate how molluscan material can be used to understand human interactions with coastal resources. However, excluding non-molluscan resources from analyses can limit the strength of the derived observations. It is possible that variation in molluscan foraging may reflect changes in other parts of the economy rather than fluctuations in population, environment, climate, or culture. To provide robust and reliable conclusions about economic intensification, the entirety of the subsistence economy needs to be considered. The observations for Yindayin, therefore, are indicative rather than conclusive proof for the presence or absence of population pressure and economic intensification. This limitation is the result of the availability of data rather than a fault with the model presented here. The economic intensification model can and should be applied to assemblages that assess the broader economy for a site or group of contemporaneous sites. The application of the economic intensification model to more complete economic data will enable researchers to better pinpoint the impact of economic intensification and population pressure on hunter-gatherer foraging patterns.

This study demonstrates the value of the Boserupian definition of economic intensification; that is, an increase in total economic production with an accompanying decrease in productivity per unit of input (Morgan 2015). If we first understand how increased production has been generated (i.e., via increasing or decreasing efficiency), then we have a chance of identifying its root causes. In practice, Boserupian economic intensification results in foragers working harder for resources—in optimal foraging theory terms, diet breadth widens to include less optimal prey as encounter rates with higher-ranked prey begin to decline. The decline in high-value resources can be caused by overexploitation (Mannino and Thomas 2002), declining habitat conditions (Broughton et al. 2008), or social factors that reduce access to prey (Whitaker and Byrd 2014). Supplementation means collecting increasing numbers of productive, reliable, smaller-bodied prey, which usually entails increased handling costs. A reliance on small prey tends to reduce mobility because small prey such as plant and molluscan resources tend to collect in fixed locations, while increased handling costs means spending more time at processing locations near the resources (Binford 2001:402). The combination of reduced mobility and reliable resources can lead to an increase in population and an increased need to reduce handling costs to increase output, a process that can lead to complex foraging and social behavior (Codding and Bird 2015). If the effects of climate and environmental change can be eliminated, then identifying these types of responses can signal the presence of population pressure at a site. The work presented here, underpinned by the predictions of optimal foraging theory and Boserupian economic intensification, provides a model for pursuing this type of analysis.

References Cited

Arnold, J. E., M. R. Walsh, and S. E. Hollimon. 2004. The Archaeology of California. *Journal of Archaeological Research* 12(1):1–73.

Ash, Jeremy, Patrick Faulkner, Liam M. Brady, and Cassandra Rowe. 2013. Morphometric Reconstructions and Size Variability Analysis of the Surf Clam, Atactodea(=Paphies) Striata, from Muralag 8, Southwestern Torres Strait, Northern Australia. *Australian Archaeology* 77(1):82–93.

Attenbrow, Val. 2004. *What's Changing: Population Size or Land-Use Patterns? The Archaeology of Upper Mangrove Creek, Sydney Basin.* Australian National University Press, Canberra.

Bailey, Geoff N., and Alan S. Craighead. 2003. Late Pleistocene and Holocene Coastal Palaeoeconomies: A Reconsideration of the Molluscan Evidence from Northern Spain. *Geoarchaeology: An International Journal* 18(2):175–204.

Barker, Bryce. 1991. Nara Inlet 1: Coastal Resource Use and the Holocene Marine Transgression in the Whitsunday Islands, Central Queensland. *Archaeology in Oceania* 26(3):102–109.

———. 2004. The Sea People: Late Holocene Maritime Specialisation in the Whitsunday Islands, Central Queensland. In *Terra Australis*, edited by S. O'Connor and J. Golson, p. 20. Australian National University Press, Canberra.

Barr, Cameron, John Tibby, Melanie J. Leng, Jonathan J. Tyler, Andrew C. G. Henderson, Jonathan T. Overpeck, Gavin L. Simpson, Julia E. Cole, Steven J. Phipps, Jonathan C. Marshall, Glen B. McGregor, Quan Hua, and Fiona H. McRobie. 2019. Holocene El Niño-Southern Oscillation Variability Reflected in Subtropical Australian Precipitation. *Scientific Reports* 9(1):1627–1627.

Beaton, John. 1985. Evidence for a Coastal Occupation Time-Lag at Princess Charlotte Bay (North Queensland) and Implications for Coastal Colonization and Population Growth Theories for Aboriginal Australia. *Archaeology in Oceania* 20(1):1–20.

Binford, Lewis R. 2001. *Constructing Frames of Reference: An Analytical Method for Archaeological Theory Building Using Hunter-Gatherer and Environmental Data Sets.* University of California Press, Berkeley.

Bird, Douglas W., and Rebecca L. Bliege Bird. 1997. Contemporary Shellfish Gathering Strategies among the Meriam of the Torres Strait Islands, Australia: Testing Predictions of a Central Place Foraging Model. *Journal of Archaeological Science* 24(1): 39–63.

Bird, Douglas W., Jennifer L. Richardson, Peter M. Veth, and Anthony J. Barham. 2002. Explaining Shellfish Variability in Middens on the Meriam Islands, Torres Strait, Australia. *Journal of Archaeological Science* 29(5):457–469.

Bocquet-Appel, Jean-Pierre, Pierre-Yves Demars, Lorette Noiret, and Dmitry Dobrowsky. 2005. Estimates of Upper Palaeolithic Meta-Population Size in Europe from Archaeological Data. *Journal of Archaeological Science* 32(11):1656–1668.

Boserup, Esther. 2003. *Conditions of Agricultural Growth: The Economics of Agrarian Change under Pressure.* Routledge, Abingdon, UK.

Bowen, James, and Margarita Bowen. 2002. *The Great Barrier Reef: History, Science, Heritage.* Cambridge University Press, Cambridge.

Braje, Todd J., and Jon M. Erlandson. 2009. Mollusks and Mass Harvesting in the Middle Holocene: Prey Size and Resource Ranking on San Miguel Island, Alta California. *California Archaeology* 1(2):269–290.

Braje, Todd J., Torben C. Rick, and Jon M. Erlandson. 2012. A Trans-Holocene Historical Ecological Record of Shellfish Harvesting on California's Northern Channel Islands. *Quaternary International* 264:109–120.

Bronk Ramsey, Christopher. 2009. Development of the Radiocarbon Calibration Program. *Radiocarbon* 43(2A): 355–363.

Broughton, Jack M., David A. Byers, Reid A. Bryson, William Eckerle, and David B. Madsen. 2008. Did Climatic Seasonality Control Late Quaternary Artiodactyl Densities in Western North America? *Quaternary Science Reviews* 27:1916–1937.

Burrows, Mark A., Jack Fenner, and Simon G. Haberle. 2014. Humification in Northeast Australia: Dating Millennial and Centennial Scale Climate Variability in the Late Holocene. *The Holocene* 24(12):1707–1718.

Butler, Virginia L., and Sarah K. Campbell. 2004. Resource Intensification and Resource

Depression in the Pacific Northwest of North America: A Zooarchaeological Review. *Journal of World Prehistory* 18(4):327–405.

Chappell, John. 1983. Evidence for Smoothly Falling Sea Level Relative to North Queensland, Australia, during the Past 6,000 Yr. *Nature* 302(5907):406.

Codding, Brian F., and Douglas W. Bird. 2015. Behavioral Ecology and the Future of Archaeological Science. *Journal of Archaeological Science* 56:9–20.

Codding, Brian F., Jim F. O'Connell, and Douglas W. Bird. 2014. Shellfishing and the Colonization of Sahul: A Multivariate Model Evaluating the Dynamic Effects of Prey Utility, Transport Considerations and Life-History on Foraging Patterns and Midden Composition. *Journal of Island and Coastal Archaeology* 9(2):238–252.

Eichhorst, Thomas E. 2016. *Neritidae of the World*. ConchBooks, Harxheim, Germany.

Erlandson, Jon M. 1988. The Role of Shellfish in Prehistoric Economies: A Protein Perspective. *American Antiquity* 53:102–109.

Faulkner, Patrick, Matthew Harris, Abdallah K. Ali, Othman Haji, Alison Crowther, Mark C. Horton, and Nicole L. Boivin. 2018. Characterising Marine Mollusc Exploitation in the Eastern African Iron Age: Archaeomalacological Evidence from Unguja Ukuu and Fukuchani, Zanzibar. *Quaternary International* 471:66–80.

Faulkner, Patrick, Matthew Harris, Othman Haji, Alison Crowther, Mark C. Horton, and Nicole L. Boivin. 2019. Towards a Historical Ecology of Intertidal Foraging in the Mafia Archipelago: Archaeomalacology and Implications for Marine Resource Management. *Journal of Ethnobiography* 39(2):182–203.

Giovas, Christina M., Meagan Clark, Scott M. Fitzpatrick, and Jessica Stone. 2013. Intensifying Collection and Size Increase of the Tessellated Nerite Snail (*Nerita tessellata*) at the Coconut Walk Site, Nevis, Northern Lesser Antilles, AD 890–1440. *Journal of Archaeological Science* 40(11):4024–4038.

Hammer, Øyvind, and David A. T. Harper. 2006. *Paleontological Data Analysis*. Blackwell, Malden, Massachusetts.

Hammer, Øyvind, David A. T. Harper, and Paul D. Ryan. 2001. Paleontological Statistics Software Package for Education and Data Analysis. *Palaeontologia Electronica* 4(1):9.

Harris, Matthew, Marshall Weisler, and Patrick Faulkner. 2015. A Refined Protocol for Calculating MNI in Archaeological Molluscan Shell Assemblages: A Marshall Islands Case Study. *Journal of Archaeological Science* 57:168–179.

Heaton, Timothy J., Peter Köhler, Martin Butzin, Edouard Bard, Ron W. Reimer, William E. N. Austin, Christopher Bronk Ramsey, Pieter M. Groote, Konrad A. Hughen, Bernd Kromer, Paula J. Reimer, Jess Adkins, Andrea Burke, Mea S. Cook, Jesper Olsen, and Luke C. Skinner. 2020. Marine20—The Marine Radiocarbon Age Calibration Curve(0–55,000 cal BP). *Radiocarbon* 62(4):779–820.

Hiscock, Peter. 2008. *The Archaeology of Ancient Australia*. Routledge, New York.

Hopley, David, Kevin E. Parnell, and Scott G. Smithers. 2007. *The Geomorphology of the Great Barrier Reef: Development, Diversity and Change*. Cambridge University Press, Cambridge.

Houbrick, Richard S. 1991. Systematic Review and Functional Morphology of the Mangrove Snails *Terebralia* and *Telescopium* (Potamidae; Prosobranchia). *Malacologia* 33: 289–338.

Jerardino, Antonieta. 2010. Large Shell Middens in Lamberts Bay, South Africa: A

Case of Hunter-Gatherer Resource Intensification. *Journal of Archaeological Science* 37(9):2291–2302.

Khan, Nicole S., Erica Ashe, Timothy A. Shaw, Matteo Vacchi, Jennifer Walker, W. R. Peltier, Robert E. Kopp, and Benjamin P. Horton. 2015. Holocene Relative Sea-Level Changes from Near-, Intermediate-, and Far-Field Locations. *Current Climate Change Reports* 1(4):247–262.

Kelly, Robert L. 2013. *The Lifeways of Hunter-Gatherers: The Foraging Spectrum.* Cambridge University Press, Cambridge.

Lewis, Stephen E., Craig R. Sloss, Colin V. Murray-Wallace, Colin D. Woodroffe, and Scott G. Smithers. 2013. Post-Glacial Sea-Level Changes around the Australian Margin: A Review. *Quaternary Science Reviews* 74:115–138.

Lewis, Stephen E., Raphael A. J. Wüst, Jody M. Webster, and Graham Anthony Shields-Zhou. 2008. Mid-Late Holocene Sea-Level Variability in Eastern Australia: Holocene Sea Levels of Eastern Australia. *Terra Nova* 20(1):74–81.

Lourandos, Harry. 1997. *Continent of Hunter-Gatherers: New Perspectives in Australian Prehistory.* Cambridge University Press, Cambridge.

Lourandos, Harry, and Anne Ross. 1994. The Great "Intensification Debate": Its History and Place in Australian Archaeology. *Australian Archaeology* 39(1):54–63.

Magurran, Anne E. 1988. *Ecological Diversity and Its Measurement.* Princeton University Press, Princeton, New Jersey.

Mannino, Marcella A., and Kenneth D. Thomas. 2002. Depletion of a Resource? The Impact of Prehistoric Human Foraging on Intertidal Mollusc Communities and Its Significance for Human Settlement, Mobility and Dispersal. *World Archaeology* 33(3):452–474.

Morgan, Christopher. 2015. Is It Intensification Yet? Current Archaeological Perspectives on the Evolution of Hunter-Gatherer Economies. *Journal of Archaeological Research* 23(2):163–213.

Moy, Christopher M., Geoffrey O. Seltzer, Donald T. Rodbell, and David M. Anderson. 2002. Variability of El Niño/Southern Oscillation Activity at Millennial Timescales during the Holocene Epoch. *Nature* 420(6912):162–165.

Munro, Natalie D., and Levent Atici. 2009. Human Subsistence Change in the Late Pleistocene Mediterranean Basin: The Status of Research on Faunal Intensification, Diversification & Specialisation. *Before Farming* 1(1):1–6.

Nagaoka, Lisa. 2002. The Effects of Resource Depression on Foraging Efficiency, Diet Breadth, and Patch Use in Southern New Zealand. *Journal of Anthropological Archaeology* 21(4):419–442.

O'Connell, James F., and Jim Allen. 2012. The Restaurant at the End of the Universe: Modelling the Colonisation of Sahul. *Australian Archaeology* 74:5–31.

Rowland, Michael J., Shelley Wright, and Robert Baker. 2015. The Timing and Use of Offshore Islands in the Great Barrier Reef Marine Province, Queensland. *Quaternary International* 385:154–165.

Shulmeister, James. 1999. Australasian Evidence for Mid-Holocene Climate Change Implies Precessional Control of Walker Circulation in the Pacific. *Quaternary International* 57–58:81–91.

Shulmeister, James, and Brian G. Lees. 1995. Pollen Evidence from Tropical Australia for the Onset of an ENSO-Dominated Climate at c. 4000 BP. *The Holocene* 5(1):10–18.

Smith, Mike. 2013. *The Archaeology of Australia's Deserts*. Cambridge University Press, Cambridge.

Smithers, Scott G., David Hopley, and Kevin E. Parnell. 2006. Fringing and Nearshore Coral Reefs of the Great Barrier Reef: Episodic Holocene Development and Future Prospects. *Journal of Coastal Research* 221:175–187.

Soemodihardjo, S., and W. Kastoro. 2008. Notes on the Terebralia Palustris (Grastropoda) from Coral Islands in the Jakarta Bay Area. *Marine Research in Indonesia* 18:131–148.

Stiner, Mary C., Natalie D. Munro, and Todd A. Surovell. 2000 The Tortoise and the Hare: Small Game Use, the Broad Spectrum Revolution, and Paleolithic Demography. *Current Anthropology* 41(1):39–79.

Tallavaara, Miikka, Petro Pesonen, and Markku Oinonen. 2010. Prehistoric Population History in Eastern Fennoscandia. *Journal of Archaeological Science* 37(2):251–260.

Thakar, Heather B. 2011. Intensification of Shellfish Exploitation: Evidence of Species-Specific Deviation from Traditional Expectations. *Journal of Archaeological Science* 38(10):2596–2605.

Thomas, Frank R. 2001. Mollusk Habitats and Fisheries in Kiribati: An Assessment from the Gilbert Islands. *Pacific Science* 55(1):77–97.

Thomas, Frank R., Patrick D. Nunn, Tamara Osborne, Roselyn Kumar, Francis Areki, Sepeti Matararaba, David Steadman, and Geoff Hope. 2004. Recent Archaeological Findings at Qaranilaca Cave, Vanuabalavu Island, Fiji. *Archaeology in Oceania* 39(1):42–49.

Torfing, Tobias. 2015. Neolithic Population and Summed Probability Distribution of ^{14}C-Dates. *Journal of Archaeological Science* 63:193–198.

Ulm, Sean. 2006. Australian Marine Reservoir Effects: A Guide to ΔR Values. *Australian Archaeology* 63(1):57–60.

———. 2011. Coastal Foragers on Southern Shores: Marine Resource Use in Northeast Australia since the Late Pleistocene. In *Trekking the Shore: Changing Coastlines and the Antiquity of Coastal Settlement*, edited by Nuno F. Bicho, Jonathan A. Haws, and Loren G. Davis, pp. 441–461. Springer, New York.

Whitaker, Adrian R. 2008. Incipient Aquaculture in Prehistoric California? Long-Term Productivity and Sustainability vs. Immediate Returns for the Harvest of Marine Invertebrates. *Journal of Archaeological Science* 35(4):1114–1123.

Whitaker, Adrian R., and Brian F. Byrd. 2014. Social Circumscription, Territoriality, and the Late Holocene Intensification of Small-Bodied Shellfish along the California Coast. *Journal of Island and Coastal Archaeology* 9(20):150–168.

Willan, Richard C. 2013. A Key to the Potamidid Snails (Longbums, Mudcreepers and Treecreepers) of Northern Australia. *Northern Territory Naturalist* 24:68–80.

Williams, Alan N. 2013. A New Population Curve for Prehistoric Australia. *Proceedings: Biological Sciences/The Royal Society* 280(1761):1–9.

Wilson, Barry R., Carina Wilson, and Patrick Baker. 1993. *Australian Marine Shells*. Odyssey, Leederville, Australia.

9

Application of the Ideal Free Distribution Model to Pacific Island Settlement Patterns

A Case Study from Tutuila Island, American Sāmoa

ALEX E. MORRISON, ROBERT J. DINAPOLI,
MELINDA S. ALLEN, AND TIMOTHY M. RIETH

Settlement pattern studies have played a crucial role in Polynesian archaeology for much of the last half century (e.g., Green 1967; Ladefoged and Graves 2002; Morrison and O'Connor 2018). Despite an emphasis on environmental and social factors and how they structure human spatial organization and land use, most of these studies have not applied theoretical principles and models from human behavioral ecology in clear or explicit ways (for exceptions, see DiNapoli and Morrison 2017; DiNapoli et al. 2018; Field 2004, 2005; Kennett and Winterhalder 2008). These models are particularly well suited for settlement studies because they provide predictions about the timing, tempo, and drivers of colonization; the expansion of settlements; and subsequent migrations that can be tested empirically using archaeological data.

The Sāmoan islands of West Polynesia (Figure 9.1) are central to our understanding of how, why, and in what ways Pacific peoples dispersed across island landscapes and archipelagoes (e.g., Sear et al. 2020). In the 1960s, Roger Green and colleagues applied the basic tenets of settlement pattern archaeology to sizable areas of the large islands of 'Upolu and Savai'i in the western part of the archipelago (see Morrison and O'Connor 2018 for a review). This seminal research established the settlement pattern approach as a highly influential conceptual framework for archaeological research in the region (e.g., Clark and Herdrich 1993; Davidson 1969; McCoy 1976; Morrison 2012).

Human behavioral ecology theories complement settlement pattern approaches by providing explanatory models for how and why human settlements vary across different socioecological contexts (DiNapoli and Morrison

2017). Through the development and application of relatively simple conceptual models, human behavioral ecology offers testable predictions and evolutionary-scale explanations (i.e., intergenerational and longer) for archaeological phenomena. While a range of substantive issues can be explored through human behavioral ecology frameworks (see Bird and O'Connell 2006; Codding and Bird 2015; DiNapoli and Morrison 2017), the ideal free distribution model has been particularly valuable in explaining large-scale inter-island migrations (e.g., Giovas and Fitzpatrick 2014; Kennett and Winterhalder 2008; Kennett et al. 2006) and smaller-scale intra-island settlement chronologies (e.g., Jazwa et al. 2016; Winterhalder et al. 2010). Variants of the ideal free distribution model have also proven useful for assessing the effects of despotic social hierarchies on settlement organization and population distributions (e.g., Bell and Winterhalder 2014; Jazwa et al. 2019; Prufer et al. 2017). In Polynesia, Kennett and Winterhalder (2008; see also Allen 2012) have used ideal free distribution to predict island settlement patterns. However, empirical applications have been limited and are currently needed. In this chapter, we use a comprehensive geospatial database of Sāmoan archaeological sites and their associated radiocarbon determinations to test ideal free distribution predictions that relate the timing and progression of initial human settlement to environmental opportunities and risks on Tutuila, the third largest island (142.3 sq km) in the Sāmoan archipelago. This volcanically young island is 653 m high.

We have applied the ideal free distribution model to address the history of Sāmoan settlement location, land use, and spatial organization. Our assumptions about whether Sāmoans followed ideal free distribution model predictions reflect our belief in the general utility of using simple conceptual models to understand complex phenomena in human history. We use the model to address whether the initial inhabitants of Tutuila followed an ideal free distribution settlement pattern, to determine which habitat qualities or geographical characteristics were important enough to influence settlement choices over time, and how these choices might have changed according to variations in human demography and ecological dynamics. Deviations from the model predictions are not unexpected and ultimately help us learn something unique about the past, including the island-specific habitat qualities that structured settlement choices over time.

Cultural Background

The Sāmoan Islands consist of six main high volcanic islands and a number of smaller islets. These islands were initially settled in the Lapita period by populations whose dispersal into Remote Oceania began around 3000 BP and ended in Sāmoa, the eastern terminus (Kirch 2017). The defining archaeological signature of the Lapita period cultural horizon is dentate-stamped ceramics, although plainware and distinctive stone and shell artifacts have also been identified (Kirch 1997). Unlike the case for neighboring Tonga and Fiji, where Lapita period ceramics are plentiful in early colonizing sites, only a single Lapita period site with decorated ceramics is known from Sāmoa, the submerged Mulifanua site off the northwestern coast of 'Upolu (see Figure 9.1; see also Cochrane et al. 2016 and Dickinson and Green 1998). Problematically, dated samples from Mulifanua are not from stratigraphic contexts but are solely from dredged sediment. These data indicate that site occupation likely occurred circa 3000–2650 cal BP (Green 1974; Petchey 2001). Slightly later, or perhaps contemporaneously, communities that produced plainware pottery occupied multiple locations on Ofu Island, at the eastern end of the archipelago, around 2900–2550 cal BP (Clark et al. 2016; Petchey and Kirch 2019).

Studies in the Sāmoan archipelago suggest that after initial colonization, settlements were primarily coastal and few in number (Rieth et al. 2008). They also suggest that within the first millennium of occupation, people initiated agricultural activities and that some activities may have extended inland (for Vainu'u and Tutuila, see Eckert and Welch 2013; for Leuluasi and Luatuanu'u and 'Upolu, see Green and Davidson 1974; for Pulemelei and Savai'i, see Martinsson-Wallin et al. 2006). Monument building, primarily large masonry and earth mounds, and the development of the "traditional" village layout observed at European contact, which features a central green and variably sized house mounds, seems to have been initiated in the past 1,000 years (Green 2002). However, while the outline of the Sāmoan sequence is fairly well established, the tempo and geography of settlement expansion, the role of resource opportunities, and the risks involved in structuring settlement patterns are still poorly understood. The ideal free distribution model provides a useful framework for investigating such relationships.

The Ideal Free Distribution Model

The ideal free distribution model considers where individuals would ideally choose to settle given variation in habitat quality and population densities in surrounding habitats (Codding and Bird 2015:15; Fretwell and Lucas 1969). A primary assumption of the model is that under ideal and free conditions, initial colonizers and subsequent migrants will settle the highest-ranking

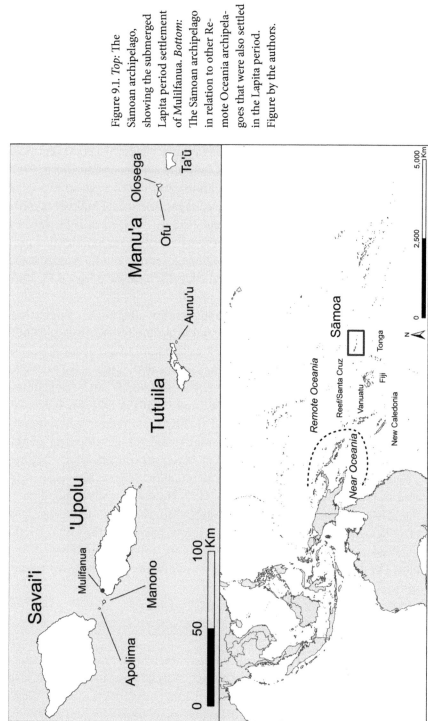

Figure 9.1. *Top:* The Sāmoan archipelago, showing the submerged Lapita period settlement of Mulifanua. *Bottom:* The Sāmoan archipelago in relation to other Remote Oceania archipelagoes that were also settled in the Lapita period. Figure by the authors.

habitats first. Individuals will move to less productive habitats only when returns from the highest-ranked areas decrease to levels that are equal to or worse than the next-lower-ranked habitats. Under the assumptions of the model (Figure 9.2), habitat quality results in negative density dependence. As in situ populations grow or immigration increases, the suitability of the highest-ranked habitat will decline until a density threshold is reached, at which point the second-ranked habitat becomes equal in suitability to the first habitat and begins to be settled. This is known as the habitat matching rule (Tregenza 1995). The result is that over time, less suitable habitats are settled in serial order of *initial* suitability.

In addition to the size and density of population, environmental perturbations such as volcanic eruptions, tropical cyclones, sea-level fluctuations, or floods can play a role in reducing habitat quality and should be considered in models that predict variation in settlement chronologies (Fitzhugh 2003). This fairly simple formulation of the ideal free distribution model can be combined with other variants of the model, such as ideal free distribution with an Allee effect, a model that relaxes the assumption of negative density dependence, and ideal despotic distribution, a model that predicts that differences in competitive ability will restrict the choices for habitat settlement.

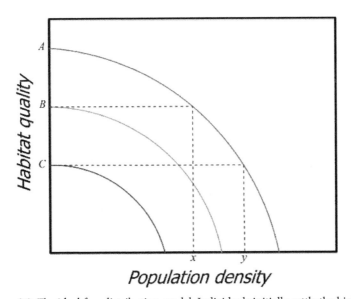

Figure 9.2. The ideal free distribution model. Individuals initially settle the highest-quality habitat (A) until a population density threshold is reached (x), when settlement in the next-highest-ranked habitat (B) is initiated. Habitat quality C is not occupied until population density y is reached. Figure by the authors.

These two variations of the ideal free distribution model are relevant for exploring changes in archaeological settlement patterns (e.g., Allee et al. 1949; Bell and Winterhalder 2014; Fretwell and Lucas 1969; Jazwa et al. 2019). We focus on variation in settlement patterns using the basic ideal free distribution model.

Methods

Geodatabase Development

To document Sāmoan settlement patterns and land use over time and space, we drew on the Sāmoan Archaeological Geospatial Database, which was developed using a GIS platform that combines data about the locations of known archaeological sites with environmental data, radiocarbon dating, and uranium-thorium series dating (Morrison et al. 2018b). This is a collaborative effort between multiple teams working in the Sāmoa archipelago. The database includes information from cultural resource management documents and academic research publications for the entirety of the archipelago. In this database, there are 291 archaeological sites with 248 associated age estimates for Tutuila Island, the focus of our study.

Modeling Habitat Quality

Archaeologically evaluating the ideal free distribution model requires chronological estimates for the serial order of settlements and estimates of habitat quality. Although access to fresh water was certainly an important factor in settlement choice, the distribution of streams across Tutuila suggests that most areas (with the exception of the Tafuna Plain) would have had readily accessible freshwater resources. Thus, fresh water was probably not a limiting factor on decisions about where to settle. For Tutuila, we have assumed that the subsistence base of the island's first settlers involved cultivated root crops (taro, the name for multiple yam species), bananas, and possibly breadfruit, along with shallow-water marine fish and shellfish (Quintus and Cochrane 2018). We have also assumed that two desirable habitat requirements were relatively flat coastal land for cultivating crops (which we modeled as areas with less than 10 degrees slope) and habitats that were close to the coast, especially to coral reefs. We used GIS to create a digital elevation model for the island that identified coastal land units with slopes of less than 10 degrees. We estimated the extent of coral reef habitat using a combination of high-resolution satellite imagery and coastal and hydrography maps in *A Coastal Zone Management Atlas of*

American Samoa (American Samoa Government, Development Planning Office, and University of Hawaii Cartographic Laboratory 1981). While we recognize that there is considerable variation in these two very general categories of habitat, this simple approach enabled us to begin testing the basic predictions of the ideal free distribution model.

We also acknowledge that the coastal geomorphology of Sāmoa was dynamic during the past three millennia (Cochrane et al. 2016) and that this may have affected coral reef abundance and quality. However, we expect that the large-scale geographical differences that are observable today also held in the past; for example, contemporary differences in the relative size of coastal flats were probably broadly similar in the past. Indeed, according to the higher-than-present sea-level stands that have been reconstructed for the Sāmoan Islands (see Goodwin and Grossman 2003), many of Tutuila's small embayments probably had even smaller coastal flats than we see today, which would have restricted both settlement and agricultural activities.

Finally, habitat quality in the central region was probably adversely affected by the Leone Volcanic series on the Tafuna Plain. While most of the subaerial parts of Tutuila were formed around 1,000,000–1,500,000 years ago (McDougall 1985), the Leone Volcanics are part of a major post-erosion volcanic rift system that extends northwest to Savai'i (see Figure 9.1) and dates to the Holocene (Stearns 1944:1313). Although no geologic work has been conducted to refine this age estimate, archaeological research by Addison and colleagues (2006; Addison 2014) identified intact ash layers up to 20 cm thick overlying ceramic-bearing archaeological deposits on the Tafuna Plain. Charcoal samples from contexts with ceramics below the ash layers date to cal AD 420–600 (Addison et al. 2006:9). The authors note that additional subsurface investigations in the vicinity of the dated deposits did not find paleosols between the initial lava substrate and subsequently deposited tuff and ash deposits. This suggests that ash and tuff deposition was frequent enough to inhibit the formation of soils. The Tafuna Plain may have been a largely barren and rocky landscape for the first 1,000–1,500 years of human occupation. Depending on the periodicity and magnitude of volcanic events, much of western and central Tutuila may have been uninhabitable for extended periods of time. The present analysis places these findings within a larger, island-wide settlement history and goes some way toward evaluating the possibility that these eruptive events both adversely affected habitat quality and may have been perceived as settlement risks by people in the past. It is possible that the Tafuna Plain was not perceived as habitable or sufficiently risk free until after volcanic action ceased.

Analytical Land Units for Chronological Modeling

We used Bayesian calibration models to document chronological patterns in settlement in Sāmoa. Before developing Bayesian chronological models and tracking settlement and land use, it is necessary to define an appropriate analytic spatial scale for aggregating dates. For example, models built at the scale of the individual deposits may be formulated at such a fine resolution that they limit comparability across an island landscape but may be useful for documenting intervalley trends in land use. For our analysis we generated analytical land units on the island of Tutuila that approximate valleys. Generally, these units are contiguous land areas that consist of coastal flats and valley bottoms. These units are largely separated by geographic features such as valley slopes and ridges. The two exceptions are the Tafuna Plain, which consists of uninterrupted flat land, and a number of upland sites that were aggregated into the general class of ridgelines even though they are not contiguous. Ridgelines include three upland settlements investigated by Pearl (2004; see also Moore and Kennedy 1999); four other settlements (Levaga, Lefutu, Old Vatia, and Masausi); and the major basalt quarry of Tatagamatau (see Best et al. 1989). Notably, units vary considerably in size; the Tafuna Plain,

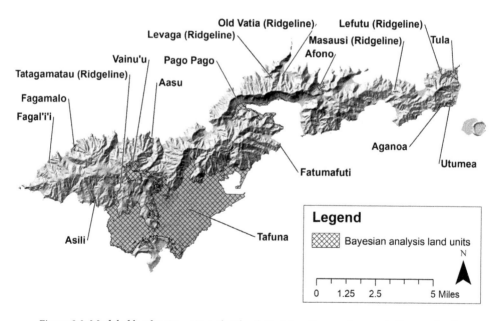

Figure 9.3. Modeled land units on Tutuila Island. Each location on the map indicates a land unit, except for the five ridgeline places, which correspond to one land unit. Figure by the authors.

for example, is quite large. Thirteen land units, which feature 39 individual archaeological sites that are associated with radiocarbon dates, met our modeling criteria (discussed later). These land units constituted the spatial units for our Bayesian chronological modeling. Figure 9.3 shows the village and/or traditional names of the key sites in these units.

Combining Land Units into Zones

Initially we attempted to assess habitat quality at the scale of individual land units, but it became apparent that modeling variation at this scale would not produce meaningful results. We hypothesized that the spatial scale of habitat variability that structured past settlement choice occurred over a larger geographic area and that our initial analysis was too fine-grained. To address this problem, we changed our analytical scale for habitat quality from individual land units to provinces or zones. We identified three zones of relatively equal size but of varying habitat quality and labeled them East, Central, and West (Figure 9.4). We excluded the Tafuna Plain land unit from this analysis because it is not known when the plain and the related landforms in the Leone Volcanic series formed. Thus, combining its settlement history with the settlement history of other land units in the Central Zone could be problematic.

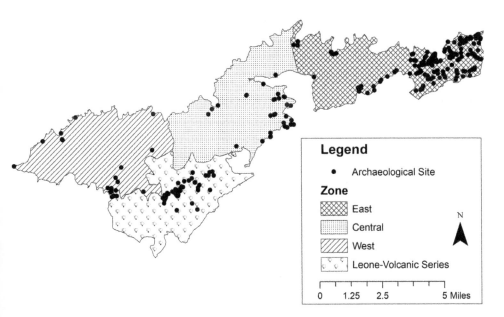

Figure 9.4. Map showing the Leone Volcanic series, analytical settlement zones, and all identified archaeological sites within each zone. Figure by the authors.

Bayesian Chronological Modeling in OxCal

To gain accurate estimates for the timing of settlement, we first filtered the available radiocarbon results according to a set of explicit criteria and then built a series of Bayesian models in OxCal 4.4.2 (Bronk Ramsey 2017).

A Priori Chronological Data

To ensure reasonable relationships between the Bayesian estimates and the target event of interest—initial settlement of each land unit—we used the oldest radiocarbon determinations from each unit and excluded dates that were more than 200 years younger than the oldest date. This criterion ensures that radiocarbon determinations associated with post-settlement activities do not skew "Boundary" start estimates for land units toward younger dates.

We also excluded radiocarbon determinations obtained from bulk soil samples and from radiocarbon laboratories known to have produced questionable results (e.g., the Gakushuin Laboratory). The resulting subset of radiocarbon determinations are all for terrestrial samples. For determinations on samples with known or potential inbuilt age (e.g., identified long-lived species or unidentified charcoal or wood) we applied a "Charcoal" outlier parameter (following Bronk Ramsey 2009; Dee and Bronk Ramsey 2014).

Because models with only one determination can produce imprecise and potentially inaccurate results, we created calibration models only for land units with two or more radiocarbon determinations that met the above criteria. (We acknowledge that models with only two determinations can still be problematic, but we accepted this as a trade-off for increased overall sample size). We excluded some areas with large radiocarbon datasets from this analysis (e.g., 'Aoa) because they did not meet our modeling criteria.

Model Parameters

We used the IntCal20 calibration curve (Reimer et al. 2020) because for radiocarbon analysis, the boundary between the atmosphere of the Southern and Northern Hemispheres is considered to lie along the Intertropical Convergence Zone (McCormac et al. 2004:1088; Petchey et al. 2009:2238). Since the Sāmoan archipelago lies within a part of the South Pacific Convergence Zone that merges with the Intertropical Convergence Zone, we have used the Northern Hemisphere calibration curve.

Given the considerable archaeological research that indicates that

Sāmoa was settled after most other islands in the Lapita geographical range (Rieth and Cochrane 2018), we used this information to constrain the "Boundary" start estimates for each land unit. We recreated a Bayesian model from Sheppard and colleagues (2015) for the timing of Lapita period colonization of the Reef Islands and Santa Cruz Islands (to the west of Sāmoa), and we used that model's start "Boundary" as a terminus post quem for settlement of each land unit using the "After" function in OxCal. Our logic is that radiocarbon chronologies for the earliest Lapita period ceramic settlements in the Santa Cruz Islands indicate that Sāmoa was likely settled later than the Reef Islands and Santa Cruz Islands (Sheppard et al. 2015). The geographical position of Sāmoa and post-settlement changes in artifact inventories that do not extend to Sāmoa support this logic. Using these criteria enabled us to create "Phase" models for all land units in which the "Boundary" start estimates provide the initial settlement dates. All chronological estimates are presented as 95.4% highest posterior density intervals.

Sheppard and colleagues' (2015) model has several marine dates that we recalibrated using the updated Marine20 calibration curve (Heaton et al. 2020). The original local marine reservoir correction (ΔR) that Sheppard and colleagues (2015) used was based on a charcoal-shell pair (unidentified charcoal in *Trochus* spp. shell). We updated the ΔR for Marine20 using an online ΔR application[1] applying the Radiocarbon Dated NoHem method (described in Reimer and Reimer 2017). We set marine radiocarbon age to 3137 ± 24 (NZA-53598, *Trochus* shell), and we set the ^{14}C BP to 2768 ± 15 (NZA-53697, the charcoal embedded in the shell). The result was in an updated ΔR of -93 ± 36. The updated colonization estimate for the Reef Islands and Santa Cruz Islands is 3005–2780 cal BP (95.4% highest posterior density, rounded to the nearest five years), which is similar to Sheppard and colleagues' (2015) estimate using Intcal13 and Marine13 with a ΔR of +122 ± 28, which produced an estimate of 2920–2793 cal BP (95.4% highest posterior density).

Model Queries

After we created individual land unit models, we extracted the "Boundary" start estimates and calculated the probability that any land unit was settled before another using the "Order" query in OxCal. The order is based on a greater than 50% probability that a particular land unit was settled before another land unit. From the results of this query, we organized the land units into a probable settlement sequence.[2]

Results

Assessment of Tutuila Geospatial Data

Figure 9.4 shows that while the 291 archaeological sites on Tutuila are widely distributed across the island, there is a greater concentration in the east. Gaps in site distribution may be attributable to a number of factors. Some areas may be insufficiently surveyed, modern development may have concealed some sites, and some sites may have been unsuitable for habitation, for example because of steep topography and limited land for settlement. Many locations along the western and northern parts of the island have not been sufficiently studied. These are areas where current settlement and associated development projects are limited compared to other areas. In contrast, today the Tafuna Plain is a densely populated area where numerous historic preservation projects have been conducted. In addition, much of the eastern portion of the island was systematically surveyed in the 1980s (Clark and Herdrich 1993). Finally, modern development in the central portion of the island near Pago Pago has likely obscured or destroyed evidence of initial settlement in what would have almost certainly been an attractive location for initial human colonists.

Figure 9.4 further illustrates that despite volcanic activity on the Tafuna Plain (see below), Sāmoan populations occupied this area. Although the Leone Volcanic series is very poorly dated, we assume that settlement on the Tafuna Plain occurred in the post-volcanic period which, based on our chronological modeling (detailed in the Chronological Modeling Results section), was likely 2245–1745 cal BP (95.4%).

Habitat Quality Assessment

Expectations of the model are predicated on variation in habitat quality. We labeled three zones of relatively equal size as East, Central, and West (Figure 9.4). Preliminary assessment of habitat quality across these three zones showed that the eastern end of the island has the greatest proportion of both coastal flat land (less than 10 degrees slope) and coral reef and thus should have been the highest-ranked habitat, assuming these two dimensions of variability were important to the island's earliest settlers. The western end of the island, in contrast, has the smallest amount of coastal flat land and coral reef and thus is the lowest-ranked habitat (Table 9.1). The amount of habitable land is not positively correlated with the size of the three zones (Table 9.1). The ideal free distribution model predicts that the initial settlement sequence for Tutuila began in the East, then extended to the central region of the island, and terminated in the West Zone. We evaluated this model using Bayesian chronological analysis.

Table 9.1. Acreage of coastal flat land and coral reef habitat in the East, Central, and West Zones of Tutuila

Zone	Coastal flat land		Coral reef habitat		Total habitat acreage
	N	%	N	%	
East	954	11.50	1,257	15.10	8,318
Central	484	0.06	590	0.07	8,556
West	226	0.02	452	0.05	9,387

Note: Ridgelines are not included in this table because although they offer limited amounts of flat land, they lack coral reef habitats.

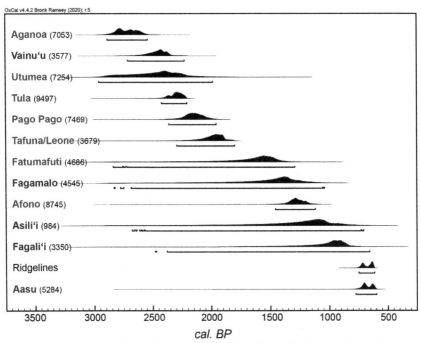

Figure 9.5. Bayesian start boundary estimates for the thirteen land units displayed in Figure 9.3. Figure by the authors.

Chronological Modeling Results

Thirteen land units met our criteria for inclusion in the Bayesian chronological analysis (Figure 9.5, Table 9.2). While the results of the Bayesian analysis produced large date ranges, the overall ordering of the settlement sequence (Figure 9.5, Tables 9.2 and 9.3) illuminates a number of important patterns.

First, most of the earliest settlements occurred on the eastern end of the island. A noticeable exception to this pattern is the early upland settlement at Vainu'u. At 2835–2490 cal BP (95.4%), Aganoa is the earliest settlement (Moore and Kennedy 1999; Pearl and Sauck 2014), followed by Vainu'u (Eckert and Welch 2013), Utumea (Moore and Kennedy 1999), and Tula (Rieth and Cochrane 2012). This was followed by settlement as much as 600 years later in central Tutuila, including Pago Pago (Addison and Asaua 2006), portions of the Tafuna Plain/Leone, and Fatumafuti (Morrison and Addison 2008, 2009). This delay in occupation may have been related to active volcanism on the Tafuna Plain. It may have been as long as another four centuries before people occupied the coastlines of small embayments in the north and west. Not surprisingly, upland ridges were the last locations to be settled. These modeled results point to a trend of early settlement in the eastern sector of the island and subsequent movement into the central, western, and upland locations (see Figure 9.3).

Table 9.2. Results of single-phase Bayesian chronological models for the thirteen land units showing highest posterior density estimates

	Initial settlement estimate				Zone
	cal BP		BC/AD		
Land unit	95.4%	68.2%	95.4%	68.2%	
Aganoa (LU-7053)	2835–2490	2760–2550	885–540 BC	810–605 BC	East
Vainu'u (LU-3577)	2655–2175	2475–2305	705–225 BC	530–355 BC	West
Utumea (LU-7254)	2910–1930	2650–2170	960 BC–AD 20	700–220 BC	East
Tula (LU-9497)	2375–2155	2280–2175	425–205 BC	330–225 BC	East
Pago Pago (LU-7469)	2315–1905	2175–2005	365 BC–AD 45	225–55 BC	Central
Tafuna/Leone (LU-3679)	2245–1745	2005–1835	295 BC–AD 205	55 BC–AD 115	Central
Fatumafuti (LU-4686)	2790–1240	1840–1345	840 BC–AD 710	AD 110–605	Central
Fagamalo (LU-4545)	2785–990	1730–1095	835 BC–AD 960	AD 220–855	West
Afono (LU-8745)	1400–1065	1290–1145	AD 550–885	AD 660–805	East
Asili'i (LU-984)	2620–655	1540–830	670 BC–AD 1295	AD 410–1120	West
Fagali'i (LU-3350)	2350–610	1200–775	400 BC–AD 1340	AD 750–1175	West
Ridgelines	700–565	685–570	AD 1250–1385	AD 1265–1380	Ridgelines
Aasu (LU-5284)	730–550	680–565	AD 1220–1400	AD 1270–1385	West

Note: Ranges have been rounded up to nearest five years. All models have agreement indices above 60. Land units are arranged from top to bottom according to the results of OxCal's "Order" query (see Table 9.3).

Table 9.3. Probabilistic rank ordering of initial settlement dates for Land Units using OxCal's "Order" query

t_1 \ t_2	LU_7053	LU_3577	LU_7254	LU_9497	LU_7469	LU_3679	LU_4686	LU_4545	LU_8745	LU_984	LU_3350	Ridgeline	LU_528
LU_7053	—	0.9562	0.8213	0.9979	0.9987	0.9943	0.9613	0.9681	0.9999	0.9756	0.9861	1.0000	1.0000
LU_3577		—	0.5056	0.9141	0.9795	0.9781	0.9141	0.9283	0.9997	0.9452	0.9692	1.0000	1.0000
LU_7254			—	0.7566	0.8948	0.9364	0.9042	0.9211	0.9983	0.9405	0.9671	1.0000	1.0000
LU_9497				—	0.9216	0.9561	0.8807	0.9000	0.9996	0.9234	0.9574	1.0000	1.0000
LU_7469					—	0.8562	0.8387	0.8647	0.9993	0.897	0.9433	1.0000	1.0000
LU_3679						—	0.786	0.8228	0.9988	0.866	0.9269	1.0000	1.0000
LU_4686							—	0.6607	0.968	0.772	0.877	1.0000	0.9999
LU_4545								—	0.8389	0.6887	0.8328	1.0000	0.9998
LU_8745									—	0.5219	0.7497	1.0000	0.9997
LU_984										—	0.6963	0.9900	0.9887
LU_3350											—	0.9861	0.9834
Ridgeline												—	0.5129
LU_5284													—

Note: The values on this table indicate the probability that t_1 is older than t_2.

Discussion

Our model includes an assessment of the spatial patterns of settlements across Tutuila and an analysis of two measures of habitat quality. The results of the Bayesian analysis indicate that the eastern portion of Tutuila Island was the locus of initial settlement and that for the most part, expansion appears to have occurred from the East to the West Zones (Figure 9.5). An exception to this trend is the early component at the upland site of Vainu'u, which may not necessarily be indicative of permanent habitation and does not appear to be continuous with later occupation of the same locale (Eckert and Welch 2013). It is possible that early use of the uplands was limited in duration and was perhaps restricted to time periods between volcanic events. A second exception to the model predictions is the placement of Afono later in the settlement sequence than expected. This surprising result is likely due to a lack of systematic archaeological data recovery in the embayment at Afono and the nature of previous work done at that location in a specifically defined historic preservation context. Previous archaeological investigations may not have been focused on acquiring early dates from previously defined locales. Overall, according to our results, the settlement history for Tutuila is consistent with theoretical predictions of the ideal free distribution model. Our results indicate the importance of coastal flats and coral reefs in decisions colonizers made about which habitats to settle.

Habitat Quality and Dynamic Environmental Processes

There are a number of points to consider with respect to our results in relation to the late Holocene Leone Volcanics. First, as discussed, although large portions of central and western Tutuila are flat and habitable today, the plain may not have formed until several centuries after initial human occupation of the island. It may also be that even after the plain formed, it was some time before the area was suitable for agriculture and that coral reefs may have taken some time to develop after volcanic activity. While volcanism was undoubtedly a major factor that limited habitability and settlement in some regions, the timing, periodicity, and extent of these events is poorly understood. Addison and colleagues' (2006; Addison 2014) archaeological observations make clear that portions of the Tafuna Plain were experiencing volcanic activity as late as 1,500 years ago. Our chronological modeling suggests that at least limited settlement had commenced on the Tafuna Plain by around 2245–1745 cal BP (95.4%). Further archaeological and geological research should be directed to resolving the timing and impact of volcanism on Tutuila in the late Holocene.

While we did not model sea-level decline in the mid- to late Holocene, it is another important variable to consider in analyses of island habitability (e.g., Allen et al. 2016; Cochrane et al. 2016; Morrison et al. 2018a). The small and narrow coastal plains that exist today on western Tutuila would have been even smaller 3,000 years ago during the 1- to 2-m-higher sea stand (Grossman et al. 1998; Dickinson 2003). However, our findings resonate with findings from Rieth and colleagues'(2008) GIS-based model of the effects of differential sea level on initial human settlement of Tutuila. Their results predicted that 3,000 years ago, more locations were suitable for settlement along the East and Central Zones of the island and that only two were present along the Tafuna Plain and west Tutuila coast.

Analytical Concerns

Several analytical issues with our findings warrant discussion. Our stringent modeling criteria required that a number of early dates at key localities like 'Aoa, located on eastern Tutuila, be excluded. However, while dating at 'Aoa is problematic, the potentially early dates of circa 3000–2800 BP (Clark and Michlovic 1996) are consistent with our general results of early settlement occurring in the East Zone of the island.

We have also focused on assessing only two of the ideal free distribution model predictions. With the data that are currently available, we have not been able to explore the role of habitat density in initiating out-migration. Codding and Bird (2015:16) comment on the challenges of estimating past population density using archaeological data. While in theory we could have assessed this prediction of the ideal free distribution model by analyzing continuity in radiocarbon distributions from each of the land units in our study, in reality biases associated with particular excavation sampling strategies and inconsistencies in the reporting of radiocarbon protocols by excavators makes it difficult to evaluate the relationship between habitat density and out-migration. Also of note is the possibility that due to the Allee effect, top-ranked habitats might have been temporarily depopulated as individuals move into lesser-ranked habitats. Another possibility is that rapid habitat switching may have occurred (Codding and Bird 2015:15; Winterhalder et al. 2010).

Our analysis points to the potential value of renewed excavations to ensure that gaps in the current settlement chronology are not a result of biased field sampling, particularly an overemphasis on the dating of early ceramic-bearing deposits. For example, at Tula, Rieth and colleagues (Rieth and Cochrane 2012; Rieth and Morrison 2017; see also Cochrane et al. 2013) documented what appears to be a continuous sequence of depositions at the seawardmost location they tested, but they dated only the basal ceramic-bearing deposit. They dated additional deposits on the coastal plain at three other locations that returned later age estimates (~620 ± 30 and ~350 ± 30), but it is unclear whether the gap in occupation (instead of a continuous sequence, as ideal free distribution model predicts) is the result of dating biases or other factors.

Conclusions

We used the ideal free distribution model to predict that two key aspects of habitat suitability, 1) flat coastal land (as a proxy for agricultural potential) and 2) the extent of coral reef (as a measure of marine resource productivity), shaped the process of human settlement across Tutuila Island in the Sāmoan archipelago. Our initial evaluations suggested that colonizers ranked the East Zone of Tutuila the highest, sequentially followed by the Central and the West Zones of the island. We also hypothesized that risks from volcanic activity in central Tutuila affected settlement adversely. To test the fit between the predictions of our model and the archaeological record, we used a geospatial database of 291 archaeological sites and 248 ^{14}C dates. Bayesian chronological modeling supported an order of settlement that fit with our initial predictions of an east-to-west settlement progression. This trend held despite the volcanic risks identified for the Central Zone, especially the Tafuna Plain. Our Bayesian analysis also indicated relatively late settlement of remote upland ridgeline locations. No ridgeline settlements returned reliable radiocarbon ages that are earlier than 3000 cal BP. This result suggests the importance of flat coastal plains and coral reef habitat for early settlers in Sāmoa. Our methodology identifies eastern Tutuila as an important locality for understanding the initial settlement of the island. This finding has value for both researchers and cultural resource managers.

Another important outcome is the finding that volcanic activity played a more consequential role in the process of island settlement than previously recognized. Our results show that volcanism on the Tafuna Plain slowed, but did not prevent, occupation in the Central Zone. Sustained settlement did not develop for some time after volcanic activity. We suggest that volcanic activity may have inhibited soil formation and the development of coral reefs for an unknown period. However, after active volcanism ceased, the fertile, well-drained volcanic ash enhanced the area's agricultural productivity. The large number of archaeological sites on the Tafuna Plain that postdate the early settlement period seems to support this analysis. Interestingly, none of these later settlements are located on the island's coasts, raising the possibility that marine resources were less important for these populations. The unexpected result that volcanic activity in the late Holocene enhanced the productivity of a large portion of central Tutuila Island and improved habitat quality points to the importance of investigating past ecological dynamics and underscores the process by which we learn from simple models such as the one we used in this study.

The ideal free distribution model also provides a foundation for investigating temporal changes in habitat quality and human diets. Although zooarchaeological analyses of fish and shellfish assemblages from Tutuila have thus far suggested considerable stability over time, Morrison and Addison (2009) found modest evidence for a decline in a reliance on fish later in the Sāmoan sequence. Other studies have suggested declines in certain fish taxa (e.g., Rieth and Morrison 2017). Isotopic studies also suggest a greater dependence on agricultural resources over time (Valentine et al. 2011), although these interpretations have been recently challenged (Eerkens et al. 2019) and sample sizes remain small.

Finally, our analysis of the ideal free distribution model suggests that Sāmoan populations increasingly faced less viable settlement opportunities over time. People did not begin to occupy habitats with limited coastal plains and poor coral reef habitat until the beginning of the first millennium AD. Shortly after (if not concomitant with) the first settlement of Tutuila's West Zone (sometime in the period 180–833 AD), Sāmoa experienced a prolonged drought that presumably adversely affected habitat suitability across the island. At the same time, the first unequivocal indicators of human activity appeared in the closest East Polynesian archipelago, the southern Cook Islands some 1,400 km to the east (Sear et al. 2020). The overlap in the timing of these processes, habitat infilling, prolonged drought in the west, and population dispersals to the east is notable. That population dispersal is consistent with predictions of the ideal free distribution model. As habitats in Sāmoa filled and population densities increased, the benefits of long-distance migrations began to outweigh the costs of persisting in an increasingly suboptimal homeland.

Notes

1. "Calculate ΔR," Queen's University Belfast Center for Climate, the Environment, and Chronology, accessed May 11, 2021, http://calib.org/JS/JSdeltar20/.

2. All Bayesian modeling code and results can be found at https://github.com/rdinapoli/Tutuila_IFD_Bayesian.

References Cited

Addison, D. J. 2014. *Late-Holocene Volcanics on Tutuila Island, American Sāmoa: An Archaeological Perspective on Their Chronological and Spatial Distribution.* Prepared for Utu Abe Malaae Executive Director. American Sāmoa Power Authority, Pago Pago.

Addison, D. J., and T. S. Asaua. 2006. 100 New Dates from Tutuila and Manua: Additional Data Addressing Chronological Issues in Samoan Prehistory. *Journal of Samoan Studies* 2:95–117.

Addison, D. J., T. Tago, J. Toloa, and E. Pearthree. 2006. Ceramic Deposits below Fifth to Sixth Century AD Volcanic Ash Fall at Pava'ia'i, Tutuila Island, American Samoa: Preliminary Results from Site AS-31-171. *New Zealand Journal of Archaeology* 27:5–18.

Allee, W. C., O. Park., A. E. Emerson, T. Park, and K. P Schmidt. 1949. *Principles of Animal Ecology.* Saunders, Philadelphia.

Allen, M. S. 2012. Molluscan Foraging Efficiency and Mobility amongst Agricultural Foragers: A Case Study from Northern New Zealand. *Journal of Archaeological Science* 39:295–307.

Allen, M. S., A. E. Morrison, A. M. Lorrey, J. X. Zhao, and G. E. Jacobsen. 2016. Timing, Magnitude and Effects of Late Holocene Sea Level Drawdown on Island Habitability, Aitutaki, Cook Islands. *Archaeology in Oceania* 51(2):108–121.

American Samoa Government, Development Planning Office, and University of Hawaii Cartographic Laboratory. 1981. *A Coastal Zone Management Atlas of American Samoa.* American Samoa Government, Development Planning Office, Pago Pago.

Bell, Adrian Viliami, and Bruce Winterhalder. 2014. The Population Ecology of Despotism. *Human Nature* 25(1):121–135.

Best, Simon, Helen M. Leach, and Daniel C. Witter. 1989. Report on the Second Phase of Fieldwork at the Tataga-matau Site, American Samoa, July–August 1988. Department of Anthropology, University of Otago, Dunedin, New Zealand.

Bird, Douglas W., and James F. O'Connell. 2006. Behavioral Ecology and Archaeology. *Journal of Archaeological Research* 14(2):143–188.

Bronk Ramsey, C. 2009. Bayesian Analysis of Radiocarbon Dates. *Radiocarbon* 51(1):337–360.

———. 2017. Methods for Summarizing Radiocarbon Datasets. *Radiocarbon* 59(6):1809–1833.

Clark, J. T., and D. J. Herdrich. 1993. Prehistoric Settlement System in Eastern Tutuila, American Samoa. *Journal of the Polynesian Society* 102(2):147–185.

———. 1993. Prehistoric Settlement System in Eastern Tutuila, American Samoa. *Journal of the Polynesian Society* 102(2):147–185.

Clark, J. T., and M. G. Michlovic. 1996. An Early Settlement in the Polynesian Homeland: Excavations at 'Aoa Valley, Tutuila Island, American Samoa. *Journal of Field Archaeology* 23(2):151–167.

Clark, J. T., S. Quintus, M. Weisler, E. St. Pierre, L. Nothdurft, and Y. Feng. 2016. Refining the Chronology for West Polynesian Colonization: New Data from the Samoan Archipelago. *Journal of Archaeological Science: Reports* 6:266–274.

Cochrane, E. E., H. Kane, C. Fletcher, M. Horrocks, J. Mills, M. Barbee, A. E. Morrison, and M. M. Ta'ūtunu. 2016. Lack of Suitable Coastal Plains Likely Influenced Lapita

(~2800 cal. BP) Settlement of Sāmoa: Evidence from South-Eastern 'Upolu. *The Holocene* 26(1):126–35.

Cochrane, E. E., T. M. Rieth, and W. R. Dickinson. 2013. Plainware Ceramics from Sāmoa: Insights into Ceramic Chronology, Cultural Transmission, and Selection among Colonizing Populations. *Journal of Anthropological Archaeology* 32(4):499–510.

Codding, Brian F., and Douglas W. Bird. 2015. Behavioral Ecology and the Future of Archaeological Science. *Journal of Archaeological Science* 56:9–20.

Davidson, J. M. 1969. Settlement Patterns in Samoa before 1840. *Journal of the Polynesian Society* 78(1):44–82.

Dee, M. W., and C. Bronk Ramsey. 2014. High-Precision Bayesian Modeling of Samples Susceptible to Inbuilt Age. *Radiocarbon* 56(1):83–94.

Dickinson, W. R. 2003. Impact of Mid-Holocene Hydro-Isostatic Highstand in Regional Sea Level on Habitability of Islands in Pacific Oceania. *Journal of Coastal Research* 19(3):489–502.

Dickinson, W. R., and R. C. Green. 1998. Geoarchaeological Context of Holocene Subsidence at the Ferry Berth Lapita Site, Mulifanua, Upolu, Samoa. *Geoarchaeology* 13(3):239–263.

DiNapoli, Robert J., and Alex E. Morrison. 2017. Human Behavioural Ecology and Pacific Archaeology. *Archaeology in Oceania* 52(1):1–12.

DiNapoli, Robert J., Alex E. Morrison, Carl P. Lipo, T. L. Hunt, and Brian G. Lane. 2018. East Polynesian Islands as Models of Cultural Divergence: The Case of Rapa Nui and Rapa Iti. *Journal of Island and Coastal Archaeology* 13(2):206–223.

Eckert, S. L., and D. R. Welch. 2013. A Commanding View of the Pacific: Highland Land Use as Viewed from Vainu'u, a Multi-Component Site on Tutuila, American Samoa. *Archaeology in Oceania* 48(1):13–25.

Eerkens, Jelmer W., Eric J. Bartelink, Julianna Bartel, and Phillip R. Johnson. 2019. Isotopic Insights into Dietary Life History, Social Status, and Food Sharing in American Samoa. *American Antiquity* 84(2):336–352.

Field, Julie S. 2004. Environmental and Climatic Considerations: A Hypothesis for Conflict and the Emergence of Social Complexity in Fijian Prehistory. *Journal of Anthropological Archaeology* 23(1):79–99.

———. 2005. Land Tenure, Competition and Ecology in Fijian Prehistory. *Antiquity* 79(305):586–600.

Fitzhugh, B. 2003. *The Evolution of Complex Hunter-Gatherers: Archaeological Evidence from the North Pacific.* Kluwer Academic/Plenum, New York.

Fretwell, S. D., and H. L. Lucas Jr. 1969. On Territorial Behavior and Other Factors Influencing Habitat Distribution in Birds, I: Theoretical Development. *Acta Biotheoretica* 19:16–36.

Giovas, Christina M., and Scott M. Fitzpatrick. 2014. Prehistoric Migration in the Caribbean: Past Perspectives, New Models and the Ideal Free Distribution of West Indian Colonization. *World Archaeology* 46(4):569–589.

Goodwin, I. D., and E. E. Grossman. 2003. Middle to Late Holocene Coastal Evolution along the South Coast of Upolu Island, Samoa. *Marine Geology* 202(1–2):1–16.

Green, R. C. 1967. Settlement Patterns: Four Case Studies from Polynesia. *Asian and Pacific Archaeology Series* 1:101–132.

———. 1974. Pottery from the Lagoon at Mulifanua, Upolu. In *Archaeology in Western Samoa*, vol. 2, edited by R. C. Green and J. M. Davidson, pp. 170–175. Auckland Institute and Museum, Auckland.

———. 2002. A Retrospective View of Settlement Pattern Studies in Samoa. In *Pacific Landscapes: Archaeological Approaches*, edited by T. N. Ladefoged and M. W. Graves, pp. 125–152. Easter Island Foundation Press, Los Osos, California.

Green, R. C., and J. Davidson. 1969/1974. *Archaeology in Western Sāmoa*. Vols. 1 and 2. Auckland Institute and Museum, Auckland.

Grossman, E. E., C. H. Fletcher III, and B. M. Richmond. 1998. The Holocene Sea-Level Highstand in the Equatorial Pacific: Analysis of the Insular Paleosea-Level Database. *Coral Reefs* 17(3):309–327.

Heaton, T. J., P. Köhler, M. Butzin, E. Bard, R. W. Reimer, W. E. Austin, C. B. Ramsey, P. M. Grootes, K. A. Hughen, B. Kromer, P. J. Reimer, J. Adkins, A. Burke, M. A. Cook, J. Olsen, and L. C. Skinner. 2020. Marine20—The Marine Radiocarbon Age Calibration Curve (0–55,000 cal BP). *Radiocarbon* 62(4):779–820.

Jazwa, C. S., D. J. Kennett, and B. Winterhalder. 2016. A Test of Ideal Free Distribution Predictions Using Targeted Survey and Excavation on California's Northern Channel Islands. *Journal of Archaeological Method and Theory* 23(4):1242–1284.

Jazwa, C. S., D. J. Kennett, B. Winterhalder, and T. L. Joslin. 2019. Territoriality and the Rise of Despotic Social Organization on Western Santa Rosa Island, California. *Quaternary International* 518(30):41–56.

Kennett, D. J., A. Anderson, and B. Winterhalder. 2006. The Ideal Free Distribution, Food Production, and the Colonization of Oceania. In *Behavioral Ecology and the Transition to Agriculture*, edited by D. J. Kennett and B. Winterhalder, pp. 265–288. University of California Press, Berkeley.

Kennett, Douglas J., and Bruce Winterhalder. 2008. Demographic Expansion, Despotism and the Colonisation of East and South Polynesia. In *Islands of Inquiry: Colonisation, Seafaring and the Archaeology of Maritime Landscapes*, edited by Geoffrey Clark, Foss Leach, and Sue O'Connor, pp. 87–96. Australia National University Press, Canberra.

Kirch, P. V. 1997. The Lapita Peoples: Ancestors of the Oceanic World. The Peoples of South-East Asia and the Pacific. Blackwell, Oxford.

Kirch, P. V. 2017. *On the Road of the Winds: An Archaeological History of the Pacific Islands before European Contact.* University of California Press, Berkeley.

Ladefoged, Thegn N., and Michael W. Graves (editors). 2002. *Pacific Landscapes: Archaeological Approaches.* Easter Island Foundation, Los Osos, California.

Martinsson-Wallin, Helene, Geoffrey Clark, and Paul Wallin. 2006. Monuments and People: The Longevity of Monuments: The Past in the Present—A Report of the State of the Pulemelei Site, Savai'i, Sāmoa. *Journal of Sāmoan Studies* (2):57–63.

McCormac, F. G., Hogg, A. G., Blackwell, P. G., Buck, C. E., Higham, T. F., and P. J. Reimer. 2004. SHCal04 Southern Hemisphere Calibration, 0–11.0 cal kyr BP. *Radiocarbon* 46(3):1087–1092.

McCoy, P. 1976. *Easter Island Settlement Patterns in the Late Prehistoric and Protohistoric Periods.* International Fund for Monuments, New York.

McDougall, I. 1985. Age and Evolution of the Volcanoes of Tutuila, American Samoa. *Pacific Science* 39(4):311–320.

Moore, J. R. and J. Kennedy. 1999. *Results of an Archaeological Cultural Resource Evaluation for the East and West Tutuila Water Line Project, Tutuila Island, American Samoa* Draft report for the American Samoa Power Authority. Haleiwa, Hawaii, Archaeological Consultants of the Pacific.

Morrison, A. E. 2012. An Archaeological Analysis of Rapa Nui (Easter Island, Chile) Settlement Structure. PhD dissertation, University of Hawaii, Manoa, Honolulu.

Morrison, A. E., and D. J. Addison. 2008. Assessing the Role of Climate Change and Human Predation on Marine Resources at the Fatu-ma-Futi Site, Tutuila Island, American Samoa: An Agent Based Model. *Archaeology in Oceania* 43(1):22–34.

———. 2009. Examining Causes and Trends in Marine Trophic Level Change: 1500 Years of Fish Exploitation at Fatu-ma-Futi, Tutuila Island, American Sāmoa. *Journal of Island and Coastal Archaeology* 4(2):177–194.

Morrison, A. E., E. E. Cochrane, T. Rieth, and M. Horrocks. 2018a. Archaeological and Sedimentological Data Indicate Lapita Settlement on a Newly Formed Coastal Plain: Tavua Island, Mamanuca Group, Fiji. *The Holocene* 28(1):44–55.

Morrison, A. E., and J. T. O'Connor. 2018. Settlement Pattern Studies in Polynesia: Past Projects, Current Progress, and Future Prospects. In *The Oxford Handbook of Prehistoric Oceania*, edited by E. E. Cochrane and T. L. Hunt, pp. 452–466. Oxford University Press, Oxford.

Morrison, A. E., T. M. Rieth, E. E. Cochrane, and R. J. DiNapoli. 2018b. The Samoa Archaeological Geospatial Database: Initial Description and Application to Settlement Pattern Studies in the Samoan Islands. *Journal of the Polynesian Society* 127(1):15.

Pearl, F. B. 2004. The Chronology of Mountain Settlements on Tutuila, American Samoa. *Journal of the Polynesian Society* 113(4):331–348.

Pearl, F. B., and W. A. Sauck. 2014. Geophysical and Geoarchaeological Investigations at Aganoa Beach, American Samoa: An Early Archaeological Site in Western Polynesia. *Geoarchaeology* 29(6):462–476.

Petchey, F. 2001. Radiocarbon Determinations from the Mulifanua Lapita Site, Upolu, Western Samoa. *Radiocarbon* 43(1):63–68.

Petchey, F., M. S. Allen, D. J. Addison, and A. Anderson. 2009. Stability in the South Pacific Surface Marine ^{14}C reservoir over the Last 750 Years: Evidence from American Samoa, the Southern Cook Islands and the Marquesas. *Journal of Archaeological Science* 36(10):2234–2243.

Petchey, F., and P. V. Kirch. 2019. The Importance of Shell: Redating of the To'aga site (Ofu Island, Manu'a) and a Revised Chronology for the Lapita to Polynesian Plainware Transition in Tonga and Sāmoa. *PLOS ONE* 14(9):e0211990.

Prufer, K. M., A. E. Thompson, C. R. Meredith, B. J. Culleton, J. M. Jordan, C. E. Ebert, B. Winterhalder, and D. J. Kennett. 2017. The Classic Period Maya Transition from an Ideal Free to an Ideal Despotic Settlement System at the Polity of Uxbenká. *Journal of Anthropological Archaeology* 45:53–68.

Quintus, S., and E. E. Cochrane. 2018. Pre-contact Samoan Cultivation Practices in Regional and Theoretical Perspective. *Journal of Island and Coastal Archaeology* 13(4):474–500.

Reimer, P. J., W. E. N. Austin, E. Bard, A. Bayliss, P. G. Blackwell, C. Bronk Ramsey, M. Butzin, H. Cheng, R. L. Edwards, M. Friedrich, P. M. Grootes, T. P. Guilderson, I. Hajdas,

T. J. Heaton, A. G. Hogg, K. A. Hughen, B. Kromer, S. W. Manning, R. Muscheler, J. G. Palmer, C. Pearson, J. van der Plicht, R. W. Reimer, D. A. Richards, E. M. Scott, J. R. Southon, C. S. M. Turney, L. Wacker, F. Adolphi, U. Büntgen, M. Capano, S. M. Fahrni, A. Fogtmann-Schulz, R. Friedrich, P. Köhler, S. Kudsk, F. Miyake, J. Olsen, F. Reinig, M. Sakamoto, A. Sookdeo, and S. Talamo. 2020. The IntCal20 Northern Hemisphere Radiocarbon Age Calibration Curve (0–55 cal kBP). *Radiocarbon* 62(4):725–757.

Reimer, R. W., and P. J. Reimer. 2017. An Online Application for ∆R Calculation. *Radiocarbon* 59(5):1623.

Rieth, T. M., and E. E. Cochrane. 2012. *Archaeological Monitoring and Data Recovery in Support of the Federal Emergency Management Agency Permanent Housing Construction Program, Tutuila Island, American Samoa.* International Archaeological Research Institute, Honolulu, Hawaii. Prepared for the Department of Homeland Security, Federal Emergency Management Agency.

———. 2018. The Chronology of Colonization in Remote Oceania. In *The Oxford Handbook of Prehistoric Oceania*, edited by Ethan E. Cochrane and Terry L. Hunt, p. 133. Oxford University Press, Oxford. DOI: 10.1093/oxfordhb/9780199925070.013.010.

Rieth, T. M., and A. E. Morrison. 2017. Pre-Contact Fish Choice and Foraging Efficiency at Tula, American Sāmoa. *Archaeology in Oceania* 52(1):22–31.

Rieth, T. M., A. E. Morrison, and D. J. Addison. 2008. The Temporal and Spatial Patterning of the Initial Settlement of Sāmoa. *Journal of Island and Coastal Archaeology* 3(2):214–239.

Sear, D. A., M. S. Allen, J. D. Hassall, A. E. Maloney, P. G. Langdon, A. E. Morrison, A. C. Henderson, H. Mackay, I. W. Croudace, C. Clarke, and J. P. Sachs. 2020. Human Settlement of East Polynesia Earlier, Incremental, and Coincident with Prolonged South Pacific Drought. *Proceedings of the National Academy of Sciences* 117(16):8813–8819.

Sheppard, P. J., S. Chiu, and R. Walter. 2015. Re-dating Lapita Movement into Remote Oceania. *Journal of Pacific Archaeology* 6(1):26–36.

Stearns, H. T. 1944. Geology of the Samoan Islands. *Geological Society of America Bulletin* 55(11):1279–1332.

Tregenza, T. 1995. Building on the Ideal Free Distribution. *Advances in Ecological Research* 26:253–307.

Valentin, F., E. Herrscher, F. Petchey, and D. J. Addison. 2011. An Analysis of the Last 1000 Years Human Diet on Tutuila (American Samoa) Using Carbon and Nitrogen Stable Isotope Data. *American Antiquity* 76(3):473–486.

Winterhalder, B., D. J. Kennett, M. N. Grote, and J. Bartruff. 2010. Ideal Free Settlement of California's Northern Channel Islands. *Journal of Anthropological Archaeology* 29(4):469–490.

Conclusion

Advances in Current Theoretical Approaches to Coastal Archaeology

HEATHER B. THAKAR AND
CAROLA FLORES FERNANDEZ

As demonstrated through the regional reviews and local case studies in this volume, coastal archaeology from around the world is well positioned to contribute to the advancement of traditional research agendas focused on 1) the environment and ecology of coastal communities, which are often at the frontlines of environmental change; 2) patterns of colonization, dispersal, and migration; 3) the innovation of specialized maritime technology; 4) patterns of settlement and resource use; and 5) the development of social and political complexity, including increased conflict and territoriality. Human behavioral ecology recognizes that there are many paths to fitness that compete for time and energy. Throughout the book we engage with theoretical models derived from human behavioral ecology to gain insights about past coastal societies, adapting them as needed to the problem and regional context at hand.

Archaeological applications of human behavioral ecology largely focus on human use and occupation of the terrestrial environment. When applied to coastal contexts, studies have been geographically concentrated and thematically focused on hunter-gatherer societies (c.f. Plekhov et al. and Gauthier and Thakar, this volume). The chapters in this book offer critical reviews from coastal regions where this theoretical approach has been previously employed and local case studies from coastal regions and time periods where this theoretical approach is still nascent. The authors interrogate the use and utility of prey and patch choice models, ideal distribution models, and niche construction theory, as well as novel perspectives (e.g., traditional ecological knowledge) and agent-based methods to reconstruct patterns of coastal adaptations. These efforts highlight considerations that shift our application or interpretation of these models in coastal contexts. In this way, coastal resources and coastal societies offer opportunities for continued refinement and integration with emerging research frameworks. Each chapter of the book explores theoretical approaches to coastal archaeology, driving advances in the use and utility of human behavioral ecology.

Volume Review

West, Gjesfjeld, Anderson, and Fitzhugh (Chapter 1) demonstrate that the Arctic and Subarctic archaeological record provides adequate evidence to ask fundamental human behavioral ecology questions about the ecological forces that drive long-term changes in diet, population, and settlement patterns. This review suggests that all three variables—diet, population, and settlement patterns—are tied to the coastal environment in critical ways and that the archaeological record of these regions has great potential to clarify these relationships in the context of human behavioral ecology. The rich zooarchaeological record of this region suggests that different hunter-gatherer groups adapted to localized climate change in different ways, but regional studies are rare, and human behavioral ecology models could help to clarify the relationship among climate, extreme seasonality, animal availability, and northern peoples' complex foodways on a broader scale. Paleodemography and settlement studies suggest that the marine environment played an important role in the growth and mobility of human populations across the Arctic and Subarctic, but the relationship between environmental changes and demographic changes remains elusive. Human behavioral ecology models should be applied more widely to understand how population dynamics, resource use, and technological change could improve our understanding of cultural change. Although optimal foraging models may not address some of the key variables driving the dynamics of Arctic and Subarctic lifeways under extreme weather conditions and seasonality (e.g., the demands of food storage for lean seasons and maintaining social networks in this context), a human behavioral ecology perspective in Arctic environments offers a number of ways to address these dynamics, including modeling future discounting, intragroup relationships, and sharing. The authors conclude that application of these tools may illuminate how people selected resources and adapted to seasonal extremes across these regions.

Tushingham (Chapter 2) demonstrates the utility of human behavioral ecology approaches and models in many archaeological studies of northeast Pacific Rim societies but argues that regional application of human behavioral ecology continues to lag behind other parts of western North America.

The nature of the aquatic resource base and highly seasonal environments of the northeast Pacific can complicate application of traditional foraging models. This is particularly true when considering the myriad of ways people pursued, processed, stored, defended, and managed or otherwise impacted coastal resources and landscapes. In this vein, the author argues that the usefulness of human behavioral ecology is contingent on consideration of alternative rankings, constraints, and currencies in traditional contingency models. Critical revision of these model components is most effective when informed by collaboration with Indigenous communities and traditional ecological knowledge, which encapsulates ideas about sustainability and stewardship of common pool resources and points to numerous ethnohistoric cases among coastal hunter-gatherers. Advocating for broader integration of human behavioral ecology, traditional ecological knowledge, feminist theory, and other complementary frameworks, Tushingham highlights how evolutionary frameworks are also being expanded to include better models that incorporate Indigenous voices and expand work on women's decision-making strategies. She argues that human behavioral ecology models, if applied realistically, can offer a relevant framework for elucidating past aquatic adaptations. Such research may help us to expand our understanding of archaeology of the region, from initial colonization to the evolution of mass harvesting techniques, human-fishery dynamics, sedentism, and storage, not to mention studies of women's decision-making, and the opportunity costs of childcare.

Plekhov, Levine, and Leppard (Chapter 3) explore the untapped applicability of human behavioral ecology approaches within Mediterranean prehistory. Despite the paucity of research driven by human behavioral ecology in the Mediterranean basin, the authors argue that the few studies that exist show the way to interesting applications considering the richness of the data in the prehistoric Mediterranean, but also because of the extent to which it provides a broad geographic sweep whose constituent components are united in their heterogeneity. The proximity of Mediterranean microecologies allows the testing of human behavioral ecology expectations under different social forms witnessed from the mid-Holocene onward. In this way, the fact that Mediterranean archaeological datasets are an excellent testing ground for anthropological theory exploring processes of growth, diversity, and interconnection, render its inclusion in global and comparative archaeologies so vital.

Daniels, Thakar, and Neff (Chapter 4) draw attention to the lasting and broader impacts of the activities of ecosystem engineers at the eastern Soconusco mangrove zone. They argue that nowhere are these effects clearer than in the dynamic environments produced where land meets ocean water, where geomorphological effects like sea-level rise, sediment discharge, longshore currents, and wave action interact with human niche construction activities. These dynamic processes were creating a new coastal landscape with new opportunities for human adaptation before 4,000 years ago. Operationalized by expectations derived from human behavioral ecology, the authors argue that niche construction theory provides an effective framework for archaeological assessment of the coevolution of coastal ecosystems and human societies because it effectively integrates anthropogenic impacts, recognizing that they become an ecological inheritance that changes the selective environment faced by future generations. In the eastern Soconusco mangrove zone, inland forest clearance was the main niche construction effect detectable in the sedimentary record. Forest clearance not only modified the inland environment but the environment and ecosystem of the coast as well. During the Early Formative, those inadvertent modifications of the coast became the ecological inheritance selected for a variety of innovations, including reduced residential mobility, colonization of the wetlands, and innovations in resource procurement and processing technology.

Flores Fernandez and Olguín (Chapter 5) discuss the potential for application of costly signaling theory to enrich interpretations about the sociopolitical context of fishing communities from the southern coast of the Atacama Desert. With particular focus on the costly and dangerous pursuit of offshore swordfish hunting, the authors posit that investment in specialized technology required for swordfish capture, such as harpoons and boats, functioned as both utilitarian and prestige goods that successful hunters depended on to gain personal prestige as worthy leaders, competitive allies, or mates in a context of growing population. Moving away from economic currency toward social valuation shifts this research into the realm of broader anthropological issues related to the role of power in structuring past coastal societies. Nevertheless, principles like the sharing context of hunting kills, the benefits achieved by hunters, the inefficiency of the hunting behavior, and the underlying qualities hunters broadcast are difficult to identify or evaluate in the archaeological record. The authors argue that costly signaling theory opens interesting questions about, for example, collective actions and social prestige among coastal hunter, gatherer, and fisher communities; future research programmed to evaluate costly signaling theory expectations will be a great contribution to enrich interpretations of past human behaviors in the study area.

Gauthier-Bérubé and Thakar (Chapter 6) engage human behavioral ecology to enhance the study of wooden remains from shipwrecks to reconstruct and interpret past behaviors linked to wood acquisition in eighteenth-century France. Maritime success of the French Navy implied an efficient use of the forest, where resource and habitat degradation implied higher costs, suboptimal products (vessels), and higher probabilities to fail. Drawing on well-established human behavioral ecology prey choice and field-processing models, this chapter explores the environmental and socioeconomic factors that influenced tree selection during the construction of a ship and how these factors interacted with one another. In addition, the study highlights how crucial terrestrial resources are for coastal and marine adaptation in its wider sense and how the ways terrestrial resources are used may affect activities performed in the sea. Contingency models derived from human behavioral ecology are useful tools to identify the different economic, social, environmental, and technological factors that weigh the complex relationship between shipbuilding and forestry practices. These models also provide a first step toward integrating shipbuilding practices into a larger discussion on resource management and selection as part of human behaviors and decision-making processes in colonial times.

Wren, Janssen, Hill, and Marean (Chapter 7) employ agent-based modeling to examine local-scale understanding of human decision-making from optimal foraging theory and bridge to a longer-term and broader-scale pattern that is more directly comparable to the archaeological record. Using the coast of South Africa as a case study, they highlight that the spatial and temporal variability of coastal resources means that human foraging may be seen as a complex system with unexpected emergent effects. They argue that the application of optimal foraging theory to human foraging societies provides a highly successful framework for understanding human decision-making in the present and in the past, often with unintuitive conclusions. They conclude that agent-based modeling has a similar potential by expanding the logic of optimal foraging theory to a broader range of research questions. While traditional optimal foraging theory asks which resources might be included in the diet and when a forager might move on to a new patch, an agent-based model may address the sustainable population size of a given resource landscape, the overall composition of the diet, or even the response of past populations to specific climatological and ecological changes with small adjustments to the model code.

Wright, Faulkner, and Westaway (Chapter 8) seek to unite predictions of the optimal foraging theory prey and patch choice models with the principles of Boserupian economic intensification to better understand human predation pressure on vulnerable mollusk populations along the Australian coast. Highlighting critical concepts related to the definition of economic intensification (specialization, diversification, innovation), which results in greater production, they seek to evaluate how increased production has been generated (i.e., via increasing or decreasing efficiency). Through close examination of the archaeomalacology assemblage, the authors explore the relationships between diet breadth, resource value, habitat conditions, prey size, handling costs, and prey mobility. Emphasizing the importance of sessile and predictable molluscan resources as dietary staples, they argue that reliance on small prey that people may collect in fixed locations (e.g., plants and mollusks) often increase handling costs, which means more time spent at processing locations near to the resources. Reduced mobility and reliable resources can lead to increased populations and an increased need to reduce handling costs to increase output, a process that has been seen to lead to complex foraging and social behavior.

Finally, Morrison, DiNapoli, Allen, and Rieth (Chapter 9) evaluate an application of the ideal free distribution model to predict the importance of two key habitats that potentially shaped the process of human settlement across the island of Tutuila in the Sāmoan Archipelago: flat coastal land (a proxy of agricultural potential) and the extent of coral reef (a measure of marine resource productivity). Such settlement studies have played a crucial role in Polynesian archaeology throughout much of the last half century. Through this analysis, they argue that human behavioral ecology provides a complementary theoretical framework to more traditional settlement pattern approaches by providing explanatory models for how and why human settlements vary across different socioecological contexts. More specifically, through the development and application of relatively simple conceptual models, human behavioral ecology offers testable predictions and evolutionary-scale explanations for archaeological phenomena. The authors argue that this approach is particularly well suited for these kinds of studies because they provide theoretically derived predictions about the timing, tempo, and drivers of colonization, settlement expansions, and subsequent migrations—predictions that can be tested empirically using distributional archaeological data.

Insights and Opportunities

No environment is constant. In addition to interannual variation, seasonal variation in the abundance, distribution, and accessibility of plant and animal resources certainly influence the quantity and quality of food available to coastal communities throughout the year. Thus, defining resource productivity and habitat suitability remains one of the greatest challenges to archaeological applications of human behavioral ecology models. Even informed assessments of environmental suitability may fail to account for highly localized valuations of resource productivity across ecological domains or how shifting degrees of economic reliance on distinct resource bases limits the predictive power of models derived from human behavioral ecology.

Representing the past environment as a static backdrop rather than a moving target obfuscates millennia of negotiation with humans and with other processes at both larger and smaller scales. Humans occupy their landscape in a dynamic manner, often altering their mobility patterns in response to environmental, cultural, and economic factors that fluctuate through time. These factors almost certainly contributed to local social and environmental historical contingencies that influenced human behavior and decision-making. Thus, the process by which ecological circumstances contribute to one array of foraging choices, technological innovations, and organizational patterns rather than others remains incomplete and obscure. Moreover, ecologists have long recognized that shifts in foraging strategies can lead to substantial population increases. Thus, how human foragers move about and exploit landscapes directly influences human reproductive efforts and population-level demography.

Recent work has explicitly recognized the difficulties of inconstant suitability and has sought to explore the relationship between suitability and subsistence economies. The inclusion of local ecological knowledge is key to enriching the expectations and constraints of several human behavioral ecology models, making them more accurate under local ecological and social realities such as extreme seasonality and the need to store and share food. Following the need for including present time local knowledge to better understand past behaviors, the application of costly signaling theory on ethnographic and archaeological contexts from the same area can provide that link with the incredible possibility to explore the endurance of behaviors such as offshore hunting through time, whether is related to contexts of signals broadcasting and the social or reproductive benefits the activity entails.

Regional Variation in Theoretical Approaches

Across the globe, past coastal societies manifested complex social, political, and economic behaviors once accorded only to agricultural societies. Effectively decoupled from dependency on domesticated plants and animals, the development of complexity is no longer a presupposed evolutionary endgame for human societies. It is clear that diverse patterns of hunter-gatherer "adaptive persistence, change, and expansion [occurred] often at the expense of agriculture" (Bettinger 2015:2–3). Nowhere is this diversity of lifeways more visible than in the archaeological literature of coastal California, where complex evolutionary landscapes presented "difficult adaptive problems to which there were often multiple solutions" and "historical contingencies pushed hunter-gatherers sometimes in one direction, sometimes another" (Bettinger 2015:2–3). Wholesale rejection of linear evolutionary schemes that once dominated theoretical approaches to sociopolitical variation has deepened appreciation for the successful organizational and economic diversity of foraging societies. This thinking drives a new wave of theoretical investment in understanding the diversity of lifeways developed by coastal societies.

Although theoretical approaches derived from human behavioral ecology are still criticized for its reductionist approach to human behavior, simplification of reality has proved to be a useful tool to identify the different factors that compound human-environment relationships. The chapters of this book evidence this. Human behavioral ecology can be applied using models of different levels of complexity to extremely different coastal settings and social contexts. These models seek to distinguish between behaviors that can and cannot be explained by biological or economic principles. Regional comparative studies enrich our understanding of the relationship between resource use, population dynamics, technological change, and cultural transformations. However, the intensity of research applying human behavioral ecology models to coastal archaeological contexts at the different locations presented throughout this volume is heterogeneous. The editors of this volume both work on the California Channel Islands, a region where research has a long and well-developed ecological and evolutionary focus. Publication of Kennett's (2005) book *The Island Chumash: Behavioral Ecology of a Maritime Society* accelerated the application of this theoretical approach on the California Channel Islands and in coastal contexts around the globe. Research interconnections along the Pacific Rim of the North American continent have also promoted the expansion of this approach across the Arctic and the Pacific Northwest Coast of the United States. These regions tend to be overrepresented in archaeological research that incorporates human behavioral ecology.

In contrast, in Europe, Central America, and South America, interesting hypotheses derived from human behavioral ecology remain understudied. South Africa and Pacific Islands such as Australia and Sāmoa fall in the middle of this research spectrum. Why these regional differences? It may be related to sociohistorical circumstances of theoretical development in archaeology and to the nature of archaeological data. In Latin America, Marxist theory focused on the social relationships of production marked the development of archaeology as a discipline, locally contemporaneous with the revolutionary political processes of the area (Bate 1977; Lumbreras 1974; Tantaleán and Aguilar 2012). This epistemology defined thinking about past societies in recent decades during which cultural ecology and neo-evolutionary theories were not considered. In Europe, frameworks from behavioral ecology have not been widely explored either, in part for the distinction between classical and anthropological archaeology and the avoidance of applying concepts related to optimal behavior and modeling when rich cultural evidence allows to reconstruct past societies in detail (see Plekhov et al., Chapter 3 herein).

Latin America, Europe, and North America have archaeological evidence from a multiplicity of types of societies from hunter-gatherers to empires who lived in harsh and mellow environments, with marked seasons and year-round resource availability. There seem to be no geographic or temporal bounds to the utility of human behavioral ecology models, as successful analyses have been conducted across western North America, Europe, South Africa, and Oceania in time periods ranging from 50,000 years ago to the early twentieth century. Not to mention contemporary ethnographic applications reviewed in the introduction. Such models are capable of generating testable hypotheses concerning the colonization of landscapes, the spatial distribution of populations, cooperation and competition, social hierarchy and inequality, and the impacts of subsistence on settlement patterns. Their success in addressing such wide-ranging research questions demonstrates that these models are helpful not only for analyzing settlement patterns in relation to environmental factors but also for better understanding social forces that impact population distribution. No matter what coastal context we study, theoretical approaches from human behavioral ecology can enrich our understanding of their past. Future investment in regional studies across diverse coastal settings will contribute further refinements and continued development of human behavioral ecology in coastal contexts.

References Cited

Bate, Luis. 1977. *Arqueología y materialismo histórico*. Ediciones de Cultura Popular, Mexico, D.F.

Bettinger, Robert L. 2015. *Orderly Anarchy Sociopolitical Evolution in Aboriginal California*. University of California Press, Los Angeles.

Kennett, Douglas. 2005. *The Island Chumash: Behavioral Ecology of a Maritime Society*. University of California Press, Los Angeles.

Lumbreras, Luis. 1974. *La arqueología como ciencia social*. Editorial Histar, Lima.

Tantaleán, Henry, and Miguel Aguilar (editors). 2012. *La arqueología social latinoamericana: De la teoría a la praxis*. Editorial Universidad de los Andes, Colombia.

Contributors

Melinda S. Allen is professor of anthropology (archaeology) at the University of Auckland, New Zealand. Her research interests include long-term human ecodynamics, human-climate interactions, processes of colonization, and post-settlement interaction and exchange. Her field work is centered in Polynesia, including New Zealand and Hawaiʻi.

Shelby Anderson is associate professor in the Department of Anthropology at Portland State University. Anderson earned her PhD from the University of Washington. Her research interests include the archaeology of past hunter-gatherer societies, human ecodynamics, forager food preparation technologies, applied archaeology, Indigenous archaeology, and archaeology of the Arctic, Subarctic, and Pacific Northwest.

James T. Daniels Jr. is a PhD candidate in the Department of Anthropology, University of California–San Diego, and senior archaeologist at ASM Affiliates. Daniels received his master of arts in anthropology from California State University–Long Beach. His research interests include ecological inheritance and Early Formative settlement patterns along the coast of southern Mesoamerica and their effects on the landscape and environment.

Robert J. DiNapoli is a postdoctoral research associate in environmental studies and anthropology at Binghamton University, State University of New York. DiNapoli earned his PhD in anthropology from the University of Oregon. His research focuses on using human behavioral ecology and computational modeling to study human-environment interactions in the Pacific and Caribbean Islands.

Patrick Faulkner is senior lecturer in archaeology at the University of Sydney in Australia. Faulkner earned his PhD from the Australian National

University. His current research interests include coastal palaeoeconomies, archaeomalacology, human-environment interactions, and historical ecology.

Ben Fitzhugh is professor of anthropology and director of the Quaternary
Research Center at the University of Washington. Fitzhugh earned his PhD
from the University of Michigan. His interests are in the historical ecology
of high-latitude maritime hunting, fishing, and gathering communities, especially around the North Pacific Rim and Arctic.

Carola Flores Fernandez is professor in the School of Archaeology at Universidad Austral de Chile, Puerto Montt; associated researcher at the Center
for Advanced Studies in Arid Zones, Chile; and deputy director for ANID
Millenniums Nucleus UPWELL, Chile. Flores Fernandez earned her PhD in
anthropology from the University of California–Santa Barbara. Her current
research focuses on human-environment interactions, archaeomalacology,
paleo-oceanographic reconstructions through isotopic analyses on mollusk
shells and on technology of ancient fishing societies.

Marijo Gauthier-Bérubé is the archeology research director at the Fort Saint-
Jean Museum in Quebec, Canada. Gauthier-Bérubé earned her PhD in anthropology from Texas A&M University. Her nautical archaeology research
focuses on the relationship between traditional knowledge and the standardization of historic shipbuilding practices.

Erik Gjesfjeld is program officer at the John Templeton Foundation. Gjesfjeld
earned his PhD from the University of Washington. His research focuses
on human ecodynamics, evolutionary approaches to the analysis of human
behavior, and the dynamics of technological change, particularly in northern
environments.

Kim Hill is professor in the School of Human Evolution and Social Change
and in the Institute for Human Origins at Arizona State University. Hill
earned his PhD in anthropology from the University of Utah. His research
interests include evolutionary cultural ecology, hunter-gatherer societies,
and evolutionary origins of human uniqueness.

Marco A. Janssen is professor in the School of Sustainability and director of
the Center for Behavior, Institutions, and the Environment, both at Arizona
State University. Janssen earned his PhD from Maastricht University, the

Netherlands. His research interests include the development of computational models of social-ecological systems.

Thomas P. Leppard is assistant professor of anthropology at Florida State University. His research focuses on the emergence of social complexity and human ecology and ecodynamics. Leppard earned his PhD in archaeology from Brown University. He is especially interested in comparative approaches to emergent social complexity, variability in forms of Holocene social organization, and how environmental adaptation drove this variability.

Evan Levine is a PhD student in the Joukowsky Institute for Archaeology and the Ancient World at Brown University and a digital humanities specialist at the American School of Classical Studies at Athens. His research interests include the interface between regional archaeological survey, spatial statistics, and remote sensing to explore the archaeology of mixed agropastoral economies.

Curtis W. Marean is professor in the School of Human Evolution and Social Change and in the Institute for Human Origins at Arizona State University and an honorary professor and international deputy director in the African Centre for Coastal Palaeoscience at Nelson Mandela University. Marean earned his PhD from the University of California–Berkeley. His research interests include human origins, the prehistory of Africa, paleoclimates and paleoenvironments, and the study of animal bones from archaeological sites.

Alex E. Morrison is principal archaeologist at Applied Earthworks Inc. in San Luis Obispo, California, and affiliate graduate faculty in the University of Hawai'i–Manoa Anthropology Department. Morrison earned his PhD from the University of Hawai'i–Manoa. His research interests include marine ecology, spatial modeling, settlement pattern and landscape archaeology, human behavioral ecology, and historic preservation.

Hector Neff is professor emeritus in the Department of Anthropology, California State University–Long Beach. Neff earned his PhD in anthropology from the University of California–Santa Barbara. His current research focuses on early human occupations and anthropogenic impacts on the landscape of Pacific coastal Central America.

Laura Olguín is a PhD student at the Universidad Católica del Norte, San Pedro de Atacama, Chile. Olguín earned her master of science from the Universidad Católica del Norte, San Pedro de Atacama, Chile. Her research interests include archaeomalacology, ichthyoarchaeology, zooarchaeology, coastal adaptations, historical archaeology, and cultural resource management.

Daniel Plekhov is a PhD student in the Joukowsky Institute for Archaeology and the Ancient World at Brown University. His research interests include the long-term socioecological impacts of agricultural infrastructure, particularly agricultural terraces, on local communities and environments in Jordan and Peru.

Timothy M. Rieth is senior archaeologist at International Archaeological Research Institute, Inc. in Honolulu, Hawai'i. Rieth earned his master of arts in anthropology from the University of Hawai'i–Manoa. His research interests include island colonization, chronological modeling, and human behavioral ecology.

Heather B. Thakar is assistant professor and director of the Radiocarbon and Isotope Sample Preparation Laboratory and the Archaeobotany Laboratories at Texas A&M University. Thakar earned her PhD in anthropology from the University of California–Santa Barbara. Her research interests encompass the development of Quaternary coastal foraging and proto-agricultural societies along the Pacific coast of North and Central America, studied through the lens of archaeobotanical, zooarchaeological, and isotopic analyses. Her approach to human behavioral ecology is informed by feminist, Indigenous, and collaborative archaeological practice.

Shannon Tushingham is assistant professor and the director of the Washington State University Museum of Anthropology. Tushingham earned her PhD in anthropology from the University of California–Davis. She is an anthropological archaeologist with research broadly centered on human-environmental relationships and the evolutionary archaeology of hunter-gatherer-fishers in western North America. Her research program involves behavioral ecology and evolution of hunter-gatherer socioeconomic systems, evolution of psychoactive plant use by human cultures worldwide, and equity and multivocality in STEM science and the dissemination of knowledge.

Catherine F. West is research assistant professor and director of the Zooarchaeology Laboratory in the Department of Anthropology and Archaeology at Brown University. West earned her PhD from the University of

Washington. Her research interests are in marine historical ecology and the applied potential of zooarchaeological data to contemporary resource management, particularly in the Arctic and Subarctic.

Michael Westaway is Australian Research Council Future Fellow in Archaeology at the University of Queensland. Westaway earned his PhD from the Australian National University. His research interests include environmental archaeology, bioarchaeology, and palaeo-anthropology.

Colin D. Wren is associate professor of anthropology at the University of Colorado–Colorado Springs and a research associate with the African Center for Coastal Palaeoscience, Nelson Mandela University. Wren earned his PhD from McGill University, Montreal, Canada. His research interests include quantitative methods, including agent-based modeling, geographic information systems, and spatial statistics, for understanding past foraging societies.

Martin Wright is senior archaeologist with the archaeological consulting firm Virtus Heritage in Sydney, Australia. Wright earned his bachelor of arts from the University of Sydney. His current research interests include archaeomalacology and coastal paleo-economies.

Index

Page numbers in *italics* refer to illustrations

Society and Ecology in Island and Coastal Archaeology

EDITED BY VICTOR D. THOMPSON AND SCOTT M. FITZPATRICK

The settlement and occupation of islands, coastlines, and archipelagoes can be traced deep into the human past. From the voyaging and seafaring peoples of the Oceania to the Mesolithic fisher-hunter-gatherers of coastal Ireland, to coastal salt production among Maya traders, the range of variation found in these societies over time is boundless. Yet, they share a commonality that links them all together—their dependence upon seas, coasts, and estuaries for life and prosperity. Thus, in all these cultures there is a fundamental link between society and the ecology of islands and coasts. Books in this series explore the nature of humanity's relationship to these environments from a global perspective. Topics in this series would range from edited volumes to single case studies covering the archaeology of initial migrations, seafaring, insularity, trade, societal complexity and collapse, early village life, aquaculture, and historical ecology, among others along islands and coasts.

The Powhatan Landscape: An Archaeological History of the Algonquian Chesapeake, by Martin D. Gallivan (2016; first paperback edition, 2018)

An Archaeology of Abundance: Reevaluating the Marginality of California's Islands, edited by Kristina M. Gill, Mikael Fauvelle, and Jon M. Erlandson (2019)

Maritime Communities of the Ancient Andes, edited by Gabriel Prieto and Daniel H. Sandweiss (2019)

The Archaeology of Human-Environmental Dynamics on the North American Atlantic Coast, edited by Leslie Reeder-Myers, John A. Turck, and Torben C. Rick (2019)

Historical Ecology and Archaeology in the Galapagos Islands: A Legacy of Human Occupation, by Peter W. Stahl, Fernando J. Astudillo, Ross W. Jamieson, Diego Quiroga, and Florencio Delgado (2020)

The Archaeology of Island Colonization: Global Approaches to Initial Human Settlement, edited by Matthew F. Napolitano, Jessica H. Stone, and Robert J. DiNapoli (2021)

Human Behavioral Ecology and Coastal Environments, edited by Heather B. Thakar and Carola Flores Fernandez (2023)